Jack in Port

sailortowns of eastern Canada

Judith Fingard

UNIVERSITY OF TORONTO PRESS

Toronto Buffalo London

ISBN 8020-2458-0 (cloth)
    8020-6467-1 (paper)

Canadian Cataloguing in Publication Data

Fingard, Judith, 1943–
    Jack in port
    (Social history of Canada, ISSN 0085–6207 ; 36)
    Bibliography: p.
    Includes index.
    ISBN 0-8020-2458-0 (bound). – ISBN 0-8020-6467-1 (pbk.)

    1. Merchant seamen – Nova Scotia – Halifax – History –
    19th century. 2. Merchant seamen – New Brunswick –
    Saint John – History – 19th century. 3. Merchant
    seamen – Quebec – Québec – History – 19th century.
    I. Title. II. Series.
    HD8039.S42C34   331.7′6162388′09715   C82-094507-2

Social History of Canada 36

This book has been published with the help of a grant
from the Social Science Federation of Canada,
using funds provided by the Social Sciences and
Humanities Research Council of Canada,
and assistance from the Publications Fund of
the University of Toronto Press.

36

Social History of Canada

H.V. Nelles, general editor

JUDITH FINGARD is a professor of history at Dalhousie University.

The boisterous presence of thousands of merchant sailors drawn from the casual labour forces of Canada and other countries enlivened the seaports of Quebec, Saint John, and Halifax during the shipping seasons of the age of sail. Their patterns of employment, shipboard and seaside misbehaviour, and serious injuries and illnesses drew a variety of responses from port society.

Jack in Port describes the social and economic environments of Canada's large nineteenth-century ocean ports where sailors sought work, jumped ship, created disturbances, and fought for a better work environment.

Characterized by seasonality and shortage of supply, the sailor labour market had to contend with official regulation and unofficial controls – a struggle between reform and tradition – in a society undergoing fundamental economic transformation. Boarding-house-keepers often acted as private shipping agents, intimidating shipmasters and crimping sailors. Governments and reformers sought to control this lucrative system, but with limited success, until the sailortowns of the crimps and the seafarers died with the passing of the sailing ship.

Judith Fingard re-creates here the world of work and the dockside environment of three generations of nineteenth-century sailors, adding another fascinating chapter to our rapidly growing knowledge of the Canadian working class.

Contents

Illustrations

Tables

Acknowledgments

The research for this book was supported by the Social Sciences and Humanities Research Council of Canada through a leave fellowship in 1975–6 and a research grant in 1978–9. Archival, library, and museum staff were always helpful, and I want in particular to acknowledge the assistance of Monica Robertson, former archivist of the New Brunswick Museum, Shirley Elliott, librarian of the Nova Scotia Legislative Library, and the members of the Atlantic Canada Shipping Project at Memorial University who facilitated my research during the summer of 1978. My friends and colleagues have contributed advice and encouragement. To Phillip Buckner, Susan Buggey, David Frank, Gregory Kealey, Ian McKay, and David Sutherland I extend my appreciation. My research assistants, Penny Hoover, Donald Lemon, and Karen Vance, performed yeoman service. Dinkie Persaud produced the typescript. At every stage Peter Burroughs could be relied on for tea, sympathy, and cogent criticism.

I wish to dedicate this book to the memory of David Alexander (1939–1980) and Leslie Upton (1931–1980), two fellow historians whose friendship in the 1970s was for me a source of confidence and inspiration which I shall always treasure.

Dalhousie University
October 1981

JACK IN PORT

Introduction

Anyone visiting the seaport towns of Quebec, Saint John, or Halifax during a mid-nineteenth-century shipping season could not have helped but be impressed by the number of sailors who crowded the nooks and crannies of the bustling dockside. This golden age of shipping – the 1850s and 1860s – was also the golden age of employment for merchant seamen. In their hundreds and thousands they moved in and out of the major Canadian seaports, creating a uniquely transient and multinational community which this book calls *sailortown*. In Canadian historical literature the merchant sailor has received little notice. His life and work do not readily conform to the models and theories favoured by social historians. His legendary indiscipline, non-productive labour, and frequent foreignness mark him out, along with naval seamen, soldiers, and prostitutes, as a misfit who was there to be seen, perhaps, but who need not be heard. The present study tries to rescue from obscurity those merchant sailors and the shoreside milieu in which they moved. Largely descriptive in nature, it portrays the way in which the institutions and demands of society shaped and conditioned the drama of seafaring and how shipboard concerns, in turn, fashioned the sailors' experiences on land.

During the course of the nineteenth century, a number of critical changes occurred in the composition of the seafaring population, the pressures of time, and the discipline and mobility to which sailors were exposed both on sea and land, as well as in the technology of seafaring. The sailors who flourished in the second quarter of the nineteenth century entered, in British North American ports, a labour market which included few non-English-speaking seamen. The sailor's experience from the 1820s to the 1840s was confined to vessels under 600 tons, on which he might sail with other men from his community, some of whom might be relatives. Whether or not he had any kinship or residential connection with the shipmaster, he might well be paid a share of the profits of the trading voyage rather than according to a monthly wage rate. Either way, his contractual arrangements were as likely to protect his interests as they were to benefit his employer. This equilibrium was attributable partly to the looseness and imprecision which characterized written agreements and partly to the nature of vice-admiralty court jurisdiction. Since the latter was specifically designed to deal with maritime disputes and protect Britain's marine manpower, it allowed sailors considerable scope for collective legal action.

During this first generation, the sailor remained a jack of all trades. There were few specialist positions aboard ship, and progression – from boy to ordinary seaman, from able seaman to bosun, and from mate to captain – was theoretically possible for the bright, diligent worker. At the same time, in port, the sailor performed the chore of handling cargo, enjoyed access to a wide range of taverns in which to drink, eat, and carouse, and, when necessary, lodged with tradesmen or resident seamen or dockside workers. The unhurried pace of the pre-industrial age meant that sailors' visits to port were sufficiently lengthy to enable them to make a significant contribution to both the economy and the character of sailortown. The port's middle-class inhabitants, to which the sailor was more often than not a stranger by virtue of his social status and his domicile, professed to be worried about his morals, but, being practical commercial people, they remained relatively tolerant towards the behaviour of men from whom they derived both profit and labour.

At the heart of this study is the second generation, the sailors of the 1850s, 1860s, and early 1870s, years in which the opportunities for seafaring grew by leaps and bounds. With that growth, the homogeneity of crews and their potential for collective action decreased as a result of the internationalization of the labour market and the extension of government restrictions on seafarers' job mobility and customary labour litigation. The larger vessels dating from this period often sailed to a tight schedule, which meant that sailors were driven harder as their masters strove to compete with rivals in the era of free trade. Dangerous steam-driven machinery was introduced to help run the vessel and work the cargo. At the same time, the resolve of shipowners to keep costs to a minimum led to a deterioration of shipboard conditions.

Another noteworthy result of the rapid expansion of shipping and shipping-related industries in eastern Canadian ports was the persistence of the wage differentials for transatlantic voyages which had begun to emerge during the time of the first-generation sailor. Although higher wages on the western rim of the Atlantic were the result of a shortage of labour rather than an artificial withholding of labour, the continued demand for sailor labour, as well as the outlawing of private-enterprise hiring, created the 'crimping' establishments for which nineteenth-century sailortowns were notorious. The disruptive turnover in seafaring jobs promoted by the sailor-snatchers left visiting vessels without their customary cargo-handlers and thereby strengthened the employment opportunities for shore-based labour. Moreover, the determination of the 'crimps' to preserve their sailor clientele from the clutches of government shipping masters led to the emergence of the specialized sailors' boarding-house which became the headquarters of their illegal operations. The second-generation sailor was therefore subject to considerable manipulation in a sailortown, where he was no longer a free agent, and to a greater sense of alienation on board ship – in the fo'c's'le he encountered foreigners and on the bridge a captain who was a manager rather than an owner.

The third-generation sailor, active in the last quarter of the century, belonged to a dying occupation. If he chose to continue, like his father and grandfather, to work on deep-sea sailing vessels, he was unlikely to be given much chance to leave his mark on the sailortowns of eastern Canada. The short stopovers characteristic of the new pace of commerce allowed the sailor little time to go ashore. If he did, he encountered pressures to act temperately and avoid boarding-houses (and their attendant social activities) and the courts for the redress of grievances arising from his work. At the same time, his sailortown cohorts were being forced to abandon crimping by a late-century evangelical-inspired 'reform' movement directed as much against sailortown as against the sailor. For both, the writing was on the wall.

If such a seafarer joined a steam vessel as an alternative to sailing, he turned his back on Quebec, Saint John, and Halifax; steamship traffic had little human impact on these ports. As a result the late 1890s saw the demise of sailortown. The sailors who now visited the former major seaports belonged to the fisheries or the coasting trade and tended to be residents rather than strangers. They had an interest in the community quite different from that of the crews who had manned the great international traders of the earlier age of sail.

While a generational overview lays bare the chronology and changing pattern of the present study, it obscures a number of persistent themes, which cut across the three generations and profoundly influenced the landward impact of sailors. The first of these was the seasonality of work. Since the seafarer, like many labourers, artisans, and primary producers, could work only during mild seasons, the seasonality of seafaring discouraged the creation of a sufficient resident work-force to man the merchant vessels of shipbuilding ports. Seasonality thus encouraged a work-force dominated by strangers. Because most seafarers were strangers in port, their life ashore was characterized by isolation and segregation. This isolation discouraged both effective unity of purpose and action among sailors and a constructive concern and respect for seafarers among landsmen. The typical landsman's response to sailors' exigencies was a blend of admiration and disdain – admiration for a work-force which provided a vital link with the world of progress and prosperity beyond the seas; disdain for a proverbially bothersome presence in the streets, taverns, and institutions of health, order, and justice. None the less, since the interests of the sailor intersected with those of some residents, to the mutual benefit of both, sailortown flourished and acted as a challenge to the bourgeois notions of order and modernity.

Another persistent theme, which influenced the merchant sailor's activities both at sea and on shore, was the contractual nature of his employment. Since breaches of contract by either party to an agreement frequently led to litigation, court actions formed a commonplace feature of port life, unparalleled in other occupations. Closely related to the excessive regulation of sailors' employment was the characteristic response of bound labour to disagreeable employment – desertion. Whatever its extent, the gallons of ink which the authorities expended on suggestions for curbing it indicate that they saw desertion as a serious threat to the achievement of a disciplined society.

In order that we may see both the change over time and the persistence of common themes in the sailor labour markets of Quebec, Saint John, and Halifax, this book focuses on five major subjects: the problem of the shortage of sailors, the nature and variety of seafaring experiences, the most common preoccupations of sailors ashore, the central role of litigation in the sailors' work-world, and the exploitation and manipulation of sailors in port. Since sailortown, not the sailing vessel, provides the context, we begin this study with, and emphasize throughout, the landward conditions that produced the labour market.

The sailor
labour market

Central to the economic life of the nineteenth-century city, dependent for its livelihood on ocean trade and activities related to shipping, was the bustling waterfront. On the wharves during daylight hours merchants conferred with stevedores, immigrants argued with carters and hotel runners, shipmasters bargained with provisioners. Coal handlers, timber towers, fish screwers, and ship labourers plied their trades amid the shipping agents' offices, warehouses, drinking dens, and oyster bars. The passageways were cluttered with imported goods awaiting the attention of customs officials and shipping clerks. Order was maintained by the harbour-master and port warden, each of whom kept an experienced eye on the movement and discipline of vessels, and by the police, who patrolled the dockside in order to protect persons and property. Alongside the wharves, visiting vessels in need of refurbishing received the attention of resident riggers, caulkers, and carpenters. Offshore, vessels were anchored near timber rafts and scows for loading or awaiting pilots to guide them to open water. On busy days the harbour resembled a smouldering, burnt-out forest of masts enveloped by the sooty exhaust from the steam tugs and donkey engines. As darkness descended, the vessels released their sailors to comb the streets of sailortown in search of wine, women, and song. The cover of night also facilitated the age-old practice by which seamen deserted from one vessel only to sign on its neighbour. The universal tendency of sailors to jump ship affected seafaring employment patterns round the world, including the Canadian ports, which experienced their own unique features of supply and demand.

Sailor labour markets, which responded to the needs of vessels on deep-sea voyages, prevailed in the timber export ports of Quebec and Saint John and in the fish export and general import centre of Halifax. The character of these labour markets was shaped in part by the patterns of trade pursued by the vessels in and out of the ports. Transatlantic vessels arriving in Quebec and Saint John brought from Europe, or from intermediate ports in Newfoundland or the eastern American seaboard, ballast (or its equivalent in salt, coal, or iron), general merchandise, or immigrants. After discharging and loading they cleared port timber-laden and destined for a wide variety of ports in the United Kingdom and western Europe. From Halifax, a smaller class of vessels than those engaged in the timber trade carried fish and general cargoes southwards to the United States and the Caribbean and coastwise rather than crossing the Atlantic. Vessels entering port carried diverse products from Europe and the Americas ranging from gin to steel rails (in the 1870s) but concentrating mainly on textiles and foodstuffs. In addition, Saint John and Halifax shared a lively and competitive involvement in the coastwise carrying trade, in both Canada and the United States and, by the 1860s, in the longer-haul West Indies and South American trades. Involvement in these latter entailed a fundamental shift in the trading patterns out of Saint John. As that city's deal trade to Great Britain declined in 1869 and 1870, the vessels in the lumber trade increased in number while declining in tonnage, which reflected a change 'from the vessels of a large tonnage, carrying timber and deals to Great Britain to those of smaller capacity, carrying sugar shooks, boards, plank, scantling, laths, pickets, shingles &c to the United States, West Indies and South America.'[1]

The variety in the patterns of trading out of the eastern Canadian ports was determined not only by the cargoes but also by the way in which the business of shipping was pursued. The complementary timber-exporting and shipbuilding activities in Quebec and Saint John were frequently managed by firms having a parent company in Britain for which they acted as colonial branches or agencies. In 1835 the firm of Pollok and Gilmour of Glasgow and Liverpool, with major branches in Saint John and Quebec, was operating a fleet of over 100 ships, the largest under the British flag. The ownership and management of vessels trading to Quebec were largely in British hands and more centralized than the shipping of the other two ports. A number of British ports had their Quebec fleets, that of Greenock in 1872 comprising about two dozen vessels. Local merchants frequently acted as agents for British and foreign vessels. Richard Dobell, timber merchant and president of the Quebec Board of Trade, supplied the loads of 220 of the 1,004 ships carrying timber cargoes from port in 1872. In both Saint John and Halifax, where a greater proportion of the fleets were locally owned, businessmen none the less sought vessels for charter on the basis of cost rather than ownership. In the 1868 shipping season in Saint John, the local timber baron, Alexander Gibson, employed seventy-eight square-rigged vessels to export deals from his own mills and those he represented. At one point in 1872 nearly all the 119 vessels in Saint John were chartered for the West Indies trade. The practice of chartering vessels for conducting the export trades of the ports introduced an increasing number of foreign vessels, particularly those flying the Norwegian and American flags. On domestic and British and foreign vessels, the pressures for maintaining speed, finding cargoes, and loading to over-capacity determined, and were determined by, the rate of freight, that crucial factor in the competitive world of nineteenth-century shipping.[2]

The vessels in question, whether directly employed or chartered, ranged in size from the small schooners favoured in the fishing trade to the brigs and brigantines of the coastwise trade and the barques, barquentines, and ships of the transatlantic and other long-haul trades. The impending obsolescence of the large-class wooden vessels was foreshadowed by the growing number of ocean-going steamers which shared their berths. At the most active times of the season, harbours and wharves were jammed with vessels of varied rigs which reflected the nature of the port's trade. During the height of the timber trade it was not unusual in the busiest loading months of late spring and late summer for more than 200 square-rigged vessels to be anchored in the stream between Cape Diamond and Point Lévis at Quebec and for eighty square-rigged vessels to be discharging and taking in deals at Saint John. The vessels involved in Saint John's wood trade included both large square-rigged vessels and smaller rigs, the former destined for transatlantic crossings, the latter for the southern routes to the United States and the tropics. A June day in 1869 saw 60 square-rigged vessels and 32 schooners over 70 tons in port, amounting to some 51,300 tons exclusive of the large fleet of smaller vessels used by local trade. On a late October day in 1872, the Saint John press recorded the presence of 2 steamers, 12 ships, 19 barques, 4 brigs, 14 brigantines, and 48 schooners. The decline in square-riggers was not offset by a significant steamer trade in Saint John, whereas in Halifax by the 1870s the trade carried in steamships was considerable, with as many as a dozen in port at a time. The early trading season of 1874 found the harbour dotted with 8 steamers, 2 ships, 11 barques, 3 brigs, 13 brigantines, 2 topsail schooners, and innumerable schooners and small craft.[3]

Despite differences in the patterns of shipping in the three ports, especially the much greater size of operations in Quebec, several common characteristics predominated. The ports enjoyed roughly the same shipping season, extending from April to November on the coast, with usually a month's additional delay in the spring in the St Lawrence. It was in these major ports that most of the ships involved in northern oceanic trade entered and cleared, were fitted out and provisioned, and many of them built or repaired. Here too the essential labour for the execution of the deep-sea shipping trades was sought and obtained. For whatever the vessels might carry, they all required seamen to get them under way, work them to their ports of call, maintain them, and, at least until late in the century, discharge and load their cargoes.[4]

The summer shipping season, annually greeted with enthusiasm in all three ports, was the major focus of nineteenth-century port life. It posed a number of problems for merchant shipping. The quest for profits encouraged shipowners involved in transatlantic trade to try to cram two return voyages into one shipping season. This tight schedule was by no means easy for the clumsy, slow-moving timber ships which, in addition to a long crossing, required a lengthy stopover in port in order to load their bulky cargoes. Captains who attempted the two crossings were therefore anxious to avoid crewing problems if possible. Sailing ships and unsophisticated steamers working in and out of the Atlantic coast ports could count on a slightly longer season, though the primitive technology of winter travel, to say nothing of the fear of storms, effectively precluded extensive merchant shipping from December to March.[5]

Not even the best-equipped and -manned vessel could be sure of withstanding the perilous winter storms in the north Atlantic. When a vessel was overladen, the chances of shipwreck were considerably increased, as was demonstrated by the fate of the deal-laden *Turkish Empire* on Partridge Island off Saint John in March 1879. Unable to lower the boats in the raging storm, the hapless vessel, with the pilot still aboard, struck against the rocks and immediately broke up. After striking broadside on, 'the next sea that came rolled her to the other side, when the three masts went by the board, literally splitting the vessel in two, and causing the deals to fly about like so many chips.' Six of the twenty-four-man crew perished, several being crushed by the unleashed timber cargo, another crushed to death in the steering gear. The captain, who had lashed himself to the rail, died as the vessel broke up, and two of the seamen, who had been recently rescued from another shipwreck, perished because they took to the mizen-mast, which went over in quick succession after the foremast and mainmast. A couple of days after the wreck, the body of the cook was picked up 'with the right leg gone at the knee, the eyes out of their sockets and the breast crushed in.' In their gruesomeness, seafaring deaths graphically illustrated the seaman's struggle with the elements.[6]

Except on the rare occasions when the harbours froze solid, there was of course movement in and out of the ports of Saint John and Halifax throughout the year, but, outside the recognized shipping season, this movement was inconsiderable as far as the commodity trades were concerned. It could not be otherwise in Saint John where the export trade was dependent on river navigation for securing timber cargoes and the freedom of the port's harbour from ice did not in itself provide access to supplies of the staple export. In Saint John and Quebec the closing date of the shipping season was also dictated until 1862, and again after 1874, first by imperial and then by dominion deckload laws which prohibited the carrying of heavy timber on deck in the autumn and winter. While the laws were often evaded by defining all sorts of extra timber as allowable ship's timber, and in Saint John by slipping across the border to secure clearances as American freight, some shipowners paid serious regard to the legislation and also favoured early sailings because of lower insurance rates. The restricted season often meant that the capital represented by the vessels lay idle for a long period each year. Winter was the time for maintenance and repairs, something that provided a degree of winter employment in the Atlantic coast ports, though the non-Canadian ownership of many of the visiting ships tended to direct wintering and repairs to British seaports. William Lord, whose father regularly commanded timber ships trading to Quebec in the middle decades of the century, claimed that it was common at the time for these ships 'to lie up for the winter' in Britain after discharging the foremast hands. A major change in the seasonal deployment of vessels was provided by the repeal of the Navigation Acts in 1849, which opened up, for both colonial-owned and British-owned ships, trades which complemented the north Atlantic timber trade. Many of these ships used what had previously been the slack season for transporting cotton and timber from the southern United States to destinations in Britain and Europe. The West Indies and South American trades out of Halifax and Saint John could also make limited use of the winter months if the vessels left the northern ports in the autumn for a two- or three-month voyage.[7]

For the sailors who manned the merchant vessels frequenting Halifax, Saint John, and Quebec, the seasonal implications were twofold. For half the year, sailors were unemployable in their seafaring occupation in these particular ports. This encouraged them either to get out of port before winter on ships sailing for foreign destinations or to return to local residences where a supplementary family livelihood saw them through. If they remained in port, they had to fit into the accustomed pattern of pre-industrial winter life as underemployed or unemployed labourers. For the other half of the year, the commerce of the ports demanded their services in large numbers and paid them relatively well for the voyages they undertook.

The chronic shortage of seafaring labour during the commercial season commanded the attention of shippers and master mariners no less than it did that of the seamen themselves. This circumstance – as worrisome to capital as it was advantageous to labour – affected Quebec to a very considerable degree, Saint John slightly less, and Halifax intermittently. At the beginning of the season these ports required more seamen to man the outgoing ships than the number who arrived in merchant vessels to take on cargo. The major contributory factor to this imbalance can be traced to local shipbuilding. This leading secondary industry, which developed rapidly in the wake of the flourishing timber trade of eastern British North America, affected the labour supply in the three ports in somewhat different ways.

THE LABOUR SUPPLY

Quebec was the shipbuilding centre of Lower Canada. Its builders employed the cheap labour of winter to construct a fleet of wooden sailing vessels that were ready for launching soon after the seven-month season of river navigation opened in May. The new ships were almost entirely exported for sale, especially on the Liverpool market, earning for Quebec the distinction of fostering comparatively few shipowners among its merchants. Quebec's interest in its vessels therefore ended as soon as they were received by the buyers' or the builders' agents in Britain. This short-term investment not only influenced the financing, construction, and rate of shipbuilding, but also shaped the attitudes of the builders towards the manning of the vessels. They had no incentive to foster a native merchant marine. The quality of the seamanship was a matter of complete indifference to them and they therefore did little to encourage Canadians to become seafarers.[8]

But the nature of the voyages (see Table 1.1) and of the cargoes also materially contributed to the absence of a local market of sailors. Not only did the navigation season coincide with the farming, fishing, and well-paid port labour seasons to produce manifold opportunities for labour in summer, but also, for obvious and for less apparent reasons, shipping on ocean vessels was accorded the lowest priority on the workingman's list of possible employments. One obvious explanation was the dangers involved. Sailoring in general was the most hazardous occupation available, with astounding mortality rates in the age of sail. Plimsoll-inspired reformism in the last quarter of the century revealed the unsafe nature of floating places of work. For one thing, rumour had it 'that fully one quarter of the larger class of vessels leaving and arriving at Canadian ports are not properly provided with seaworthy boats.' In 1886 the crew of the Quebec barque *Gaspé* were unable to rescue a drowning seaman because of the condition of its boats. It was claimed 'that at the time the sailor fell overboard the boats were turned bottom up on their skeeds, that no tackle or davits were ready, the tackle being unshipped and stowed away in the hold. A boat, it is said, was got out after 20 minutes delay, but being in such a bad and leaky state, she could not be kept from sinking and returned to the ship again, leaving the poor man to his fate.'[9]

Certainly, timber ships had the distinction of being the worst hulks on the open sea. Many were disrated vessels, old, leaky, and rotten, the largest of which began their sailing careers as full-rigged ships but had been reduced to barques for carrying timber. Others were newly built Quebec vessels inadequately equipped, often without life-saving apparatus or a proper forecastle for the accommodation of the crew. William Lord subscribed to the widely held belief that the aged Quebec timber ships were encircled by chains to keep them from falling apart,

TABLE 1.1
Ocean shipping; Quebec

Year*	Vessels	Tons	Seamen	Vessels with cargoes	Vessels in ballast	British flag	Foreign flag	Major origins and destinations of voyages
1840 Inwards	1,255	430,951	16,827					1,052 from UK
Outwards	1,314	449,085	17,317					1,186 to UK
1845 Inwards	1,439	576,541	20,932					1,209 from UK
Outwards	1,499	584,540	21,131					1,409 to UK
1850 Inwards	1,196	465,804	16,092					717 from UK
Outwards	1,275	494,021	16,991					1,057 to UK
1855 Inwards	750	354,202	11,212	371	379	676	74	442 from UK
Outwards	877	366,631	11,750	877	0	798	79	717 to UK
1860 Inwards	1,252	666,958	21,299	548	707	1,072	180	836 from UK
Outwards	1,293	671,137	21,012	1,293	0	1,119	174	1,136 to UK
1865 Inwards	1,466	775,676	23,238	770	696	1,245	221	738 from UK
Outwards	1,690	964,387	25,260	1,690	0	1,435	255	1,217 to UK
1870 Inwards	1,091	756,078	21,931	639	452	820	271 (225 NOR†)	847 from UK
Outwards	999	674,894	18,865	999	0	756	243 (194 NOR)	848 to UK
1875 Inwards	854	639,235	19,818	384	470	540	314 (269 NOR and SWED‡)	639 from UK
Outwards	1,041	840,065	22,888	1,039	2	686	355 (303 NOR and SWED)	943 to UK
1880 Inwards	657	675,634	17,221	336	321	475 (65 CAN§)	182 (168 NOR and SWED)	496 from UK
Outwards	611	572,562	14,587	610	1	349 (75 CAN)	187 (170 NOR and SWED)	529 to UK
1885 Inwards	541	620,352	15,963	288	253	294 (24 CAN)	247 (214 NOR and SWED)	
Outwards	561	562,122	14,026	560	1	285 (70 CAN)	276 (232 NOR and SWED)	
1890 Inwards	477	617,510	14,339	233	244	246 (38 CAN)	231 (201 NOR and SWED)	
Outwards	403	439,092	10,048	401	2	191 (51 CAN)	212 (191 NOR and SWED)	

SOURCE: Trade and Navigation statistics, Canada *Sessional Papers*
*Figures for 1870, 1875, 1880, 1885, and 1890 are for year ending 30 June.
†Norwegian
‡Swedish.
§Canadian

'for some that I saw in Quebec looked as if they were ready on the slightest strain to break in two, having curves in them like the humps on the back of a dromedary.' As for the new vessels, Joseph Wetmore, captain of the fine new ship *Atlantic*, which had to put into Halifax with a mutinous crew in November 1868 en route from Quebec to Liverpool, admitted that the ship carried no lifebuoys and was incompletely fitted out, though 'she is fitted as is usual with new vessels going home.' Her temporary fitments included an insecure forecastle perched on the deck which had flooded 'breast-high' during a heavy gale. The inundation spelled potential disaster for the twenty-one men who had to live there and who feared that the next stormy sea would wash away their frail quarters.[10]

Timber itself was a notoriously dangerous cargo. It was liable to shift in bad seas and throw the vessel on to its beam ends. The deckloads of spars and masts – as threatening to human life as were mines without safety regulations – provided an additional and capricious hazard to the crew. Most sailors engaged in the timber 'droghers' who lived to tell the tale could describe the horrors of their voyages in overloaded ships. William Lord made his first return crossing from Quebec to Britain as an ordinary seaman on an archetypal unseaworthy vessel, the *Dorchester*, 'an antiquated Noah's ark kind of craft' of barque rig which was too old, heavy, and leaky to withstand the storms she encountered. About 300 miles off the coast of Ireland she became waterlogged and began to break up. The first victim was the galley, 'a hut on top of the ship,' which was washed overboard complete with cook. The next victim was the deckload on one side of the ship. After it had been dumped over, the resulting list necessitated the exceedingly hazardous release by the crew of the other portion of the deckload. This operation cost the lives of another two men washed over with the timber. By then the perilous state of the ship forced the remainder of the crew, together with the captain's wife, to take to the customary refuge in the tops where they languished for five days. Luckily their vessel drifted close to shore and they were rescued by Irish fishermen. Many thousands of sailors in similar circumstances met the ghastly fate of the *Dorchester*'s cook and the two unfortunate seamen before the mast. If a young Lower Canadian felt a taste for open water, he would naturally prefer the opportunities provided by the tamer inland navigation or, if he lived down river, he could go fishing in local waters.[11]

The less obvious but more critical reason for the failure of the local labour market to remedy the shortage of sailors can be found in the one-way nature of the voyages. The crews of the ships sent across the Atlantic to be sold were discharged on arrival in Britain. Although these one-way voyages made by new Quebec-built vessels comprised only a minority of departures from Quebec during the navigation season, all employment available on visiting British ships was in fact similarly one-way in nature. British shipowners, for a variety of complex economic and strategic reasons, shipped their seamen in British ports for a round voyage, the agreements specifying discharge and payment in a British port. For the aspiring Canadian sailor, this meant that on arrival in Britain, he would be discharged and thrown upon a glutted sailor market, with no chance for a westbound crossing at wages comparable to those paid for the Quebec-United Kingdom run, and with no possibility of shipping to his home port without incurring the risk of having to return in the same vessel to Britain in order to receive his outstanding wages. In other words, the nature of Quebec shipping in the nineteenth century rendered the occupation of mariner unattractive to a man wishing to retain a domicile and family in Quebec and hoping at the same time to better himself. Such opportunities simply did not exist. Furthermore, since the prospective Canadian sailors would need to come from the ranks of those inward-looking, home-loving French Canadians who worked the timber and built the ships, or the clannish Irish immigrants recently escaped from the United Kingdom who dominated dock labour in the latter half of the century, the chances of nurturing a pool of native seamen were even further reduced.[12]

In these circumstances the Quebec shipbuilder or his captain sought a crew from among the sailors arriving in the packets or timber ships in the spring fleet. Their willingness to filch from the legally bound crews of British or foreign vessels had far-ranging effects on the port and important implications for the sailors engaged in the Quebec trade. The first visiting ship that lost crew members to a new vessel had in turn to seek its complement from among the crews of neighbouring vessels. Captains shipped deserters to replace the men they themselves lost through desertion. The multiplier effect continued throughout the season, with the situation at its most extreme in June, when the first arrivals got away, and in the autumn, when the remaining vessels competed to wind up their business and escape from the St Lawrence before the freeze-up. Wage rates accordingly rose to compensate for the shortage of sailors and the shortage of time. A master experienced in the Quebec trade itemized in 1847 the costs incurred by owners whose crews deserted in the midst of their contracted voyage from Britain to Quebec and back again:

A ship between 500 and 600 tons, number of seamen 16, at £3 per month; each man had a month's advance, and half-pay note for his family, which note, if the man should desert, cannot be stopped for two months afterwards, making an advance to each man £6, or for sixteen men £96. On arriving at Quebec the crew are prevailed upon by lodging-house-keepers and others to leave, and who promise to get them from £12 to £15 per month; they then desert, and the master is obliged to hire a stevedore and labourers to load his ship, which will cost £100. When loaded he is compelled to call to his aid these selfsame lodging-house-keepers to find him a crew, say at the lowest wages £12 per month, which will be £9 more than the crew shipped for in England. If a good return voyage is made, and the crew discharged in 1½ months, each man will have cost £13.10s additional, which, multiplied by 16, is equal to £216; total cost of wages for the voyage of four months, £412. Had the original crew remained by the ship during the voyage, each man's wages would have amounted to £12, which, multiplied by 16, is £192. Loss to the owner for the voyage, £220. A ship generally makes two voyages in the season, and if the same practice should be repeated the owner is a loser of £440.[13]

During busy years such as 1851 and 1855 the higher costs in both wages and port charges accompanying the frequent delay in sailing were covered by increases in rates of freight. This development adversely affected the export merchants of Quebec at the same time as their less prominent brethren – shopkeepers, publicans, and boarding-house-keepers of the Lower Town – enjoyed the expenditure of the sailors' advances for the new voyages. Conversely, during the years of business recession, when few new ships were launched from the Quebec yards, the diminished demand for crews produced a sharp fall in seamen's wages, as for example in 1858 and 1859.[14]

Since many captains were strangers to the port of Quebec, or at best infrequent seasonal visitors, a class of local sailor-broker was nurtured to find the ship its crew and to provide the absconding sailor with a more remunerative berth. The registrar-general of seamen claimed that the demand for seamen encouraged the Quebec middlemen in the mid-1840s to induce about one-quarter of the seamen visiting Quebec (excluding mates and apprentices) to desert from their vessels.[15] These brokers or agents, popularly called 'crimps,' a term that stigmatized them as sailor-stealers, may have been beneficial to the sailor during the rise of Quebec's timber-based prosperity. But amid its wildly fluctuating fortunes from the 1850s to the 1870s, the crimps became bold, brutal, and unrestrained. Apart from this change in the nature of crimping, the repercussions attending the shortage of seamen remained amazingly constant throughout the period from the 1830s to the 1890s. The end thereafter of the shortage of sailors was more attributable to Quebec's own demise as a port and to the greater mobility of labour in the steam age than to reforms in the merchant service.

None the less, the failure to alleviate the costly and long-standing labour shortage in the shipping fleets of Quebec requires some further explanation. An effective attempt to cope with the deficiency would have entailed a rigid enforcement of imperial shipping law, which was being evaded or distorted locally to meet the self-interested aims of sailortown society. Moreover, Pollok and Gilmour believed in the 1850s that imperial law itself was inadequate and that the chief responsibility for counteracting desertion rested with the negligent British government. There were, to be sure, specific measures taken to alleviate the shortage. One was the dangerous tendency of desperate, hard-pressed sea captains facing the November freeze-up to sail short-handed in order to meet their schedules. Contemporaries attributed many a fatal shipwreck to the undermanning of the timber vessels bent on fleeing the St Lawrence.[16]

A range of less perilous remedies was put forward to overcome the labour problem. Some interested parties thought it might be worthwhile to investigate long-term solutions to the shortage, such as the introduction of an apprenticeship system similar to that used in the British merchant marine (and suggested for the US merchant service). The Quebec Board of Trade, in its usual pragmatic vein, pointed out that apprenticeship would not work in the Quebec trade 'because all or nearly all vessels built here are sent home for immediate sale and the apprentices would have to be sent back to Quebec at a very heavy expense.' It would work only on Canadian vessels 'clearing out for ports or places not in the United Kingdom.' Another popular notion for meeting the demand was derived from an English practice, begun in the late eighteenth century, which turned suitable vessels into training ships for pauper boys and in the second half of the nineteenth century provided an alternative to conventional reformatories for delinquent youth. More patient observers put their faith in the emergent steam age, which would direct surplus labour to undermanned ports with the speed and certainty required to protect the interests of commerce. The most radical suggestion by far came from a shipmaster who thought the remedy lay in fixing the wage rate at Quebec at a maximum of four pounds a month.[17]

Two major proposals relentlessly discussed throughout the period were discharge of sailors on arrival in port and importation of surplus seamen by the shipbuilders who had caused the problem to begin with. With a few notable exceptions, the advocates of discharge included Canadian shipbuilders and shipowners and the variegated elements in the port economy, from shopkeepers to ship labourers, who already depended on desertion and on discharges (which captains granted under threat of legal proceedings) for generating a significant portion of their summer livelihood. The opponents of discharge included, again with exceptions, visiting sea captains, who found it tedious and expensive to replace part of a crew, let alone a whole one, and agents of such important British shipowners as Pollok and Gilmour, whose first loyalty was to the imperial counting-house, not to the colonial port. The colonial advocates of free trade in sailors upbraided the British shipping interests for being 'monopolists and usurers when labor is the commodity, instead of "wares, goods and merchandise"' and for denying sailors participation 'in the modern changes in the relations existing between capital and labor' solely because they were politically insignificant. Canadians claimed to be 'in favour of dropping outdated controls and leaving the supply of seamen to operations of the free market economy in so far as the very nature of the sea service allows for such a policy.'[18]

For their part, the British thought of their seamen as part of the manpower of the British nation: their wages supported their families and contributed to the well-being of their home communities. Their terms of employment ensured a constant supply of labour to British shipowners, whose world-view could hardly be expected to bend to accommodate one geographic area of their commercial empire. And, overriding all other considerations, was state policy, which still subscribed to the time-honoured view that the merchant service existed to supply the Royal Navy in wartime. It was in the interest of the nation to retain British seamen in British ships; discharge in British North America would only accelerate the already established practice of British seamen looking for better opportunities on vessels belonging to the United States, a commercial rival of growing importance.[19]

The long debate over the advantages of discharging sailors became an academic one in which the Quebec advocates never attempted to hide their self-interest. Quebec businessman H.J. Jameson claimed in 1859 that discharging seamen would promote 'the spending of from £800,000 to £1,000,000 in our port, by the increased employments afforded our working men throughout the season of navigation.' Newspaper editors sometimes claimed discharge would have miraculous results for seamen. The editor of the *Quebec Mercury* argued in 1870 that it would diminish the 'demoralization' associated with the seafaring life and greatly improve 'the general character of the merchant marine.' The demoralization in question was equated with desertion, the only way sailors could achieve the equivalent of discharge, except that when they were unsuccessful they were either 'incarcerated in common prisons where they necessarily associate with vagabonds, bad characters and even felons, or else are subjected to a penal discipline destructive of all self respect.' In the mean time, in 1854, the British government explicitly prohibited discharge abroad in order to discourage 'the accumulation in foreign ports of distressed British subjects, to be sent home at the public charge.' By protecting British seamen in distant ports against forcible eviction from their vessels, the law rendered unlikely the acceptance of the general principle of discharge abroad.[20]

The second major proposal, that of importing crews for new vessels, was long favoured by British shipowners trading to Quebec and also by those Quebec business interests, represented by the Quebec Board of Trade, which were not involved in shipbuilding. These proponents claimed that Quebec shipbuilders should feel a special obligation to man their vessels in an orderly, legal fashion. To some extent the British practised what they required of their Quebec counterparts. The large companies engaged in the timber trade, which sent annual fleets to the St Lawrence, often carried extra hands in the hope that the inevitable losses through desertion might thereby be supplied. During seasons when the wage rates out of Quebec were considered especially exorbitant and when time allowed, extra hands were sought in less favoured labour markets on the east coast. For their part, Quebec shipbuilders did occasionally bring in sailors to man their vessels, but the method was found unsatisfactory: 'One gentleman has said that he had repeatedly imported crews from England for his new ships, and that he never could retain them. On one occasion a crew on their arrival marched up to the Police Office and demanded and obtained their discharge only because the vessel for which they had been hired had not been named.' The major obstacle in the way of a regular policy of importation of labour was not the local opposition but rather the necessity of enshrining the practice in legal garb. Further statutory regulation of an occupation already legislated into hopeless confusion promised to be unpopular. Moreover, as an attempt in Saint John in 1840 showed, the British Board of Trade, which controlled marine affairs, did not favour the removal of disengaged sailors from the British labour market even for the limited and patently imperially biased purpose of bringing home to market the ships built in the colonies. British government opposition to systematized importation proved to be intractable.[21]

Saint John was a hybrid port, combining dependence on the timber trade and shipbuilding (like Quebec) with participation in the short-range and long-haul carrying trades in the Americas (like Halifax). The manning of its fleets was influenced by shipbuilding, the entrepreneurial activities of its merchants, and the geographical features of its location. Unlike Quebec at its commercial height, Saint John was not the only shipbuilding centre in its province, but it was the major one. A large proportion of vessels built outside Saint John, particularly on the Fundy shore, did however visit Saint John for fitting out, cargo, and manning. Since many new ships sought their crews in Saint John, the labour shortage resembled that of Quebec. As in Quebec, shipbuilding was a winter activity and the shipbuilders were anxious to dispatch the completed vessels to the United Kingdom market with the opening of the spring trade. During the years when shipbuilding boomed, the demand for seamen invariably exceeded the supply, wages rose, and incoming seamen seized the better opportunities that emerged. (Table 1.2 gives details of ocean shipping from Saint John from 1840 to 1890.) But here the similarity with Quebec ends, because Saint John was much better situated than Quebec for supplying its merchant fleets. For one thing, New Brunswick raised its own complement of native seamen: there were ample chances to sail in merchantmen and maintain a domicile in Saint John. Vessels engaged in coasting and the West Indies trade often terminated their contracted voyages in Saint John. Even the transatlantic timber trade was not closed to native seamen, since Saint John, again in contrast to Quebec, was a shipowning port, the shipowners and shipmasters of which were willing to compensate the sailors for one-way voyages entailing discharges abroad. Admittedly,

TABLE 1.2
Ocean shipping: Saint John

Year*	Vessels	Tons	Seamen	Vessels with cargoes	Vessels in ballast	British flag	Foreign flag	Major origins and destinations of voyages					
								UK	BNA	USA	British colonies	Spanish West Indies	South America
1840 Inwards	1,693	188,605	10,293			1,599	94	211	1,123	326			
Outwards	1,779	225,347	10,639			1,688	91	312	1,154	258			
1845 Inwards	1,758	280,379	12,145			1,677	81	412	967	306			
Outwards	1,764	296,558	12,677			1,686	78	558	912	249			
1850 Inwards	1,695	260,429	11,172					133		694	831		
Outwards	1,720	284,793	12,192					457		405	840		
1855 Inwards	1,886	367,521	13,558										
Outwards	1,870	420,624	14,897										
1860 Inwards	1,757	365,041	13,361	1,383	374	1,529	228						
Outwards	1,676	386,828	13,575	1,289	387	1,453	223						
1865 Inwards	1,856	433,834	13,869	1,236	620	1,628	228						
Outwards	1,883	475,775	14,878	1,743	140	1,659	224						
1870 Inwards	1,613	471,297	13,382	1,103	510†								
Outwards	1,141	417,388	10,747	1,135	6	842	299 (279 US)	258		638			30
1875 Inwards	1,131	377,614	10,593	712	419	797	334 (257 US)	113		935		188	
Outwards	1,157	450,516	11,803	1,141	16	799	358 (251 US)	335		622		90	
1880 Inwards	1,424	462,880	12,337	583	841	1,001 (950 CAN‡)	423 (372 US)	102		1,187			
Outwards	1,364	458,880	11,799	1,356	8	958 (910 CAN)	406	252		976			
1885 Inwards	1,740	401,545	15,391	676	1,064	1,311 (1264 CAN)	429 (396 US)						
Outwards	1,777	428,521	15,806	1,723	54	1,353 (1300 CAN)	424 (395 US)						
1890 Inwards	1,766	500,641	17,468	705	1,078	1,334 (1288 CAN)	432 (385 US)						
Outwards	1,791	504,494	17,659	1,061	314	1,377 (1342 CAN)	414 (376 US)						

SOURCE: Trade and Navigation statistics, New Brunswick and Canada *Sessional Papers*
*Figures for 1870, 1875, 1880, 1885, and 1890 are for year ending 30 June.
†Statistics conflicting
‡Canadian

one-way voyages from Saint John to Britain without compensation, for the purpose of selling new ships or in British-owned vessels, constituted a significant proportion of departures. Saint John sailors, too, could be stranded in Britain. In 1841 Seaman Raghan, whose family resided in Saint John, had to wait three or four weeks in Liverpool until he found a suitable means of returning to his native city. In the mean time he ran up a considerable debt at his boarding-house and laboured as a tidesman at the docks. This work finally led him to a New Brunswick vessel and he returned to Saint John on the *Lady Milton* in December by working his passage as a supernumerary, ostensibly against the captain's desire and without signing articles. Subsequently he was awarded full wages for the voyage by the magistrate's court in Saint John. Alderman Benjamin Peters, who presided over Raghan's suit for wages and who earned a reputation in the 1840s as a solid friend of seamen, sympathized with Raghan's determination to seize the opportunity to work his passage home instead of continuing his vigil in Liverpool for another Saint John ship.[22]

By the mid-1870s, after the overseas market for New Brunswick's wooden sailing vessels had contracted, ship ownership increased in Saint John, giving the port a brief distinction as the fourth ship-owning port in the British Empire, surpassed only by Liverpool, London, and Glasgow. Harmony between shipowners and shipbuilders and the concentration of owning and building in the same hands prevented Quebec-style tensions in the sailor labour market. Moreover, Saint John had ready access to other labour markets. Its regular contact with the many Nova Scotia ports enabled it to draw on that considerable source of seamen. The newspapers of Halifax kept local seamen well informed concerning the labour conditions of the Saint John sailor market. The mobility between those two centres was matched by that between Saint John and the large ports of the American seaboard, where local shipping agents recruited seamen. Shipping connections with Boston, New York, and the ports of the American south provided opportunities for the movement of labour closed to Quebec before the advent of rail travel.[23]

Although the shortage of sailors in Saint John in the nineteenth century seldom appeared as critical as that in the larger port of Quebec, it was severe enough to spawn a parallel range of remedies. None was more successful there than at Quebec, but one demands some comment: legislation requiring local shipowners to import crew members to man the new ships they built or purchased. The New Brunswick statute of 1840 which embodied this stipulation extended to shipowners throughout the province, but since the British government, in its imperial wisdom, disallowed the act, it remained on the statute book too short a time to make a discernible impact on local shipping. None the less some shipowners, temporarily affected, noted that imported seamen, too, deserted from their intended vessels or proved to be too expensive to retain when the ship was not ready to launch by the expected date. The 1840 statute, 'to provide for a regular supply of seamen for new ships fitted out or loaded in the Province,' imposed harsh financial penalties for failure to comply with the obligation to import four hands for each new vessel of 300 tons and one man for each additional 100 tons. Despite this, the act had the support of the Saint John Chamber of Commerce, and available evidence indicates that shipowners tried to comply with its regulations and did not protest against or resent this government interference in their labour problems. Those Saint John shipowners who petitioned in 1842 and 1843 for reimbursement of their fines or expenses incurred unnecessarily in importing seamen did so because the statute had been annulled, not because they considered themselves to have been unjustly treated. What both the legislation and the local response to it amply demonstrated was the deeply felt interest of shipowners in solving the problem of manning their vessels. Had the local legislature been permitted to pursue this policy, the importation of seamen might have created an environment far more favourable to the employer than to labour. Britain's refusal to countenance such regulation thus protected the sailor as much as it did the shipping interests of the mother country. The legislature continued for several years to toy with the possibility of reintroducing the legislation, with bounties (raised by a tax on newly built tonnage) rather than penalties. The plans disappeared in 1849 when a government shipping office was established to regulate the manning of ships. Thereafter the shortage of sailors continued in Saint John until the problem was alleviated by the decline in the building of wooden ships, the prolonged trade depression of the late 1870s, and the tendency of visiting steamships to retain their crews.[24]

Halifax, the entrepôt of the northeast Atlantic, was noted neither as a timber nor as a shipbuilding port, but none the less timber was loaded and reshipped and ships were built, repaired, and fitted out there. Had it been a major shipbuilding port it might still have escaped the chronic shortage of seamen that affected Quebec and Saint John. For sailoring, like shipbuilding, was both an important and a respectable occupation in Nova Scotia. While we must not romanticize the 'iron men' of Nova Scotia shipping, all Nova Scotia's commercial centres were seaports in the pre-railway age, and their youth, be they the sons of farmers, fishermen, shipbuilders, merchants, or sea captains, were bred to the sea. Few lived far from the smell of the salty sea air, and few resisted the temptation of an exciting and hazardous, if temporary, acquaintance with life before the mast. The *Novascotian* claimed in 1856 that 'no country employs comparatively a larger number of native seamen in manning its craft.' Many of the native sailors engaged in trading voyages considered themselves to be primarily fishermen. Indeed the seasonal features of the two types of seafaring were complementary, since seamen who fished in the summer could augment their meagre earnings by undertaking an autumn voyage to the West Indies. The nature of merchant shipping therefore encouraged the development of a native merchant marine, unlike the pattern of trade in Quebec which positively discouraged it.[25] (Table 1.3 gives data on Halifax shipping from 1850 to 1890.)

As one observer noted, the dangers of seafaring did not deter Nova Scotians: 'They take to the water as naturally as a brood of young ducks.' And yet in the 'Lights and Shadows of Sea Life' described in the press, the shadows took the kind of toll which must have encouraged Maritime youth to look for other options once the wanderlust was out of their systems. In 1877 a Halifax newspaper recorded the chequered career of one of its native career sailors as an illustration of the risks of seafaring. As an apprentice on an English brig, this sailor entered hospital in Trinidad with yellow fever at the same time that an apprentice with the same name, from a vessel of the same name, died of this same affliction in Port of Spain, and the Halifax family mistakenly went into mourning. Wrecked on a Halifax brig returning from the West Indies some years later, the surviving sailor and his mates were picked up by an American whaleship outward-bound to the Pacific whaling grounds and eventually landed at the port of Talcuhauna on the Chilean coast. By the time they returned home via the United States they were received 'as if risen from the dead.' When the same sailor was mate of a brig bound for Halifax from Liverpool, one protracted crossing ended just in time to prevent cannibalism among the crew. After he became a master, this sailor was wrecked off Cape Hatteras where he clung to the capsized West Indiaman for many weeks before being rescued by a Liverpool-bound cotton ship. 'At last and finally

TABLE 1.3
Ocean shipping: Halifax

Year*	Vessels	Tons	Seamen	Vessels with cargoes	Vessels in ballast	British flag	Foreign flag	UK	BWI	BNA	Sea fisheries	USA	Foreign West Indies	Spanish West Indies	Nfld.
1850 Inwards	1,194	176,604	13,646					99	630 ⎰			294			
Outwards	1,068	161,394	12,746					45	721 ⎰			208			
1858 Inwards	1,398	208,516	14,709	1,301	97	1,330	68	102	70	684		352			
Outwards	1,243	166,483	13,631	1,213	30	1,221	22	36	136	721		208			
1860 Inwards	1,471	224,186	15,768	1,333	138	1,409	62	94	89	685		379			
Outwards	1,435	209,936	17,040	1,346	89	1,415	20	40	167	831		251			
1865 Inwards	1,481	292,091	18,351	1,298	183	1,348	133	123	155	577		446	149		
Outwards	1,150	260,776	18,250	1,004	146	1,086	64	56	225	486		266	88		
1870 Inwards	1,251	311,357	16,319	1,104	147	1,036	215 (192 US)	93	116			428		130	192
Outwards	1,014	275,062	14,940	935	79	873	141 (126 US)	58	176			255		114	201
1875 Inwards	1,215	354,274	18,188	1,055	160	861	354 (312 US)	94	207			421		93	313
Outwards	771	300,374	13,859	737	34	620	151 (116 US)	70	149			186		93	193
1880 Inwards	1,070	529,663	21,140	949	121	881	189 (134 US)	159	141			350		127	141
Outwards	1,139	478,875	19,858	1,120	19	994 (794 CAN†)	145 (99 US)	132	126		86	204		153	164
1885 Inwards	942	601,112	21,896	865	77	724 (427 CAN)	218 (143 US)								
Outwards	1,098	585,921	22,901	1,069	29	907 (627 CAN)	191 (110 US)				245				
1890 Inwards	1,065	682,408	24,261	923	142	856 (484 CAN)	209 (87 US; 74 NOR‡ and SWED§)								
Outwards	1,273	658,340	26,731	1,252	21	1,089 (736 CAN)	184 (80 US; 64 NOR and SWED)								

Major origins and destinations of voyages

SOURCE: Trade and Navigation statistics, Nova Scotia and Canada *Sessional Papers*

*No statistics are available for 1840s or 1854–57 inclusive. Figures for 1858, 1860, 1865 are for year ending 30 September; for 1870 on, for year ending 30 June.

†Canadian
‡Norwegian
§Swedish

his adventurous career was brought to a close in the West Indies where his old enemy "Yellow Jack" met him and conquered.'[26]

As if natural disasters were not bad enough, locally owned vessels had a reputation for being needlessly dangerous places to work. The editor of the Halifax *Morning Chronicle* alleged in 1873 that 'our Nova Scotian coasting traders and short voyagers, say to West Indies ports and the United States, are short-manned and provided with no effective lifesaving apparatus, and without proper lamps, and are too often over-laden.' Poor food and inadequate accommodation also made employment on Halifax vessels uncomfortable. 'Every shipmaster and seaman sailing out of the port knows,' the same editor continued in a later article, 'that our vessels are not well fitted; every man who has anything to do with shipping knows it, every shipowner knows it, and most of them privately acknowledge it, and try to justify it by the excuse that the closeness of competition necessitates the shaving of expenses down to the lowest possible figure.'[27]

If Nova Scotia seafarers experienced the usual dangers of seafaring in an age when shipowners showed little regard for their welfare, the seamen could look forward to at least the kind of advancement in their careers which the maritime nature of Halifax enterprises encouraged. For those sailors who stayed with the sea, such advantages as commanding a vessel, buying shares in a vessel, and utimately owning a vessel existed because shipping was not centralized or monopolistic. How widespread such opportunities were is not at all clear. For the sons of Halifax's leading merchants and shipowners apprenticeship in the West Indies trade was a prelude to rapid upward mobility. But one old salt complained in 1856 that vessels sailing out of Halifax were, for the most part, commanded by foreigners, not natives, and that advancement was rare among Halifax sailors.[28]

Whatever the likelihood of promotion, foremast hands were at a premium in Halifax during the busiest weeks of the shipping season, especially after the Washington Treaty of 1871 admitted undermanned American fishing schooners to port and during the decades when the steam age made Halifax an important coaling station. Moreover, the success with which Halifax merchants imposed their hegemony over the provincial fishing industry produced the kind of centralization of Nova Scotia's fish export business that increased the need for seamen in Halifax. At the same time Halifax demonstrably functioned as the sailor market for the province as a whole, since the natural tendency of

outport and riverside shipbuilders and shippers was to seek their
seamen in the major centre of population and business.[29]

In addition to the different nature of its shipbuilding and export
trades, Halifax enjoyed one other distinction: it was a naval port. The
presence there of Britain's North American squadron during the very
months of the merchant shipping season had a number of implications
for sailors. For one thing, the proverbial prankishness and group
riotousness of Jolly Tars ashore tended to command a larger share of
public attention than the activities of merchant sailors. One cannot
help speculating to what extent the naval presence might also have
discouraged the desertion of merchant seamen in Halifax. Clearly the
port enjoyed the services of an unofficial marine police force during the
summer visits of the admiral of the squadron. When the *Excelsior* entered port in 1864 with a crew which had stopped work to protest
against the leaky condition of the vessel, the captain was sent a posse
of officers and men of the HMS *Duncan* to guard the seamen until they
could be arrested by civilian law officers. The navy itself was plagued
by desertion. The admiral threatened during a flood of desertions in
1861 to search every merchant vessel leaving Halifax for his missing
men. In 1872, eighty desertions in Halifax were reported from the HMS
Royal Alfred alone. It seems that the high rate of naval desertions during
boom years for commercial shipping meant that naval sailors not only
deserted, but also were crimped or enticed by high wages into the
merchant service. With the Royal Navy acting in part as a source of
supply for the merchant fleets operating out of Halifax, it is difficult to
see the naval presence as a deterrent to the desertion of merchant
seamen. Rather the navy acted for Halifax as an illegal source of supply
not available on a regular basis in Saint John or Quebec. Paid-off naval
sailors were known also to seek employment in merchant vessels
crewing in their port of discharge. When the *Excelsior* left Halifax after
the trial of its seamen for insubordination, the reconstituted crew
contained a number of ex-naval sailors.[30]

In the absence of large-scale civilian desertion, the shortage of
merchant sailors in Halifax can still be inferred from the same kind, if
not the same degree, of sailors' strikes, crimping, and litigation as
in Saint John and Quebec, which operated under the same imperial or
similar colonial merchant shipping acts. Over time the problem
receded. When the shipping master claimed in the mid-1880s that a
scarcity of men existed every year except in January and February, he

implied that the shortage was confined to the declining number of sailing vessels. Seamen shipped in Britain for the return voyage did not desert from the briefly berthed steamers as they had formerly done from sailing ships. Wages and conditions of work were marginally better, laws were stricter, and the wage differential on opposite sides of the Atlantic was no longer so significant.[31]

GOVERNMENT CONTROL

Although the labour shortage variously affecting the merchant fleets of the three ports in the nineteenth century was never resolved by the shipping interests, attempts were made to control the sailor market. In circumstances where the free operation of the market favoured labour over capital, the govenment stepped in, ostensibly to promote order and fairness in the shipping of seamen, but in reality to discourage desertion and crimping and thereby serve the needs of capital. Two types of controls were introduced over and above the traditional resort to legal punishment for desertion and crimping. On the punitive side, in Quebec an attempt was made to prevent desertion by maintaining a river police force. On the regulatory side, government shipping offices, staffed by shipping masters, were established at mid-century in Quebec and Saint John, with British blessing, and later adopted by the dominion government for Halifax as a prelude to being extended to all other Canadian ports.

The river police force initiated in Quebec in 1838 never received a very good press – its membership reflected a local community which benefited from the practices it was meant to contain. It is indeed debatable whether the force aided and abetted rather than curbed crimping and desertion. Both local and British business interests lacked confidence in the integrity of the force and called unsuccessfully for the stationing of British ships-of-war in the St Lawrence as a more effective deterrent.[32] None the less, the force lasted, largely on a seasonal basis, until 1893 and was, after Confederation, along with its Montreal counterpart, a federally supervised and subsidized law enforcement agency.

Encouragement for the formation of the Quebec river police force had first come from Lord Durham. Visiting shipmasters concluded that the force organized by Durham in 1838 reduced the amount of desertion, and they therefore put pressure on government to continue it. The necessary resident interest in the seasonal force was supplied by the Quebec Board of Trade, the main motivation of which may have been to extend the duties of the force to protect the property of the timber merchants. In 1840 the board came out in favour of a compulsory tax on shipping for the support of the force and suggested the idea of using the police office as the sole shipping office. Through the 1840s, however, the force remained a seasonal body supported by a voluntary tax on shipping. Its control was vested in the Board of Trade in 1846 but the board's expectation that the British Mercantile Marine Act of 1850 would lessen desertion at Quebec led to a unilateral reduction in the force in 1851, which greatly annoyed shipmasters and caused a strike of the fourteen policemen. After being attacked by the crew of a vessel they had been sent to search for deserters, the policemen walked off the job complaining that 'they were not sufficiently numerous for the discharge of their duties' and were 'not being adequately remunerated.'[33]

The Board of Trade's high-handedness ended its interference with the force. The legislature regularized the force's operation in 1852 under the judge of the sessions and introduced a compulsory tax on shipping tonnage. These measures did not stop the criticism, which was directed mainly at the seasonal nature of the force. Organized early in May, it disbanded each November after the men had 'just been drilled and trained by their experienced Chief, in the routine of their peculiar duties.' The local newspapers drew an unfavourable comparison with Montreal, the only other port with a civilian water police force, where a much larger force was retained year round despite the considerably smaller volume of shipping. The occasional use of the Quebec force during the winter – in 1864–5 for frontier duty to prevent the crimping of British subjects into the us (Union) army and in the late 1860s to patrol the Lower Town – did not lead to permanent establishment. Certainly the suggestion that the force be used for winter patrol duty to replace the British garrison recalled in 1871 fell on deaf ears. And indeed, after the offices of chief of the force and shipping master were joined in 1870, the force came under increasing pressure as its effectiveness, its composition, and its cost became matters for debate.[34]

The diligence of the river police was called into question particularly during the summer of 1872 when crimping reached violent proportions. The failure of the police to prevent the disorder and apprehend its perpetrators was attributed to the inadequate size of the force.

While its seasonal nature also continued to be a cause for concern, the more vociferous critics claimed that the growing inefficiency was tied to its increasingly French-Canadian composition. At the same time reductions in the numbers of the force and in the wages of the men and the appointment of a French-Canadian chief raised questions about the police's ability to suppress crimping, by then 'one of the greatest, hydra-headed, evils of trade.' The annual reports of the chief of the river police in papers of the Department of Marine indicate, however, that on average over 500 arrests of sailors and crimps were made by the police during the shipping seasons of the 1870s. Raiding boarding-houses in search of runaway sailors became a specialty in the early 1880s.[35]

Although the potential for wider use of the force was illustrated in 1878 and 1879 when it was used to suppress land-based strikes of ship labourers, it was abolished in 1893; the city had refused to take it over from the federal government, on the ground that it patrolled the harbour rather than the town. Pressure for termination had come from members of parliament, who had no interest in favouring Quebec over other ports (the Montreal water police had already been dismantled, and neither Saint John nor Halifax, with its ready-made naval patrol, had ever established a harbour police force).[36] The MPs were supported in their demand by Quebec shipowners, who faced heavier dues in American ports in retaliation against the tonnage duty levied on American vessels in Quebec for the support of the police.[36]

All the ports eventually boasted shipping offices (see Table 1.4), the purpose of which was to regulate hiring and eliminate irregular practices of the free-enterprise employment brokers. Staffed by a shipping master and his deputies, the office was designed to oversee the engagement of crewmen within its port, endorse changes in the contract between captain and sailors, and superintend the paying off of arriving sailors who were entitled to discharge by virtue of the contract or by rights established in a local court case.

The first such office came into existence in Quebec in 1848 with the appointment of Alfred Hawkins as shipping master. Created by Canadian legislation of 1847, it gave Quebec the distinction of being the first British or colonial port to regulate the sailor market directly by a government agency.[37] Immediately, the shipping office was abhorred by all the local parties who profited from the status quo and by the

TABLE 1.4
Number of sailors shipped by government shipping masters

Year*	Quebec	Saint John	Halifax	Montreal	Yarmouth
1848	2,255				
1849	2,602				
1850	1,871				
1851	1,773				
1852	1,329	3,230			
1853	1,814	3,823			
1854		3,802			
–					
1869	854	4,745			
1870		4,020			
1871		4,471†			
1872	2,127	3,962†			
1873	2,330	4,957†	3,137‡		
1874	2,264	4,168	3,188		
1875	3,511§	4,417	2,825	686	
1876	1,728	4,170	2,547	614	712
1877	1,771	3,904	2,879	480	
1878	1,151	3,664	2,660	396	
1879	925	2,842	2,532	516	
1880	1,307	4,279	3,339	1,491	540
1881	1,030	4,314	3,579	676	780
1882	1,544	4,375	3,329	539	736
1883	1,881	4,615	3,423	545	525
1887	798	3,910	2,651	897	671
1889		3,658	3,404	1,355	700

SOURCES: Sixth Annual Report of the Shipping Master's Office, Quebec for 1853; Public Archives of Canada, RG 4, C 1, vol. 331, No. 355; List of Men Shipped at the Port of St. John for the Three Years ending Jan. 1855 by Patrick Comerford, Provincial Archives of New Brunswick, RLE/854-5, re 3; Canada *Sessional Papers*, Annual Reports of Department of Marine
*1869–74: fiscal year; 1875–89: calendar year
†Includes discharges
‡15 months
§17 months

seamen themselves, who clung to customary practices. The office enjoyed a stormy career until vested interests found they could ignore it with impunity. Its ineffectiveness, apparent as early as 1850, continued until its decreasing business was assumed by the resident Department of Marine official in 1889.

During the first year in operation, however, the office appeared to threaten existing desertion and hiring patterns and disrupt considerably the traditional customs of Quebec. Some sailors, fearing the threat of prosecution in Britain if they shipped through the new office as deserters, and resenting in principle the interference with their customary methods for finding employment, deserted to the United States via up river steamer routes instead of to other vessels in port. Others felt sufficiently cowed by the new legislation to stay by their ships in port, an unheard-of circumstance. The combination of desertion out of the port, on the one hand, and continued service in the visiting vessels, on the other, was interpreted by the locals as having disastrous effects on the economy of the Lower Town and the resident working class. Whichever course the sailors took, the business interests of the Lower Town, especially outfitters and publicans, were deprived of the advantages usually occasioned by the expenditure of the advance of wages given rehired deserters. In addition to the tens of thousands of pounds allegedly lost to trade, residents claimed that the usual ship labouring jobs were unavailable for the local labour force. Several thousand casual labourers lost their crucial seasonal employment of loading the timber ships because sailors remained at their posts. Not only was this a great hardship for the labouring poor, but it also deprived the trade of the town of the expenditure of the earnings of the timber stowers and many influential residents of the rents of their large property holdings in the Lower Town. The impact of the new legislation coincided with a poor commercial season, and the depression of the Lower Town was probably as much owing to business recession as to the new shipping office. The public, however, was adamant in its condemnation of the unwanted institution and the ruinous monopoly it created.[38]

During the shipping season of 1849, the memory of the previous year's experience created more positive displays of disapproval of the new legislation. Alfred Hawkins became the target of the seething discontent. Hated by a community that did not want him and an embarrassment to the government that employed him, Hawkins tried in vain to maintain the integrity of his office. After being intimidated out of several buildings Hawkins saw his fourth office, along with some £40,000 to £60,000 of surrounding property, destroyed in July 1849 by the work of incendiaries. A rioting mob damaged his next premises and a third attempt to put an end to the office by force was only just diverted in late August when a procession of sailors bent on destruction was stopped by the intervention of the magistrates, who read the riot act. That summer saw much rioting and incendiarism against authority in Quebec and other Canadian cities. This wider epidemic of disorder should not however be permitted to detract from the political importance of the attempts to wreck the shipping office. Not only did sailors join with townspeople to destroy the shipping office but also local interest groups succeeded in securing a legislative inquiry into the operation of the shipping act.[39]

Nothing as dramatic as those events happened again. Townspeople and sailors learned to live with the shipping office and to flout its authority. The impotence of that office is clearly demonstrated in the unimpressive statistics of the shipping master, which are particularly revealing when compared to Saint John, where the government shipping master handled a large proportion of the turnover in the local sailor labour market. Through the early 1850s in Quebec the apprehensions of the local populace slowly abated as the shipping office figures began to reveal the ineffectiveness of the shipping act. In 1851, one critic claimed that 1,000 men were needed to man the new ships but that the shipping master had been able to supply only one-tenth that number. Of twenty-six new vessels launched in Quebec in 1852 before 1 October, only three were supplied by the shipping office. The number of sailors recruited by the office declined, the shipping master being unable to capture more than two-thirds of the business of shipping seamen, and that degree of success pretty well confined to its initial years of operation. Many local residents continued to demand the abolition of the office on the ground that it created a monopoly ruinous to the shipping interests and the city. Their failure to achieve abolition encouraged them either to countenance more aggressive crimping, or, in the case of the Quebec Board of Trade, to condemn utterly the undesirable institution.[40]

The emergence of illegal crimping had crippling effects on the shipping office. For one thing, the crimps had little difficulty in persuading sailors to avoid the office altogether; sailors were, in any case, opposed to the office in principle and no amount of telling them what was good for them would change this. As a result, the prevailing scarcity of sailors seeking employment through the shipping office drove up the wages quoted there to hitherto unknown levels, which hardly endeared the office to the shipping interests it was designed to benefit. Crimps were therefore able to offer lower wages to shipmasters outside the government shipping office and capture back their custom and an increasing proportion of the whole business of shipping seamen. Not content to allow the resulting limited supply of sailors to determine the wages offered at the shipping office, the crimps encouraged sailors to combine and demand even higher wages when they went to the shipping office.

While sailors' strikes for higher wages had occurred in Quebec before the advent of the shipping office – in 1841, for example – the protest against the office was the most effective in uniting sailors in a demand for higher wages. One season's experience with Shipping Master Hawkins in 1848 precipitated efforts by the boarding-house-keepers and other interested parties on shore to reinstitute a higher wage rate during the summer of 1849, and the seamen were naturally willing to refuse to ship in order to enforce the better rates. During the strike, sailors resorted to persuasion to convince their fellow seamen that holding out for an increased rate of wages was for the common good of all concerned. In one incident, a number of seamen boarded the *John and Eleanor* at night and forced a sailor who had shipped below the desired rate to go ashore with them. The reluctant sailor ran away and two of his abductors were subsequently arrested. For several years thereafter sporadic disorder continued to mark sailor resistance to the Quebec shipping office. In the early summer of 1851, for example, about 200 striking seamen stayed on shore, 'parading the streets and congregating on the Plains adjacent to the city, armed with clubs, and colors flying, bidding defiance to the masters and authorities.'[41]

This course of events meant that the initial supporters of the shipping office – shipmasters, owners, and merchants – became aggravated by its inefficiency and began to make their own private arrangements. Hawkins found that captains, who left their ships' articles with him on which to enter the names of the newly engaged seamen, frequently became annoyed at his inability to man their ships expeditiously and at reasonable wages and accordingly withdrew their articles from his office. Thwarted on all sides, Hawkins became more interested in tracking down crimps and delinquent seamen who avoided the shipping office than in the seemingly hopeless task of improving the efficiency of his office. In 1850 he wrote to the registrar-general of seamen in London: 'I cannot express to you how ambitious I am to accomplish the intentions of the Act and put down a system of open and monstrous plunder which has so long disgraced the port of Quebec.' The popular image of the office became one of a police establishment rather than a labour exchange, especially after

1852, when the shipping master was given the services of two constables paid for out of the funds of the river police force. Moreover, the shipping master dispatched to the registrar-general of seamen regular lists of deserters known to have shipped through the shipping office. To curb former practices the office would have to stop shipping these deserters. Yet it was 'necessarily dependent for its supply of seamen on desertion, the very evil which it was designed to remedy.' Even during the first year of its operations the office shipped 408 deserters, almost one-third of the total desertions reported. At the end of each shipping season the engagement of deserters was essential in order to provide employment for seamen before the freeze-up and to relieve the city of Quebec of the prospective burden of their maintenance or transportation to ice-free ports. As a result, according to one observer, 'it has been found absolutely necessary, with the view of getting vessels off, late in the fall, for the shipping master to enter into a *sub rosa* arrangement with the crimps to procure men.'[42]

For the legislation affecting the shipping office to have had at least a chance to work, one serious loophole in the act of 1847, which was not corrected by Canadian legislation for almost thirty years, would have required alteration. By clause 8 of the statute the business of shipping seamen was limited not solely to the official shipping master but to the shipping master *or* the ship's captain, owner, or accredited agent. In theory, the master went to the shipping master if he was unable to find his own men; in practice, despairing of the efficiency of the shipping office and unable usually to recruit sailors directly, he continued without interruption to rely on the services of more knowledgeable middlemen, now labelled *crimps*.[43]

Indeed the legislation created crimping as it existed in Quebec in the second half of the nineteenth century. While the form of the legislation was therefore such that it rendered the shipping office ineffective right from the beginning, the nonsensical nature of so loose a piece of legislation became fully apparent only after the monumental consolidation and revision of British shipping regulations in the Merchant Shipping Act of 1854. This legislation required sailors in British-registered vessels to be shipped before a public shipping officer. In Quebec the existing shipping master discharged this responsibility under the aegis of the colonial legislation. The anomaly arose, then, of British vessels visiting Quebec having to use the shipping office, keeping it in business as it were, while masters of new vessels or Quebec-owned vessels (subject to colonial rather than British law) did not need to darken its doors with their manning arrangements. Since the Quebec shipping office exacted a much higher fee for shipping a seaman than was current in other British ports, the parties that complained most in the long run about the Quebec shipping office were British: masters, owners, and British marine boards who kept the marine department of the British Board of Trade fully informed on the inequities of arrangements in notorious Quebec. One shipmaster sailing out of Liverpool claimed in 1858 not only that the Quebec shipping office supplied seamen at twice the rate available through unofficial sources (£9 a run rather than £4 to £5 a month) but also that desertion was encouraged by the shipping master in order to increase his engagement fees.[44]

As time went on it became clear that the shipping office survived only because it conformed to the British regulations of 1854. Despite its existence, the traditions of the sailor labour market went on much as before, except that crew changes on British ships were endorsed by the shipping master. For a time in the 1850s it looked as though the office might in fact disappear. Hawkins died unlamented by sailors and populace in 1854. Instead of the government appointing a successor, the duties of the office were the next year added to those of the collector of customs, John W. Dunscomb, as the British Merchant Shipping Act allowed. This change practically obliterated the office since it appears that Dunscomb turned a blind eye to the casual arrangements deriving from the previous decade which re-emerged after Hawkins' death. Moreover, the custom house was not equipped to cope with the peculiar features of shipping seamen. Its office hours were from ten to four on weekdays only, and since 'wind and tide wait for no man' shipmasters were forced to procure their men from the crimps outside regular hours.[45]

A successor to Hawkins was found in the person of Ralph B. Johnson, a septuagenarian from Sherbrooke, who was appointed half-way through the summer of 1858. In 1868 Johnson reported that the office was handling only about one-half of the business of the Quebec sailor market, the rest being transacted unlawfully by the crimps. During the eleven years he retained his post, Johnson claimed he was offered bribes hundreds of times, threatened by anonymous letters, and assaulted by one of Quebec's best-known crimps, Thomas O'Leary. He was able to make little headway in the face of the customary collusion between masters and crimps. One effect of the decline in the business of the shipping office was Johnson's inability to finance it by shipping fees alone. The Canadian government had to vote an annual grant to keep the office solvent. After Confederation the minister of marine, Peter Mitchell, a New Brunswicker, was left to draw an unfavourable comparison between the Saint John office which supported itself and the Quebec establishment which appeared to be grossly inefficient.[46]

Johnson was superannuated in 1870 and his removal effectively marked the transformation of the office of shipping master at Quebec. The new government policy towards the shipping office demonstrated that the attempt to regulate the sailor market had been abandoned. For Johnson's successor, R.H. Russell, another septuagenarian, was already the chief constable of the Quebec river police force and it was in his continued role as a law enforcement officer rather than as the shipping master that he was expected to interfere with the illegal practices of manning the Quebec fleet. Russell accepted a nominal role and made no attempt to supply the special needs of shipmasters. The captain of the *Harvest Home*, for example, had to ship his own replacements for deserters on a June Sunday in 1873, when Russell's shipping office was closed.[47] By the time the shipping and discharge of seamen in Canadian ports had been regularized and standardized in 1874 by the federal Seamen's Act of 1873, the shipping office at Quebec had become an anachronism. The shipping master-cum-police chief continued to go through the motions but the tightening of the regulations, particularly the provision that finally required that all seamen's engagements without exception must be endorsed in the shipping office, made no appreciable effect on the sailor market of the port of Quebec. As a result, Russell's successor, Benjamin Trudel, appointed in 1878, was dismissed as shipping master in 1889. Thereafter the local Department of Marine official acted as shipping master but crusades against irregularities were no longer necessary now that the shipping had declined and the crimps, as we shall see, had been routed.

The ignominious career of the government shipping office at Quebec was not repeated by that at Saint John. Established – as a result of pressure from shipowners, builders, and merchants – only two years after the Quebec one, and closely modelled on it, including the ambiguous nature of the shipping master's authority, it enjoyed an uneventful career. The first minister of marine thought he knew the reason for the difference between the two offices. He suggested that while 'neither Quebec nor New Brunswick produce seamen to any extent,' none the less 'in New Brunswick, no serious difficulty ever occurs, as the shipping master at Saint John has got the crimps under control, and in very few cases has he ever any trouble with them.'[48] Despite the fact that Mitchell had the story the wrong way round – it was the shipping master who was under the control of the crimps – he was correct in noting the absence of antagonism in Saint John. The close identity of interest between shipowners, merchants, and shipbuilders contributed to the harmony. If countenance can be given to the claim of contemporaries who increasingly blamed the shipmasters for the decline of the Quebec shipping office, the attitude of the captains visiting Saint John must have been one of greater co-operation. Essentially, then, fewer aggravations existed there. Initial co-operation was not converted into disenchantment as was the case at Quebec after the failure of the shipping office to accommodate masters' requirements. We can assume that the wages established at the shipping office did not repel the custom of the captains. Wages seem to have reflected supply and demand as created by the exigencies of trade, and not by artificial means. Moreover the shipping fee at Saint John was only half that at Quebec. We know that captains and shippers involved in the Quebec trade resented a fee which seemed to be so out of line with practice elsewhere. This irritant was avoided at Saint John and it was this lower fee that the Department of Marine adopted in its Seamen's Act of 1873.

The extent to which the shipping master was responsible for the accommodation with the Saint John crimps remains open to speculation. He seems to have come to terms with them because he soon discovered that he could not recruit seamen directly. Sailors looking for ships did not usually walk into his office as independent candidates for employment. There is no evidence that the shipping master even attempted to find his own men, except by leading occasional recruiting forays into other ports. The first shipping master had been a free-lance shipping agent, the type of intermediary who had supplied captains with men before the establishment of the shipping office. Before 1850 he had depended on the boarding-house-keepers for his recruits; he continued to depend on them after 1850. The influence of the boarding-house-keepers on the shipping office increased rather than decreased. In 1882, for example, the shipping master engaged 2,431 seamen as crew members on foreign-going vessels: 64 per cent were referred to the shipping office by twenty-five boarding-house-keepers and half the seamen so supplied came from the houses of six boarding masters situated in the dockside area between York Point and Reed's Point.

The Saint John shipping office therefore became a clearing house which rubber-stamped the arrangements made between captains and suppliers. The only tension between the shipping master and the boarding-house-keepers occurred in the early 1860s when Allan McLean served as deputy shipping master to his father, James McLean, whom he ultimately succeeded in 1865. Two assault cases in the shipping office, each involving the deputy and a boarding master, reveal that the younger McLean did not take kindly to interference in such matters as the determination of the amount of sailors' advances. And he did not appreciate the tendency of boarding masters to treat the shipping master as a clerk available for the convenience of business transactions between themselves and the shipmasters. For their part, the boarding masters considered themselves the muscle and conscience of the shipping office. They worked round the clock, unlike the shipping master, to make sure the vessels were supplied with men. As boarding-house-keeper William McFadden explained in 1864: 'We are always, day and night, ready to assist men on board of vessels leaving this port or any bye port, when the shipping master of this port is laying in his bed and we attending to his duty of seeing the men on board.'[49]

Allan McLean's conflict with the boarding-house-keepers while he was deputy was translated into a certain zeal for prosecuting shipmasters who failed to use his office after he himself became the shipping master. Although these actions were based on custom rather than law, all the captains prosecuted by McLean were fined for each man they engaged outside the shipping office, with the exception of one who was ignorant of the rules of the port. These prosecutions demonstrate that the shipmasters were a good deal more vulnerable than the boarding masters who, after the formation of their association in 1864, were able to control completely the supply of non-resident sailors in Saint John.[50]

When a shortage of sailors prevailed in Saint John, employers looked for the necessary labour to the nearby overstocked American ports, thereby ignoring both the shipping master, who was helpless to intervene, and the local crimps, who apparently failed to anticipate the shortage. The success with which captains and shippers were able to hire seamen in the United States gave Saint John a decided advantage over Quebec. As Peter Mitchell reported in 1870, sailors engaged in American ports for service in Quebec had innumerable opportunities for breaking the agreement on the train journey to the port. The sailor going to Saint John, in contrast, was not afforded the same facilities for changing his mind once he embarked on one of the three weekly steamers operating between Boston and Saint John.[51]

None the less, the Saint John shipping master continued to ship sailors numbering three or four thousand annually during the second half of the nineteenth century. His success, particularly his ability to avoid ugly incidents involving crimps, may mean that Saint John was a more law-abiding port. Or perhaps, as Shipping Master Allan McLean noted in 1870, it was the lack of a resort to law rather than the study to observe it which tempered the potential conflict in Saint John. He claimed that crimping was considerable but that the deserters were not pursued by captains, with the result that an exchange of ships and men continued to take place similar to the practice in Quebec before mid-century, entirely in the open and without undue fear of reprisals. This tendency, he said, also discouraged crimps from secreting the men and thereby artificially forcing up wages. In other words, the community of interest in Saint John left shipmasters relatively free to make their own arrangements, encouraged them to use the shipping office as a recording office, and made them wary of applying the letter of the law which might hamper, more than facilitate, the manning of their ships.[52]

Given its innocuous nature, the shipping office in Saint John was not accorded much respect locally and was not an intrusive addition to port life. It went about its business with such little clamour that legislators and crimps in the sister port of Quebec were of the opinion that it closed down soon after it had opened. During a change of shipping masters in 1865, there was a move within the commercial community to have the office abolished. It seemed to be unnecessary, not because it worked so badly, as in Quebec, but because a new generation of merchants, come to prominence since its inception, regarded it as a wholly superfluous piece of bureaucracy. In the 1870s, however, the office received a new lease on life as a federal institution when the discharge of sailors was accorded stricter regulation and became another one of the shipping master's fee-generating responsibilities. As a result, the income of the Saint John shipping master soon doubled. Moreover, despite the fact that the shipping of seamen remained fairly constant, with only a slow decline perceptible in the late 1880s, the

TABLE 1.5
Business transacted in the major shipping offices in 1885 and 1887

Shipping office	1885		1887	
	Shipped	Discharged	Shipped	Discharged
Quebec	761	174	798	279
Saint John	3,716	2,632	3,910	2,700
Halifax	2,972	1,980	2,651	1,933
Montreal	517	652	897	1,756
Yarmouth	564	419	671	569

SOURCE: Canada *Sessional Papers*, 18th and 20th Reports of Department of Marine

discharge of seamen increased (see Tables 1.4, 1.5). In 1875 20 per cent of the business of the Saint John office was devoted to discharge, and by 1889, 40 per cent. This is a small but important shift. It may reflect a number of things about the nature of trade and manning in that port: that more seamen from Saint John and nearby were joining a declining trade, as timber lost its prominence, particularly on the British route; that shipbuilding had declined to such an extent that the pressures to desert no longer obtained; that the increasing significance of local ship ownership in the city's trade meant that a larger amount of the employment of sailors was conducted in Saint John rather than in British ports; or that the shift in shipping southwards instead of eastwards concentrated more of the legal manning of ships in Saint John. By late century the Saint John shipping office had become very similar in its operations to its counterpart (opened in 1872) in Halifax, where the discharge of seamen constantly represented between 40 and 45 per cent of the business.[53]

The establishment of the Halifax office was called for as early as the mid-1860s when the rate of desertion on vessels from Britain reached serious proportions. The office was created in response to local demand as well as in accordance with the new Department of Marine's intention to regulate the sailor market in every port in the dominion. Irregularities in the shipping of seamen had encouraged seamen to engage on more than one vessel in port and collect advances for each engagement. The editor of the *Morning Chronicle* speculated that John D. Cummins, the new shipping master, would 'prevent the perpetration of such frauds by seamen. All seamen must be shipped by the

Shipping Officer and after they have signed articles for one voyage they cannot ship for another without producing a discharge, which must be given by the same officer.' The shipping master was also empowered to regulate arrangements made by employers. When J.B. Oxley of Messrs Oxley & Co paid off three crewmen of the Yarmouth barque *Argo* in 1874, Cummins sued for violation of the law which stated 'that all seamen shall be discharged, and receive their wages in the presence of the Shipping Master duly appointed for the port.'[54]

As in Quebec a quarter-century earlier, the sailors showed their disapproval of wage regulation practised by the new shipping master by going out on strike in 1873. For several months they held out for higher wages. Early in the strike the seamen were demanding $25, $5 above the prevailing rate. When Huston Stairs reluctantly tried to ship for $20, he was upbraided outside the shipping office by one of the strikers, Patrick Carroll, who 'abused the man for accepting the low rate, threatened him and attempted to take his advance note from him.' The press comment on Carroll's conviction under Nova Scotia's anti-combination legislation was typical of nineteenth-century advocacy of freedom of labour: 'It's all very well for a man to fix his own value, but when he undertakes to fix the value of other men and to intimidate them the strong arm of the law is necessary to deal with him.' By March the going rate was $18 a month, with the seamen demanding $22. Joseph Atkins signed articles at the lower rate but tried to insist on the higher wages when his advance was paid. When the shipping master threatened him with court proceedings, he was cowed into joining his vessel.[55]

Overt resistance by sailors in Halifax was short-lived. By the time A.B. Bligh, the second shipping master, appointed in 1879, described his functions to the Labor Commission in 1888, he was shipping about 2,800 sailors a year but, as had always been the case with shipping masters, his authority was confined to crews involved in the foreign trades. The regulations governing the domestic coasting trade did not require that the crew be shipped before the government officer. Moreover, even in the foreign trades, the authority of the shipping offices effectively extended only to ships registered in the empire. Captains of foreign ships, European and American, were encouraged to complete their local employment formalities before the shipping master but such a course depended on consular co-operation. If the American consul in Halifax, for example, did not wish to employ the services of the shipping master, there was no way Canadian jurisdiction could be extended to the manning of American ships in a Canadian port. And indeed the American government took a hard line on this matter in respect to the Saint John shipping office in the late 1880s.[56]

The prominent British sailors' union organizer J. Havelock Wilson claimed in his autobiography that British shipping offices (known as mercantile marine offices) were no better than government crimping agencies. Like the free enterprise crimps, he claimed, they neither consulted the interests of the sailor nor respected any sailor-based combinations to raise wages. Much the same could be said for the Canadian counterparts. Quebec residents described Hawkins as the greatest crimp in town and the aim of the shipping offices in Quebec and Saint John at mid-century was unabashedly to force down wages. Evidence tends to suggest, however, that the shipping offices were unsuccessful in fixing wages. The first shipping master in Quebec found himself having to entice seamen to his office with offers of higher wages in order to break into the sailor labour market.[57] If the Quebec shipping office can be described as an anachronism, the Saint John one, instead of regulating employment, merely recorded sailors' engagements and discharges, and the Halifax office appeared too late to make a significant impact on the manning of sailing vessels. Then again, the offices could not alter the tendency for wage rates to remain higher on this side of the Atlantic than in Britain and Europe, and they did not discriminate against deserters despite their raison d'être as discouragements to desertion. Furthermore the dependence of the shipping masters on fees aided and abetted mobility rather than stability in the labour market. For these reasons, the potential of the shipping offices as the focus for sailor dissatisfaction was not realized. Only initially did they unite sailors in militant opposition. Over the long term, however, they failed to control sailors and thereby failed to foster labour consciousness among a disparate, unorganized workforce. At the same time, the inability of the shipping offices to alleviate the shortage of sailors helped to focus public attention on the quality of seafaring labour as an explanation for its deficient quantity.

2

Patterns of
seafaring life

Nineteenth-century commentators tended to agree that the quality of merchant seamen was progressively deteriorating. To some extent their pessimism reflects the timeless disposition of moderns to exaggerate the virtues of the past to the disadvantage of the present. But there may have been a grain of truth in the claim because the rate of expansion in merchant shipping in the middle part of the century was rapid enough to affect the level of competence of the work-force. Not enough men came forward to sign on the increasing number of vessels. Despite the many opportunities, potential seafarers were undoubtedly deterred from committing themselves to the merchant service because working conditions remained primitive and wage rates paid in Britain continued to be little better than a soldier's. The work was more like slavery than free labour and the discipline was derived from military rather than civilian life.

In circumstances where demand almost invariably exceeded supply, inexperienced men as well as burnt-out, unfit individuals were bound to be hired as seamen. The crew shipped aboard the *Janet Kidston* in Quebec in 1859 revealed both the ineptitude and intransigence of poor-quality seamen. Difficult to muster initially and set to work, the Quebec hirelings resisted orders, resorted to abusive and 'saucy' language, and refused to work. As the voyage proceeded, the captain discovered that most of them were incompetent seamen. He ended up disrating and reducing the pay of seven of the twelve men hired at Quebec.[1]

For native Canadians the acquisition of seafaring skills was a hit-and-miss affair. There were no local traditions of formal apprenticeship, no successful navigation schools, and, for masters and mates, no specifically Canadian examinations until 1871. Not only did seafaring attract the unskilled, but it also drew to its ranks, because of the hardness, uncertainty, and transiency of the life, individuals who were tough, vulgar, and even wild when given the opportunity. The image of the typical seafarer was therefore far from flattering. Among our three ports, the greatest concern about the alleged decline in the quality of seamen was expressed in Halifax, the most important of the native labour pools. To their credit, observers in that port were in the forefront of the campaign to urge the reform of the merchant service, claiming that it was the poor conditions which produced the deterioration in manpower, not the reverse. The unsatisfactory conditions were experienced by many thousands of seafarers who moved in and out of Halifax, Saint John, and Quebec in the age of sail.

TYPES OF SAILORS

Yet among these observers no single portrait emerges of the typical Jack Tar. Sailors were drawn from all levels of society in both major seafaring nations and minor island communities. The most common characteristics of the men before the mast were youthfulness, a proletarian or agrarian background, and a restless disposition. On the basis of individual and group case studies and statistical data a fairly accurate impression can be gained of the kinds of seafarers who frequented Canadian ports. They were either career sailors or casual sailors, of British descent or foreign, and male or, in very small numbers, female.

The career sailor was distinguished by his ambition and frequently also his status in life as the son or close relative of a shipmaster or merchant. During his years before the mast he tended to show an exceptional faithfulness to his vessel and to be critical of the customary practices of sailortown. His actions were governed by his vision of the future which included the probability of the command of his own vessel. Casual sailors, in contrast, tended to regard seafaring either as an escape from the pressures of society or as a short-term prospect for adventure or employment. While these two types of casual sailor might differ markedly in class background and personality, they were similar in their lack of commitment to seafaring as a career and in their lack of prospects for advancement through the ranks. Drawn usually from the unskilled dockside and countryside populations of seafaring nations, they went to sea sporadically or on a seasonal basis. The escapist was usually a misfit or scallywag who ran away to sea to avoid the constraints of society. For his part, the adventurer tended to be a footloose, but generally respectable, young man who spent the first five to ten years of his independence gaining experience of the world through varied voyages. He was the kind of lad who wrote letters to his mother and adapted himself readily to both the congenial and disagreeable aspects of life among mariners and landsharks. He knew he would leave the sea when he had worked the wanderlust out of his system. If by chance he continued to rove the seven seas, he provided the skill and experience found among fo'c's'le labour.

Jack could also be a foreigner. If a native of a country with an alien language and an alien culture, he crewed visiting vessels of his own nation or contributed to the cosmopolitan mixture of crews of English-speaking vessels. Poorly paid and eminently exploitable, he was the natural prey for the crimps and harpies of sailortown. When he got into trouble he aroused the concern of middle-class society, which often felt sorry for the stranger it failed to protect. The sailor was not always a man. By the time detailed records were preserved in the 1860s stewardesses were common on vessels of the British Empire and the United States. The stewardess did not find employment only on passenger vessels with large support crews. She worked also on wooden sailing vessels earning wages which ranged from the nominal shilling a month to a rate which compared favourably with that of the ordinary seaman. She represents the least-known and most enigmatic element in Neptune's work-force.

Our first type of sailor, the career sailor, is personified by William Lord, a native of Newport in Wales. From the first day he stepped aboard a vessel he was a member of the sailor élite. He worked as hard and risked as much as any other sailor but the end in view was not to drink, whore, or frolic in the next port: it was to ascend the seafaring hierarchy as rapidly as possible. The son of a veteran shipmaster in the Quebec timber trade, Lord began his seafaring about the middle of the nineteenth century as a boy both in age and in rating. For two years he performed the menial, back-breaking jobs associated with this initial position. At the beck and call of the whole crew, he was knocked about and exploited in a typically ruthless fashion.

Lord's first voyage as an ordinary seaman was aboard the 700-ton timber vessel the *Dorchester*, which carried a crew of fourteen together with the captain's wife and several animals. On the voyage from Newport to Quebec via Lisbon, the vessel leaked like a sieve and the crew wore themselves out with constant pumping. On his overdue arrival in Quebec in late June, Lord was greeted by his anxious father, whose own vessel, the *Juno*, was loading timber. Lord, unlike his mates, was treated to several days' living like a prince on his father's ship. On his return to the *Dorchester*, Lord helped to discharge the ballast, which was standard procedure for the crew. This was followed by another regular practice at Quebec, the desertion of the crew. With the exception of the officers and Ordinary Seaman Lord, the crew were induced to leave their vessel by the crimps for which Quebec was especially notorious. Depleted crew notwithstanding, the vessel was towed to the timber booms at Diamond Harbour where it was loaded by hired labourers who finished the stowing, including the deckload, by mid-August. When the vessel was ready to clear, the new crew that came on board were, according to Lord, 'of a very motley description.' The eastbound voyage across the Atlantic was an eventful one for Lord. The steward was disrated, a common occurrence among crimp-shipped crews, and Lord was appointed in his stead. Then, as we have seen, 300 miles off the coast of Ireland, the pre-eminently 'unsea-worthy' vessel encountered a storm with devastating results.

After the rescue of the *Dorchester*'s shipwrecked crew, Lord spent the ensuing winter engaged in tedious maintenance work on his father's vessel which was laid up in Britain during the freeze-up of the St Lawrence. The following summer he made two return voyages across the Atlantic in the *Juno*. On the first occasion the vessel picked up coal at Cardiff and sailed to Quebec carrying Lord as steward. The second voyage began in Britain in June with the sixteen-year-old Lord's promotion to able seaman. During the unloading and loading, which involved discharging the Quebec timber at Bristol and taking on another cargo of coal at Cardiff, Lord fell overboard and narrowly escaped drowning, being, like so many sailors, unable to swim. The vessel left Cardiff with the usual drunken crew, put aboard by the port's boarding-house-keepers. On this voyage out to Quebec, helmsman Lord was injured when the vessel shipped a huge wave which struck the rudder and caused the steering wheel to revolve so rapidly that it threw Lord against the lee sides with sufficient violence to cause concussion.

Despite his mishaps, Lord enjoyed his service on the *Juno* much better than on the *Dorchester*. Not only was his father master, but also this 1,500-ton ship, now rigged as a barque, was much faster and less leaky than the ill-fated *Dorchester*. Lord's time in Quebec was not spent pursuing the pastimes of the casual sailor. His father introduced him to the mercantile élite and he spent a pleasant time hob-nobbing with Upper Town society. On the return to Britain, the *Juno* was again laid up for the winter.

According to his memoirs, Lord made only one more trip to Quebec as a seaman, and while the chronology is vague, this voyage apparently occurred after a period of several years during which he acquired experience on a variety of routes, including the West Indies. Lord described his vessel on this last visit, the *Madras Packet*, as a timber drogher. He joined her in Cardiff, as a second mate, for a voyage to Quebec via Cadiz and Newfoundland. Because of his youthfulness, he had difficulty making the sailors obey his orders. Fortunately he was able to establish his authority through a bloody fist fight with an insubordinate 'packet rat,' the most hardened and vicious breed of transatlantic sailor. Much to Lord's relief, no doubt, the packet rat deserted at Quebec. Again his stopover in port was not characteristic of the run-of-the-mill sailor. He renewed old friendships with members of Quebec society and visited places of historical interest. After the vessel had shipped its cargo of timber, it returned uneventfully to Caernarvon.

Lord eventually became a commander and made the transition from sailing vessels to steamships. By the time he wrote his memoirs in 1894, he was secretary of the British Shipping Federation and of the North of England Steamship Owners Association. His advancement as a sailor had been rapid and carefully plotted. His four voyages to Quebec involved port calls which differed markedly in quality from the stopovers of the average sailor in the nineteenth century.[2]

For a scallywag among the casual sailors, we turn to James Prendergast, a Haligonian, who spent more time in jail than at sea, but who worked on both sailing vessels and coastal steamships during the years which saw the transition from wind to steam power. How and why he ran foul of the established order are impossible to say. A pathological trouble-maker, at his worst when excited to violence by drink, Prendergast directed his chronic anti-social behaviour more often against members of his own family than against representatives of authority and respectability. By 1874, when he was still in his early twenties, he had been dubbed 'notorious' by a newspaper reporter who made his regular acquaintance as a defendant in court. In May of that year he committed the sailor's most serious port offence when he deserted from the schooner *Kate* and was sentenced to three weeks in prison. He was also found guilty on at least four other occasions in 1874 of drunkenness and disorderly behaviour; breaking window glass; stabbing his wife, a local prostitute; and assaulting a man in the street after which he resisted arrest and attacked a policeman. One of his innumerable prison escapes occurred in November of that year.

Until 1891 Prendergast was repeatedly before the Halifax magistrate's court. His rebelliousness took a number of extrovert forms. He continued to smash windows, he threw stones at passers-by, and he thieved far and wide. Not content with stabbing and frequently beating his wife, he also assaulted his father-in-law, his mother, and his father, robbed them, and despoiled their property. He refused to settle his accounts at public houses, offended local morals by indecently exposing his person in the street, and in 1881 proclaimed himself an atheist to the court clerk. His frequent escapes from prison were not always the fault of careless jailers. Indeed he appears to have been something of a escapologist, freeing himself in 1879 from chains in a locked cell and in 1880 getting away through a stove pipe hole in the wall.

Prendergast was such a liability to the city that the authorities let him go whenever he entered a shipping agreement which seemed likely to remove him at least temporarily from Halifax. He shipped on the steamer *Faraday* in the summer of 1887 but had returned to town by mid-November, appropriately announcing his arrival with a window-smashing spree in an Albemarle Street tavern and, after his arrest, a repeat of the performance in the police station. Charged in 1878 with beating his father-in-law with a shoe, he was let go when the authorities learned that he had shipped on a steamer. In 1882 he deserted ship again in Halifax after boarding a timber vessel bound for Liverpool. The crew was relieved of his disruptive presence when, bent on desertion, he stole a skiff alongside in the harbour and escaped through Dartmouth. The editor of the *Morning Herald* remarked on this occasion that it was 'a great pity that the city was not clear of this miscreant as he is one of the worst characters we have.'[3] In the autumn Prendergast was released from prison (in the middle of a sentence for drunken and disorderly behaviour and escaping from prison) in order that he could join a Norwegian timber barque bound for Britain. In 1888, towards the end of his known escapades in Halifax, he had graduated from being a sailor to serving as an agent for supplying seamen to visiting captains, an activity that situated him on the road to becoming a crimp, sailortown's most infamous figure.[4]

For incorrigibles such as Prendergast the civic authorities considered seafaring to be the ideal prescription. Similar characters could be found in Saint John. William Walsh, described as 'a notorious protégé of the police,' was released from custody in 1859 when he signed articles as a sailor. Similarly in 1863 the shipping master deliberately shipped a recidivist thief to relieve the city of the care of a man who generally spent eleven months out of twelve in the penitentiary.[5] For the misfits of society, therefore, the push towards the sea could be as strong, if not stronger, than the pull.

The other type of casual sailor, the one less disposed to mischief, was the stalwart young adventurer who was probably the most common of nineteenth-century sailors. Because sailoring for him represented but one stage in his working life, he was inclined to put up with his working conditions, however bad they might be. The brief but varied seafaring experience of Harris H. Barnes provides our example of the venturesome lad for whom the sea was a frontier to be conquered and an initial source of livelihood. Barnes was born in Halifax in 1843 and when fourteen went to live on a farm with his uncle in Five Islands, Colchester County, an outport with a seafaring tradition. Most farmers' sons served informal apprenticeships at sea and at least half of the inhabitants of that village were sailors. Not surprisingly in these circumstances, Barnes decided to seek his fortune as a sailor. He undertook his first engagement from John Bartlett's boarding-house in Saint John in the spring of 1862 as steward on the new schooner the *Duke of Newcastle,* on articles that took him on a voyage to Boston and back to Saint John. He next engaged on the schooner *Boston* for a return voyage to New York. The vessel being damaged on the home run, Barnes made his way back to Five Islands in late September, wintering over at his uncle's farm. In the spring he shipped on the schooner *Will o' the Wisp* as a seaman. The schooner ran between Parrsboro and Windsor twice a week on a regular basis. It offered little in the way of glamour and Barnes soon decided he 'wanted to get away and see more of the world.'

Accordingly, at the age of twenty he shipped as an ordinary seaman in the summer of 1863 on the new brigantine *Hutoka*, a 126-ton vessel, which was loading timber at Parrsboro to transport to a northern English port on her maiden voyage. The vessel was in fact to share the fate of many contemporary Canadian-built vessels: it was to be sold in England. The crew was not apprised of this plan until they were in mid-Atlantic. On arrival in Preston in September, they were 'huddled into a third class compartment of a railroad train going to Liverpool,' where they were paid off at the sailors' home, a combined boarding-house and shipping office, on 3 October. Here the deception was compensated for by an extra month's wages for all hands, a payment which conformed to the standard arrangement out of the leading Fundy port of Saint John for reimbursing native crews for the run to Britain.

Barnes and his shipmates then had to find new jobs. Seafaring engagements in Britain were at very low wages, and, for the North American voyages, as we have seen, the seamen were required to sign articles for a return voyage, meaning discharge once again in the mother country. Barnes found the options extremely discouraging and, being a worthy young man, appears not to have considered the possibility of shipping to North America on round-trip articles with the intention of deserting on arrival. Instead he followed the custom of others, particularly of the officers of vessels sold in Britain, and bought a passage back to North America in an emigrant vessel. On the *Chancellor*, a Black Ball Line packet vessel, he sampled life in the steerage, a grisly experience which made seafaring seem like heaven.

After a journey of a month he arrived in New York, verminous and penniless. In order to secure a new set of clothes he worked for a month as a railway navvy, before returning to New York to ship at Christmas-time on the *Belle* which was sailing to Saint John. Succumbing to typhus soon after he shipped, Barnes woke up the next February in Saint John in the Kent Marine Hospital, maintained exclusively for seamen. He learned that on the arrival of the *Belle* on New Year's Day, he had been recognized and taken to hospital by John Bartlett, whose boarding-house business had taken him abroad the vessel looking for clients. Bartlett secured his sea chest and balance of wages which he safeguarded until Barnes could leave hospital and move to the boarding-house. With his health undoubtedly in a delicate state, he returned home to Halifax before going to Five Islands to re-engage on the *Will o' the Wisp* for the summer of 1864.

He abandoned seafaring for the winter but the following spring he signed on as a hand on the brig *Thames*, on which he coasted twice between Pictou and Boston before growing 'tired of coasting, weary of hauling through bridges and up narrow rivers, and wishing for more of the open sea' and so took his newly achieved able seaman status off to Halifax. In the year since his last visit to his native city, his mother had died, his only brother had moved to Boston, and his sister had abandoned the port for the country to teach school. With his family gone, Barnes's appreciation of the class connotation attached by the middle class to hands before the mast made him realize that he had few options of where he might stay during his visit. 'I had many wealthy connections in the city of Halifax,' he recorded in his memoirs, 'but I was only a poor sailor boy, so I went directly to Tom Ward's sailors boarding house on Water Street.' It is in Halifax that we find Barnes engaging on the last two voyages that he recorded in his reminiscences. In December 1865 he signed on the brig *Gondolier*, which, after a hazardous winter voyage, arrived in Baltimore with fish and took on a general cargo for transport to Port of Spain. From Trinidad, the *Gondolier* sailed in ballast to Cienfuegos to load sugar for New York. In April the vessel reached New York, where Barnes was appointed second mate for the run to Halifax. Arriving there in May, Barnes was paid off and signed on as seaman on the brig *Lady Franklyn* for a voyage to Barbados with a cargo of lumber. Here the record of Barnes's seafaring ends. While he may have continued to go to sea for some time thereafter, he is known to have soon joined the Canadian migration westwards to the prairies away from the coast and away from seafaring.[6]

A third category of sailor comprised non-English-speaking, non-Canadian seamen. The number of foreign sailors visiting port increased dramatically during the century. Before the repeal of the navigation laws in 1849 their numbers were legally limited on British vessels and the foreign traffic in colonial ports made up only a small percentage of the vessels entering and clearing. By the 1890s, however, about one-third of the sailors in the British merchant marine were foreigners who among them spoke over 300 languages, and the percentage of foreign-registered vessels found in Canadian ports amounted to almost one-quarter of the recorded entrances. The foreign names of these sailors became an indicator of their numerical significance late in the century, but earlier in the century the tendency of many foreigners in the British mercantile marine to anglicize their names often hid their identity.

The foreigner on an English-speaking vessel was more prominently subjected to exploitation in an occupation that was often uncomfortable even for the most representative British or Canadian sailor. A black man, Hippolita Rapha, was detained on board the schooner *J.L. Cotter* in 1879 after helping to load the vessel at Martinique. Having been tricked into sailing to Saint John, his ignorance of shipping articles allowed the captain to get out of paying him wages as a seaman.[7] In 1894 a Portuguese sailor on the *Nicanor* successfully defended himself against a reduction in wages, on the ground that disrating for inability to speak English was forbidden, a regulation that recognized the importance of foreign labour to British shipping.[8] English-speakers were not the only people to mistreat foreign sailors. A lone Frenchman on a schooner in Halifax crewed by Germans came off second best in the Franco-Prussian war on board his vesel. The Germans 'put kedge anchors in his berth, soup pots in his bag, cut vent-holes in his boots and burnt "powder monkeys" in close proximity to his head when he slept.' The magistrate who heard the story was amused by pranks which he considered to resemble his boarding-school experience.[9]

Like their Canadian and British counterparts, foreign sailors looked for justice in Canadian ports. In the case of the barque *Gladstone* in 1870, they were not disappointed. Four seamen, including three continental Europeans named Cornelius Vondersteen (Dutch), Karl Kreuse (Prussian), and Franz Tadejevich (Austrian), sued for wages totalling nearly $900. Refused their pay earlier by their captain, Peter York, the men had endured unjustified imprisonment in Matanzas and insufficient food and a fireless fo'c's'le on a voyage from Matanzas to Saint John with their drunken master. Tadejevich had been forced against his will to act as mate on the voyage and in that capacity had been coerced into signing various entries in the log relating to the misbehaviour of his comrades without being able to read the captain's English. As a result of the withholding of their wages, the seamen were without decent clothing. 'The result,' according to one observer,' was that their intelligent faces contrasted strongly with their filthy and meagre apparel.' As soon as they had recovered their wages they could be 'seen upon the streets with good clothes upon their backs and smiles of happiness upon their faces.' While the people of Saint John were ashamed of Captain York, the seamen claimed 'to have strong faith in the government that could secure justice to poor and friendless foreigners.'[10]

The unfortunate victim in the celebrated *King Ceolric* murder case in Saint John in 1875 was a foreign sailor, an Austro-Italian named John Yealch. From accounts of the incidents aboard the newly built ship shortly after it sailed on its maiden voyage to Liverpool, a number of characteristics of foreign sailors emerge. First, foreign sailors, whatever flag they flew under, tended to work in international crews. The crew of the *King Ceolric* included, in addition to the one Austro-Italian, five Irishmen, four Americans, two Englishmen, two Frenchmen, one Belgian, one Welshman, one Newfoundlander, and two Saint John men, one of whom was George McNutt, the accused murderer.[11] Second, foreign sailors, certainly when in a minority on an English vessel, were under peer pressure to anglicize their names. Although most accounts in the course of the murder trial refer to the victim as John Yealch, the first press releases after the murder named him Jean Yealch and indicated that he was better known as John Jeffry.[12] Another feature that should be noted is that Yealch shared with most seamen before the mast a youthful age and a disposition for drunkenness whenever the opportunity offered and for rowdiness as a means of protesting his grievances.

The Yealch case also provides us with evidence that this sailor, and by implication many others like him, was a lad who took pains to keep in touch with his kinfolk. The existence of a letter written by Yealch on the eve of the fateful sailing of the *King Ceolric* was discovered after the vessel returned to port with its victim. It was signed Jovane Yelich, yet another variation in nomenclature, and addressed to his father Signor Biachi Yelich in Trieste. Besides reporting on his health and his shipping engagements, Yealch sought information on the whereabouts of his brother Antonio and gave his parents a Liverpool address where they could write him. The letter had been entrusted to Yealch's Saint John boarding master for posting and the latter submitted it to the coroner when the vessel returned to port the day after it sailed. Since sailors' boarding-house-keepers often received a bad press, it is worth noting that the transient sailor far from his native home trusted his boarding master and relied on him for a range of essential services.[13]

Although it is useful to try to arrive at an understanding of the special problems which related to foreign sailors, separating them out in this discussion is not meant to imply that they cannot be fitted into the more general categories of career or casual sailor. Rather we should be aware that until the period of international immigration to Canada commenced late in the nineteenth century, sailors tended to form the most cosmopolitan of Canadian residents, brief though those residences were. Where foreign sailors of one nationality or linguistic group frequented port in sufficient numbers, they introduced the local population to various aspects of their culture. To attend to their needs, a host of services developed ranging from consular offices (normally staffed by resident merchants) to ethnic boarding-houses.

Any portrait of the fourth category, female seafarers, must be a composite one since they were few in number but shared common characteristics. A combination of ships' articles for vessels visiting Saint John in the 1880s and the engagement books of Saint John Shipping Master W.H. Purdy for the same period gives us information on twenty-five women hired in Saint John in the decade between June 1881 and June 1891. In all these cases, and on voyages to other parts of the world recorded in related articles, the women were rated as stewardesses, and in an overwhelming majority of cases they shared the same surname as the cook, cook/steward, or steward. The exception was the passenger steamship which regularly carried single stewardesses who were never very long removed from a port of call and who found protection in numbers. The presence of women on board merchant vessels tends to undermine the popular notion of women being regarded as harbingers of bad luck by seafarers. Exactly what the duties of the stewardesses were on board is a matter for speculation. Their relationship with the cook or steward would tend to suggest that they acted as helpers in the galley and officers' quarters. They may have been a substitute for the ship's boy. Possibly they served on vessels where the captain was accompanied by a wife who required female companionship. Sometimes the captain himself wanted the company. A case in Saint John in 1875 reveals that the master of the barque *Daphne* purloined his steward's wife for his own purposes and kept her on board his vessel until the steward threatened to shoot him.[14] In the 1880s, however, there is no hint of such scandal on vessels served by stewardesses in Saint John.

Table 2.1 includes most of the information available on the stewardesses from the shipping master's engagement books. Two major questions emerge from the data: what can we make of the cases where husband and wife had served previously on different vessels? and

TABLE 2.1
Engagement of stewardesses by the Saint John shipping master 1881–91

Name, age, and residence*	Wife	First voyage	Previous voyage was with husband	Previous voyage was not husband's	Wages per month (year in parentheses)
Alice McMaster*† (27) Saint John (D)‡	x		x		$15 (1881); $10 on articles
Francois Amero (28) Weymouth (D)	x	x			$4 (1882)
Elizabeth Frances (20) Saint John	x	x			$15 (1882)
Mary Schultz (41) Liverpool	x		x		$10 (1882)
Annie Rogers² (28) Fredericton	x	x			$15 (1882)
Janet Woods (18) Saint John (D)	x	x			$5 (1882)
A. Julia Horsey (22) Yarmouth (D)	x			x	$5 (1882)
Carrie Martin (27) Halifax (D)	x			x	£3 (1882)
Catherine Crosby (30) Yarmouth			(with son)		$5 (1882)
Emily Germain³ (23) Pictou (D)	x		x		1s (1883)
Annie Rogers² (27) Fredericton (D)	x		x		$15 (1883)
Maggie Trask (17) Weymouth (D)	x	x			$40 run (1883)
Emily Germain³ (23) Pictou (D)	x		x		$5 (1883)
C. Sampson (19) Windsor	x		x		$8 (1883)
Alice McMaster¹ (29) Dorchester	x		x		$15 (1883)
Maria Cruikshank⁴ (40) Saint John	x			x	$10 (1883)
Florence Scovell (29) Liverpool (D)	x			x	$10 (1884)
Maria Cruikshank⁴ (45) Saint John (D)	x		x		$25 (1884)
Eliza B. Talbot (50) Boston					$20 (1884)
Jane Thompson (28) Londonderry	x		x		$15 (1885)
Sarah E. Laskie (47) Yarmouth (D)	x			x	$18 (1886)
Rachel Reid (35) Roseway, NS (D)	x	x			$1 run (1888)
May Estabrook§ (17) Saint John	x	x			$15 (1888)
Catherine Ellis (30) Wilmot, NS	x	x			$10 (1890)
Annie Rogers² (30) Saint John (D)	x			x	$10 (1890)

SOURCE: New Brunswick Museum, Saint John, Port of Saint John, Shipping Registers, No. 2, 1881–1887 and No. 3, 1887–1895.
*The inconsistency in the data relating to age and residence is typical of nineteenth-century records.
†McMaster, Rogers, Germain, and Cruikshank (superscript 1, 2, 3, and 4 respectively) had two engagements each.
‡Discharge information is available in the articles.
§Did not join

what significance can we assign to the variety of wage rates for stewardesses? The first question can be satisfactorily explained in one case which may help us understand the others. Maria and Patrick Cruikshank were hired on the Saint John ship *Hudson* in December 1883. Maria claimed that her previous vessel was the *J.V. Troop*; Patrick's was the *Privateer*. Cruikshank's service on the *Privateer* can be traced through that vessel's crew agreement for that particular voyage and there we find him stating that his previous vessel had been the *J.V. Troop*.[15] It seems likely therefore that Maria Cruikshank had shared her previous voyage with her husband but that she had stayed ashore during his previous engagement on the *Privateer*. This being the case, we might conclude that the employment of women was erratic and dependent on the arrangements their husbands were able to make on their behalf. Two of the other four women clearly saw themselves as appendages of their husbands. Both Carrie Martin of the *Marabout* and Sarah Laskie of the *Celeste Burrill* signed on discharge as Mrs Carrie Martin and Mrs C.R. (Charles R.) Laskie respectively.[16]

This dependence of the woman on her husband may also help to explain the wide fluctuations in the wage rates. The lowest wages probably occurred when the captain reluctantly hired the wife. In most cases the stewardess was the lowest-paid crew member and the wages in Table 2.1 of one shilling a month and one dollar for the run to Britain paid in two cases in the Saint John shipping office undoubtedly denote that the woman was on board on sufferance of the master. Other women, however, were able to command a wage rate almost as high as that of ordinary seamen and they must have been expected to do their fair share of the work, whatever that work might have been.

Elizabeth Frances, a young single woman, whose hiring on the American ship *Gettysburg* in 1882 for a voyage from Saint John to Australia is recorded in the shipping master's register, was paid a wage which was only one dollar less a month than that of most of the crew. Maggie Trask, who is listed as being seventeen and making her first voyage on the *Mary L. Burrill* in 1883, received on discharge about £1.5s less in wages than the able seamen for the month-long voyage to Liverpool.[17] Maria Cruikshank was paid the same wages as her husband – $25 a month – for her engagement on the Saint John ship *Creedmoor* in 1884. The previous year on the *Hudson* she had received only one-quarter as much. Eliza Talbot, apparently an experienced stewardess on the New England-Maritime coastal steamers earned $20 a month on the ss *Dominion*, the same rate paid the waiters and the assistant cooks on this passenger vessel. Sarah Laskie, another older woman, was hired on the *Celeste Burrill* in 1886 at $18 a month, only $2 less than the wages of her husband.

Besides the women entering service in Saint John, the agreements of incoming vessels record additional information on the employment patterns of women. In 1883, for example, stewardesses arriving in Saint John did not desert. Mary Pierott of Cork had been hired in Britain and a couple of weeks after arriving in Saint John on the *Abbie S. Hart* in April 1883 she was discharged along with her husband. A stewardess on the *Ecuador*, Sarah Porter from south Wales, arrived with her cook-husband William, a West Indian, on a voyage from Glasgow, and they remained by the vessel for its return voyage to Liverpool. Pierott had shipped in Britain for wages one-third those of the seamen; Porter received two-thirds of the seamen's rate.[18]

The ships' articles for those hired in Saint John indicate that the employment of women was not accidental. Emily Germain, the stewardess with the token wage of one shilling on the *Lottie Stewart*, was discharged, along with her husband, in Dublin in late May 1883. They reshipped the same day on the same vessel and returned to Saint John, Emily again at one shilling a month, and were discharged on 16 July 1883.[19] They remained two weeks in Saint John before signing on the Halifax barque *Bonito* on 1 August 1883.

Annie Rogers, hired on the barque *Robert S. Besnard* in September 1882, was discharged in New York in January 1883 after a voyage which involved two Atlantic crossings. She was paid off with $32, which in total wages (including a $15 advance) gave her $47 for four months' work.[20] As the table indicates, the Rogers team made a career of seafaring. So did the Horseys. They stayed by the *Vendome* for two voyages after their engagement in Saint John in October 1882. Similarly the Reids repeated their service on the *City Camp*. Rachel was hired at one dollar for the run to Britain in April 1888 and discharged with her husband in Bristol in May. They both shipped for the *City Camp*'s next voyage from Cardiff to Montevideo to New York to Bordeaux to Cardiff. This time Rachel was paid a better wage of £1.5s a month and collected £12.13s.4d at the end of the nine-month voyage. The *City Camp* continued to hire steward-stewardess teams for the next two voyages. In the early and mid-1880s the masters of the *Constance*, the *Kelverdale*, and the *Marabout* also engaged stewardesses for two or more successive voyages.[21]

Apart from this record, which creates the impression that stewardesses were cheap, reliable, and regular crew members, little evidence exists to provide a basis for evaluating women seafarers. An official log of the Saint John vessel *Wealth of Nations* in 1868 described one stewardess who was discharged in Boston en route to Saint John from Liverpool. Her character was recorded by a captain who expected a degree of civility if not gentility from female crew members. According to him, 'Albertine Neilson the stewardess [is] filthy, wasteful and incompetent and when spoken to uses most disgusting and obscene language such as "stick it up my ass" and threatens to black the eyes of some of the officers.'[22] She appears unlikely to have been the type who made the vessel seem like a home away from home. Women who followed the sea must of necessity have been able to hand out abuse since they were no doubt subjected to their own share of it from the members of the other sex who outnumbered them by at least twenty to one.

VESSELS AND VOYAGES

While motivation, ethnicity, and gender were factors which distinguished seafarers, so also was the type of vessel on which they served. The rig and source of power of the vessels in turn were related to the nature of the voyages. In the main, deep-sea vessels and voyages were of three different categories, and so were the men who sailed them. We shall look at sailors on these three types of vessel: the small vessel, primarily engaged in coasting or in fishing; the steamship, which was, by the last quarter of the century, carrying an increasing volume of the water-borne traffic of the seaports; and the ocean-going sailing vessel, which can tell us most about life in sailortown.

The small vessels were primarily schooners, which at mid-century were still crossing the Atlantic and making West Indies voyages but which by late century tended to be involved in what the shipping master of Saint John, at any rate, called coasting voyages.[23] These entailed following the coastline, without crossing large stretches of open water, but were by no means confined to Canadian waters. The voyages undertaken by these vessels in purely local waters, for which the newspapers tended to reserve the label *coasting*, are largely unrecorded and include voyages such as Barnes's frequent crossings of the Bay of Fundy in the *Will o' the Wisp* and fishing expeditions. Only the larger class of schooners trading outside Canadian waters were required by law to complete written contracts with their crews before the shipping master but most of these agreements have not been preserved in the original form. In the late-century records of the Saint John shipping master, however, the engagements on those coasting vessels involved in 'international' voyages are registered. If we sample these records for 1883, we find that the overwhelming majority of the sailors engaged on coasting vessels under 200 tons were native sailors, men such as Harris Barnes.[24] If that was the case for the documented, international coasters, we can infer that it was even more characteristic of the undocumented, local coasting vessels.

The seamen on the international coasters hailed from Saint John and its maritime hinterland on both sides of the Bay of Fundy. They were generally hired on articles of six months' duration but were only infrequently out of the home port for a period longer than a month. According to Shipping Master Bligh of Halifax, sailors tended to stay by their vessels for the full six-month coasting engagement.[25] In the course of a year such vessels operating out of Saint John brought their sailors back to that port more than a half-dozen times and very often they were laid up in Saint John for two or three winter months during which their crews were probably discharged. In a random sample from the shipping master's records, of thirty of the 177 international coasting vessels trading out of Saint John in 1883, the shipping columns of the port's newspapers show that at least eighteen returned to port six times or more in the course of the year and at least eight of the thirty were laid up in Saint John for several months in the winter.[26] Two of the vessels are known to have engaged for part of the year in local waters in coasting voyages which are undocumented in the port records but turn up, sometimes in detail, in the newspaper listings.

These coasting vessels are not ones to which we would look for deserters and the rowdier elements of sailortown. To judge from their consistently native crews and the account of the names of the vessels on which the seamen had previously served, the sailors on the coasting vessels were not part of the international sailor labour market which flourished in the three ports. What may have most distinguished the crews of these vessels in this regard was their immunity from the crimping establishment. They do not appear to have been the denizens of boarding-houses; or if they were their treatment was different from that of their counterparts on ocean-going voyages. In our thirty-vessel sample we find that in 382 hirings only six sailors are recorded as being supplied by boarding-house-keepers. Four of the six were men from continental Europe. Only twenty-two other seamen were listed as from outside the Canadian Atlantic region: four were American, three were Irish, nine were from the Baltic, five were British, and one claimed Montreal as home. (In 1886 nearly 90 per cent of the seamen hired on coasting vessels were from the Atlantic region.)[27]

Not only were the crews of the coasting vessels frequenting the port of Saint John preponderantly Maritimers, but they were also younger than those drawn into the international labour market. Only 21 per cent of the 382 sailors in the 1883 sample were thirty-one and over, which compares with 30 to 35 per cent of the seamen crewing on large sailing and steam vessels in Saint John during the 1880s. The shipping master's records indicate also that the masters of the schooners were often in their twenties and that seamen, regardless of age, could one month be making their first voyage and the next month be commanding the vessel. Clearly, the relationship between owning, commanding, and crewing the local, smaller-class vessels was very close and a flexibility between the various functions applies uniquely to this type of vessel and sets it apart from the other types.

Out of Saint John, carrying cargoes of boards, planks, pickets, laths, cordwood, deals, shingles, railway ties, staves, clapboards, barrels, pailings, scantling, timber, and piling, these vessels seldom took their crews farther than New England ports or New York whence they returned almost always in ballast, the only other notable inward cargo being American coal. The rapidity with which they returned to Saint John and turned round to carry their small cargoes again to the United States imposed a regular discipline on their crews. This again distinguished them from their counterparts on the ocean-going sailing vessels, which made much longer port calls.

As in the case of the small trading vessels, so for steamers our knowledge of service is limited. The regular passenger steamers operating out of Saint John appear not to have crewed in that port to any considerable extent: it could be that they engaged crews cheaper in American ports or smaller ports of the Atlantic region. These regular coasting steamers, like the schooners trading out of Saint John, visited port frequently, and while they therefore swelled the number of entrances and clearances, including number of crew, they would not have introduced to the port the number of different seamen who came ashore from the long-range sailing and steam vessels.

The problems relating to statistics for coasting steamers were perceptively explained by the controller of customs in Saint John in his report for 1860:

In making up these Returns of Shipping now submitted, every time a vessel arrives or clears from, or to, Ports outside the Province, the tonnage and number of men are inserted, so that a Steamer trading frequently to one particular Port, swells up the tonnage entering and clearing at that Port, and would give a very erroneous idea of the number of mariners actually engaged in the trade of the county. For instance, the American steamers *Eastern City* and *Admiral* run between Saint John and Boston, and during last year the *Admiral* made 36 trips, and the *Eastern City*, 34 trips. In these shipping returns therefore they represent 70 vessels, 47,260 tons, 1,508 men, whereas in reality there are only two vessels, 1,347 tons and 53 men employed.[28]

The newspaper shipping columns in Saint John in 1883 record about sixty entrances each for the Boston and Eastport steamers, the *State of Maine* and the *Falmouth*, yet neither hired any crew members in Saint John that year. The same was true of the other coasting steamers – the *City of Portland*, on the Eastport run (about twenty-five entrances), the *Dominion*, on the Yarmouth run (twenty times), and the *Hiawatha* and *Empress*, which served Annapolis (at least fifteen entrances between them). The *Dominion* engaged crew in port in 1884 but such sporadic use of the Saint John shipping master's services is no help in determining the impact of steamer crews on ports of call.

That the coasting steamer crews were employed on a regular rather than a casual basis can be inferred. For example, the steamship crews went out on strike in Saint John in 1883 to demand higher wages to compensate for greater productivity. They wanted an increase from $30 to $35 per month 'on the ground that the steamers are now making an extra trip every week.' In the case of the *Falmouth*, the strikers left the vessel when they failed to achieve their object, but their substitutes were in fact paid at the new rate, which was 75 per cent higher than that of the crews on our thirty sailing coasters.[29]

More can be learned about the crews of the *international* steam freighters entering Saint John. In 1883 the shipping master recorded the entry of thirty-three such steamers, which arrived in ballast and cleared carrying mainly deals.[30] Only seven of these vessels engaged crew members in Saint John, the most extensive hiring being that of five men on the ss *Beaconsfield*. Ships' articles exist for sixteen of the British vessels among the steamers.[31] Thirteen others were non-British vessels, of which nine were Spanish. Since none of the voyages of this group of ocean-going steamers originated in Saint John, the minimal crewing indicates that few desertions occurred on steam vessels. The fact that the steamers provided little business for the shipping master's office probably means that they needed few of the other port facilities for their crews. Of the sixteen steamers for which articles exist, six of the vessels accounted for the twenty recorded desertions from steamers and ten of these desertions occurred on two of the ships, the *Beaconsfield* and the *Cydonia*. The *Bessarabia, Borghese, Broomhaugh, Caduceus, Hesleden, Minnie Irvine, Rossend Castle, Stanmore, Widdrington,* and *Winchester,* manned on average by about twenty-five seamen each, reported no desertions on clearing from the port of Saint John.

The stability of the steamer crews contrasts sharply with the unreliability of the crews of the ocean-going sailing ships. Since there is nothing in the composition of the crews which provides a basis for contrast, the faithfulness of steamer crews and their resultant lack of contribution to the disorderly flavour of port life must be explained by other than human factors. One reason is provided by the nature of the voyages undertaken by steamers. In eight of ten cases where no deserters were reported, each of the vessels had visited a large American port before entering Saint John, and sailors looking for new opportunities or exciting adventures were more likely to try their luck in places such as New York and Boston than in Saint John. As a desertion port for the widely travelled steamship seaman, Saint John would have been fairly low on the list.

There is reason also for thinking that seamen were probably more content with their berths on steamships than on sailing vessels. Although the work might seem less skilled and more unpleasant and divisive, steamships made frequent stops which helped to allay the frustration that affected sailors. The speed of steam travel considerably shortened the length of voyages and it was the reduction in the period afloat which helped to make steamer crews more sanguine about their working conditions than the crews on sailing vessels. The length of turn-round time in port was also reduced, but for trading steamers visiting Saint John in 1883, the usual port stop of ten days to two weeks was still long enough for the steamer crews to get into trouble and leave their imprint on sailortown if they were so inclined. Since the proportion of Saint John's trade carried in steamers was still very small, the low desertion rate on steamers was significant as a portent of things to come rather than as a force for change in the 1880s.

But Saint John's limited experience of desertions among steamer crews tends to be confirmed by evidence relating to Halifax in the same decade. Shipping Master Bligh claimed that he engaged only a few men on steamers.[32] An examination of the articles of a sample of fifteen of the sixty-six steamships of which the Halifax entry in 1886 was noted in a short-term run of registers of the shipping firm of Pickford and Black reveals very stable crews and extremely short stopovers.[33] In the approximately thirty-five visits accounted for by these fifteen steamers, only one visit was for two days, the rest turned round in a twenty-four-hour period. The total number of crew changes recorded for the Halifax visits was four discharges and four engagements. Significantly, therefore, steamers, which varied greatly in size (from crews of twenty to ninety) and in the nature of the voyages (from Britain to Halifax direct to complicated Mediterranean-American dozen-stop voyages before calling at Halifax) varied not at all in the pattern of crew behaviour. Not one desertion was recorded in Halifax and the large total of seamen and seawomen which these passenger and freight steamers carried were given virtually no opportunity to explore Halifax's sailortown. Moreover, the steamers coming direct from England were on their way to a major American port via Halifax, a significant factor for prospective deserters.[34]

Given the ephemeral port experience of steamship crews, we must look for the sailortown habitués among the crews of the large sailing vessels, which entered Saint John in ballast and departed timber-laden. Shipping Master Purdy's records provide us with some indication of the nature of sailing vessel crews out of the port of Saint John in the 1880s.

Although the ocean-going engagements included some schooner and steamer crews, the vast majority were engagements on large sailing vessels, usually British, but with a sprinkling of American and Scandinavian vessels. A small proportion of the hirings were for vessels leaving neighbouring ports but the personnel in these cases did not vary from that supplied to vessels in the port of Saint John. One characteristic was the youthfulness of the seamen. Sixty-eight to 70 per cent of the sailor work-force on ocean-going vessels was no more than thirty years of age (see Table 2.2). About one-third of the sailors engaged on ocean-going vessels were residents of the Atlantic region (see Table 2.3), a proportion which is significantly lower than that for sailors engaging on the coasting vessels where the regularity of the return home may have been the major attraction.[35]

TABLE 2.2
Age of sailors hired in Saint John in the 1880s

Age (in years)	1883		1886		1889	
	No.	%	No.	%	No.	%
Under 20	264	10.3	201	11.0	199	12.3
20–30	1,470	57.4	1,086	59.3	897	55.6
31–40	582	22.7	374	20.4	304	18.8
41+	246	9.6	167	9.1	214	13.3
Unknown	1	0.04	5	0.3		
Total	2,563		1,833		1,614	

SOURCE: Shipping Master's Registers of Engagements, New Brunswick Museum, Saint John

TABLE 2.3
Residence of sailors hired in Saint John in the 1880s

Place of residence	1883		1886		1889	
	No.	%	No.	%	No.	%
Saint John	313	12.2	265	14.5	175	10.8
Rest of Atlantic region	629	24.5	501	27.3	356	22.1
Other parts of Canada	23	1.0	15	0.8	4	0.3
United States	195	7.6	156	8.5	149	9.2
United Kingdom	722	28.2	422	23.0	437	27.1
Other	681	26.6	474	25.9	493	30.6
Unknown					1	0.06
Total	2,563		1,833		1,614	

SOURCE: Shipping Master's Registers of Engagements, New Brunswick Museum, Saint John

Engagements in 1883 included 320 seamen from the Scandinavian
states; in 1889 there were 230. This proportion of Scandinavians (12 to
15 per cent) is lower than Bligh's claim for Halifax, where he stated in
the mid-1880s that one-third of the sailors he shipped were Scandinavian.[36] There is no way of verifying Bligh's figure since Halifax
shipping registers exist only for the period since 1912. Findings of the
Atlantic Canada Shipping Project for the Yarmouth-registered fleet,
which are unrelated to the port of entry, indicate that the number of
Scandinavians increased significantly in the 1870s to 21 per cent from
14.5 per cent in the 1860s but that there was then a slow decline to 20.1
per cent in the 1880s and 19.6 per cent in the 1890s.[37]

Whatever their age or nationality, the sailors' impact on the port depended to a large extent on the length of time they stayed. Since they seldom sailed on the same vessel in which they had arrived, the duration of the sailors' visits to port is not easy to determine. We know that sailing vessels often remained for several weeks. In 1886, for example, at least half the ocean-going vessels entering Saint John berthed for three weeks or more. In 1890 over 70 per cent stayed three weeks or more.[38] Evidence indicates that the sailors who manned these vessels remained in port for a much shorter period. Of deserters named in crew agreements in 1883 who were found being hired in the shipping master's office after leaving their vessels, the majority stayed less than a week. Discharged men, identified in the same way, tended to linger somewhat longer (one to three weeks for the majority) before they entered new engagements. Their longer stopovers may be partly attributable to the greater proportion of local residents among dischargees than among deserters.

For a more detailed examination of the crews of sailing vessels, we shall again use the sample year 1883 in Saint John. The nature of the hiring performed by the shipping office in Saint John was affected by three factors. First, Saint John, like Quebec, was a shipbuilding and outfitting port and even as late as the 1880s, when the building of large wooden freighters had passed its peak, some of the vessels crewing in Saint John were about to set out on their maiden voyages. In 1883, about twenty of the 297 voyages recorded in the shipping master's entry book were those of new vessels built in the Bay of Fundy area.[39] Second, for a large number of vessels crewing in Saint John the voyages, like those of the new vessels, originated in Saint John. Both these types of voyages – by new vessels and by older, locally owned vessels, which had discharged their seamen in port – meant considerable business for the shipping master and the boarding-houses which supplied him, because they entailed the provision of complete crews. Third, vessels in the midst of their voyages in Saint John required replacements for lost crew members. The loss might be occasioned by discharge or death but the more common reason for depleted crews in Saint John in the 1880s was still desertion.

The routine nature of desertion in eastern Canadian ports is recorded in the crew agreements of 113 of the 297 ocean-going voyages entered in the shipping master's book for 1883.[40] Omitting the sixteen steamship voyages mentioned above seventy-nine of the ninety-seven sailing voyages recorded the status of the crew on entering port and changes occurring in Saint John. Of the seventy-nine, sixty-eight listed deserters, amounting to some 558 seamen. By nominal linkage, 196 of the 558 men can be readily identified in Shipping Master Purdy's records as entering soon after into new engagements on other ocean-going vessels (as well as seven on coasting voyages). Since sailors frequently changed their names and many of the signatures on the articles are impossible to decipher, it seems likely that many more of the 558 deserters – including those who joined foreign vessels unbeknown to the shipping master – also reshipped within a short space of time.

Desertion remained, then, a major source of supply for manning vessels in Saint John. This does not mean that the shipping master necessarily violated the law. Desertions were not officially reported at his office by the captain until the vessel was on the point of clearing, perhaps weeks after the seamen had absconded and reshipped. Moreover, the federal Seamen's Act of 1873 explicitly absolved the shipping master from asking to see the seaman's certificate of discharge from his last ship unless he had reason to suspect the sailor was a deserter. Clearly most deserters were not asked for proof of lawful discharge and reshipped quickly enough to escape detection.

The pattern of employment on fifty-two of the sixty-eight voyages with desertions was a straightforward round trip from a port in the United Kingdom or nearby continental Europe to Saint John and back to a port of discharge in the United Kingdom or Europe. Another five voyages included a stop at the Azores, North Sydney, or Yarmouth before reaching Saint John, and a sixth altered its destination on arrival in Saint John and sailed instead for Africa. The refusal of the sailors on these fifty-eight voyages to stay by their vessels for the return trip was based largely on the higher wage rates they could obtain under new engagements in Saint John. They went on deserting as long as it was to their economic advantage to do so.

The westbound wage rates in the 1880s remained very much the same as they had been for half a century (see Table 2.4). In the 1883 sample the lowest monthly wage for an able seaman embarking in the United Kingdom or Europe was £2.15s, the highest £4, but the most prevalent by far was £3. The wages sailors gambled to obtain through desertion in Saint John in 1883, when paid on a monthly basis, were somewhat higher than English wages, being between $18 and $22 for an able seaman (see Table 2.5). (For purposes of comparison an exchange rate

TABLE 2.4
Wages of able seamen on vessels clearing English ports for North America, June, 1847–66

	Out of London		Out of Liverpool		Out of Hull	Out of Tyne	
	Sail	ss	Sail	ss	Sail	Sail	ss
1847	£2.10s	–*	£2.15s	–	–	£3	–
1848	£2.10s	–	£2.12s.6d	£3.10s	£2.15s	£3	–
1849	–	–	£2.12s.6d	£3.10s	£2.15s	£2.15s	–
1850	–	–	£2.5s	£3.10s	£2.17s.6d	£2.10s	–
1851	£2.10s	–	£2.17s.6d	£3.10s	£2.15s	£2.17s.6d	–
1852	£3	–	£3	£3.10s	£3	–	–
1853	£2.15s	–	£3.10s	£3.10s	£3.10s	–	–
1854†	£3.17s.6d	–	£4	£4.10s	£5	£5	–
1855	£3.15s	–	£3.10s	£4.10s	–	–	–
1856	£2.15s	–	£3.10s	£4.10s	–	–	–
1857	£3	£4	£3.10s	£4	–	£3.7s.6d	–
1858	£3	£4	£3.15s	£4	–	–	–
1859	£3	£4	£3.15s	£4	£3.10s	£3.5s	–
1860	£3	£4	£3.15s	£4	£3.10s	£3	–
1861	£3	£4	£2.15s	£4	£4	£3.5s	–
1862	£3	£4	£3.5s	£4	£3.10s	£3.10s	–
1863	£3	£4	£3.10s	£4	£3	£3	–
1864	£3	£4	£4	£4	£3.10s	–	–
1865	£3	£4	£3	£4	£3.10s	£4	–
1866†	£3.15s	£4	£4	£5	£3.10s	£4	£4

SOURCE: MT 9/4/1822/67 (Papers of the Marine Department, Board of Trade, Public Record Office, London, England)
*'Where no entry appears against the year, no vessels engaged crews in the month of June for North America.'
†'The high rate of wages in 1854 was during the Crimean War, and in 1866 was in consequence of the seamen's strike for higher wages.'

of $4 = £1 is assumed.) But the vast majority of seamen before the mast shipped in Saint John were paid by the run and only bad luck made the lump sum payment unprofitable for the one-way voyage. Run rates in 1883 fluctuated from $30 during February, March, and April to $40 in May, July, and October, to a normal high season rate of $50, but with considerable variation, during the hectic months of June, August, and September. At the end of the season, November and December run money was down to $35. While the advances varied too, they tended to cluster around $20, whether the rate of the wage was as low as $30 or as

TABLE 2.5
Average wages for the run from Saint John to Britain in the 1870s

Year	1870	1871	1872	1873	1874	1875	1877	1878
Average wage	$45	$55	$60.50	$55	$30	$40	$30	$25

SOURCE: Canada *Sessional Papers*, Annual Reports of the Department of Marine

TABLE 2.6
Rate of wages paid at the shipping office, Quebec in 1852 and 1853

1852 Dates	Wage	1853 Dates	Wage
Opening of season to 18 May	£5	Opening of season to 16 July	£10
18 May to 2 June	£6	16 July to 17 Aug.	£12
2 to 30 June	£5.10s	19 Aug. (on 2 ships only)	£10
30 June to 3 July	£6 to £7.10s	19 Aug. to 9 Nov.	£11
3 July to 10 Sept.	£8	9 to 19 Nov.	£14 to £15
10 to 25 Sept.	£7	20 Nov. to close of navigation	£16 to £22
25 Sept. to 11 Oct.	£6.10s		
11 Oct. to 15 Nov.	£6		
20 to 22 Nov.	£6 to £7.10s		

SOURCE: Fifth and Sixth Annual Reports of the Shipping Master's Office, Quebec, Public Archives of Canada, RG 4, C I, vol. 327, No. 2931, and vol. 331, No. 355

high as $60. On discharge on the other side of the Atlantic, sailors hired by the run normally collected around £5.[41]

Available data on wage rates in the nineteenth century indicate considerable fluctuation by month and year (see Table 2.6). But the Canadian rates were, with rare exceptions, always higher than the British. The contrast comes out most graphically in individual cases. When Thomas Paget of the *Golden Age* was committed to prison in London in 1871 for refusing to go to sea, it was revealed that he had shipped for £3.10s a month, deserted at Quebec, and shipped in another vessel to England for £13 a month.[42] The argument used in the Canadian ports to discredit desertion was that the crimps got most of the money. The discharge pay for sailors is noted on the crew agreements (from Saint John in 1883 and from another 200 ships' articles from the 1850s to the 1890s used in this study) and referred to in British court cases involving shipping infractions (reported in the *Shipping and Mercantile Gazette*); even if most of the advance went to the crimp, the average sailor still ended up with more money in his pocket at the end of the voyage than if he had abided by the British rates. Securing higher eastbound rates (through desertion) was one way the sailor had for occasionally supplementing the continuously low wages available in Britain and on the continent.

The patterns that emerge among the Saint John deserters in 1883 confirm not only their low British wages but also their youthfulness and national heterogeneity. The sixty-eight deserter-prone voyages produced an average of eight deserters each. One of the fifty-eight standard transatlantic timber voyages was made by the Saint John ship *Asiania*, which lost seventeen of its twenty-two-man crew. Eleven were thirty years old or younger and the deserters came from Saint John, Nova Scotia, Canada, the United States, Antigua, Ireland, England, Scotland, Sweden, and Germany. The *G.S. Penry*, a Saint John barque, declared seven deserters out of a crew of ten, all under thirty years, with a majority claiming Finland as home, the rest coming from Sweden, Norway, and the United States. Another Saint John barque, the *Katahdin*, reported the desertion of all twelve able and ordinary seamen, three of whom were over thirty years. They were all 'foreigners' from Norway, Russia, Germany, France, and Manila (Philippine Islands). In March, the *Lottie Stewart*, also a Saint John barque, lost all ten of its young seamen (only one was over thirty), half of whom were Finns; the rest came from Sweden, Germany, Russia, and Ireland. On its next visit in July the vessel lost seven men: six of its eight able seamen and the boy. Two were over age thirty. These deserters were Irish, Spanish, Swedish, Russian, English, and American. The *Twilight*, a barque registered in Londonderry, Ireland, lost six of its sixteen-man crew early in the season. On its next visit it lost eleven of a total crew of fifteen; two were over thirty years. Nine of these deserters from a voyage which originated in Londonderry were Irish. The new Saint John ship *Wildwood* lost twenty-five men of twenty-six, including six stowaways hired after clearing from Liverpool. Eleven were English, four American, and four Irish. The rest came from France, Chile, Nova Scotia, and Saint John. While over all, the greatest number of deserters were English, Irish, and American in that order, the Baltic (Norway, Sweden, Finland, Germany, and Russia combined) was responsible for 66 per cent more deserters than was England.

Most of the other ten, more diverse voyages which produced deserters in Saint John, bear some resemblance to the eleven sailing voyages without desertions. Seven of the ten lost less than five men each after arriving in Saint John from a variety of exotic locations in the tropics and more attractive desertion ports in the United States. The voyage pattern of the *Napier* will suffice as an example. It had sailed from Penarth to Port Elizabeth to St Helena to Boston to Saint John. Its one deserter was the cook-steward who had been hired in Boston by the month. The rest of the crew were discharged in Saint John after signing on in Boston for the run to the Fundy port. Clearly Boston had been the major desertion port for this vessel. An obvious conclusion which emerges from the connection between voyage patterns and rates of desertion is that without its status as a one-stop timber port for transatlantic sailing freighters, Saint John would not have been a major deserters' port.

The eleven sailing vessels which reported no desertions at all in Saint John in 1883 included six in which the sailors did not need to succumb to the temptations to desert because their engagements terminated in Saint John. The whole crew of the *City of Charlottetown*, a Prince Edward Island barquentine, were discharged and paid off in Saint John after an eight-month voyage from London via Natal and Pernambuco. During a port visit in March the Saint John barque *Director* discharged its crew, most of whom had been hired in Boston for the run to Saint John on the final leg of a nine-month voyage which had begun in Hamburg and taken the vessel to New York, Alicante, Tupani, Gloucester, and Boston, before reaching Saint John. The Annapolis barque *Palermo* terminated a voyage in Saint John in April after having been to Matanzas and Boston. Most of this crew also had been hired in Boston for the run to Saint John. For one of the final five vessels in our survey of seventy-nine voyages, Boston again is relevant. The Newcastle barque *Gateshead* arrived after a two-week stopover in Boston during which six desertions had occurred. No one deserted from the vessel in Saint John.

We should note also that the crews of two other vessels without deserters were characterized by an unusual degree of homogeneity for international freighters. The men were Welsh sailors, noted for their reliability. The Liverpool vessel *Dusty Miller* sailed out of Caernarvon, and its visit in September and October was the third voyage of the year, the two earlier ones having taken the vessel to Savannah and Quebec. No desertions were recorded in any of these three voyages. The Welsh sailors stood by their vessel which was skippered by the same Caernarvon master on the three voyages. Another Liverpool vessel, the *Plevna*, did a round voyage Caernarvon-Saint John-Caernarvon between April and July 1883. With a Welsh master and eleven Welshmen among its twelve sailors, no desertions occurred in Saint John. In contrast, on its second visit to port late in the autumn manned with a mixed crew from Canada, England, Ireland, Sweden, and Germany, seven desertions were recorded.

In 1883, therefore, Jack's desertion in Saint John depended on that port being the first landfall and the crew being an international one. These were features which applied almost exclusively to the deep-sea trading vessels. The international mixture of crews was widely recognized and was as much characteristic of the ports of Halifax, Quebec, and ports in the British and American trading empires as it was of Saint John. As the *Shipping and Mercantile Gazette* reported in the early 1870s: 'Sailors of all nations are migratory beings, and in these days there is hardly a seagoing vessel which has not amongst her crew the subjects of half a dozen different States, and there are not perhaps, half a dozen of a whole ship's company who belong to the same port.'[43]

THE SEAFARER'S OUTLOOK

The seafaring life produced a distinctive outlook – ribald, careless, matter-of-fact – which neither sketchy case studies nor laborious statistics can capture. Some of the best of the seafaring novels and memoirs convincingly describe the life at sea – the hardships and excitements, the conflicts and the camaraderie. They follow the sailor to shore, too, and treat the vicissitudes of that part of his experience. But authors such as Frederick Marryatt, Richard Dana, and Herman Melville were literate, educated men who spoke through the mouth of the respectable, genteel sailor. They fail to capture the language and manners of humble sailors before the mast. The vulgarity and coarseness of sailors' talk emerges instead from lusty sea songs and shanties, important to sailors as entertainment during their brief leisure moments at sea and as accompaniments to their back-breaking labour both at sea and in port.

The oral traditions of seafaring, represented by song, knew no national boundaries. The familiar 'A-rovin' A-rovin','in an explicit and earthy version, belonged equally to seamen visiting Canadian, American, European, or far eastern ports:

In Amsterdam there lived a maid,
[Chorus] Mark well what I do say!

In Amsterdam there lived a maid,
An' she wuz mistress of her trade.
  [Chorus] We'll go no more a-rovin with you fair maid!

[Full Chorus] A-rovin' a-rovin',
             Since rovin's bin me ru-eye-in,
             We'll go no more a-rovin',
             Wid you fair maid.

One night I crept from my abode,
To meet this fair maid down the road,

I met this fair maid after dark,
She took me to her favourite park.

I took this fair maid for a walk,
An' we had such a lovin' talk.

I put me arm around her waist,
Sez she, 'Young man yer in great haste!'

I put me hand upon her knee,
Sez she, 'Young man yer rather free!'

I put me hand upon her breast,
Sez she, 'The wind is verrin' sou'-sou'-west!'

'The wind is verrin' sou'-sou'-west,'
Her voice was as deep as an ol' sea-chest.

The cheeks of her ass wuz as tight as a drum,
The lips o' her mouth wuz as red as a plum.

Her skin wuz as white an' as creamy as milk,
The hair o' her legs wuz as soft as silk.

I put me hand upon her thigh,
Sez she, 'Young man yer rather high!'

I pushed her over on her back,
An' then she let me have me whack.

Such songs may have entertained port society but they also confirmed
the worst prejudices about sailors, especially their sexual indulgences.

As we shall soon discover, the official logs frequently recorded the
venereal complaints of the foremast hands. These reports contrast
sharply with the seafaring jargon used to describe whoring and
venereal disease in 'Ratcliffe Highway,' one of the most popular
fo'c's'le songs of the age of sail:

As I wuz a-rollin' down the Highway one morn,
I spied a flash packet from ol' Wapping town,
As soon as I seed her I slacked me main brace,
An' I hoisted me stuns'ls an' to her gave chase.

[Chorus] Oh, me riggin's slack,
   Aye, me rattlin's are frayed,
   I've rattled me rigging down Ratcliffe Highway!

Her flag wuz three colours, her masthead wuz low,
She wuz round at the counter an' bluff at the bow;
From larboard to starboard an' so rolled she,
She wuz sailin' at large, she wuz runnin' free.

I fired me bow-chaser, the signal she knew,
She backed her main tops'l an' for me hove to;
I lowered down me jolly-boat an' rowed alongside,
An' I found madam's gangway wuz open an' wide.

I hailed her in English, she answered me clear,
'I'm from the Black Arrow bound to the Shakespeare';
So I wore ship wid a what d'yer know,
An' I passed her me hawser an' took her in tow.

I tipped her me flipper, me towrope an' all,
She then let her hand on me reel-tackle fall;
She then took me up to her lily-white room,
An' in her main riggin' I fouled me jibboom.

I entered her little cubby-hole, an' swore damn yer eyes,
She wuz nothin' but a fireship rigged up in disguise,
She had a foul bottom, from sternpost to fore,
'Tween wind and water she ran me ashore.

She set fire to me riggin', as well as me hull,
An' away to the lazareet I had to scull;
Wid me helm hard-a-starboard as I rolled along,
Me shipmates cried, 'Hey, Jack, yer mainyard is sprung!'

Now I'm safe in harbour, me moorings all fast,
I lay here quite snug, boys, till all danger is past;
With me mainyard all served, boys, an' parcelled an' tarred,
Wasn't that a stiff breeze, boys, that sprung me mainyard?

Here's a health to the gal wid the black, curly locks,
Here's a health to the gal who ran me on the rocks;
Here's a health to the quack, boys, who eased me from pain,
If I meet that flash packet I'll board her again.

Work songs also demonstrate that sailors' language was unlikely to resemble polite parlour talk. Two verses of the pumping song 'The *Ebenezer*' run:

The Ol' Man wuz a drunken geezer
Couldn't sail the *Ebenezer*;
Learnt his trade on a Chinese junk,
Spent most time, sir, in his bunk.

[Chorus] Ooh! Git along boys, git along do,
          Handy, me boys, so handy!
          Git along, boys, git along do,
          Handy, me boys, so handy!

The Chief Mate's name wuz Dickie Green, sir,
The dirtiest bugger ye've ever seen, sir;
Walkin' his poop wid a bucko roll,
May the sharks have his body, an' the devil have his soul!

The halyard shanty 'Blow, Boys, Blow' also describes the captain and mate in unflattering terms:

Who d'yer think's the skipper of her?
[Chorus] Blow, boys, blow!
A bow-legged bastard from the Bowery.
[Chorus] Blow, me bully boys, blow!

Who d'yer think's the chief mate of her?
Why Pompey Squash, that big, buck nigger.[44]

An illustration of sailors' more spontaneous obscenities is contained in the log of the *Ben Lomond,* a Greenock vessel which visited Quebec in 1858. One obstreperous member of the crew, James Killian, vigorously expressed his reluctance to take orders while the vessel was in port. He spent the day of 26 October employed in operating the vessel's winch as the vessel was being stowed with timber at Sillery Cove. The mate recorded that 'when called to heave he would call out heave your sister[s] cunt dam[n] you and other such language.' When the mate told him he was not to swear, Killian answered 'that he did not care a damn for any mate in the *Ben Lomond* and that the *Ben Lomond* had turned damned religious.'[45]

Killian's apparent surprise at the mate's objection to his choice of epithets would seem to indicate that the *Ben Lomond* was not normally run like a moral prison. None the less, life on board was rigidly regulated in theory if not in practice. No vessel for which papers exist condoned the consumption of alcohol on board ship.[46] The articles of other vessels specified restrictions which were meant to deal with problems such as that posed by Killian. The articles of the *Lady Hincks* in 1883, for example, specified 'No swearing or clothes to be washed on Sundays,' an interesting blend of restrictions.[47] Deprived of liquor, the sailor had to do without other comforts while he was at sea. With the occasional exception of the cook or steward among the crew, the sailor lacked the right to have his woman with him, unlike his shipmaster. Nor were pet animals welcome. When William Doace took his dog aboard the *Simonds* for a voyage from Saint John to Liverpool in 1867, the captain charged him £2.10s for the animal's passage.[48]

Songs, obscenities, and restrictions can be extracted from the historical record. But the common sailor was not a prime subject for art and photography, with the result that our impressions of what sailors looked like are far from clear. Did they have a distinctive working garb or was the nature of their employment too casual to produce an acknowledged uniform? While meagre pictorial sources suggest variety in the style of dress, sailors adopted a similar attitude to their clothes. Most sailors, far from home and unable often to collect wages until the end of a long voyage, placed what might seem like an exaggerated importance on the personal belongings they carried with them. The sailor's concern about the loss of his clothes, either individual items or the contents of his chest or duffle bag, was frequently recorded in court cases.

For most sailors the contents of the sea chest represented the sum total of their worldly possessions and descriptions of those possessions therefore provide us with some insight into the material world of the sailor, especially his wearing apparel. The effects of Adam Lindberg, killed by the wheel of the gin block used for discharging coal from his vessel, the *Milton Lockhart*, at Quebec in 1871, were sold to the members of the crew after the vessel sailed. The men, identified by name, bought:

C. Thompson: one singlet 2s.3d; one shirt 1s.6d; one pr mittens 6d.
Olef Nealson: one singlet 1s.3d; one reefing jacket 1s; one pr mittens 2d.
Sam Olsen: one singlet 1s.4d; one pr drawers 3s; one pr drawers 10d; one singlet 5d; one pr trousers 3s.2d; Book 4d.
J. Carleberg: one singlet 1s.8d; knives and spoons 1s.3d; sundry articles 2s.4d.
J. Swanson: one pr drawers 3s; one shirt 4s.10d; one coat 6s.2d; oilskins 1s.8d; one pr blankets 1s.8d; razor 6d.; one pr stockings 1s.8d; tinpot 1½d.
J. Christie: one shirt 1s; one guernsey frock 6s; southwester 8d.
H. Svenger, carpenter: one coat 3s.3d; muffler and handkerchief 1s.3d.
R. Eddy: one pr boots 10s; clothes bag 2s.8d.
J. Richardson: meershum [sic] pipe 1s.6d.

The proceeds of the sale amounted to £3.6s.11½d, which, added to Lindberg's wages (two months, five days at £3.5s per month), totalled £10.7s.9½d. From this amount the captain deducted 10s.2d for the advance note Lindberg had received in North Shields, 1s for the shipping fee payable to the mercantile marine office; 9s advanced to Lindberg in cash at Quebec; 10s for four pounds of tobacco doled out to the seaman; and 1s.3d for a bar of soap. The remaining £8.16s.4½d was to be delivered to the marine department of the British Board of Trade for transmission to Lindberg's next of kin.[49]

James Thomson, a twenty-year-old Shetlander drowned while securing timber at Sillery Cove in 1857, left effects not dissimilar in variety to Lindberg's. They included: one chest, one reefing jacket, two cloth coats, one bed cover, one blanket, one pair of cloth trousers, two flannel shirts, two cotton shirts, two cloth vests, one pair of stockings, one clothes bag, two cloth caps, two cravats, one silk handkerchief, one pair of cotton trousers, one looking glass, two pairs of boots, one pair of shoes, one towel, one southwester, two brushes, one razor, one spoon, and one needle case. This inventory suggests that Thomson had enjoyed dressing up and attending to his toilet when the occasion afforded.[50]

Not all sailors who died on the job left so many possessions as Lindberg and Thomson, though the common clothing items tended to be oilskins, sou'westers, guernsey frocks, and reefing jackets. John Giles, a Londoner, who fell from the foretop-gallant yard to his death in the sea on the voyage of the *Bellcarrigg* from Liverpool to Quebec in 1863, left a more modest stock of effects: one pair of blue trousers, one blue shirt, one bag, one set of oilskin coat and trousers, one old guernsey frock, one singlet, one white shirt, one pair of flannel drawers, two blankets, and one bed.[51]

None of these sailors was a deserter and had not therefore risked the loss of his possessions while in Quebec. William Timlin, a lad who died on the *Lady Falkland* in 1858, after shipping at Quebec, was less fortunate. The absence of an inventory of belongings would suggest that he had probably deserted at Quebec and had not been supplied with an appropriate kit by the crimp who found him alternative employment. Listed on the articles as only fourteen years old, Timlin was killed at sea when he fell from the futtock mizen onto the deckload. The log recorded that at 4 p.m. the crew 'committed his body to the deep, having no effects, only what he had on his back when coming on board in Quebec.'[52]

The stark descriptions of burials at sea indicate that the seafaring occupation was short on ceremonial, particularly that important nineteenth-century celebration, the Victorian way of death. Death at sea always resulted in a hasty dispatch of the body to the briny deep: no wake, no mourners, no comradely processions. On shore there was some scope for public display but the sailor's status as a poor stranger militated against the provision of a fancy funeral. The description of a sailor's funeral contained in a Halifax newspaper in 1845 emphasizes the matter-of-fact seafaring attitude towards death at the same time as it satisfies the contemporary appetite for pathos and melodrama.

We speak of a funeral we saw yesterday in Water Street. There was something peculiarly striking in its appearance that rivited [sic] our attention as we turned up opposite the Commercial Wharf. The procession moved along towards us. It came more rapidly than usual, and we were not surprised at this, when as the hearse approached, one could tell at a glance that a Sailor was driving.

Yes! it was a poor Sailor's Funeral! There were more evidences of the fact than the glazed hat and weather beaten features of the hearse-driver. There was a very meagre attendance of mourners in the train – and a glance in at the plain black coffin, with the lid but carelessly tightened down, told plainly that the helpless inmate was not one who had amassed a large share of the wealth of mammon.

But five couple of his messmates followed him to the grave; poor fellow! perhaps they had subscribed together to procure for him the rites of decent burial. A storm of snow and sleet was whirling in fitful eddies through the streets – and the dashing and gurgling of the waves at the docks and wharves could be distinctly heard, everything looked bleak and desolate – and the east wind moaned dismally. The elements seemed to sympathise with the woe-begone appearance of the train which followed the remains of the poor sailor to the grave ...

Among all classes of men, none more deserve our pity and support than the weather beaten mariner – he who to bring us the luxuries of foreign climes, risks health, and life, and comfort on the boundless ocean ... Oh think! benevolent hearted reader for a moment how desolate and gloomy must often be the death bed of the adventurous, uncomplaining, kind hearted, generous sailor, and sure we are that the call of humanity will ever go more directly to your hearts, and there will be more good Samaritans among us than there are.[53]

The rhythm of
port life

Society took cognizance of the comings and goings, the employment
and unemployment, and the sickness and death of sailors. The
seasonal quality of port life heightened local awareness of the
seafarers' impact on the port, which began with the arrival of the
merchant fleet in the spring. In May 1872, the Quebec *Morning
Chronicle* reported:

The arrival yesterday of the first ship from sea caused great excitement among
our fellow citizens. Thousands crowded the wharves to see her coming round
the Point. As soon as she hove in sight, with her sailors aloft furling her sails,
there was a murmur of delight and satisfaction from the crowd, which is only
heard but once a year. Scarcely had this murmur died away when everyone
seemed to think that he had suddenly become busy, that their prospects had
brightened; and the thought of soon turning over the shining dollar loosened
every tongue. The ship's anchor was soon cast, and ere the sound had died
away o'er the waters every voice was hushed; and, if a question were, by
chance, asked it was only in a whisper lest they would not hear the lowering of
the boat that brought the Captain to our shore. In a few moments, however, the
Captain's gig was seen leaving the ship's side; and at every stroke of their oars
the excitement from the crowd became greater until he reached the landing,
where a general rush was made to welcome the newcomer. Every eye
brightened as they saw him land, and he had soon around him – ship-
chandlers, stevedores, timber-towers, butchers and others who were welcom-
ing and endeavouring to persuade him what they could do for him. But, as he

continued walking, quite a procession was formed, in whose wake a few of our crimps were seen quite as gay as the rest, in fact, everything had become quite lively on his landing.[1]

The sailors prominent on the deck of the first vessel to reach Quebec in the shipping season of 1872 would have spent over a month on the perilous late-winter voyage across the Atlantic. For them the prospect of going ashore was as welcome as was the appearance of their ship to the people of the port, especially to the crimps. From May until November Quebec residents were seldom allowed to forget the presence of merchant sailors.

Although the season was longer in Saint John and Halifax, their ice-free harbours did not protect them from a winter slowdown. Here seasonality was caused by physical, geographical, and environmental factors: the supply of goods for export diminished in winter, regulations relating to winter sailings restricted deckloads and increased insurance rates, and no sailing vessel crossed the north Atlantic in winter unless it had to. The same enthusiasm greeted the beginning of the navigation season in Halifax. The *Morning Journal* recorded in April 1857:

Our harbour wears a very different appearance from what it did a few weeks ago. There are many fine vessels now in the stream and at the wharves, discharging valuable cargoes – and the coasters and fishing crafts are numerous. The country dealers are beginning to arrive to carry off a share of the late transportations, and the dry goods merchants and their staffs are in full employment.[2]

The excitement and expectations felt in port at the opening of the season differed markedly from the anxieties experienced at the close of the season. In Quebec, sailors remaining in port after the freeze-up of the St Lawrence exacerbated seasonal poverty and unemployment. Seamen figured prominently among the poor in the winter of 1835–6, some of them as a result of late season shipwrecks, the most unfortunate having been involved in two successive disasters on the *Cumberland* and the *Merlin*. In the winter of 1848, deserters unable to secure employment were found to be 'perishing in the woods or out-houses with cold and hunger.'[3]

Lone sailors lacking prospects of employment in winter frequently went or were taken to the Saint John police station for 'protection.' John Weatherspoon, lately arrived in Saint John from England, claimed in December 1866 to be looking for a job or for a chance to work his passage home. David Mill, a sailor from Dundee, who also sought protection in the police station in January 1867, complained that his late captain owed him twenty dollars. A German sailor who went to the station for protection in December 1873 was thought to be a fit object for the Saint John almshouse. George Wood deserted from his vessel early in January 1874 in the hope of improving his wages by getting a 'good run' home. Not only did he fail to find a ship but he was also unable to find employment of any kind ashore. A Danish sailor who deserted from his ship also in January 1874 was excluded from the Saint John boarding-houses, a policy the local Boarding House Keepers Association maintained against those who broke locally arranged engagements. As a renegade defying the customs of the port he found a cold welcome awaiting him when he went to the police station for protection.[4]

The usual local response to the prospect of having to support unemployed seamen through the winter was to suggest that they should be sent to seaboard ports in the United States on the ground that the expense of forwarding them was much less than maintaining them in Quebec. In December 1853 the editor of the Quebec *Morning Chronicle* objected to this suggestion and claimed that 'British seamen if willing to work can always secure employment and might be advantageously engaged, at any rate as riggers, in our ship-yards during the winter months. They will be much wanted in the spring to man not only the new vessels, but those that have remained here during the winter.'[5] A marooned sailor with a particular skill, such as a ship's carpenter, might indeed join the ranks of resident shipwrights if enough winter work were available. Such a course was not necessarily involuntary and accidental. A case in point is provided by the experience of a ship's carpenter in Saint John, a 'Dutchman' named William Williams, who commanded public attention in 1841 when he murdered a local shoemaker, William Blair, with whom he lodged in winter. It was apparently Williams's custom to ship out of Saint John during the summer and work in Saint John shipyards during the winter.[6]

The editor of the *Morning Chronicle*, who objected to the removal of unemployed sailors from Quebec in the winter of 1853–4, endorsed such a policy three years later. Because of the success of the crimps in the 1856 season in withholding sailors from the labour market and driving up wages, a large number of 'deluded' sailors were left without vessels at the close of navigation when the last departing vessels were able to hire both hands and officers for next to nothing. The prospect of maintaining 200 unemployed sailors through the winter encouraged the newspaperman to suggest that the crimps should be licensed, like European courtesans, and required to pay a tax for the support of their victims. In the absence of such a system, he took comfort in Quebec's possession of a railway by which some of the sailors could be dispatched to Atlantic ports.[7]

In the case of late season shipwreck and ice damage, wintering at Quebec was unavoidable. During the winter of 1853–4, the ice formed unusually early and some twenty or thirty vessels had to winter over.[8] While the port of Quebec was noted as a winter shipbuilding port, it did not normally function as a wintering port for idle timber vessels. The latter usually returned to Britain with their cargoes and discharged their seamen in order to keep wintering expenses at a minimum.

The end of the season at Quebec also sent 'into winter quarters' 'ship-chandlers, tug-steam boat owners, timber towers, market boat-men' and even timber merchants.[9] Similarly, the seasonal patterns of shipping at Quebec disrupted the activities of a number of sailortown residents who made their living off the sailors in the summer. Like sailors accidently stranded in Quebec, boarding-house-keepers, crimps, and runners were deprived in winter of their accustomed employment and had to devise a means of keeping alive. Many resorted to seasonal migration. The pattern of moving to southern American ports to engage in similar types of business in the off-season was well established by the 1850s. Certainly the crimps cleared out in winter and were said to make for New Orleans, the reputed headquarters of the dockside underworld.[10] In the summer of 1859, three weeks after arriving in Quebec from New Orleans, Christopher Sheridan, a runner for a sailors' boarding-house in Champlain Street, was before the magistrate charged with assaulting the master of the ship *Spartan*. In the early autumn he was tried on a charge of receiving a seaman's clothing, a euphemism for crimping, and the police magistrate claimed:

It was not to the interest of the city to have here, during the winter, persons of the class to which the defendant belonged. He would not, therefore, sentence him, as he should have done were it earlier in the season, to the full term of imprisonment awarded by the statute but only to 40 days plus a $10 fine, so that he might be able to quit Quebec before the close of navigation.[11]

By the 1870s the ship labourers too had acknowledged the established rhythm of seasonal work. In the autumn when the last sailor joined the last stowed vessel, the stevedores and labourers packed up and went south until April to attend to timber cargoes during 'the southern season.' The exodus increased with the decline of commercial activity in Quebec, particularly the demise of wooden shipuilding, which had previously provided winter employment.[12] A further acknowledgement of the complementary nature of the two major Atlantic timber shipping seasons was provided in 1876 when the Norwegian government sent out a missionary to Quebec to attend to the spiritual needs of Norwegian nationals who visited the port as sailors – in the winter the Reverend M. Wormdahl was posted to Pensacola, Florida.[13]

Whether the interruption in trade entailed migration abroad or distress at home, the lot of the seasonally employed worker was not a comfortable one. Finding themselves confronted with winter unemployment, the Quebec river police force adopted a militant stand in 1854 in order to cope with their uncertain prospects. The force went on strike for higher wages in the summer, a demand specifically tied to the wholly seasonal nature of their employment.[14] Given the police force's annual disbandment in the autumn, the port authorities found it difficult to maintain the desired degree of continuity and quality in the composition of the force. As a correspondent to the *Quebec Mercury* explained in 1856:

Even with the best rule and able assistance of active chiefs, how can you expect the men to be independent in the discharge of their duty or to act with determination when you call to mind that there are six long months of winter, when they do not know where fate may cast their lot to earn a livelihood for their families. If it happens that you meet in your walks through this city, that stirring individual, F.B. McNamee, ask him and he will tell you, as I have seen them, that the water policeman and the boarding master of last summer, toil together on his work in the trenches of the city water works. Again, ask their chief how many of those men are gone out South or to sea, for the winter, and will be back in time to get on in the spring, and I will be bound to say, that he will tell you, that more than three quarters of them are gone. And these men, knowing that this is their fate for the winter months, is it reasonable to suppose that they will or can become efficient in the performance of their duty during the summer months?[15]

The varied length of stay by vessels complicated the activity of the shipping season by introducing a myriad of subsidiary rhythms as each individual vessel entered and cleared port, unloading and loading during its stopover not just freight but also members of a labour force overwhelmed by overwork, tedium, illness, enforced temperance, and dissatisfaction with fellow workers or superiors or working conditions or seafaring per se. As the shipping columns of the newspapers amply confirm, almost every day during the shipping season vessels entered port. Passenger liners, particularly the steamers, turned round quickly, but the larger freighters, sail or steam, stayed for ten days to a month. The log of the Saint John barque *Achilles* in Quebec in 1846 illustrates the typical occupations of a visiting timber ship whose port work entailed no steam-driven machinery:

24 Aug. 1846 Came to anchor off Charles River. Discharged
             Charles Brown, ordinary seaman.
25 Aug. 1846 Commenced to discharge ballast
26   People [i.e. sailors] employed at the ballast
27   ditto
28   Noon weighed anchor and drop'd down alongside of the
             Block and Moored
29   Put out all the ballast
30   [Sunday]
31   People employed clearing away the hold and getting
             up the derricks. Four seamen deserted: Thomas Atwood,
             William Christian, John Nugent, William Duncan.
             Thomas Johnson absent
1 Sept.   Thomas Johnson deserted. Commenced to take in. Took
             in 32 piece white pine and 1,480 pipe staves; 50 pieces outside.
2   Took in 45 pieces and 5,480 West Indian staves. 46 outside.
             Two seamen deserted. Names Charles Lyon, William Williams
3 Sept.   Took in 66 pieces of white pine. 114 pieces outside.
4   "   Took in 60 pieces. 118 pieces outside
5   "   Took in 42 pieces. 110 outside
6   "   [Sunday]
7   "   Took in 46 pieces. Finished the lower hold. 102 pieces outside
8 Sept.   Took in the beam filling, 54 pieces and two on 1st tier.
             Took in 3000 plank. 91 pieces outside.
9   "   Took in 50 pieces. 83 outside.

10	"	Took in 44 pieces and two chord lathwood. 79 pieces outside.
11	"	Took in 23 pieces. Took in 1,704 West Indian staves and 406 pipe staves, 200 deal ends. 78 pieces outside.
12	"	Took in 36 pieces. 39 pieces outside.
13	"	Sunday
14 Sept.		Took in 35 pieces and finished loading. 7 pieces outside
15	"	People and labourers employed cleaning away the decks, securing the spars and water casks and filling them. One gang setting up the jibboom gear.
16	"	Pilot came on board, stores and crew — seven seamen: Alex Mitchell, Henry Pearson, John Owen, Robert Dunn, George Robertson, John Johnston and Wm. Clynk. At 4 p.m. Charles Fowler, seaman fell from the mizen crosstrays, struck the Poop rail and fell overboard and was drowned.
17	"	Weighed anchor and got underway.[16]

New technology and increased competition combined to halve the stopover of timber vessels by the 1880s. Eight steamers in Saint John in April 1882 were in port on average for twelve and a quarter days.[17]

The numbers of sailors who came ashore from the visiting vessels (see Table 3.1) vastly increased the populace of each city. For a large portion of the year in Halifax the population was swollen by several hundred, often over a thousand.[18] The population of Quebec was, according to one newspaper account, augmented by 10,000 sailors during the summer: 'hardy, athletic fellows, who, being less actively employed, have every temptation to be disorderly.'[19] If the port calls of sailors encouraged them to go on sprees and make hay while the sun shone, the transiency of those calls also profoundly affected their reception in port. Since the vast majority of seamen in all three ports were not only transient but also non-resident, society tended to look on those who followed the sea not as men with individual characteristics but as the stereotyped characters prevalent in seafaring lore. With the exception of soldiers, sailors constituted the only members of society, who, when involved in court or creating disturbances or laid low by accident or illness, were always identified by their occupation. Their distance from society was thereby enhanced. They did not belong; they were not allowed to merge into the general population.

To some extent the distancing was reinforced by the location of sailortown. In Quebec, for example, a sailor in the Upper Town was a

TABLE 3.1
Entrances and clearances (including coasting vessels) 1880–95

Year ending 30 June	Saint John				Halifax				Quebec			
	Vessels inwards	Seamen inwards	Vessels outwards	Seamen outwards	Vessels inwards	Seamen inwards	Vessels outwards	Seamen outwards	Vessels inwards	Seamen inwards	Vessels outwards	Seamen outwards
1880	3,340	20,728	3,110	20,548	3,286	32,351	2,964	31,460	3,748	40,341	3,702	37,707
1885	3,797	26,942	3,811	27,231	3,587	36,558	3,842	37,875	2,918	37,565	2,938	35,628
1890	4,199	30,376	4,200	29,130	4,465	44,131	4,446	46,307	2,329	35,009	2,255	30,718
1895	3,743	30,751	3,766	32,089	4,700	43,181	4,564	44,712	761	24,686	707	19,275

SOURCE: Trade and Navigation statistics, Canada *Sessional Papers*

rare sight and the local citizenry wanted to keep it that way. In the middle of the century considerable local disapproval existed of the way the sailors had to be marched from the lock-up in the Lower Town to the court in the Upper Town to be tried for their various misdemeanours and shipping offences. The residents saw this as in some way degrading sailors, but one wonders to what extent their views reflected a distaste at seeing seafaring riff-raff in their neighbourhood. One such comment contains the usual blend of abhorrence and paternalism.

We allude to the, at present unavoidable, practice of parading sailors through the streets of the Lower and Upper Town, to and from the Court-House, in charge of the police. Scarcely a day passes, during the summer season, that a body of seamen, guarded by police, are not seen wending their way to and from the tribunal before which they have to appear. This is not as it should be. In most cases sailors' cases are matters of civil suit, and in very many of these, from various causes, they obtain for themselves a favourable result. In others – where breaches of the local laws are concerned – exposure to the public gaze is an unavoidable consequence, and the penalty must be borne, and that unpitied by the looker-on. We should wish to see it otherwise. Our desire is to approximate our attempts at improvement of the condition of the sailors, while with us, to those made elsewhere; and the first step towards this should be the establishment of a Court in the Lower Town, for the summary adjudication of seamen's cases; and, thus, not only avoid the painful and needless parade of which we complain, but also save much time to both masters and consignees.[20]

Transiency had another dimension. The large numbers of sailors on long-range vessels who visited the three major ports of Atlantic Canada during the age of sail very seldom manned the same vessels more than once. They may have regularly crossed the Atlantic but they exercised their freedom to change ship as often as they liked or could get away with. As we have seen, one result of this pattern of changing ships was that the crews of the vessels leaving the big ports of Great Britain or western Europe tended to come from very mixed places of origin. The same diversified crews entered the labour market of eastern Canada to man vessels clearing from Quebec, Saint John, and Halifax. In addition, the patterns of behaviour of the crews which manned the regular traders were as variable as their composition. The desertion rates and wage fluctuations of two ships, the *Zambesi* (Table 3.2) and the *Red Jacket* (Table 3.3), which were regular Quebec traders for ten years or more, illustrate the erratic rhythm of crew changes. Even the masters on these vessels rarely served more than two years.

TABLE 3.2

Canadian voyages 1867–82 of the *Zambesi* (official no. 35207, 1,089 registered tons, Newcastle registry)

Year	Port	Crew (AB* monthly wages)	Deserted	Discharged	Hired (AB wages)	Log detail on port work
1867 (1)	Quebec	23 (£3)	nil	5 (4 ill)	2 (£3 run)	Local laborers hired to replace unfit and absent crew
1867 (2)	Quebec	22 (£3)	4	4	4; 1 did not join (£3 month)	—
1868 (1)	Quebec	23 (£2.15s)	nil	2	nil	Local laborers hired to replace unfit seamen
1868 (2)	Quebec	19 (£3)	7	nil	8 (£7 run)	—
1870	Quebec	20 (£2.17s.6d)	5	1 (ill)	5 (£10 run)	Local laborers hired to replace drunken seamen
1871	Quebec	19 (£2.17s.6d)	12	nil	11 (£8 run)	—
1872	Quebec	20 (£3)	2	nil	1 (£11 run)	Local laborers hired to replace drunk and jailed seamen at $2 per day
1873	Quebec	21 (£4.5s)	9	nil	9 (£10 run)	Local laborers hired to replace absent seamen at $3 per day
1874	Quebec	21 (£4.5s)	nil	1	nil	Local laborers hired to replace absent seamen at $3 per day
1875 (1)	Quebec	24	nil	1	2	—
1875 (2)	Quebec	20	2	1	3	—
1876 (1)	Quebec	22 (£4)	4	3	4 (£8 run)	—
1876 (2)	Quebec	23 (£4.5s)	1	nil	nil	—
1878	Quebec	20 (£3.10s)	4	nil	4 (£6 run)	—
1880 (1)	Quebec	19 (£2.15s)	4	1	7 (£5 run)	—
1880 (2)	Quebec	21 (£2.15s)	5	2 (1 in jail)	4 (£6 run)	—
1882 (1)	Quebec	20 (£3)	nil	nil	nil	—
1882 (2)	Quebec	19 (£3.5s)	6	nil	6; 2 did not join (£8 run)	—

SOURCE: Crew agreements and official logs (when extant) were obtained from the Maritime History Group Archives, Memorial University, St John's, except for 1875, the documents for which are in the National Maritime Museum in London, England.

*Able seaman

TABLE 3.3

Canadian voyages 1872–82 of the *Red Jacket* (official no. 25758, 2,035 registered tons, Liverpool registry till 1876, Newcastle registry thereafter)

Year	Port	Crew (AB* monthly wages)	Deserted	Discharged	Hired (AB wages)	Log detail on port work
1872	Quebec	31 (£4)	3	nil	3; 2 did not join (£11 run)	–
1873	Quebec	34 (£3.5s)	8	nil	6; 1 did not join (£10 run)	Local laborers hired to replace unfit and absent seamen at $3 per day
1874 (1)†	Quebec	36 (£4)	18	nil	14 ($50 run)	–
1874 (2)	Quebec	33 (£3.10s)	15	nil	16; 1 did not join (£10 run)	Local laborers hired to replace drunken seamen
1875 (1)	Quebec	32	2	nil	nil	–
1875 (2)	Quebec	40	nil	3 (2 ill)	3	–
1876 (1)	Quebec	34 (£4)	5	nil	4 (£6 run)	–
1876 (2)	Quebec	34 (£3.10s)	nil	nil	nil	–
1878	Quebec	33 (£3)	nil	nil	nil	–
1880 (1)	Saint John	33 (£2.10s)	13	1 (sick)	12 ($20 run)	–
1880 (2)	Quebec	33 (£2.15s)	3	2	2 (£5 run)	–
1880 (3)	Quebec	32 (£2.15s)	2	nil	2 (£6 run)	–
1882 (1)	Quebec	33 (£3.5s)	3	18 (2 ill)	17 (£8 run)	–
1882 (2)	Quebec	32 (£3.5s)	18	1	17 (£8 run)	–

SOURCE: Same as for Table 3.2

*Able seaman

†(1), (2), or (3) after year indicates first, second, or third voyage to Canada that year.

The isolation of sailors, which accompanied their transiency, meant that as an easily identifiable group they were considered a nuisance in port society and were labelled as such regardles of individual qualities. Their very transiency contributed substantially to their victimization in port. When a sailor belonging to the *Odessa* missed the ferry from downtown Saint John across the harbour to Carleton in 1852, he was picked up by the police for his late-night wanderings and fined twenty shillings. One newspaper censured the authorities for their 'undue severity towards the hardy sons of Neptune ... The sailor was not committing any impropriety: his only *crime* consisted in walking the streets after midnight.' When a stipendiary magistrate was first appointed in Quebec in 1852, the editor of the *Morning Chronicle* suggested that the Lower Town would preoccupy his attention in summer as a result of the 'misdeeds of sailors and raftsmen, and other strangers of that neighbourhood.'[21] Opportunities for victimization were in any case provided by the merchant shipping legislation which regulated seafarers to a greater extent than workmen in any other trade and reinforced a sailor's special status. His misbehaviour, his deeds of violence, even when directed against his own kind, were not allowed to flourish unimpeded. A sailor's life ashore was fraught with restrictions.

Society's view of the sailor ashore was also conditioned by the position assigned him in the class structure. The dissolute habits, improvidence, and rowdiness of seamen marked them out as members of the disreputable poor. They also achieved this status through association, since many inhabitants of dockside were considered petty criminals whose existence was tolerated uneasily.[22] To the extent, therefore, that the sailor was regarded as a member of a larger grouping, it was not the respectable working class. His haunts were located in the roughest and shadiest neighbourhoods. Facilities for boarding, eating, and drinking often existed on the wharves themselves. Beyond the wharves the adjoining streets formed the heart of each port's sailortown. Most of the sailors' boarding-houses were located on these adjacent streets. In Quebec they were clustered in Champlain Street, which extended from the Lower Town to the timber coves, an area of the city deficient in municipal services and a hazard to public health.[23] Saint John's boarding-houses stretched along the harbour of the peninsula from York Point in the north to Reed's Point in the south, with the heaviest concentration in Sydney ward at the south end of the city. Halifax's boarding-houses were largely confined to Water Street, particularly Upper Water Street.

Exposed by his transiency, isolation, and class association, Jack seldom met with much approval for his activities ashore. Yet the landsman's critical view of sailors was tempered by an appreciation of the hardships of seafaring life and, in Saint John and Halifax at least, by an acquaintance with resident seamen and respect for those who became officers and ultimately worthy residents after leaving the sea. The vicissitudes of a sailor's life included shipwreck, murder on the high seas, and the ravages of disease. Sensational accounts of what happened to poor Jack at sea frequently filled columns of the newspapers. Some incidents referred to members of a port's own merchant fleet sailing the seven seas; others concerned incidents which brought the vessels in question to port; others again were simply fictional. But together they portrayed seafaring as a mixture of danger and romance; they awakened feelings of sympathy and pride in the reading public who knew that their own lives were affected, however indirectly, by the work of seamen. In these circumstances, Jack's carefree and careless habits ashore were viewed with some ambivalence. Local society was not totally despondent about his chances for improvement. Sailors were known to escape from the fo'c's'le, either through their own efforts as they moved up the chain of command to become officers, or through their contribution to port society from the landward side after they had stopped following the sea and had settled down to pursue a trade or commercial venture.

So long as he remained before the mast, Jack occupied one of three positions when he came to port: an employed sailor working about his vessel and spending some time on shore; a sailor incapacitated through illness or accident; or an unemployed sailor who had been discharged or had deserted from his last ship but had not yet reshipped. An exploration of the work he did, the illnesses he suffered, and the public attention he commanded, largely by his rowdiness, provides a way of portraying the relations between sailors and society.

WORK

For articled seamen and the seamen on foreign vessels, stopovers in port normally entailed the continuation of shipboard work, but instead of being constantly on call, as at sea, they now shared with day labourers ashore a regular working day which ran from 6 a.m. to 6 p.m. This meant that, at the captain's discretion, shore leave was usually restricted to evenings. Port work for sailors involved a range of duties, depending on the condition of the vessel and the nature of the inward-bound and outward-bound cargoes. One way to identify their responsibilities is through the use of the official logs of British-registered vessels which have been preserved on a fairly systematic basis for the period between the late 1850s and the early 1870s. The logs do not specifically record the work of the sailors; rather they indicate cases in which the accustomed work was not being done and the nature of the disciplinary action that ensued.

In the case of the *Signet* in October 1861 in Quebec, Samuel Hatfield, the master, complained: 'My crews conduct has become very bad, careless of any orders, constantly running on shore and in every way neglectful of duty by being constantly the worse for drink. I am obligated to employ riggers to do the work of the ship which might have been done by my crew had they performed their duty.' His seamen also refused to load the timber, put up the masts, and, when the vessel was ready to sail, unmoor it and raise the anchor. Subsequently, the mutinous crew deliberately wrecked the vessel in the St Lawrence. In the same port in June 1868, five members of the crew of the *Jessie Boyle* refused to pump out the ship for which they were sent to prison for seven days. The supervisory duties of the officers also varied in scope. Francis McIntyre, mate of the *Chevalier*, absented himself for a weekend during the vessel's July stopover in Quebec in July 1869, so that no account was kept of the intake of the cargo. For their part, the support staff were expected to continue their normal duties while in port. When the steward of the *Laura B.* failed to replenish the fire in the vessel's cabin in mid-December in Saint John, the captain demanded an explanation. The captain recorded that Bond, the steward, answered 'in abusive language saying that he would cut my guts out,' whereupon he was slapped into irons and carted off to magistrate's court, but not before he 'jumped up and struck at my face with all his force with the hand cuffs and had I not caught him he would have done me considerable injury.' The seamen's collective recognition of certain basic labour standards also governed their willingness to perform port work. Six seamen of the ship *Mary Jane* temporarily refused to continue scraping the ship's bottom one February 1873 afternoon in Saint John on the ground that they were being blinded by the pitch they were using. A week later the same six men knocked off work, saying 'that they would not work in the rain for any one,' for which refusal of duty they were fined two dollars each before the police magistrate.[24]

In most instances, disobedient or absent crewmen were apparently important enough to the ship's operations in port for their labour to be replaced during the period they failed to perform their duties. If absence from work was the seaman's fault, then the wages paid his substitute were docked from his own wages. While some of the labour required was skilled work – carpentry, for example – much of it was unskilled and the substitutes were presumably hired from among the pool of casual labour which thronged the docks during the shipping season. It is impossible to tell if the substitutes were the same ship labourers who handled the cargo, since the work went well beyond loading and discharging to encompass a full range of seamen's duties – rigging, painting, caulking, cooking, caretaking, pumping, scraping, and carpentry.

The specific reasons for the employment of substitutes were as varied as the work itself. In keeping with the conventional image of the sailor's behaviour ashore, his failure to perform duties often resulted from drunkenness. Whether he had been ashore with or without permission, the intoxicated seaman was of little use to his ship and could be a positive hindrance or annoyance. Hugh Small of the *James McHenry* in Quebec in the summer of 1858 was off duty through intoxication by 10 a.m. on 27 August. He thereafter indulged in abusive language and absence without leave until he deserted on 1 September, still the worse for liquor. The drinking of John Elsey, seaman, and Patrick Flynn, carpenter, of the *Agenora*, also in Quebec in the summer of 1858, resulted in neglect of duty and repeated 'French leave' (a euphemism for absence without leave). Flynn was jailed for a week, whereas Elsey deserted after a week of unauthorized comings and goings.[25]

Drunken behaviour interfered greatly with the preparations for clearing port. It was not at all unusual for the new crew members as well as the old to arrive on board completely incapacitated, as was the case with three seamen of the *Cap Rouge*, a Plymouth vessel sailing from Quebec in September 1860. Among the turbulent crew of the *Signet* of London during its final voyage to Quebec drunkenness was an additional problem. Carpenter Moyle went on a binge for a week and when he was not drinking he lay in bed, unable to do his duty. As a result of this inability to perform his accustomed port work, the master had to employ two Quebec carpenters as substitutes. Similarly, James Yates of the *Margaret Ann*, in Quebec in 1868, 'left off His duty & went to his bed Intoxicated & remained all the Day off Duty a labourer

Employed in his Room.' The next day Yates returned to his duty briefly but on being refused a shilling by the captain he went to bed and remained there for the rest of the working day. When the master met him on shore at 7 p.m. and challenged him, Yates replied that he was going 'to get a Glass of Grog,' claiming that if he had been allowed that indulgence in the morning, he would not have spent the day in bed.[26]

While isolated cases of drunkenness were disruptive, sometimes a group of crewmen drank themselves insensible together. This happened with six highly volatile seamen of the *Mary Jane*, who apparently went on a Christmas spree in Saint John in 1872 and were all too drunk to work on the 26th. Labourers were hired as replacements at $2.50 for the day. The suggestion that a substitute be hired came from the seaman himself in the case of E.A. Corry of the *Lady Westmoreland* who drank too much on 20 June 1866 in Quebec to be able to work. He asked the chief mate to employ a man in his place which was done at a cost of $1.60. A similar proposal was made by Alfred Rolph of the *Flying Foam* in Saint John in September 1869 when he admitted that he was too intoxicated to be fit for duty. When drunkenness extended to the galley, it aroused the ire of the seamen as well as the officers. John Bowe, cook of the Liverpool-registered *Astoria*, failed to provide meals for the crew, whereupon the captain invoked the British regulations for maintaining discipline, which meant forfeiture of two days' pay for the second drunkenness offence and six days' pay for the third offence.[27] (Table 3.4 lists fines for various offences as given in Canada's Seamen's Act of 1873.)

Since liquor was not permitted aboard British and Canadian ships, it was necessarily obtained ashore and usually imbibed there. As a result the connection between drunkenness and unauthorized absence from work was close. Both Howell Evans and Matthew Briggs of the *Birmingham* in Quebec in the spring of 1860 went ashore without leave on 17 May and came on board drunk and incapable of doing duty. The master used the AWOL offence rather than the drunkenness offence to punish them. He succeeded in having them committed to prison, Briggs for seven days, Evans for fourteen. It cost £7 to provide a substitute for Evans. Briggs's substitute cost £3.10s and his week in jail did nothing to cure him of his taste for liquor, since he was again so drunk and incapable of duty on 30 May that he had to be confined within the ship until he became sober.

One major reason for the jailing of a seaman on the ostensible charge of absence without leave, rather than simply docking his pay for

TABLE 3.4
Table of fines contained in the (Canadian) Seamen's Act of 1873

Offence	Amount of fine or punishment
1 Not being on board at the time fixed by the agreement	Two days' pay
2 Not returning on board at the expiration of leave	One day's pay
3 Insolence or contemptuous language or behaviour towards the master or any mate	One day's pay
4 Striking or assaulting any person on board or belonging to the ship	Two days' pay
5 Quarrelling or provoking to quarrel	One day's pay
6 Swearing or using improper language	One day's pay
7 Bringing or having on board spirituous liquors	Three days' pay
8 Carrying a sheath-knife	One day's pay
9 Drunkenness. First offence	Two days' half-allowance of provisions
Drunkenness. Second offence	Two days' pay
10 Neglect on the part of officer in charge of the watch to place the look-out properly	Two days' pay
11 Sleeping or gross negligence while on the look-out	Two days' pay
12 Not extinguishing lights at the time ordered	One day's pay
13 Smoking below	One day's pay

drunkenness, was the captain's fear of rowdy behaviour or worse. This apprehension explains the action of the master of the *Squando* in Halifax in May 1860 when two seamen, both twenty-six-year-old natives of Lerwick, left work without leave, shortly to return the worse for liquor. Since both resorted to abusive language and one, James Tait, threatened 'to thrash every son of a bitch that belonged in the ship,' the captain reported them to the mayor who had them arrested and confined to prison for a few days. Similarly, the master of the London vessel *Whirlwind*, in Saint John in the summer of 1866, took no chances when John Edmunds, who had been pestering him for his discharge, came on board beastly drunk after a day's AWOL. In response to Edmunds's threatening entry to the captain's cabin to demand money, the master sent for a police officer who took the culprit to prison.[28]

Boozing was not the only reason why seamen left their vessels temporarily without authorization, but it was the most frequently

TABLE 3.4 (*Concluded*)

Offence	Amount of fine or punishment
14 Neglecting to bring up, open out, and air bedding, when ordered	A half-day's pay
15 (For the cook) – not having any meal of the crew ready at the appointed time	One day's pay
16 Not attending divine service on Sunday, unless prevented by sickness or duty of the ship	One day's pay
17 Interrupting divine service by indecorous conduct	One day's pay
18 Not being cleaned, shaved, and washed on Sundays	One day's pay
19 Washing clothes on Sunday	One day's pay
20 Secreting contraband goods on board with intent to smuggle	One month's pay
21 Destroying or defacing the copy of the agreement which is made accessible to the crew	One day's pay
22 If any officer is guilty of any act or default which is made subject to a fine, he shall be liable to a fine of twice the number of days which would be exacted for a like act or default from a Seaman, and such fine shall be paid and applied in the same manner as other fines.	

documented. Day-long absences interfered with the work of the ship and had to be offset through the hire of local labourers. Even vessels which reported no desertions whatsoever had to hire, as the occasion arose, landsmen as substitutes for men temporarily absent. The Hull vessel *Effingham* in Quebec in the autumn of 1860 provides a useful illustration. The vessel carried a crew of eighteen, none of whom successfully deserted at Quebec. During its stopover from 3 to 25 October John McCarthy, James Riley, and Henry English spent three days in jail for which they had to provide substitutes out of their wages; James Riley deserted, was apprehended, and remained seven days in jail; Francis Mero and William Mennell absented themselves for a day at an expense to themselves of 5s.2d each for substitutes. Mennell stayed away for a second day during which he was joined by McCarthy and they again forfeited part of their wages to cover the cost of the hiring of substitutes. The *Whirlwind* employed local men to perform the work of temporarily absent seamen in the same manner as the *Effingham*. Peter Johnson was on shore without leave for five days, a sojourn which cost him £2 of his £2.10s monthly wages to pay for his substitute and he was lucky not to be charged with desertion. Robert Cobbet and William Stewart took shorter leaves but were, like Johnson, docked eight shillings a day for the pay of the hired labourers.[29]

One important shipboard duty, often assigned to a hired labourer in the case of vessels which experienced a high rate of desertion, was that of night watchman. He served as the vessel's main defence against crimps, desertions, and accidents among inebriated seamen returning on board. In normal circumstances, the watches in port would be assigned to the crewmen. Here again the vessel could not depend on the seaman's loyalty. Seaman Frederick Carlson left his watch and absented himself without leave from the *Astoria* in Saint John in 1862. He was fined the customary one day's pay (two shillings) for absence and neglect of duty.[30]

Substitutes had to be hired to perform the essential shipboard work not only of sailors unfit for duty through drunkenness or absent without leave, but also of those ill or confined to hospital, those in jail, and those who failed to join their vessel at the agreed time. Most vessels whose logs were kept in sufficient detail recorded the illness of at least one crew member who required treatment in port. The *Signet*, with its crew of 17, sent several men to hospital on both its visits to Quebec in 1861. In May Stephen Johnson went to hospital with a bad leg which was, according to the captain, 'entirely brought on by his wanton neglect,' since he failed to apply the poultices supplied him during the voyage. John Simmons's complaint was rheumatic pains, the scourge of the seafaring life. Both these seamen were in such bad shape that they were discharged after the chief medical officer certified them unfit to proceed to sea. On its second arrival in Quebec in October, the *Signet* carried three seamen who required brief hospitalization, though for quite different reasons. John Sinclair had 'clap,' William Lindsey had swollen testicles, and John Swift had skin disease. For most of the voyage from Liverpool to Saint John in the *Almira* in the autumn of 1859, Robert Thompson was laid up with pains in his back and sides, probably an attack of rheumatism. John McFarlane was suffering from venereal disease, having swellings in his groin. A couple of days after their admission to hospital in December, they were discharged from the vessel on grounds of illness. Three crew members of the *James McHenry* were sent to hospital in Quebec in the summer of

1858. Two obtained discharges on grounds of illness, one of them, James Kelly, being laid up with venereal disease. Another man off duty at sea with VD and treated in hospital for three weeks while in Quebec in 1869 was William Brown of the *Chevalier*. The captain described his complaint as being 'of a dangerous nature and apparently of long standing.'[31]

The frequent confinement of sailors to jail for desertion meant increased employment for the dockside casual labour force. In Halifax in May 1859, three sailors deserted from the vessel *Madawaska* and were discovered by the captain, armed with a warrant, in a boarding-house and sent to the Bridewell until the ship was ready for sea. The captain released them after six days but in the mean time labourers were employed in their place at 5s.6d a day to assist with the discharging of the cargo. In September 1863, shortly after the arrival of the *Bellcarrigg* at the ballast ground in Quebec harbour, Thomas Jones and Edward Warren deserted with the assistance of the crimping establishment. Jones was taken into custody after being pursued by the river police. He was tried, found guilty, and confined to jail for one month or until the vessel sailed. During the eighteen days he spent in jail the captain paid ten shillings a day for a replacement. Thirteen members of the twenty-two-man crew of the *Chevalier* deserted in Saint John in the autumn of 1869 but a fourteenth, Joseph Emons, was apprehended three days after he had absconded and sent to jail until the vessel was ready to sail. During these twenty-three days a substitute labourer was employed at the rate of $1.80 per day. The captain, Robert Allen, recorded a total cost of $49.45 on account of the desertion of Emons; this included, in addition to the cost of hiring a labourer, court and jail expenses and debts incurred by the seaman on shore as well as the cost of recovering his clothes from his concealer. 'All of the above sum,' wrote Allen in the log, 'I intend to deduct from his wages, or as much as will meet the expenses incurred by his desertion.' Clearly, if insufficient wages were owing to cover the cost, the vessel would be out of pocket. It was probably cheaper to allow deserters their freedom.[32]

Sailors imprisoned for reasons other than desertion also had to bear the cost of substitutes. Henry Morris, seaman on the *Simonds* which was in Saint John in April 1867, was jailed for assaulting the ship's carpenter. A man was employed in his place from 9 to 29 April at $1.80 a day by which time the vessel was ready to sail. With still slightly over a week of his sentence to serve, Morris (a Liverpudlian) was discharged from the *Simonds* against his will and left behind in Saint John when the vessel cleared for Liverpool. In Quebec in October 1870, nine seamen of the *Strathblane* refused to begin work one morning before 9 a.m. on the ground that they had worked two and a half hours overtime the previous night taking the ship off the gridiron. The captain 'sent for a police boat, to take the men before a magistrate to settle the question of who commands this ship – the crew or I.' The nine were sentenced to three weeks in prison with hard labour or until the departure of the vessel. The captain had them released early, five after six days and the other four after ten days; only one subsequently deserted. They were charged the legal expenses and the cost of the substitutes hired while they were in jail. A somewhat similar hiring of local workers because of a labour dispute occurred on the *Jessie Boyle* in Quebec in 1868 when George Morgan and Jeremiah Denaugh refused to lash in the bow ports of the vessel on 2 October because it was after six o'clock, seamen being very vigilant in port about their twelve-hour day. The next day the two men were sent to prison for two weeks (one week of which they served) for refusing to do the required duty and two men were employed as substitutes at the rate of eight shillings each a day.[33]

The absence from duty of a number of the crew of the *Eliza* in Quebec in 1869 resulted when the master, John Monday, was summonsed by a seaman for wages and discharge on the ground that his life was in danger if he went home in the ship. The plaintiff, Matthew Clooney, had six witnesses, the captain had three, all of whom had to be replaced for that afternoon in order to get the vessel ready for sea, the loading having been completed. After Thomas Milne, seaman of the *Lady Westmoreland*, stabbed one of his mates, Joseph Paterson, on 17 June 1866 in Quebec, substitutes had to be hired for both the incarcerated assailant and the wounded man at a rate of $1.60 a day. The court proceedings took three days, and labourers had also to be hired for the seamen who acted as witnesses at the trial. The work they did was explicitly stated as putting in the cargo. By the 25th Paterson was fit enough to return to his duty but the captain recorded that the sailor would be held 'responsible for all Labourage incurred for himself while off duty, likewise the time the witnesses was [sic] absent from the Ship.' Shipboard fighting was clearly unacceptable behaviour.[34]

In the final stages of a vessel's stopover in port, as she unmoored for clearance, local labourers were sometimes required because of the deliberate failure of seamen to be at their posts. This happened in the case of the *Almira* in Saint John in January 1860 when ten local tidesmen had to be employed to unmoor the ship and get her under way because the crew had not joined the vessel at the agreed time. Similarly the master of the *G.M. Carins* hired fifteen seamen in Quebec on 13 and 14 October 1871 to replace fifteen deserters. When two of them, William Shannon and Louis Highes, failed to join on the 15th as agreed, labourers had to be hired in their places until they finally showed up on the 18th.[35]

A general idea of the duties of seamen in port, their predilection for avoiding such work to the benefit of local labourers, and the various difficulties into which they got themselves can be gleaned from the entries in the official log of the *John Davies* kept by the master, Owen Rowlands, during a visit to Quebec, 8 June–6 July 1860:

9 June 7 pm. James McCauley, seaman, and John Brown carpenter, went on shore in the boat. Went away from the boat without leave.

10 June   They came on board at 9 am

13 June 7 pm. James Stanley, cook went on shore without leave

14 June   All day – Stanley drunk and off duty, hired a substitute @ 10s.od. per day.

15 June 10 am. Stanley went on shore without leave. Got drunk and returned but on going on shore was stopped by me, but still insisted on going ashore. Also refused to do my orders. I ordered the police boat to come to take him in charge. He went on shore before the boat arrived.

16 June   John Flaherty went on shore without leave and did not turn to his duty. Laborer employed in his room @ 10s. per day. Stanley came on board after being absent without leave 22 hours. I sent for the police boat and gave him in charge. Stanley tried by the judge and ordered on board the ship to do his duty.

16 June 6 am. John Flaherty, Edward Lynch, Charles Kelly, Laurence Ryan and James Bresham refused to do their duty and went on shore without leave. Laborers hired in their place. The above came on board – called them into the cabin. Read the entry to them. They replied that they did not want their discharge and asked me to allow them to go to their duty.

17 June   Stanley went on shore without leave, returned beastly drunk and on account of having divine services on board, I told the chief officer to set his room door and not allow him to come out until he was sober. After the service was over, I saw him going forward. Said to me, he should make me sweat before he was done with me. Hired a substitute in his place.

17 June   Edward Lynch absent without leave.

17 June 6:30 pm Brown went on shore without leave.

18 June 4 am   Stanley was absent without leave when called by Owen Ellis who was keeping watch – was not found on board.

18 June   Called Lynch and read to him the entries. He acknowledges they were all true and that he wanted to leave the ship on account of being disagreeable amongst themselves and that being caused by drinking grog.

18 June   Brown absent at 6 am when the men were turned to their duty.

19 June   Stanley not on board, hired a substitute. Stanley appeared in court against me, he having summonsed me for his discharge on the ground of the voyage being done – was ordered on board by the magistrate. He resumed duty at 1 pm. Substitute hired in his place @ $1.50 per day.

19 June   The above named [Brown] on board at 6 am and resumed duty. 6:30 am Edward Lynch, John Flaherty, James Bresham, Charles Kelly, Laurence Ryan refused duty and went on shore without leave. Hired men in their room @ 10s. per day. Noon – The above named seamen returned on board, resumed duty after being ordered on board by the judge.

20 June   John Flaherty on shore without leave – hired a substitute in his place at 7s.6d. per day.

23 June at 5 pm Owen Ellis who was keeping watch, went on shore, returned drunk and unable to do duty – hired a watchman in his room @ 10s.

    John Flaherty went on shore without leave and according to the statement of Stanley (cook) returned on board between 12 pm and 1 am, being then worst of liquor and on going to the Head, fell overboard and was drowned.

    Stanley drunk and neglecting his duty.

24 June   Stanley went on shore without leave and neglected his duty. He returned on board worst of liquor. I ordered the police boat alongside and gave him in charge (10s.).

26 June   Francis Cameron off duty drunk – hired a laborer in his place @ 7s.6d. per day.

27 June at 8 am I went down into the hold, I found James McCauley quarrelling with Mr. Knowles, the stevedore. I ordered him on deck, he said that he would not go. I called him on one side and asked what was the matter with him and why disobey my orders. He told me that I was working him up by sending him to attend the pitch pott for the carpenter. (The reason

that I did send him to that light duty was because he was sick and off duty yesterday morning). I told him so and ordered him on deck again. He would not go, but wanted to fight me, I put my hand on his shoulder and told him not to make so much noise but to go on deck to his duty, whilst my face was turned from him he struck me in the right eye, my feet slipped between the beam fillings and he fell himself on top of me repeatedly striking at me and scratching my face with his nails, until some of the men took him off me. 10 minutes after the first assault he (after coming up on the upper deck) took up a work stave and struck me a very severe blow right over the left kidney. I took a warrant and had the man apprehended.

28 June   The body of John Flaherty was picked up and identified by the crew.

29 June   The body was buried, part of the crew being in attendance, the expense of the funeral being £3.3s.0d.

30 June 7 am.   Thomas Jones, 2nd mate being drunk when the crew was ordered to duty by the chief officer, I went and spoke to him when he began to abuse me. I asked him to go on board. He said that he would go when he liked. (8 am) I asked him to come to the cabin and ordered him to his room. He then began to abuse and threaten to strike me. Also attempted to do it twice. I then put him under arrest and ordered the police boat away and told him that he might resume his duty and furthermore I gave him particular orders not to go on shore. (At 9 am) Thomas Jones went on shore without leave and remained until about 7 pm when he came on board. I ordered him into the cabin and told him to take his clothes &c out of the cabin. He refused to do so, and used high language. I ordered the steward to shut the cabin windows to prevent the noise from being heard in ships alongside and ordered him out of the cabin into the cuddy. He refused to go, but took hold of him by the right shoulder, I then shoved him out towards the door. He then struck me. I then called for help, when the chief mate came down he ran ashore. About midnight he returned on board. I sent for the police and gave him in charge for drunkenness and absence without leave.

2 July 10 am   I appeared in court against Thomas Jones, 2nd officer – case adjourned.

2 July noon   James McCauley was brought on board by a police officer. He resumed his duty.

3 July   James McCauley, James Bresham, Edward Lynch, Laurence Ryan, Charles Kelly, Robert Cooper deserted the ship taking their effects

with them. I shall also remark that the above-named seamen have been constantly absenting themselves parts of each day since we commenced to take in cargo and sometimes all day.

4 July   Joseph Walker and James Stanley (cook) deserted the ship taking their effects, the same remark as the above is applicable to these two men.

Owen Ellis drunk and off duty – Laborer hired @ 7.6d.

I discharged the case against Thomas Jones 2nd mate on the ground of him paying all expenses.[36]

Rowlands's reference to the repeated unofficial absence of his crew when the cargo was being loaded and their ultimate desertion emphasizes the considerable disruption which the erratic behaviour of seamen caused when it came to their most critical port work. It was usually the rate with which the cargo could be loaded which determined the turn-round time of the vessel and the ship's full complement were employed in this work, augmented often by local ship labourers, because cargo-handling was an integral part of the seaman's responsibilities. It was detested work and often as dangerous as operating the ship on a stormy sea. Sailors expressed their aversion in song:

Wuz ye ever in Quebec,
Launchin' timber on the deck,
Where y'd break yer bleedin' neck,
[Chorus] Ridin' on a donkey?

When William Deomer, steward of the *Commerce*, was ordered to join the crew in loading the cargo at Blais Booms in Quebec in June 1858 as a reprimand for going on shore without leave, he refused and deserted the vessel. The constant disobedience and unruliness of the crew of the *Signet* in Quebec in the autumn of 1861 meant that the loading was neglected along with all other work. As a result the captain was 'obliged to have on board 20 men in order to expedite the loading,' work which his crew could have 'performed had these men diligently attended their duty.' For local labourers, therefore, employment as cargo-handlers on the vessels was as casual a job before the 1870s as were the other shipboard jobs made available through the unwillingness or inability of seamen to perform them.[37]

Thereafter, despite the growing militancy of ship labourers in the three ports and their assumption of the status of the primary rather than secondary work-force, sailors continued to retain a share of the cargo-handling into the 1890s at least. The work by sailors persisted in two main circumstances: during ship labourers' strikes and on foreign, particularly Scandinavian, vessels.[38] During strikes, the sympathy of the sailors could by no means be assured. It was aroused in 1877 when four sailors of the *Ada Barton* loading timber in Saint John walked off the job in response to a call for solidarity by the striking ship labourers. But during the labourers' strike in Saint John in July 1886, the crew of the ship *Rossignol* began to discharge a cargo of salt after the labourers quit work. In this case the sailors stopped work only when the labourers successfully persuaded the dockside cartmen to refuse to remove the cargo. In Quebec that same month ship labourers forced sailors who had stowed one batteau-load of deals in their vessel after regular working hours to transfer the timber back to the batteau.[39]

The problems posed by foreign vessels required more concerted efforts on the part of the local labourers. Quebec stevedores, the boss labourers, accepted the importance of Norway's role in the port's timber trade by the 1890s and began to learn the Norwegian language and visit Norway in order to secure through public relations the work normally performed by the foreign crews. In Halifax in 1905 the city authorities lent their support to the local longshoremen: the city council proposed a prohibition on loading by crews of foreign vessels.[40] Whenever cargo-handling by sailors recurred, as it did from time to time as shipowners attempted to cut costs, ship labourers were prone to argue that working cargo was 'not the legitimate business of sailors.'[41] It was however only through the combination of sailors' intransigence and the increase in the pressure for speed imposed by the steam age that sailors were finally released from this chore.

Throughout the century ship labour was the activity that brought seamen most frequently into contact with workers resident in the ports. It was also work which sailors performed as casual labourers when they were between vessels. They slipped in and out of ship labouring while they continued to follow the sea; as unskilled casual labourers they often became ship labourers when they left the sea. John Barry, for example, remembered in 1878 as one of Halifax's oldest mariners, took up a livelihood as rigger and stevedore when he retired from the merchant service. None the less little evidence exists of fraternal relationships between ship labourers and sailors. Even resident Canadian sailors probably did not participate in the dockside unionization movements in the nineteenth century, unlike their counterparts in some of the major British ports. Despite the prominence of ex-sailors in their ranks, the longshoremen's lack of fellow feeling for sailors reflected a growing Canadian view that tolerance rather than encouragement was good enough for the merchant marine.[42]

SICKNESS AND ACCIDENTS

If he was not working in port or carousing in the town, the chances were that the employed seaman might be sick or injured. Illnesses and accidents resulting from a sailor's working conditions fell into two categories: those brought to the north Atlantic ports from the seaward and those that occurred on board the moored vessel as a result of duties performed in port. Among the infirmities plaguing the sailor on arrival were the rheumatic complaints and venereal diseases documented in the official logs. Other occupational hazards for the sailors engaged in the trades of the eastern Canadian ports were the contagious diseases rampant on north Atlantic routes, the tropical fevers contracted on voyages to the West Indies, and the effects of exposure to the elements in the winter.

Quarantine regulations protected the host port from such perils as typhus, yellow fever, and smallpox but increased the chances of spreading the disease among the incarcerated crew.[43] The *Little Fury*, a 349-ton vessel with an eight-man crew, brought four cases of smallpox from England to Halifax and then to Saint John in late 1871 and early 1872. Although the captain's two-year-old son had succumbed to the affliction before the vessel made its first stop in Halifax, the owners, Troop and Son of Saint John, complained bitterly at having to maintain the healthy seamen in quarantine 'in order that the public may be guarded against any danger of smallpox.' Three of the four seamen recovered, the fourth dying in Halifax, but not primarily from the fever. Rather 'he was bad from an old sore of venereal disease & the top of his head was all rotten.'[44] Some incoming crews were devastated by disease. The ship *David G. Fleming* which arrived in Saint John in July 1876 after a prolonged voyage from Liverpool had lost four of its largely black crew from smallpox on the passage and carried another ten seamen into port sick with the same fever.[45]

The other complaint which put whole crews out of action was frost-bite. Its incidence tended to increase on sailing vessels because of the lengthening of the shipping season in Maritime ports in the face of competition with steam. In 1859 the *Almira* sailed from Saint John very late in the season. Before it cleared the mainland, six of its crew were badly frost-bitten and had to be sent to hospital. The 1870s saw innumerable cases of frost-bitten crews in Halifax and Saint John. The *Monteagle* brought one to Saint John in March 1872 and the *Three Sisters* delivered the same (two of whom were saved by amputations) to Halifax in January 1873. Matthew Scott, the mate of the Liverpool vessel *Mary Jane*, had his hands frost-bitten in Saint John in January 1873. In December 1873, nine seamen of the twenty-five-man crew of the ship *Chancellor* went to hospital in Saint John frost-bitten, a ground which seven of them unsuccessfully used in court the next month in an attempt to secure their discharge. In February 1874, five badly frost-bitten seamen arrived in Halifax, on board the brigantine *Thalia*. The crew of the brigantine *William Mason* aroused a good deal of sympathy in Saint John in February 1875 when it arrived with one seaman and the second mate badly frozen. On the passage from Cuba, 'three times the deck was covered with ice from 18 to 24 inches in thickness ... The forecastle was like an ice house and the crew it is thought would have been frozen to death had not the captain given them quarters in the cabin.'[46]

As a result of the contemporary interest in the connection between climate and race, the press took particular pains to note the colour of frost-bite victims. Three sailors, one east Indian and two blacks, underwent amputations in Halifax in February 1876 after the wreck of their American ship, the *Progress*. The following winter a frost-bitten black sailor and his Italian mate turned up at the Halifax police station with stories of ill-treatment on the brigantine *Arthur* on a passage from Puerto Rico.[47] The large number of frost-bitten blacks can probably be explained by the nature of the voyages which most vessels undertook in winter. These tended to be southern ones which would mean that many of the crewmen signed on in the southern United States or the West Indies.

The danger to the health of blacks and whites alike posed by winter was exacerbated by the primitive conditions of the fo'c's'les. Very few enjoyed the luxury of a fireplace or stove. One old sea captain in Saint John in January 1888 described the lack of fire as cruelty to seamen:

Just think of it, said he, a large vessel sailing out of the port of St. John last Friday, that very cold day, when the vapor was so thick in the harbor that you could scarcely see anything before you, and the cold intense, and yet, to think of it, in that ship's forecastle there was no stove of any kind to warm the sailors, and now where are they? ... They are in the marine hospital, nearly all badly frozen.[48]

Frost-bitten sailors were not found only on ships with the worst accommodations. Debilitating exposure was also a danger associated with winter shipwreck. Many sailors escaped from seafaring disasters with their lives only to find that, as victims of severe frost-bite, their seafaring days were over. Their predicament was chronic if they happened to be stranded and disabled as well as shipwrecked in a foreign port, as happened to many seafarers in eastern Canada in the nineteenth century. With the increased resort to steam navigation and reciprocal agreements with foreign governments, shipwrecked crews could at least look foward to a speedy return to their home ports, and the Canadian ports were reimbursed for the relief they had in the mean time granted them, their own crews being returned to Canada in a like manner. Shipwrecked seamen from a vessel en route to Limerick from Quebec in December 1872 were brought to Halifax whence they were sent home in the steamer *Austrian* by the Department of Marine. A steamer arrived in Halifax in December 1875 with twenty-six ship-wrecked seamen from three different vessels. Similarly a steamer from Bermuda brought fifty-six shipwrecked men from four vessels to Halifax in January 1879. At least a shipwrecked sailor could secure help from port authorities as 'an object of especial regard to a commercial community.'[49]

Other illnesses and accidents befell seamen while in port. Indeed there was a good chance that an employed seaman would end up in hospital or the morgue after a healthy arrival in port. This turn of events is strikingly illustrated by the death of a seaman of the *Astoria* in Saint John in September 1862. 'Edwin Ryder seaman fell from the starboard main yard arm when in the act of unscrewing the studding sail boom iron and came onto the wharf.' Earlier Ryder had escaped the ravages of yellow fever which had devastated the crew after the vessel had left the Bahamas en route to New York and Saint John. Five of his thirteen shipmates as well as the master had fallen victim to that dreadful disease.[50] Ryder's fall represented one of the three main kinds of accidents which occurred to sailors on the job. The other maimings and deaths resulted from loading and discharging cargo and from using faulty or improperly handled machinery.

The dangers of a sailor's work at sea were therefore replicated in port. The falls which claimed limbs and lives were from aloft to the deck, wharf, or water, from the deck into the hold, or from the deck over the side. Falls from the rigging like Ryder's were the most common, usually fatal, and were described in the press in gory detail. A young Irish sailor, working aloft the foretop-gallant mast of the barque *Drusus* arranging the gear for hoisting out ballast in Saint John in May 1874 lost his footing and plummeted to the deck, where he died instantly of a broken neck. In Halifax in the autumn of 1879 an English sailor, Albert Crane, was aloft reeving a new brace on the brig *Como* when he lost his footing and crashed down against the booby hatch, cracking his skull 'so that the deck was be-spattered with brains and blood.'[51]

With no safety standards enforced aboard vessels, the business of discharging and loading bulky cargoes could be extremely dangerous. The vessel's winch, used in the loading operations, became a deadly weapon if the team at work suddenly let go, as happened on the ship *Agamemnon* in Quebec harbour in June 1859, killing one of the crew. Seamen were injured when they became entangled in the hoisting chains, were crushed by falling equipment, or jammed their hands in machinery. Loading from timber rafts or scows increased the likelihood of death by drowning. In most serious accidents involving cargo, coal or timber was the villain. Falling coals and pieces of timber put sailors out of commission with injuries ranging from bruises to broken limbs.[52] In Quebec two serious accidents to seamen occurred during the 1871 season on vessels discharging coal from Britain. In June the brains of Adam Lindberg, a Swedish seaman, were spattered across the deck of the ship *Milton Lockhart*, when 'the pin of the gin block broke which caused the wheel to come down' and strike him on the head. Less than four months later a sailor belonging to the ship *G.M. Carins* was more lucky: 'While pushing the coal tub towards the main-hatch, he slipped and fell into the hold, breaking both his legs.'[53]

Three accidents that happened while loading cargoes in Saint John in the 1880s serve to illustrate the dangers of heaving timber about. Williams Ross, mate of the Windsor barquentine *Canning*, came to grief in the winter of 1880 when the guy line he was holding on a piece of square timber proved to be too short. Ross was jerked into the air as the timber swung and was precipitated over the bow of the vessel, landing on his back on a raft of square timber twenty-five feet below. Helping to load timber in March 1885, James Landers, mate of the Yarmouth packet, was knocked off the wharf by a deal onto the rail of his vessel and then into the slip. He got off lightly. The same cannot be said for a young Nova Scotia sailor, Charles Morrell, who, while loading a schooner, fell off a pile of deals, twenty feet high, and struck the rail of the vessel before landing fatally in the harbour.[54]

Other cargoes caused fatal mishaps. When John Leitz, deck-hand of the ss *City of Portland*, wheeled a truck of freight over the gangway to the shore in Saint John in 1883, he unfortunately encountered a truck moving in the opposite direction. He was thrown off the gangway into the water between the pier and the steamer and was drowned. The death of John Landen of the Norwegian barque *Arvill* in Halifax harbour in 1893 occurred while he was helping to unload salt. As he was attempting to clear the rope, attached to a heavy tub, from the staging, the horse on the wharf used for hoisting started and moved the tub which hit Landen and knocked him head first eighteen feet into the hold.[55]

Seamen also suffered fatalities when they used machinery for loading and unloading or the vessel's own winches, capstans, donkey engines, and mooring equipment. Staging suspended by blocks and tackling from the masts of the Greenock ship *Albion* gave way in Quebec in 1847 while the sailors were unloading bales of dry goods. The men were precipitated into the hold and onto the deck and one young seaman, James Wilson, nephew of a Montreal publican, was killed by the falling bales. Several years later four crewmen of the ship *Cap Rouge* were injured when they were caught in the mooring chain after a rope broke during the mooring operation. In 1865 John Kennedy, a young seaman on the London steamer *St. Lawrence*, died when he was struck by one of the bars of the capstan which broke while the anchor was being lowered.[56]

The age of steam introduced new dangers to the sailors' place of work. In 1868 a seaman on board the ss *Acadia* in Saint John sustained severe injuries to his hand in the steam-driven winch and had part of his hand amputated, an operation which was, fortunately, conducted with the aid of ether. When the mate of the brig *Toronto* in Quebec in 1875 cut the tow-line attached to the steam tug after a seaman became entangled, it 'recoiled with such terrible force that it broke the leg of another sailor and absolutely cut in half the body of the first seaman,' Robert McVicar of Sydney, Nova Scotia. In 1882 the donkey engine used on board the ship *Queen of the North* for discharging ballast in Quebec exploded, wreaking havoc on the vessel. The ship's carpenter, who was working the engine, was killed instantly and two other seamen were injured. The *Quebec Mercury* reported: 'Poor Anderson presented a fearful spectacle of the violence of the death he met with, the body being much bruised and crushed.'[57]

Drowning, usually associated with the high seas, was an ever-present danger for sailors even in port. As we have seen, sailors engaged in loading timber from smaller vessels or from rafts or booms in the stream sometimes lost their lives through drowning. The same applied to some of those who, while anchored in the harbour, had to row or scull to shore. Others simply fell overboard unnoticed or were the victims of unsuccessful rescue attempts. The failure of the port authorities uniformly to hold inquests in such cases, as well as in the case of deaths from falls, was occasionally criticized.[58] The press also found fault with the masters of sailors who drowned in port. Some sailed without leaving a crew member behind to identify the victim. Others left port without making inquiries about the fate of missing sailors, assuming desertion, even though sailors very seldom deserted without taking their effects. The identification of decomposed bodies floating in the water or washed ashore was therefore virtually impossible. The headless body found in Saint John harbour in January 1866 was supposed to be that of a sailor who had fallen from Robertson's wharf in attempting to go on board his vessel, the *John Bunyan*, two months earlier. An inquest held on a body found in the river at Quebec in October 1874 had to depend on the testimony of a local ship labourer who knew about the drowning of a sailor of the *Demerara*, a vessel on which he had been working two weeks before. But as he could not identify the body and the ship had sailed, the inquiry had to be abandoned. A badly decomposed body found in the river the next summer was said 'to be that of a sailor, as a sailor's belt with knife in it still encircled the body.'[59]

In the main, the properly reported drownings occurred when sailors were attempting to board their vessels from the shore. If a sailor lost his footing and fell between wharf and vessel, he was likely to hit his head on the fender, knock himself out, and, if the hard fall itself did not kill him, slide into the water and drown. Inquests into this type of accident led to repeated controversies over the reason for a sailor's losing his footing on the gangplank or wharf. What was to blame: inadequate lighting or excess of drink? If the evidence given to the coroner's jury or the press hinted that the drowned man had been drinking, the inquest concluded that his death was clearly his own fault and no further action need be taken.

It is easy to imagine how an intoxicated seaman might have difficulty negotiating a two-foot wide plank, as did a Boston man attempting to board his steamer, the *New England*, in Saint John in 1870. His case provoked a certain amount of satisfied gloating about the fact that a lantern stood at the end of the plank. Since most of the drownings occurred at night, inquests commonly concluded that lighting was needed on the wharves. All dockside habitués, not just sailors, were endangered by the darkness which, of course, prevailed especially on moonless nights. Civic authorities and owners of wharves displayed little sense of responsibility in the matter, unlike the city missionary in Quebec who made sure that the approaches to the vessel used for night-time bethel services were well lighted. Over and over again coroner's juries in all three ports claimed that the fatal accidents were preventable: all that was needed was lighting on the wharves and in some places railings.[60]

The sporadic interest in illuminating the wharves had little practical effect. The editor of the Quebec *Morning Chronicle* suggested in 1876 that it would take the drowning of a more important individual than a sailor to accomplish the desired reforms. Honoré LeBlanc of the brigantine *A.J. White* had missed his turning in the dark and had fallen off the wharf at the end of Dalhousie Street. The night was 'pitchy dark,' and no light existed 'to illuminate what is a perfect mantrap. We have frequently called attention to the urgent necessity there is for lights being placed along all our wharves. Are we to wait until the Lieutenant-Governor, the Premier, the Mayor, or other high dignitary is drowned, before this matter, which is a requisite for the protection of hundreds of lives, is attended to?'[61] In the mean time avoidable drownings in port swelled the statistics which made seafaring look the most dangerous of occupations. British Board of Trade figures revealed, for example, that of 47,000 deceased seamen whose names were recorded during the twelve years ending 1864, no less than 20,000 died from drowning.[62]

Those sailors who were fortunate enough to escape death from fevers, frost-bite, falls, and accidents often required medical attention. At sea the sailor was usually at the mercy of the captain's medical chest; in Quebec and Saint John he was the beneficiary of the nineteenth-century equivalent of a hospital plan, a system which was extended to Halifax and other ports after Confederation. The major feature of the plan, known under Department of Marine administration as the Sick and Disabled Seamen's Fund, was the levy of a tonnage duty on shipping.[63] The rules governing the sailor's eligibility to hospital care or doctor's fees, in cases where hospitalization was not necessary, specified that he be employed, suffered from a disability contracted in the service of his vessel, and sought medical attention with the permission of his shipmaster. In these circumstances he was not charged for the expenses incurred. Sailors who did have difficulties in securing treatment and securing it gratis were those sick with 'social' diseases or diseases contracted before they shipped, those whose status was that of deserter or unemployed, and those who failed to convince their masters that they needed medical attention. Considerable confusion entered into the picture naturally enough. Some masters appear willingly to have paid medical bills or to have sent their men to hospital. Others were unsure what diseases might legitimately be related to the service of the vessel. A captain in Quebec in 1880 who had to send four of his men to hospital suffering from diarrhoea, rheumatism, dyspepsia, and pleurodynia respectively wondered if he could charge them both for the hospital expenses and the hire of substitutes in port, since their ailments were neither contagious nor the result of accident on board ship. Merchant shipping law, however, clearly stated that the men were not liable if they were 'removed for the convenience of the ship and subsequently returned to their duties.'[64]

Those who were proclaimed 'unfit to proceed' to sea were given their discharge with wages paid up to the day of discharge. This happened in the case of two seamen (discharged in hospital) of the vessel *Spruce Bud* in Halifax in 1869, Francis Vantin being ill with sciatica and Hansen Clausen Osberg suffering from epilepsy.[65] British Board of Trade guide-lines dictated that men discharged suffering from venereal disease should also have their wages paid up to the date of discharge but less any expenses borne by the vessel because of their illness.[66] The official logs indicate that many of the sailors sent to hospital with VD, who were returned to their vessels after treatment, deserted ship shortly thereafter, a course which may be attributable to their liability for expenses.[67] Articled seamen who were still ill in hospital when their vessel was ready for sea were discharged from their jobs whether they liked it or not. If they emerged from hospital fit and cured, they could join the local labour market. In Saint John, in fact, they were often shipped directly from the hospital.[68] Other captains preferred to abandon their incapacitated crewmen in an irregular manner. In 1870 a sailor in Saint John turned up at the police station for protection after he had been left behind by his vessel because he was ill. Only then did he secure admission to hospital.[69]

Usually, then, hospitalization depended on the good will of the master. This benevolence was singularly lacking in John Olive, master of the *Elizabeth Ann Bright*, who refused to allow James Stewart, a young seaman, to go to hospital and threatened to stop his wages if he did so. A victim of tuberculosis, Stewart was treated by the vessel's surgeon but he was also mistreated by the boatswain. On the sailor's death the boatswain was charged with manslaughter by the coroner's jury and the master was censured 'for neglecting to provide the deceased with necessary care' and failing to send him to hospital on arrival in Quebec. In Halifax in 1872 the captain of the schooner *Dauntless* thought that one of his seamen, Joseph Shea, was faking a broken leg in order to avoid going to sea. The opinion of a doctor settled the matter and Shea was sent to hospital.[70]

Admission to hospital also depended on compliance with port rules and regulations. In Saint John

Seamen are admitted only from vessels which pay into the Sick and Disabled Seamen's Fund through the Custom House, the rate being: for vessels over 100 tons, 2 cents per ton, paid once a year, for vessels of and under 100 tons, 2 cents per ton paid twice a year. The captain applied to the collector for the admission of his sick men, and his tonnage dues being paid, receives from the Collector a permit which has to be presented at the Hospital. Seamen deserting their vessels cannot be admitted, this precaution being taken to prevent crimps from inducing sailors to desert.[71]

Discrimination was not confined to deserters. A case occurred in 1880 which indicated the injustice of excessive rigidity. It concerned seaman Robert Grinlinton of Liverpool who arrived in Saint John from Boston in the barque *MacLeod*. After apparently being discharged, he became an invalid and applied to his former captain for a permit to enter the hospital. The collector of customs refused to issue the permit to the captain on the ground that Grinlinton was no longer actually employed on the vessel. This decision placed the sailor in an unfortunate state of limbo. 'Because he is a sailor,' wrote 'Mariner' to the *Daily Sun*, 'he cannot gain admission to the Public Hospital, and because he is a sailor laid up and unable to do duty as a sailor he cannot gain admission to the Marine hospital.'[72]

The Grinlinton case may have been an exception. But clearly the restriction of the services of the hospital to active seamen was designed to differentiate between 'good' seamen who deserved the facilities available to them and 'bad' seamen whose status was unclear and who might be erstwhile deserters. On the whole, however, the sick sailor enjoyed considerable advantages over other sick and incapacitated workers during this period. He was allowed sick leave and had access to special facilities for the restoration of his health. He lost his job through sickness only if his vessel had to leave port or if he was discharged as unfit. When cured, he could usually re-enter the sailor labour market with ease unless he found himself in Quebec in winter. If he was in danger of suffering further distress, his return home could be arranged through his consul or under the provisions of British shipping law. Not surprisingly, then, he did not feel the need for a mutual benefit society whereby he could join his fellows in organizing his own sickness benefits. The nature of the work dictated against such organization, it is true, though the membership of a Saint John sailor in that city's ship labourers association indicates that home port organizations held some appeal for resident sailors.[73] Unlike his landside counterpart, the sailor was never asked to subscribe to a 'company' benefit society. His health care was directly under the supervision of the government, an arrangement which foreshadowed modern social insurance. A detailed look at the hospitals in each of the ports will provide us with a better picture of the uniqueness of the mariners' health care system during the age of sail.

Although Quebec did not have a hospital devoted exclusively to the use of sailors, sick and wounded mariners made up a large proportion (normally well over half) of the patients in the Quebec Marine and Emigrant Hospital and were its most dependable basis of financial support as a result of the shipping tax. Although convalescents did sometimes have to winter over, the major obstacle in the way of establishing a hospital exclusively for seamen was the seasonal nature of the need. Most seamen themselves asked for early release in order to get out of Quebec before the river froze. Suggestions therefore that a seamen's hospital be established in a disused government building or in a dismasted hulk were never taken up.[74] The reluctance of the authorities to establish such an institution was not based on the inadequacy of the finances. The tax on shipping provided ample funds for a hospital and for two decades before the closure of the hospital in 1890, federal MPs charged that the seamen's fund was being used to subsidize the care of the civilian population in Quebec, a population which avidly sought accommodation in the hospital as the number of seamen visiting the port of Quebec declined. The discontinuance of the hospital was caused largely by the failure of the federal government to work out with the city of Quebec what the former considered to be an equitable cost-sharing arrangement for an institution which catered increasingly to the poor of Quebec. After its closure, Protestant seamen were sent to Jeffrey Hale Hospital and Catholic seamen found the care they needed in the Hôtel-Dieu, each at a cost of ninety cents a day defrayed from the Sick and Disabled Seamen's Fund.[75]

Between the 1830s and the 1880s the Quebec hospital catered to many thousands of merchant seamen, far greater numbers than in the other ports. The frequency with which the official logs record the dispatch of sick and injured sailors to the hospital gives some indication of its extensive use by the seafaring population. In the shipping season of 1843 (May to October inclusive) the hospital accommodated 748 sailors. During a similar period in 1862, 621 of the 825 patients in the hospital were seamen. Quebec Board of Trade figures record its continued importance thereafter: 1879–80, 498 of 886; 1880–1, 651 of 1,017; 1881–2, 415 of 853; 1882–3, 459 of 834; 1883–4, 418 of 729; 1884–5, 362 of 659; 1885–6, 248 of 459; 1886–7, 185 of 548; 1887–8, 318 of 665; and 1888–9, 211 of 351.[76]

The variety of ailments which sent seamen to hospital included the accidents which were an everyday part of the dangers of a seaman's occupation. The Quebec Board of Trade was surprised to discover, however, that accidents made up only a small proportion of hospital cases. An investigation conducted in 1843 to measure the feasibility of implementing conveyance by water of accident victims from shipboard to hospital revealed that only thirty-eight of the 748 cases were accident cases: thirty-three fractures, two dislocations, two concussions, and one gun-shot wound. A reporter for the *Morning Chronicle* visited the hospital one day in August 1877 when twenty-five of the forty-six patients were seamen. He described at some length the ailments of fifteen of the twenty-five, the rest of which, we can speculate would have included a high proportion of the publicly unmentionable venereal diseases which so frequently turn up in the vessels' official logs. None the less, the partial report of the investigation provides some insight into the illnesses which took seamen of many different nations to the Marine and Emigrant Hospital. Adam George, an Englishman and seaman of the ss *Redewater* had been three days in hospital with diarrhoea, a complaint he shared with a Norwegian sailor of the ship *Johan Hensen*, who had been confined for three weeks. Another Norwegian, Neil Anderson of the *Martin Luther*, had been admitted three months before with a disease of the rectum. That ubiquitous sailors' ailment, rheumatism, was also represented on this occasion by Michael Hennessey, a young Irish sailor of the *Primrose* who had been admitted a month before. Two seamen interviewed were suffering from ulcers on their legs and feet, the one an American of the *Perseverance* named Magnus Baines and the other, Theophile Desforest, a seaman of the *Miramichi*. Alfred Wells, a young Londoner lately employed on the *Minnehaha* was 'suffering from a white swelling.' Another seaman of the *Martin Luther*, a Swede named Christopher Jensen, was confined to bed with chronic pleurisy. And then there were the accidents associated with seafaring. Thomas Beynon of the *Greyhound* had spent two months recovering from a skull fracture sustained when he fell into the hold of his vessel. A seventeen-year-old sailor lad, Hugh Robertson, had arrived in port three months earlier on the *Macedonia* with two fractured legs and a severe gash on his head acquired when he fell from the upper topsail yard onto the ship's railing. Another young seaman, Frank Roche, was recuperating from a fracture of the clavicle caused by a severe blow of a winch-handle on board ship.[77]

The *Chronicle* reporter was pleased to report that all the seamen to whom he talked claimed to be favourably impressed with the care they were receiving in the hospital. Given the few opportunities they had to make known their opinions, sailors' attitudes towards their hospitalization are hard to discover. The bequest of his unpaid wages to the hospital by a Scottish sailor, Robert Barkley, in 1835 appears to have been made more in recognition of the sufferings of his fellow mariners than as a testimony to the quality of the care that had been afforded him before he died.[78] Complaints were far more likely to be reported by external critics of the hospital than by the patients.

Between the late 1840s, when the management of the hospital became largely French, and Confederation, at which time the hospital came under the supervision of the federal Department of Marine, the criticisms voiced in the press, by the Quebec Board of Trade, and by colonial authorities and shipping interests in Britain were tinged with francophobia. The French management of the hospital was roundly condemned in the correspondence columns of the London *Shipping and Mercantile Gazette* in 1849. Even the reasonably moderate *Quebec Gazette* shifted its position from praise for the French doctors in 1848 to demanding in 1854 that 'the French Canadian gang who now infest the establishment ought to be rooted out.' James Dean, the president of the Quebec Board of Trade, found plenty to complain about in the French, Catholic management of the hospital in 1851. 'Malpractices' included the provision of wretched and deficient food served out to sailors 'like dogs, with scarce a knife or fork for 150 patients' and attempts by the totally Catholic staff to convert deathbed patients, nine-tenths of whom were Protestant. Dean also accused members of the hospital staff, including the house surgeon, of forcing a dying sailor to make out a will in their favour. After dividing up the dead man's £15.9s, the culprits falsified the register to read that the man had been discharged and the money paid to him.

The shipping master in Quebec was also suspicious about the hospital staff acting as guardians of the effects and balance of wages of 'unfit' seamen who had been discharged in the port in order to recuperate from their infirmities. R.B. Johnson attempted unsuccessfully in 1864 to gain the British Board of Trade's approval for the suggestion that he should replace the hospital authorities as the custodian of seamen's property. He cited two cases to support the irresponsibility of the hospital authorities. When Henry Avery, a seaman discharged sick from the barque Stad Zeiricgee, 'demanded his clothes from the hospital authorities he was told they had been stolen, and that he might go to sea in the clothes he had on.' He valued his missing kit at £12.2s.6d, whereas the hospital offered him only £3.1s.7d as compensation. Similarly, Charles Smith, seaman on the barque Dominica, who knew his clothes had been delivered to the hospital by the pilot, was told they had been stolen and offered the same compensation.[79]

Another criticism related to the disposal of the bodies of seamen who died in the hospital. As transients without friends or relatives to guard their interests, they were a natural source of laboratory material for training the Quebec medical profession. Indeed, the availability of cadavers may explain the interest of the French-Canadian medical men in the hospital. James Sykes, the Church of England seamen's chaplain at the hospital, revealed what he knew about the irregularities relating to bodies in 1870. He got the permission of a government inspector of asylums and prisons to open the grave of Louis Beynon, a seaman of the ship Historia, whose burial he had conducted in December 1869. 'When the coffin lid was removed we found as a substitution of the body several pieces of firewood put in the coffin in such a manner that it could not move. The above disgraceful transaction being the act of those in authority at, and done within the walls of the Marine Hospital, where the sailor pays for, and has a right to expect protection.'[80] When the use of cadavers became approved local practice later in the century, the federal Department of Marine intervened on behalf of sailors. The bodies of three men who died in the Quebec hospital in the autumn of 1883 were 'decently interred' after the minister of marine refused to give them up for dissection, claiming that 'in all civilized and marine countries, the State is considered the guardian of the seamen.'[81]

Perhaps the criticism which most accurately reflected the concerns of sailors was that related to the location of the hospital. The various parties which proposed alternative locations were moved to do so largely because of the agonies that badly injured seamen had to endure in order to be conveyed from the wharves to the hospital at Hare Point in St Roch's ward. As the editor of the *Chronicle* so graphically pointed out:

The great distance of the Marine Hospital from the Lower Town renders the removal thither of persons who have sustained severe injuries on board ship or on the wharves a task involving the most agonizing pain, and frequently very great danger to the unfortunate victims of those accidents which are of daily occurrence in a large sea-port. There is scarcely a person, whose avocations bring him to the business part of the city, but must have frequently witnessed the harrowing spectacle of an unfortunate seaman or ship-laborer with blanched countenance and shattered, bleeding limbs, being jolted along, in a rickety caleche, over bad roads, on his way to the hospital at Hare Point.[82]

While the seamen in Quebec always shared hospital accommodation with immigrants and local residents, those sailors who had to be hospitalized in Saint John were sent to the one exclusive seamen's hospital in a major Canadian port. The career of the Kent Marine Hospital mirrored the rise and fall of the age of sail. Established in 1822 to replace poor-house accommodation for seamen, it was finally closed by the federal government in 1893.[83] At mid-century it operated as one of the most highly regarded institutions in the city. Thereafter it went through a period of dilapidation until a new building was erected in 1884. This modern establishment, under the control of the Department of Marine, became the object of severe criticism by reformers.

TABLE 3.5
Admissions, Saint John Marine Hospital

Year	Admissions	Deaths
1841	215	7
1847	486	29
1854	252	16
1857	185	7
1858	177	5
1859	256	3

SOURCE: Reports of the Marine Hospital,
Appendix to *Journals* of the
New Brunswick House of Assembly,
1842, 1848, 1854, and 1860

Unlike its counterpart in Quebec, the Saint John hospital remained open year round, year in and year out. Supported by the tonnage tax on shipping, it was managed in the pre-Confederation period by a board of commissioners, local men who had a direct interest in the health of seamen, whom they considered to be the bone and sinew of the economy. The hospital treated all cases with the exception of contagious fevers, which were referred to the pest house at Partridge Island. The admission of sailors to the two hospitals fluctuated according to the general health of the port and the volume of shipping[84] (see Table 3.5).

The bona-fide sailors admitted to the Kent hospital over the years included blacks and whites, residents and non-residents, English-speakers and 'foreigners.' As a year-round institution it treated more frost-bite victims than the hospital at Quebec. Four black sailors among the 14 patients being treated in mid-April 1872 were suffering from frost-bitten limbs. One of them, the sole survivor of the eleven-man crew of the *Sarah Sloan*, wrecked off Grand Manan in March, had suffered the amputation of both his feet. Another belonging to the *Edith Hall* had lost one foot and a part of the other. The other two, both seamen on the *Monteagle*, were not so badly frost-bitten, though one had lost all the fingers of one hand. For derelicts such as these, seafaring days were over.[85]

The thirteen men in the Kent hospital on 30 June 1880 were 'chiefly Norwegians, Swedes, Austrians and French, there being only one

English speaking seaman in the lot.' The report of the hospital for 1883 indicated that very few of the 115 seamen admitted that year were 'natives of Canada, the largest number belonging to Great Britain, Norway, Sweden, Germany and the United States.'[86] This evidence tends to confirm the prominence of foreigners in carrying the trade of Saint John in the last quarter of the century.

The residents of Saint John were attached to their marine hospital largely because of its setting in fine gardens which became a favourite resort of the citizenry in summer. 'We paid a visit to this rural asylum of the sick on Friday morning,' wrote the editor of the *Morning News* in 1850, 'and Egad when we first got a peep of, and a smell of, the flowers, spread out on all sides, we almost imagined it was a good thing to be a sick sailor, just for the sake of breathing the fine atmosphere of these "Elysian Fields".'

It was probably by way of the gardens that the interest of a number of local parties was aroused in the welfare of the sailor inmates themselves. One was the crimping establishment. It was revealed in 1880 that the keeper of the hospital 'has in past times been a good deal bothered by parties loitering about the grounds outside, talking to the men through the fence and handing them tobacco and liquor.'[87] The other major party was made up of middle-class reformers, especially women, who began to find fault with the management of the hospital in the 1880s after the original building had been replaced. The wooden structure of the 1820s had survived the great fire of 1877, which destroyed two-thirds of the heart of the city, an escape considered unfortunate since the hospital was one public building much in need of replacement. Practical problems inherent in the old structure (such as indoor earth closets) were corrected when a new building was opened in July 1884. The first Christmas in the new hospital saw the sailors treated to 'a substantial tea – turkey, blancmange, jelly etc.' by the ladies of the Church of England institute.[88]

More than new facilities, however, were needed to reform the management of an institution in which the patients were essentially 'farmed-out.' Beginning in 1882, the keeper, Milton Barnes (who had been employed in the hospital for over forty years), was given the contract by the federal government to run the hospital, a change in procedure designed to reduce costs. For him this meant a salary of $300 a year, 'free residence, free coal, free water and free gas, together with the free use of a prolific vegetable and flower garden,' and, in addition, $3 a week for boarding each patient. Dissatisfied sailors, do-good

TABLE 3.6
Diet table, Saint John Marine Hospital

Menu as described by Barnes	Menu as seen by a critic
Breakfast	*Breakfast*
Tea, with sugar and milk.	¼ loaf baker's bread
Eight ounces of bread.	1 oz. butter
Butter one ounce,	Warm water flavoured with tea,
or	containing a suggestion of milk.
Porridge and milk instead	
Dinner	*Dinner*
Monday, Tuesday, Wednesday,	Broth with a trifle of barley
Thursday and Saturday	and turnips in it.
Twelve ounces of beef.	3 wretched potatoes
Four potatoes according to size	Coarse meat boiled to shreds,
Bowl vegetable soup containing one	replaced on Friday by dry
ounce of barley, also turnips, summer	codfish and on Sunday by
savory and cabbage.	baked meat.
Friday – Codfish and potatoes with	
drawn butter	
Sunday – Roast veal, lamb or mutton	
with potatoes and gravy	
Supper	*Supper*
Same as breakfast, and in same	¼ loaf baker's bread
quantities	1 oz. butter.
	Warm water flavoured with tea, containing
	the suggestion of milk.

SOURCE: Saint John *Daily Sun*, 13 Oct., 15 Dec. 1888

female visitors to the hospital, members of the press, and ultimately the local members of Parliament raised complaints: in return for the $3, the patients were fed a diet that contained none of the nutrients necessary for nursing them back to health, left pretty much to take care of one another and without any attendance during the night when they were locked in their wards, and attended when necessary but often tardily by a doctor who was unresponsive to their needs. The criticisms by female visitors and discharged patients in 1888 led to an investigation by a *Daily Sun* reporter in October which turned up a dead rat on the kitchen floor. The official diet table was subjected to critical scrutiny (see Table 3.6).

In the spring of 1889, the members of Parliament for Saint John city and county brought the unsatisfactory management of the federally regulated hospital to the attention of the House of Commons. The Department of Marine conducted its own inquiry which concluded that a house surgeon and local supervising committee were necessary. After the investigation the days of this specialized institution were numbered. Better medical care and a more suitable environment at a lower cost were available in the public hospital. Early in 1893 the marine hospital was closed and the seamen-patients transferred to the Saint John General Public Hospital where they, like their counterparts in Halifax and Quebec, continued to be supported by government at ninety cents a day.[89]

In Halifax, meanwhile, hospital development in general was slow and the health care of sailors was further retarded by the failure of the government to implement a tonnage duty on vessels entering the port. A private hospital for merchant seamen conducted by a respected medical doctor was opened early in the century, but, for most of the period before Confederation, injured and ailing seamen in Halifax had to share the facilities of the poor-house with every other infirm, incapacitated, and helpless creature unlucky enough to find himself in that city without private means.[90] Between 1852 and 1859, estimates suggested, the average number of sailors received in the poor-house per year was thirty-five, the average term of residence twenty-eight days, and the average total amount paid by all the sailors per year nine pounds. Those who could not afford to pay were cared for out of the provincial subsidy.[91]

Halifax shipowners and other members of the shipping fraternity intermittently and ineffectually complained about the lack of hospital facilities for seamen.[92] When a hospital was finally established in 1865, it was a general hospital very much dependent after Confederation on the sailors for the regular subsidies of five dollars a week until 1879 and ninety cents a day thereafter which they brought with them out of the Sick and Disabled Seamen's Fund. For the next couple of decades seamen formed the largest single group of patients in the City and Provincial Hospital, a factor which one inhabitant assumed must surely be to the detriment of the local sick. Particularly distasteful to this Haligonian was the preponderance of 'foreign' seamen. In 1881 the seamen's missionary claimed that one-half of the male patients in the hospital were seamen.[93]

As in the other ports, the foreign sailor's vulnerability to victimization in an institution to which he indirectly contributed was amply documented in Halifax. When the hospital management came under investigation in 1886, Seaman Harris provided the legislative committee with some damning evidence relating to his own treatment. Despite his status as a paying patient, he was 'engaged in scraping the floor and in some other kinds of disgusting work.' When he had to return to the hospital after making his revelations, the house surgeon and house steward criticized by him denied him the usual weekly pass. As a result he had no clean clothes for a month. When, in desperation, he took French leave to fetch some clothes from the sailors' home where his effects were stored, he was peremptorily discharged from the hospital for disobeying the house rules.[94]

With improvements in hospital management, the grumblings of the dissatisfied became weaker. By the end of the age of sail, the Department of Marine had withdrawn from the business of supervising hospitals, and sailors, as patients, had become fully integrated into the routine of the public general hospitals. Statistics would seem to indicate that by the early 1890s the Victoria General Hospital in Halifax was taking care of the largest number of infirm seamen, whereas the number of seamen succoured in Quebec had been reduced by about two-thirds in less than twenty-five years.[95] Despite the abuses which occurred, the provision of hospital care for seamen stands out as one of the few enlightened aspects of government marine policies.

'ROWDINESS' AND VIOLENCE

While a sailor's work and a sailor's illness involved varying degrees of contact with port society, it was the sailor's rowdiness which remained the best-known feature of his port activities. He neatly fitted the stereotype of Jack ashore when he was involved in drunken brawls; when he was being carried aboard his vessel senseless; when he was monopolizing the time of the magistracy in police court; and when he was gracing the city lock-up or prison with his presence.

All appearances would seem to indicate that the sailor was more prone to troublemaking and more likely to be in the dock than his shoreside contemporaries. This may be an illusion created by two factors. The first, noted earlier, was the consistency with which he was identified as a sailor, not just in official records unavailable to the public, but in the daily press which conveyed the impression that he was unusually delinquent. The second factor relates to shipping law and crimping practices, both of which meant that the sailor was frequently before the court for violations of his contract or for being a victim of the local sailor-snatchers. No other type of worker was subject to similar restrictions and pressures. None the less, when it came to assaults and violent behaviour, the sailor was more likely than his shoreside equivalents to be beating up his superiors or fighting with his fellow workers. To help to explain this behaviour we need to appreciate the inability of individual sailors to settle their grievances at sea. Resort to fisticuffs there was likely to land the sailor in irons. Since there was no escape from disagreements at sea, many of the quarrels were saved up for resolution in port. As a result the degree of violence among sailors seems to have been disproportionately high.

Before examining the kind of rowdiness and violence indulged in by sailors, it may be useful to try to establish some sense of proportion by referring to court statistics. While Halifax in the 1880s may not be representative of the period as a whole and may differ from the other two ports, the registers of defendants before the magistrate's court does provide us with some valuable evidence. In the eleven years 1880 to 1890 merchant seamen of all ranks accounted for 8 per cent of the 14,790 cases before the stipendiary magistrate. Thirty-eight per cent of the 1,237 sailor defendants were natives of the Atlantic provinces and two-thirds of all the seamen were under the age of thirty. Drunkenness and drinking-related offences such as disorderly conduct, obscene language, breaking glass, and fighting made up 58 per cent of the sailor cases, a figure which is 10 per cent higher than that for the defendants as a whole. Another 22 per cent of the sailor cases consisted of desertion and refusal of duty cases, which were governed by merchant shipping law and will be treated in chapter 4. The bulk of the remaining offences was made up of assault cases, with only 4 per cent of sailors' offences pertaining to larceny and theft. Since Halifax was a year-round port by this period, the seasonality of the offences by sailors was not particularly marked, with some 57.5 per cent of the appearances before the court occurring between June and November.[96]

Not all examples of sailors' 'rowdiness,' however, ended up in court. Port society was willing to turn a blind eye to a certain amount of the sailors' exuberance and, as long as no one thought they were creating a disturbance, they could practise the more innocent of their antics ashore. This is not to imply that all the public displays were either recreational or violent ones. One of the major characteristics of seamen's land-based strikes, for example, was the resort to street processions in which the seamen gave expression to their wage demands. The marchers were accompanied by 'mottoes, banners, devices' and music, symbols which seemed to combine martial and religious elements. The mottoes ranged from 'Sailors' Rights' in Halifax in 1859 to 'Corkey is dead' in Quebec in 1876. They were inscribed on banners or flags, the flags themselves giving some indication of the international nature of seafaring, with British, American, and French flags appearing in the 31 January 1859 Halifax parade. One seaman in this procession also carried a miniature ship 'as an emblem of the errand in which they had banded together,' a device reminiscent of the mendicant sailors of Regency London.[97] In this case the music was provided by a fife and drum. The parades were by no means processions of stragglers. In Saint John in 1843, the seamen 'paraded through the streets in droves'; the participants in the 1859 parade in Halifax numbered nearly 200 'men of all colours'; the procession which left Diamond Harbour in Quebec in 1876 intent on reaching St Peter Street to draw attention to the seamen's wage problems included about 80 men. The parades met with a mixed reception. Newspaper comments on the Halifax strike in 1859 described that parade either as orderly or comical, and certainly unusual, one editor claiming that no strikers of any description had ever before 'to our knowledge paraded their claims publicly through the streets of Halifax.' The sailor demonstration in Quebec in 1876 ended abruptly when the police arrested the two flag-bearers who led the procession.[98]

On the lighter side, the editor of the *Novascotian* described the frolics of sailors in the streets of Halifax in 1846:

A few days since some of the streets of the town were made unusually hilarious, by a group of sailors and a crowd of boys. The former were, evidently, taking relaxation, after labour, in their own fashion, – and the latter were so amused by that fashion, that they accompanied and hurraed and showed abundant evidence of being in a congenial element. The sailors had become boys again, – if ever they had lost the juvenility of their feelings, – and the boys were only too proud and too amused, at such an assimilation. On went the Jacks, with 'some kind or other' standard hoisted – reminding of the 'some kind or other of responsibility,' which some politicians take the credit of setting up; – with the standard went antics, and shouts and grimaces, for which none but such supporters would like to be responsible, – and after and about it went, 'Tom, Dick and Harry', white, black and brown, in very republican equality. Heads peered from windows, smiles and laughs saluted the merry-makers, and on went the Jacks and Toms, under a scorching July sun, performing, in their way, a very large amount of amateur labour. The shouts were heard, repeatedly, during the afternoon, from the cross streets, as the odd procession toiled north and south, and south and north, with a most pertinacious idea of making fun out of anything, if nothing appropriate was accessible.[99]

Pranks were less readily tolerated. In 1854 'A Sailor Boy from one of the Boarding-houses in Water Street was brought up before the Police for tying a kettle and basket to a dog's tail, and setting him at large, which caused a countryman's horse to run away, and which would have resulted in serious consequences had not the horse fallen and the dog been captured.' The sailor too had been captured and fined twenty dollars.[100]

More often sailors' high spirits took on a pugnacious flavour. Citizens of Saint John's sailortown were provided with free entertainment on a summer's evening in 1871 when two sailors 'between whom a grudge of some kind existed' resorted to a formal boxing match as a way of resolving their differences. On a wharf in Reed's Point, accompanied by a referee, seconds, umpires, and spectators, they fought some twelve or fourteen rounds in half an hour and concluded their contest for the day when darkness descended and expectations of police intervention arose. About two weeks later a sailors' fight on the railway wharf attracted a large crowd, but no police until it was all over. A row in York Point in 1878, between two sailors from a local boarding-house, which consisted of 'knocking each other around the street and cursing and swearing,' drew a crowd of about 150. The spring of 1879 found the sailors of the vessels at Queen's wharf in Quebec indulging in a general row in which 'Handspikes, belaying pins and other weapons were brought freely into use.' While sailors were known to perform both with and for the locals, they also performed against them, a case in point being an evening row in Saint John in December 1870 when sailors and landsmen clashed on the corner of Dock and Union streets until the sailors fled at the sight of local reinforcements. The police arrived only after the affray was over. If the townspeople failed to witness these 'entertainments,' the local press diverted them with accounts of other sailors' disturbances, usually obtained from closely following the business of the police court. In an account entitled 'Hilarious Mariners,' the Saint John *Morning News* described a scene of 'uproarious jollity' in a boarding-house on Long wharf, where the 'sons of Neptune' went a little too far, especially in insulting the boarding mistress, and the police intervened.[101]

Most reported disturbances, however, ended up in police court where, if convicted, sailors were either fined, sent aboard their vessels, or imprisoned until their vessels sailed. Cases of a serious nature such as aggravated assaults and murders were of course transferred to the superior courts. As the survey of cases brought before the magistrate in Halifax indicated, the largest proportion of convictions was for drunkenness and various forms of disreputable behaviour combined with drunkenness. In Saint John on 30 April 1866, for example, twenty-seven defendants sat in the police court dock. They were principally sailors from visiting vessels and nearly all of them had nothing more serious than drunkenness charged against them.[102] Disorderly behaviour was the activity most frequently paired with drunkenness.

In the poorly policed days before the middle of the century, the disorderliness of sailors and their friends often amounted, in the opinion of respectable middle-class elements, to disturbing the peace and creating a nuisance. On the St Louis road in Quebec in 1836, sailors teamed up with women of abandoned character to parade with flags, singing, blaspheming, and uttering obscenities as they went. Local residents felt intimidated and shocked by this behaviour, especially when it occurred on Sunday, and felt that the shoreside activities of sailors should be brought under control. The opportunity for doing so began in 1838 with the formation of the river police force. In June the new law officers rounded up sailors and their women on the Plains of Abraham, much to the relief of local residents, one of whom claimed: 'The scenes which are there constantly exhibited are of a nature not to be described, and in fact so annoying to the neighbourhood as to depreciate property, by deterring respectable persons from hiring the houses facing the said field.' By 1847 the residents of Champlain ward were asking for a police station to restrain 'the scenes of lawless violence, drunkenness and depravity, that we were compelled to witness during the season of navigation last year.' Sunday evenings were said to be particularly bad; drunken sailors and others went so far as to interfere with the services in the Mariners' Chapel at Diamond Harbour. Similar 'disgraceful scenes' were reported in the Reed's Point area of Saint John where a respectable resident called on the boarding-house-keepers to maintain order and prevent such 'shocking' scenes as sailors 'stripped naked to the skin, slaughtering each other like brute beasts.'[103]

While the strengthening of police forces undoubtedly curbed disorderliness in the streets and other public places, the drunken brawls which occurred aboard ship within sight and earshot of local residents continued throughout the century since police interference in these fights depended on the disposition of the shipmaster.[104] 'A Protracted Row' described in a Halifax paper in 1878 provides a typical illustration of drunken fighting aboard ship:

Part of the crew of a fishing schooner, just in from a tedious trip, went up town yesterday afternoon and returned to their vessel visibly the braver for liquor. The skipper, assisted by some of his men, hustled them on board after a fashion; but do his utmost he could not get them stowed quietly. At last, fighting became a necessity. Twice the skipper started to call the police, but recollecting that he was going to sail last evening, thought it best not to surrender his men, warlike though they were. So the fight went on 'two hours by Shrewsbury clock'; shreds of garments and bloody noses were the only trophies, till an armistice was finally concluded.[105]

When a shipboard affray got out of hand in Halifax in 1869, however, soldiers on duty in the area of the Queen's wharf were called upon to suppress it.[106]

The most serious disturbances were the self-contained incidents of violence, that is those which occurred either on anchored ship or on shore between the members of the same crew. Fighting, assaults, shootings, stabbings, murders, abusive or threatening language, and larceny were offences which were frequently reported as involving sailors only. They pitted seaman against seaman, crew against officers, individual sailors against individual officers, cooks against seamen, blacks against whites. In addition to these forms of violence there were much less frequent conflicts between sailors and landsmen, particularly the police, boarding-house-keepers, and prostitutes. Since the incidence of all these forms of violence and crime are legion, we can but provide illustrations to portray the rumbustious side of the sailors' life in port.

The newspapers for the period 1860 to 1865 provide us with a variety of examples of assault cases. In Quebec in October 1860, Joseph Bryne, cook of the *John Davies*, was sentenced to one month in prison at hard labour after he stabbed one of his comrades, Michael Griffiths, who had rowed back to the vessel without him following an evening's debauch. An African sailor, John De Costa, was stabbed on board his vessel, the *Prince of Wales*, in Saint John in October 1862 by a seaman, H.W. Sewell, who had been plaguing De Costa about the tendency of his countrymen to kill missionaries and eat them and had thereby precipitated a serious quarrel. Sewell was committed for trial in the supreme court. In June 1863 Maurice Hogan, a seaman, was sentenced in Quebec to three months' hard labour for stabbing another man. That same month George Green, steward of the *Hibernia*, charged the master and chief mate with an assault which included placing him in irons, tying him with a rope, and otherwise ill-treating him. In July Antoine Riboli, seaman of the *Patrician*, was given the option of a $10 fine or one month in jail for assaulting the boatswain during the voyage up the St Lawrence, while a shipmaster, convicted of assault, was offered the choice of a five shilling fine or eight days in prison. Two masters were involved in assault cases in August. John Rees, of the *Ford Mill*, of Swansea, charged one of his seamen, Isaac Thomas, with having assaulted him on the way up the St Lawrence, a charge which resulted in a sentence of two months' hard labour for the seaman. In contrast, a steamship master was fined $2 for an assault on his second engineer. In Saint John in 1863, three black seamen of the *Black Prince* got eight weeks in the penitentiary for assaulting the first mate. When Stephen Sullivan, a young sailor of the barque *Charlotte*, was fined $6 for assaulting the steward, a boy named McCarthy, the magistrate waived the fine because Sullivan was a married man and earned 'only $6 per month.'[107]

A serious case of a sea captain cutting down one of his men with a cutlass, thereby maiming him for life, preoccupied the attention of the editor of the *Quebec Mercury* in July 1864. Because the wounded seaman was in hospital, the trial before the Court of Queen's Bench could not proceed. As a result the three vital witnesses could not be held in port and the captain, who had been allowed out on bail, also sailed away. Disturbed at the injustice of Canadian law to strangers, the newspaper suggested that the only remedy was to pass legislation requiring the detention of non-resident witnesses and the collection of bail in all criminal cases. In the autumn of 1864 a seaman was cut up with a carving knife by two women during a row in Quebec's sailortown. In Saint John William Baker, sailor of the Prussian ship *Dolphin*, was arraigned for assaulting the captain but was sent aboard the vessel when the captain expressed his unwillingness to prosecute. James Taylor, cook of the ship *Eleanor*, was fined $20 for striking his captain, who was endeavouring to find out the contents of a bag the cook was taking ashore. In March 1865 a sailor named Neal was given a $20 fine or imprisonment for ninety days for committing a 'grievous' assault upon one of his shipmates on board the *Margaret Ann* in Halifax harbour. Two months later four sailors in Saint John were committed for trial in the supreme court on a murder charge. Last but not least of our examples, David Smith, chief mate of the ship *Anna Frances*, was arraigned for assaulting one of the seamen, George Robertson, on board the vessel on the passage from Liverpool to Saint John and, despite the difficulty of judging violence at sea, he was convicted and fined $20.[108]

As the provocation of John De Costa aboard the *Prince of Wales* illustrates, violence based on racial tensions was likely to erupt between black and white seamen. In Quebec in 1835 a mulatto seaman, David Alexander, was saved from a conviction of assaulting and battering the mate of his vessel when a ship labourer testified that the mate had precipitated the attack by calling the defendant a 'black son of gun.' The French-Canadian jury in the quarter sessions trial, cognizant no doubt of the problems of the underdog, found Alexander not guilty. Tension could run very high at times on vessels where the crew were all black and the officers white. The shooting assault by the mate of a black man on board the barque *Stampede* in Saint John in 1872 occurred, according to the accused, because he could not go among the all-black crew to rescue the captain from attack with 'nothing but his two hands' to aid him. A row on the *Hypatia* a couple of months later involved another all-black crew, but the prosecution of the troublemakers did differ slightly from similar cases in that the seamen complained of police brutality and the press indulged in some racial epithets such as 'ugly customers,' 'refractory negroes,' and 'sable Nautiouses.'[109]

Black sailors sometimes refused to serve on vessels in which they constituted a minority of the crew and the abuse often heaped upon black cooks helps to establish the reason why. Racial provocation led to violence in the galley. Adam Thom, black cook of the ship *Minnesota*, was so enraged by the mate during a stopover in Quebec in 1863 that he trounced his superior soundly. In Saint John in 1878 a young seaman on board the barque *Henrietta* upbraided the cook for the poor quality of the tea. The cook resisted the insult; the sailor replied that the tea might be 'good enough for a nigger but not for a white man' and went on to stab the cook. Violence in the galley was not however entirely attributable to race. As the crucial purveyor of the sailors' rations, the cook tended to serve as a convenient scapegoat when the men were dissatisfied with the regimen aboard ship. His difficult role is illustrated in the case of the *Montezuma* in Saint John in 1873. The cook, Alfred Loftus, was charged with cutting two of the seamen with an axe during a shipboard affray, but he was acquitted of the charge of assault because of the provocation he had to endure when the drunken seamen infringed on the rights of the cook in his galley. The captain testified that Loftus had complete control of the galley, subject only to the directions of the captain and mate, and the magistrate attributed much of the difficulty to Loftus's superior intelligence and his practice of siding with the officers of the vessel during all shipboard disturbances.[110]

Sailors' troubles in port frequently involved the women who entertained them and lived with them ashore. While the sources for sailortown activity in the nineteenth century do not provide an adequate basis for assessing sailors' liaisons with prostitutes, some indirect insights into their relationships are provided by robberies and assaults. Three prostitutes in Halifax were implicated in the murder of a seaman, Alexander Allan of the *Cumberland*, in a Barrack Street brothel in 1853. The crime was universally condemned and resulted in pressure being applied to the authorities to clear out 'the detestable houses of infamy which pollute our midst.' Apart from incidents of fatal assault, the brothels made the news when they were raided or the troubles within spilled out into the street. In Quebec in 1867, for example, several sailors visited a brothel in St John's suburbs and a knife fight ensued. One of the sailors, named Fitzgerald, left the house, but was pursued and assaulted with sling-shot, feet, and fists.[111]

The fights which occurred between individual sailors and their women were private affairs, the extent of which must remain a mystery: only occasional examples come to light. Court cases arising from such encounters pitted two socially outcast elements against one another. Prostitutes were likely to be more sympathetically treated by the courts when they were assaulted by transients than by residents. One such case in Saint John in 1871 found the magistrate advising the sailor 'that if he consorted with that class of women, he must treat them kindly and he should put the same penalty upon him as if the assault had been made upon the most respectable lady in the city.' When a Nova Scotia sailor named Morey was severely injured in a Sheffield Street, Saint

John, den in 1883, he refused to lay a charge against his female assailant
on the ground that he had 'offered to fight her and had been worsted.'
Another violent encounter on the same brothel street two years later
resulted this time in the stabbing of Eva Merrill, locally known as
Circus Eva. The night before her boyfriend, Robert Normansel, was
due to sail, he inflicted nine stab wounds on her head, face, left arm,
and hands. 'I am going away tomorrow,' he said as he held her down,
'and want to leave my mark on you.' A sailor's transiency also
produced rival claims to the same woman and conflicts over female
property. In Halifax in 1868 a young black seaman from St Thomas,
named Edwards Symonds, defeated his rival for the affection of a City
Street resident in a late-night knife fight on the street.[112]

Halifax also provides us with examples of theft in which sailors,
overpowered by passion, drink, drugs, or all three, were relieved of
their cash and valuables by their lady companions. The sequence of
events is described in a ballad from Halifax called 'Barrack Street,' after
the brothel district below the east slope of the Citadel.

You sailors all, come lend an ear, come listen to my song,
A trick of late was played on me, it won't detain you long.
I came from sea the other day, a girl I chanced to meet,
'My friends will be expecting me to a dance on Barrack Street'.

I said, 'My pretty fair one, I cannot dance too well,
Besides, I am to Windsor bound, where all my friends do dwell.
I've been to sea these last two years, I've save up £30,
My friends will be expecting me this night in Windsor town.'

...

At eight o'clock that evening the drinking did begin,
And when all hands had got their fill the dancing did begin.
Me and my love danced all around unto a merry tune,
When she says, 'Dear, we will retire to a chamber all alone'.

The dancing being over, to bed we did repair,
And there I fell fast asleep, the truth I will declare.
My darling with my £30, gold watch and chain had fled,
And left me here, poor Jack alone, left naked in the bed.

I looked all around me, nothing could I spy
But a women's shirt and apron upon the bed did lie.
I wrung my hands and tore my hair, crying, 'What shall I do?
Fare you well, sweet Windsor town, I'm sure I'll ne'er see you'.

Everything being silent, and the hour but twelve o'clock,
I put on my shirt and apron and steered for Cronan's wharf,
And when I did get on board the sailors all did say,
'I think, old chap, you've had a duck since you have been away'.

'Is those the new spring fashions which have lately come on shore?
Where is the shop you bought them at, do you think there's any more?'
The captain, he says, 'Jack, I thought you were to Windsor bound,
You might have got a better suit than that for £30'.

'I might have got a better suit if I'd a had a chance.
I met a girl in Water Street; she asked me to a dance.
I danced my own destruction; I'm stripped from head to feet,
I'll take my oath I'll go no more to a dance on Barrack Street'.

Come, all you young sailor lads, a warning take by me,
Be sure and choose your company when you go on a spree;
Be sure keep out of Barrack Street, or else you'll rue the day,
With a women's shirt and apron they'll rig you out for sea.[113]

Another Maritimer, John Greer, a Prince Edward Islander, was robbed of his wages of eighteen dollars while in a drunken stupor in a Water Street grog shop, by Carrie Ferguson, an inmate of a house which was cosily called the 'Mariner's home.' Foreigners were a natural prey. A West Indian sailor was robbed by a prostitute in a Halifax brothel in 1871. Two Albemarle Street prostitutes, Sarah Saint and Kate McKenzie, combined their talents to rob two Norwegian sailors in 1884. When a sailor was relieved of his watch in another Albemarle Street brothel in 1876, he refused to prosecute once the watch had been recovered. Except in extreme cases, the courts were not considered the best mode of resolving differences with one's class associates.[114]

Likewise, sailors robbed their lady friends. Two cases from the 1850s and 1860s involving gold watches tend to suggest that the sailors assumed their relationships with prostitutes entitled them to a share of their women's property. A sailor charged with stealing the gold watch of his girlfriend from her room in Halifax's Barrack Street 'protested that he had only borrowed it, thinking that he could take that liberty with the fair one's property.' Somewhat similarly, in Saint John in 1867, Joshua Ferguson, seaman on the *Cordelia*, took a watch and chain from Elizabeth Jones of Sheffield Street on the promise that he would take her out driving. When he failed to fulfil his promise she charged him with robbery.[115]

If sailors felt they had proprietorial rights to their women's property, they revealed similar sentiments about the contents of their vessels. They usually received jail sentences of from three to twelve months for stealing property from their captains or shipmates while their vessels were in port. They also used their accessibility to cargoes, stores, and provisions to engage in some illicit entrepreneurial activities. The irresistible temptation to broach cargo, particularly liquor, is fairly well documented. The amounts stolen in several cases in the 1880s indicate that embezzled cargo was being disposed of locally. Two sailors of the barque *Lavinia* of Greenock, which was discharging sugar at the railway wharf in the Richmond district of Halifax in February 1883, acquired some fifteen-pound cans of raw sugar and offered them for sale on the upper streets. In Saint John a black sailor who deserted from his vessel and proceeded to steal several sets of gloves and fur hats in the city was also found to have taken from his vessel eight gallons of molasses, sixty pounds of coffee, fifteen pounds of sugar, and the captain's walking stick. Another sailor was captured in Halifax in 1889 in possession of 750 cigars and twelve bottles of bay rum. He was apparently only one sailor of many who engaged in an extensive trade in contraband cigars. Since the smugglers were usually successful in eluding detection, they may have been protected by an organized black market in sailortown. The items most commonly taken from ships' stores included rope and meat. Two court cases involving pork and beef in Halifax in 1873 indicate that sailors found a market for their ill-gotten gain among the petty shop- and tavern-keepers of sailortown.[116]

What seems like the sailor's penchant for getting into trouble was enhanced by a range of considerations, two of which – his occupational identity and his shipping offences – have already been mentioned. The sailor's transiency and foreignness also placed him at a disadvantage and meant he was not treated like local rowdies. For one thing he was locked away much more readily. If found on the street at night, he was almost automatically charged with drunkenness. A case in point is that of John Gaines, a forty-seven-year-old sailor, who was charged with drunkenness on a Saint John street in November 1869. He vehemently denied the charge and complained of the treatment he received, which had the effect of encouraging the magistrate to excuse him. 'In London or Liverpool,' he claimed in court, 'the Police would take the trouble to direct him to his vessel or a place of safety for the night, but here, when he requested such a favour he was marched off to the lock-up.' New sailor-visitors to port considered that some leniency should be allowed for their lack of familiarity with local regulations, which were designed to protect local society against foreigners. In Saint John, for example, foreigners were not allowed to wander the streets at night, and if they refused to take themselves off to their vessels or boarding-houses, they were arrested.[117]

Sailors regarded their own rowdy actions in quite a different manner from the local law enforcement officers. In this they may not have differed significantly from other working-class people who were used to venting their frustrations and resolving their problems in the most direct manner. What the police interpreted as fighting, sailors regarded as 'skylarking.' In their battle against the regulations and restrictions of port life, sailors occasionally won the support of the mob whose ambivalent attitude towards them meant that alliances were possible when the sailors were being victimized by the police or were contributing to the amusement of local residents. The mob was known to rescue or attempt to rescue sailors – both residents and foreigners – from arrest in the streets and other public places. When Thomas McAleer, a sailor lad, found picking dandelions in a Portland cemetery in Saint John on a summer evening in 1883, put up a 'plucky defence' against a squad of police sent to evict him, sympathetic onlookers joined in the mêlée. Their failure to rescue McAleer led to the issue of warrants for their own arrest. Bystanders also took it upon themselves to control sailors' street fights in the absence of the police and to denounce police brutality in instances of sailors' arrests in public.[118]

Another factor which may have produced the illusion of the excessive nature of sailors' misbehaviour was the summary jurisdiction over their felonies given to police magistrates by Canadian law. What this meant in practice was that sailors, as transients, non-residents, or as shipboard offenders, were tried in the lowest criminal court in the port for offences which, when committed by most citizens, were tried in the superior courts. As a result, seafarers were the only class of persons to appear in the police court reports charged with aggravated assaults or serious larcenies. To a public which was used to recitals of the day-to-day business of the police court and only occasional accounts of the sittings of the higher courts, sailors may have appeared as the only persons who were regularly being tried for such offences.[119] Summary trials were not of course deliberately designed by government to discredit sailors. They were held for the convenience of trade, and, in the major ports, where the viability of commerce was held to depend upon speed, the law obligingly bent over backwards to accommodate the mercantile class. Magistrates asleep in their beds were sought out specially to dispose of cases which were otherwise going to delay the sailing of ships. In cases of drunkenness, the police were willing to collect the fine and allow the offender to sail with his vessel if an appearance in court were likely to be detrimental to the ship.[120]

Intoxicated sailors in trouble or misbehaving were a common sight in the ports. They left no doubt that they preferred the tavern to the ship; they thought nothing of running up bills in public houses that they could not afford to pay.[121] Sailors clearly considered excessive indulgence to be their prerogative, one which would make up for all those dry, lonely weeks at sea. The host society was most critical of sailors who had gone through hell at sea only to dissipate themselves with alcohol ashore.[122] Instead of spending their time giving thanks to the Almighty for their deliverance, they became besotted and acted no different from the most vulgar layabout. The contrast of courage at sea with fecklessness on shore, of providential deliverance with heathenish ingratitude, informed the response of the public to the sailor-strangers in their midst. The resulting ambivalence displayed by port society did as much to characterize the rhythm of port life as did summer and winter, the sailors' work and leisure, sickness and health, rowdiness and punishment.

4

The sailor's labour rights

Mindless disorderliness often brought the sailor to court. Indeed sailors' cases usually comprised a very considerable proportion of the work of the lower courts. To the generality of landsmen, the sailor's court appearances strengthened his image as a nuisance, a scallywag, a nonconformist, an incorrigible misfit unable to act moderately and responsibly when released from his floating prison. This was an erroneous impression, for merchant seamen were as likely to be in court in response to the dictates of maritime labour law as they were to answer to 'disorderly' charges.

The year 1854 in Quebec provides a revealing illustration. Of the 3,363 individuals brought before the magistrates 1,222 were merchant seamen, all of whom appeared between May and November. Some 664 of the cases were for 'disorderly' offences, including 556 for drunkenness, 48 for vagrancy, and 52 for creating a disturbance. The other 558 cases, however, were shipping cases governed by British and Canadian merchant shipping legislation. They included 511 sailors' defences against charges for 170 desertions, 95 absences without leave, 78 refusals to proceed to sea, and 160 refusals to do duty. The remaining 47 were sailors' complaints for the non-payment of wages. The excess of 'disorderly' cases over shipping offences belies the far greater importance assigned to the work-related cases by the court. Some 442 of the 664 disorderly sailors were discharged. In contrast, only 32 of the 511 sailors tried on shipping offences were acquitted and only 13 of the 47 sailors who brought wage cases won theirs. To illustrate it in another way: for every sailor who went to Quebec jail on a 'disorderly' charge in 1854, one and two-thirds were incarcerated for a violation of maritime labour law.[1]

While most of Jack's 1854 court appearances in shipping cases in Quebec were for desertion and other acts of disobedience, the wage cases were suits initiated by him and represented his own resort to litigation. Indeed, the two traditional ways in which the sailor sought to remedy grievances relating to his working conditions and his wages were either to desert from his vessel or to take advantage of the legal remedies available to him under shipping law. The resort to desertion or to litigation continued to be favoured by sailors throughout the nineteenth century as it had been during the eighteenth. They were discouraged from adopting different approaches to their problems by a number of factors. The international mixture of the labour force and its transiency operated against rudimentary trade unionism. Moreover, the last quarter of the century saw a steady decline of the carrying trade in wooden vessels in which most of the sailors were employed. Their replacements on steam freighters made brief port calls in Canada and this reduced the opportunity not only for fraternity but also for the customary desertion and litigation.

While forms of protest did not change much in the nineteenth century, the environment in which they occurred became more restrictive. Not only had the sailors shipping offices to contend with, but they were also faced with the continual revision and emendation of the merchant shipping laws as the state stepped up its campaign against deserters and crimps and against the litigation they concocted in concert. In order to illustrate how sailors tried to uphold their labouring rights, in this chapter we shall examine the extra-legal and legal actions common among seafarers which led to their frequent appearances in court as defendants, acknowledging their breach of contract or resisting charges of desertion and refusal to work, or as plaintiffs pressing their own cases relating to ill-treatment, wages, and customary rights.

EXTRA-LEGAL ACTION

The most common and effective form of extra-legal protest was desertion, the high rate of which continuously alarmed the shipping interests and law enforcement agencies in the major British North American ports. It was highest in Quebec where it was complemented by a low rate of apprehensions. Reported desertions of British and colonial seamen in Quebec between 1845 and 1853 averaged 1,800 a season, a figure which represented between 10 and 20 per cent of the total seamen in port, including foreigners for whom desertion rates are unavailable. The attempts by the authorities to interfere with customary desertion in Quebec by means of the river police force and the government shipping office proved to be unsuccessful. In 1857 desertions were said to be occurring at the rate of 500 seamen per month during the seven-month shipping season.[2]

Apprehensions of deserters represented only a minor proportion of reported desertions; reported desertions, in turn, did not approximate actual desertions. Recovering escapers depended on the initiative of captains, who were unlikely to act if absconding sailors had no wages owing to them out of which court, jail, and cartage costs could be defrayed. Ships' logs and crew agreements list deserters by name, but only in a minority of cases is any indication given that police warrants were obtained and recapture attempted. The captain of the *Commerce* took the Quebec river police boat in 1858 to enable him to search the schooner *Mary Govier* for one of his missing seamen, whom he found stowed away in a locker in the fo'c's'le and whom the magistrate sent to jail until the *Commerce* was ready to sail. Occasionally masters pursued deserters with fanatical zeal. The master of the *Brave* apprehended his runaway apprentice, William Hutchinson, in Quebec in 1858 on the *Kilblain* which he had joined as a deserter in Alicante, Spain. Edward Johns, master of the *Birmingham*, went aboard the barque *Gipsy Queen* in Quebec in 1860 to recover a seaman who had deserted from the *Birmingham* two years earlier. Evans also captured another deserter in the street and, on his second voyage to Quebec that season, this resourceful master successfully searched a Champlain Street boarding-house for two deserters. But he was the exception, not the rule.[3] Masters usually preferred to admit the desertion of their absent men only when they were on the point of clearing port when it was too late to begin a search for delinquents.

Throughout the nineteenth century prevailing opinion and the testimony of sailors themselves held that the sailor, who signed his contract for a round trip at modest wages, deserted in order to take advantage of the higher wage rates on vessels crewing in Canada. In evidence to a British parliamentary inquiry in 1848, the registrar-general of seamen, Lt J.H. Brown, claimed that nearly all men who went to Quebec and New Brunswick ports deserted. The questioning continued:

Q: What becomes of them?
A: They come home in other ships. They get £12 or £14 for the voyage home a month.
Q: 'Desertion' in that case only means coming home in other ships?
A: Yes. In fact, many seamen are attracted from foreign service to the port of Quebec owing to the high wages. Since the magistrates have come to the decision of fining men who cannot produce their registered tickets of discharge from Quebec, I have investigated the cases very strictly and found, by reference to different lists, that men have gone out to Boston and New York and made their way to Quebec to get those higher wages.[4]

Brown's view was confirmed by sailors, magistrates, and the press. James Nichols, a seaman on the *Juliet*, stated in London in 1847 that after four years in the American service he had been attracted to Quebec from Boston by reading 'an advertisement in a newspaper that seamen were required at Quebec, and that large wages were given.' One of the magistrates of the London docks' Thames police court summed up the general feeling of the bench when he claimed in 1849 'that a very bad state of things existed at Quebec, and that seamen deserted to obtain larger wages coming home.' Of the two major reasons cited in Saint John for desertion in 1883, one was higher wages, the other enticement by crimps, which in itself was achieved through the promise of higher wages.[5]

But sailors also deserted on account of unfortunate experiences on their vessels. In many cases it would be impossible to say that the 'pull' of higher wages was more persuasive than the 'push' provided by feuding on the vessel, bad relations with the officers, squalid working conditions, or inhumane treatment. The editor of the *Quebec Gazette* asserted in 1857 that the most important cause of desertion was 'the general bearing of the commander of a vessel towards his crew and his treatment of them at sea.' Desertion was therefore often analogous to escape. A Scotsman who deserted in Halifax in 1862, leaving nine pounds in wages behind, explained that he had 'run away from his vessel because the captain had put him in irons and placed mustard plasters upon him.' In Quebec in 1867, Owen Humphreys, a sailor on the *Westmoreland*, was found floating near Crane Island 'on a deal and a piece of stairs.' He had jumped overboard the previous night because 'he was in danger of his life by the cruelty of the master, and thought that he might as well risk being drowned as of being made miserable by the brutal treatment of the captain.' Ebenezer Samuels, a deserter from the barque *Eunomia* in Saint John, jumped into the harbour during his conveyance back to his vessel only to be recaptured and returned, this time in irons. A sailor discovered drowned in 1851 below Quebec had tried to buoy himself up with a cork fender fastened to his breast and a piece of board lashed transversely across his thighs. We can only speculate that it was mistreatment that caused him to resort to such a desperate attempt to escape from his vessel after it had cleared port. The officers also mistreated the men. It was the mate who violently attacked William Glass on the barque *Russia* in Saint John as it began to sail in December 1889. After being struck several times and attacked with a brass knuckle, which inflicted a deep gash over his left eye, Glass jumped overboard, swam up Market Slip, and refused to return to his vesssel.[6]

Whatever their reasons for leaving or refusing to join their vessels, a very great number of seamen ended up in magistrate's court on charges of desertion, absence without leave, or refusal to proceed.[7] In the vast majority of cases, sailors pleaded guilty when charged and, depending on the inclination of the shipmaster, the vessel's anticipated length of stay, and its nationality, they were either sent on board their vessel or confined in jail at their own expense on the understanding that they would be required to rejoin their vessel when it was ready to sail. A jail sentence was not a dismissal, the contract taking precedence over all other considerations, and it was not an excuse for the master to abandon his errant seamen.[8] Apart from death or change of owner or master in port, the contract could be legally terminated only with the mutual agreement of both parties (which usually resulted from mutually antagonistic relations), by incarceration for an illness or for a crime (as opposed to an infraction of the shipping law), or if just cause could be proved in court (which was the object of most sailors' defence cases and many of their complaints, and of some of the court actions initiated by masters).

Captains were known to go to great lengths to prevent deserters released from jail from escaping reunion with their vessel. Three determined deserters in Halifax in 1866 filed off their handcuffs after they had been delivered from the jail to the brigantine *Aristos*. In response to the captain's orders to come on deck, one of the delinquents, William Jones, 'threw a handful of pepper in the Captain's eyes, and laid hold of him with his hands and teeth, and bit him severely on the left wrist – he then called upon the other two men and said *"Murder the son of a bitch, we wont go to sea with him".'* For the indiscretion of drawing his knife, Jones received a pistol ball through the lung. One newspaper commented that 'This we hope will be a warning to Seamen.' Since the captain was well known in the community (he was a member of the seafaring Crowell family), the grand jury failed to indict him on Jones's subsequent death, agreeing no doubt with the press 'that nothing but the fact of his own life being in imminent peril, would have induced him to discharge his revolver.'[9] Seven black sailors of the American ship *Bridgewater* jumped over the side of the vessel in Saint John in 1887 on their return from two weeks in jail for desertion. This time the captain preferred to sail without them, leaving them behind to undergo another term of imprisonment for desertion.[10]

The minority of sailors who pleaded not guilty to charges of desertion attempted to prove just cause for being absent from their vessels. Their testimony forms the basis for examining their motivations and their attitudes towards their contracts. Sailors' defence evidence confirms the contemporary view that the most important work-related reason for desertion in Canadian ports was the attraction of higher wages. Sailors received three to five times the British rate when they shipped for transatlantic voyages in Quebec and Saint John. Seaman Wilkins, who shipped from Liverpool to Saint John in 1847 for £3 a month, deserted and signed on in Saint John for £7 (currency) for the run to London with a guarantee of another £7 if he was discharged in London.[11] Sailors also regarded desertion as the most effective way of protesting against specific conditions of employment. They left their vessels without permission after being unreasonably denied shore leave by their officers. They left when they were ill, often after an unsuccessful application to the captain to be sent ashore for medical aid. They left to protest or escape from maltreatment by their officers, a course of action which sailors often found more appealing than the legal redress available to them under the merchant shipping acts. When they were worried about the safety of their vessel they left, again despite regular procedures for determining the seaworthiness of vessels. They also absconded when they failed to improve the wages in their existing contracts. In one case this amounted to a discovery that a uniform rate did not prevail on the vessel; in another case, where a crew had been shipped by the run rather than the month, the vessel had to put back to port for repairs and the sailors were faced with the prospect of vastly inadequate wages for the length of their engagement. Sailors also deserted to protest against demotion, inadequate food, failure to negotiate a legal discharge with the captain, and changes in the nature or duration of the voyage. Given the variety of causes, desertion arguably proved the sailors' lack of faith in litigation as a means of remedying their grievances.[12]

Officers also felt the need to protest against their working conditions in ways which incorporated extra-legal procedures. George Gordon, the black second mate of the barque *John Ross*, requested his discharge in Saint John in 1866 after several black sailors deserted and were replaced by whites. Gordon argued that 'he being a coloured man the white men would not obey his orders.' Denied his discharge, Gordon openly went absent without leave. When the master refused to give him his clothes, Gordon laid a complaint at the police court where he was found to be entitled to his discharge and his property. When the captain continued to object to giving him his clothes he went again to the police court. The sitting magistrate this time reversed the earlier decision of his colleague and ordered Gordon on board the vessel.[13]

In those cases where desertion had clearly been chosen over litigation, the sailors' chances of successfully defending themselves in court were considerably decreased. Even successful litigation might prove to be illusory and cause desertion. As in the Gordon case, there was always the possibility that the captain would not comply with the decision of the magistrate. In Halifax in 1864, for example, a captain failed to respond to a court order relating to wages and the discouraged sailor finally deserted.[14] While the overriding impetus for desertion in Quebec was always wages, sailors also deserted to avoid arduous cargo-handling, particularly in the first half of the century when such work was considered to be their prime responsibility. And this aversion to cargo-handling was not confined to Quebec. In Halifax in 1855, nine seamen deserted from their vessel in order to escape their customary discharging of cargo.[15] Last but not least, sailors sometimes had to take 'French leave' in order to seek legal advice about summonsing their captains to court.[16]

Whether they pleaded guilty or not guilty to desertion charges, most sailors were convicted and the sentences for desertion and absence without leave were very much of a piece. A willing seaman was usually returned to his vessel, a more obstinate or less trustworthy seaman went to jail to await the sailing of his vessel. But there were variations and exceptions. Sentences ranged anywhere from a couple of days to two, three, four, six, seven, eight, and even twelve weeks. If the sailor was tried before his vessel left port, he would probably be in jail only until the vessel was ready to sail regardless of the length of sentence. His sentence therefore bore little relation to the actual time he spent in jail. Only if his vessel were unduly delayed was he likely to be incarcerated for more than a month. If, however, he was caught after his vessel had left port, an occurrence that increased in the shipowning ports with the appointment of shipping masters, he could be more severely penalized.[17]

None the less, the sailor who was charged after the departure of his vessel did enjoy some advantages. If a copy of the articles had not been lodged with the shipping master or collector of customs, he automatically secured his freedom. If he was apprehended a long time after the warrant had been issued, he could not be punished in the master's absence. In cases where he was caught in the act of jumping overboard as his vessel was clearing port, the sailor was not so lucky. One such sailor was seized by the Saint John owner of his vessel as he reached the shore, and largely because he had received an advance of eighteen dollars, which was unrecoverable under the cash advance system then prevailing in Saint John, he was sentenced to twelve weeks in the provincial penitentiary. Another sailor, who tried the same desperate escape from his moving vessel, was followed by his captain in a boat, and because he was either not given the option or refused to return to the vessel, he was sentenced to four months at hard labour. A man who jumped off his vessel in Halifax as it cleared for Puerto Rico got a sixty-day sentence. For a short time following his appointment in 1873, the zealous Halifax shipping master took full advantage of his power to charge deserters whose vessels had sailed. The standard sentence was thirty days, though one sailor was given the option of paying a month's wages. By the 1880s, however, a deserter in Halifax, captured after his vessel sailed, got off with the relatively short sentence of two weeks in prison.[18]

While it might seem that deserters were subjected to fairly light sentences, many of them serving only token time and many others being allowed to pay fines instead of going to jail, this is not to suggest that seafarers cheerfully accepted their punishment. They had their pride. They resented the morass of regulations which turned them into criminals for the occasional lapse in conduct. A British sailor, Joseph

Brierley, sent to jail for five days for being absent without leave from the *Minia* in Halifax in 1893, expressed his chagrin in the form of a poem entitled 'A Briton's Lament':

I am a sailor free, and ashore I like to be,
Sometimes on pleasure bent;
And when I've got the coin I like a bit of a rout,
And sometimes stay ashore the mate's consent without.
I belong to the steamer *Minia* of cable fame renowned,
And for being ashore without leave in the police court I was found.
And there I saw a shipmate, McInnis is his name.
He being charged with an offence, just the very same.
In the prisoner's dock there we stood up
To answer to our charge;
And the magistrate said he to me
How long were you at large?
My chum said two days, I said three;
When I heard it whispered in the court
For which in jail you'll be.
The mate in the witness box was called,
To charge us with our crime (!)
And then he told the magistrate to give us quite a time.
The magistrate he then turned round
And asked what we'd to say
Why sentence it should not be passed
On us in the usual way?
Now, thirteen years I've been to sea,
And been in many a gale,
I felt it worse when I heard him say:
'Five days in the County Jail!'
And here we are in durance vile,
Awaiting for the day
Our freedom we will get,
And go away to sea.[19]

When Thomas Lake was charged with deserting from the ship *Ariadne* in Saint John in 1862, he attributed his action to intoxication and influence exerted by parties unconnected with the vessel. In common with Joseph Brierley, Lake became a victim of his own human frailty. Two sailors in Saint John who went on a spree in 1876 returned to the wharves to find their vessel had sailed without them. Missing the vessel, they claimed, was accidental, not intentional, an excuse they substantiated by willingly paying back their ten-dollar advances to the vessel's consignees.[20]

While Canadian court cases dealt with sailors who deserted unsuccessfully, a sailor on a non-Canadian vessel who evaded the law and got out of the port in which he had deserted could be charged in the vessel's home port. From the 1830s to the 1850s many cases of desertion which occurred in British North American ports were brought to light in the courts of British seaports. Interestingly enough, the initiative for the prosecutions lay more often with the government shipping authorities than with the shipowners, who were no more disposed to pursue their deserters at home than abroad. In the absence of action by the shipowner who had suffered from the breach of contract, the only way the government authorities could intervene was by penalizing the seaman for the loss of his register ticket. Suits against suspected deserters were accordingly brought by the registrar-general of seamen to whose office the register tickets of missing seamen were returned by shipmasters. But the maximum penalty the magistrate could exact in these civil actions was a ten-shilling fine.

A number of cases in the summer and autumn of 1850 illustrate the features of these prosecutions, including the reasons for desertion. Anthony Bainbridge and William John Tidder, who had been imprisoned in Quebec, had not joined their own vessels on their release. Henry Stanley had deserted at Halifax, complaining of bad usage and bad provisions. Michael Donovan, who had deserted at Quebec, also complained of bad provisions. Daniel Hill and E.H. Williamson who had deserted at Quebec and Thomas Tyson who had absconded three years earlier at Saint John all claimed ill usage or poor relations with their masters. But the lord mayor of London sitting in his Mansion-House court clearly blamed the higher wages which each seaman had obtained through his desertion.[21] Seamen were also fined the standard ten shillings when they applied for a new register ticket without an adequate excuse for the loss of their previous one. The incorrigible Fawcett Twentyman had possessed six register tickets, each of which had been lost through desertion: twice at Quebec, and once each at Saint John, Trinidad, Bahia, and Valparaiso. In reporting the prosecution on a November day in 1851 of a room full of seamen for losing their tickets, the editor of the *Shipping and Mercantile Gazette* bewailed the fact that 'Notwithstanding that the authorities of the Registry-office had adopted every vigilance to acquaint the owners and captains of the vessels from which the seamen had deserted to prosecute, not a single individual attended to urge and sustain a conviction.'[22]

When deserters were in fact prosecuted by their aggrieved shipowners in Britain, the punishment of convicted deserters often took the form of thirty days' imprisonment at hard labour. John Toogood, whose conduct in Quebec was 'found to have been the reverse of his name,' went to labour on the treadmill in Plymouth jail for his Canadian desertion in 1839. Seaman DeShiel, who was one of six deserters who left the barque *Lochibo* in the Saguenay river, received a thirty-day sentence in the Thames police court in London in 1847. Four of the forty seamen who had deserted from the large troop ship the *Java* in Quebec in 1850 were similarly sentenced in the Mansion-House court. The legislation also empowered the magistrates to declare forfeited the deserter's wages, part of which could be claimed in a summary action as compensation by the injured shipowner, part by the Seamen's Hospital Society. Such cases usually occurred as wage disputes. The master of the barque *Helen* succeeded in avoiding the payment of balances of £11 and £13 due for wages from Quebec to London, claimed by two seamen complainants, by producing as a witness the master of the *Thomas Fielding* from which the two men had earlier deserted in Quebec. Having obtained a portion of their forfeited wages from the master of the *Helen*, the master of the *Thomas Fielding* then had the right to prosecute the seamen for desertion for which they would receive the additional punishment of imprisonment.[23]

In cases of prosecution for desertion the Mercantile Marine Act of 1850 gave considerable encouragement to the magistrates to pass harsher sentences. A seaman who had deserted from the *Bude* in Saint John in 1851 was, on conviction in London, committed to six weeks at hard labour. The Gloucester magistrates took advantage of the new legislation to impose eight- and twelve-week sentences on Quebec deserters in 1851. Henry Crossland, who deserted from the barque *Bride* with the rest of the crew in Saint John in July 1851, was sentenced in London to three months at hard labour. In Liverpool in 1857, Ralph Wilson was convicted of desertion from the *Lady Blaney* at Saint John. In addition to the standard three-month sentence, he forfeited the wages he had earned both in the *Lady Blaney* and the *Alexander* in which he returned to Britain, the latter being handed over to his former captain to cover the cost of a substitute. A Quebec deserter of the ship *St. Lawrence* was tried in Glasgow the same winter. He received also the twelve-week sentence, forfeited the balance of wages due him at the date of his desertion (this was applied to offset the costs of the shipowner-complainant), and he was ordered to pay eleven pounds for the substitute who had replaced him on the *St. Lawrence*.[24] The forfeiture of wages earned on the westbound voyage proves that it was not just sailors indebted to their ships who deserted in Canadian ports.

Foreign sailors on foreign vessels in the Canadian trades could also be prosecuted for desertion in Britain under the Foreign Deserters Act of 1852, the provisions of which applied in all cases where reciprocal arrangements existed, the major exception being seamen on American vessels and foreign sailors who had deserted from their British vessels in their own country and returned to British territories in ships of their own country. A prosecution under this act occurred in Bristol in 1854 when five Prussian sailors were charged with desertion from the Prussian ship *William* at Quebec at the instigation of the Prussian vice-consul on behalf of the captain. The five seamen, who had all returned to Britain 'at exorbitant wages' in the *Sir Henry Pottinger*, were, according to the provisions of the act, conveyed to their captain at Sunderland under a police guard paid by the captain.[25]

Deserters brought before the magistrates in Canada or in Britain were encouraged to state their motivations in case they constituted grounds for dismissing the complaint, for securing a discharge from the vessel in question, or, on acquittal, for prosecuting the captain or owners. This meant that the onus was on the sailor to provide a just cause for his absence if he pleaded not guilty. Pleas which elicited a sympathetic response from the magistrate included sickness and forcible conveyance to the vessel in an inebriated or drugged condition. Magistrates seem also to have been guided by a sense of fairness when it came to financial considerations. For example, in those instances where sailors had been shipped locally by the run but had to put back with their vessel and faced several weeks in port, during which they would in effect be receiving no remuneration, the magistrate tended to order the captain to discharge the sailors. Evidence of serious ill-treatment was also likely to secure an acquittal for deserters. One notorious case in the Halifax police court included testimony by the sailors that the captain had already caused the death of one sailor by jumping on his genitals.[26]

But the most successful defence was to find, with the help of legal advice, those loopholes in the articles of agreement, required on all British and Canadian vessels over eighty tons, which the merchant shipping legislation identified as just cause for the cancellation of the contract. The articles were absolutely essential for proving the desertion – no articles, no proof, no desertion. The written agreement, which had to be read to the seamen and signed by them, contained the following information, taken in this case from the Canadian federal Seamen's Act of 1873, which is typical of nineteenth-century shipping acts.

1. The nature, and as far as practicable, the duration of the intended voyage or engagement;
2. The number and description of the crew, specifying how many are engaged as sailors;
3. The time at which each seaman is to be on aboard or to begin work;
4. The capacity in which each seaman is to serve;
5. The amount of wages which each seaman is to receive;
6. A scale of provisions which are to be furnished to each seaman;
7. Any regulations as to conduct on board, and as to fines, short allowance of provisions, or other lawful punishments for misconduct which the parties agree to adopt.

Irregularities in the articles arose in numerous ways and it was very seldom that an irregularity, once established, could act in any other way than as a justification for acquittal. Some of the most common irregularities in the agreements used to secure dismissal of desertion and absence-without-leave cases, and which indeed were employed in all other types of defences relating to terms and conditions of employment, were the absence or alteration of the appropriate signatures of master and seamen on the articles, the failure of the captain to ensure that the articles had been read over to the crew, or a deviation in the voyage as specified in the written description. In the case of George Mitchell, charged with wilfully absenting himself from the brig *Eclipse* in 1854, the articles given in evidence were adjudged by his counsel not to conform to the format required by law. They had, in addition, been altered without Mitchell's consent and were not the articles under which the vessel had gone to sea. Since the magistrate agreed, Mitchell was acquitted.[27]

Inundated with cases, many of which were clearly spurious, the Quebec police magistrate, William McCord, had to decide whom he was going to believe in respect to the observance of the shipping regulations. He explained his position thus:

The articles are frequently signed without being read to the seamen; I have, however, ruled that when the man could and did sign his name, he could not repudiate the contract; but I have ruled otherwise when the man has been an illiterate person and only made his cross. I have decided that when the articles were only read when out of port, and the steamer alongside, to be fatal, as although the man might go ashore, yet the Captain would not have his complement of men. When the captain and one officer have testified that all formalities have been complied with, I have given judgment in favour of the ship, although several seamen have testified to the contrary. Reading part of the articles, and not reading the scale of provisions, I consider fatal, but only in favor of those men who were illiterate and made their cross.[28]

The extensive occurrence of defences and complaints based on purely technical grounds would seem to have been sufficient to produce counter-measures by the state. But the British authorities, emulated after Confederation by the Canadian, claimed that they could not take 'the right of the first opportunity of redress away from seamen' and blamed masters for the irregularities, calling on them to be 'more careful in making out and adhering to agreements.'[29]

While desertion and absence without leave were more common shipping offences than refusal to proceed, the latter was considered the most insubordinate among this triumvirate of offences, and, as a violation of the sacred bond of obedience, it was the most severely punished in court, with jail sentences ranging up to ten weeks unless mitigating circumstances could be proved.[30] Charles Brown, arraigned on a refusal-to-proceed charge in 1872, was unable to convince the magistrate in Saint John that sickness prevented him from going to sea. His Honour concluded that Brown's 'chief object seemed to be to defraud the owners of the vessel out of the advance wages paid to him.' Four black sailors refused to go aboard their vessel, the *Lyman Cann*, in Saint John in 1870 – they had been given assurances that the crew would include six, not four, black sailors – but the white magistrate turned a deaf ear to the sailors' desire to protect their vulnerable position by bolstering their numbers. Another Saint John magistrate in 1867 was more sympathetic to a sailor who refused to go to sea after he was released from jail where he had been confined for debts to his boarding master. Faced with the prospect of having to cross the ocean in December with insufficient clothing because his creditor had retained his advance of wages, the sailor insisted that 'he had no idea of endangering his life on the "briny deep" while others lived in luxury ashore on the proceeds of his toil.' As in desertion cases, the articles could be the decisive factor in determining contested cases of refusal to proceed. In Halifax in 1856, two seamen of James West's brigantine, the *Lady Ogle*, refused to embark on a voyage to the West Indies; it became clear during the cross-examination that the articles had not been read to them and the case was dismissed.[31]

The obstinacy inherent in sailors' refusal to proceed was often associated in the contemporary press with drunkenness, many departing vessels having taken aboard well-soused crewmen. 'Lively' scenes often ensued, such as the fracas which accompanied the refusal to proceed of two seamen on the ship *Gatineau* off Saint John's Partridge Island in 1873. The men jumped aboard the steam tug and hid in the coal bunkers. They were pursued by the second mate, who drove them out of their refuge with a hose and withstood their attack until five or six of the other crewmen came to the sailors' rescue. In this particular case all the sailors eventually ended up back on board, where they were expected by onlookers to resume their usual tasks once they had 'got the liquor out of them.' A deserter who resisted an officer trying to put him on board the schooner *Ulalume* in Saint John began to co-operate when the policeman told him: 'There was an old horse about, and when men refused to proceed quietly, they were dragged along by the feet.'[32]

Desertion, leave, and refusal to proceed represented individual responses to unsatisfactory conditions of employment. Yet they were not insignificant as incipient forms of collective action. Perhaps as many as one-third of the desertions prosecuted involved two or more seamen, individuals who often had neither nationality nor language in common but who had learned to act together as short-term shipmates. For more marked expressions of collective protest, however, we must consider the other major form of extra-legal protest: the sailors' work stoppage.

Analogous to sit-down strikes by land-based workers, work stoppages were labelled by the bosses and the law as instances of refusal of duty, insubordination, disobedience, or mutiny. As a form of group protest, the suspension of work by a vessel's crew was far more common than the port strike, at least a dozen of which occurred among crews of various vessels and disengaged seamen in the streets of Halifax, Saint John, and Quebec. Moreover, as a traditional form of collective protest by seamen, work stoppages were subject to merchant shipping law which prosecuted and punished seamen more severely than the criminal law dealt with combinations of land-based workers. As workers transgressing the rigid bond of shipboard obedience, 'striking' seamen were therefore more likely than their shoreside counterparts to end up in court and in jail.

Work stoppages were sparked by a range of causes and varied in their degree of militancy. An examination follows of the four problems they addressed: human failings and personal relationships; uncertainties concerning the safety of the vessel; violation of the customary times and conditions of work; dissatisfaction with the shipping contract. We shall then give separate consideration to the characteristics of some of the most serious work stoppages: large-scale shipboard strikes or mutinies by desperate crews driven to extreme lengths.[33]

The human factors precipitating work stoppages included involuntary sickness and inebriation. Sometimes these conditions resulted in legal charges of refusal to work. When drunken crews refused to work and became obstreperous on clearing port, the ensuing rowdiness could produce serious injuries and hefty jail sentences. Other work stoppages in this category concerned such things as the sailors' lack of confidence in the master and their worries about the composition of the crew. Shortly after the brigantine *Annie* sailed from Saint John for Havana in the autumn of 1869, the captain became ill and had to relinquish his command. When the new captain joined the vessel at anchor off Partridge Island, six of the crew refused to work, 'alleging as their reason that having returned to port, their engagement was no longer binding.' The port authorities, however, considered Partridge Island outside the port of Saint John and, instead of allowing the men to go ashore to put their case to litigation, they sent aboard three policemen who coerced the crew into resuming their work. When four sailors of the *Annie Maud* were charged with disobedience after a seventy-four-day voyage from Liverpool to Saint John in 1875, the evidence indicated that their captain was incompetent: he had last commanded an ocean vessel in 1849 and that ship he had lost off Cape Clear. The complexities of this case never got aired in court; the captain had failed to read over to the seamen the charges he recorded in the official log book during the voyage. As a result he had to drop the charges.[34]

The seamen on the brigantine *Fortuna* were worried, not about the captain, but about two of their shipmates as the vessel left Halifax for Demerara in January 1883. They were so concerned about the unruliness and violent behaviour of Patrick Mullens and Michael Jones that they refused to proceed with them on board. The captain returned to port where he chose to charge only the two refractory seamen, the others being content to resume their duty once two substitutes had been hired. Similarly, the crew of the *John Givan* refused to proceed on their voyage after one of the sailors tried to stab another. The matter was resolved by discharging the assailant from the vessel. When fourteen sailors of the ship *Vancouver* were sentenced to twelve weeks in jail for refusing duty in Saint John in 1888, eleven of them took the option of returning to their vessel. Once on board the six black sailors among that portion of the crew again refused to work, resuming only after a 'little' police persuasion was applied. While no direct reasons for the behaviour of the blacks were included in the reports, it seems likely that they were in a racial minority among the crew, a situation which, we have seen, was feared by black sailors.[35]

Since seamen before the mast were not always without faults, refusal cases did sometimes arise as a result of the downright troublesome and perverse behaviour of the individual crew members. The reaction of the rest of the seamen was not always as loyal to the vessel as was the response of the crew of the *Fortuna* to their two misfits. Three cases in Halifax in the mid-1870s illustrate this point. The first concerns Bernard Hirsey, seaman on the cable steamer *Faraday*, who refused to do duty and threatened violence to the officers during the return voyage from Newfoundland. After he was placed in irons en route to Halifax, other members of the crew became 'disaffected.' Responsibility for the trouble was however blamed entirely on Hirsey, who alone was tried and sentenced to eight weeks in prison. The implication was that he was the 'ringleader' of a crew with grievances. Such a relationship was much clearer in the second example, that of Alfred Thomson of the barque *Glenralloch*. He was described as the 'spokesman' for a crew which refused to heave up the anchor and get the vessel under way. For some unspecified reason Thomson was determined not to proceed with the voyage and his shipmates stoutly supported him in his stand. His grievance became their grievance. He was beaten by the mate with a belaying pin and left the vessel at his own request on the steam tug, still exhorting the crew not to work as the vessel sailed to Liverpool. In the third case three seamen of the brigantine *Montrose* supported their fellow seaman, a Lascar (Indian seaman), who was struck by the mate when he refused to loose the jib, by stopping work and leaving the vessel, with their possessions.[36]

Cases of refusal were sometimes more specifically linked to instances of ill-treatment. Ill-treatment is a whole area for litigation on its own; here we will just make the connections relevant to work stoppages. Since mistreatment frequently involved physical force which produced an inability to work, it was an involuntary cause for withdrawal of services. A case occurred in Saint John in 1857 of a seaman who, having been struck over the head with a belaying pin by the mate on a voyage from Boston and then put in irons and kept on bread and water for four days, was expected to work in his badly injured and weakened state. His inability to do so led to a charge of refusing to do duty, which the magistrate must have considered untenable because he dismissed the case. Sailors were also known to counteract charges of refusal of duty by citing instances of physical mistreatment. Joseph Beattie, cook of the *John*, claimed that he had been abused by the mate for most of the voyage to Quebec in 1848, a plea that did not convince the magistrate, largely because of Beattie's dirty and slovenly appearance. Verbal abuse also affected work. Nine sailors of the ship *Juno* in Saint John in 1866 stopped work and became unruly because the two mates were constantly in the habit of using very provocative language to them, particularly the first mate, whom they described as a 'scoundrel' unfit to be placed over men.[37]

A second cause of work stoppages was the sailors' unease over the seaworthiness of their vessels. Sailors stopped work to protest against undermanning and insufficient ballast, but usually the complaints of crews in the wooden sailing vessels had to do with leaky conditions which threatened their safety during a long voyage. In most instances the crew's refusal to continue on the voyage was designed to force the captain to return to the nearest port.[38]

Once in port a number of things could happen. Sometimes when surveys of vessels agreed with the sailors' estimate of unseaworthiness or the articles fortuitously contained irregularities, the crews were vindicated and normally discharged. Other sailors who got the chance deserted, leaving nothing to the vagaries of local justice.[39] This is what happened in the case of the *Mary Stewart* which put into Halifax in November 1858 with deck leakage problems after having sailed from Saint John en route to Glasgow. For whatever reason, the captain chose not to prosecute his men, and after they deserted he hired a new crew which safely guided the vessel to its destination. The log of the events between Saint John and Halifax is interesting for demonstrating the reasonableness and humanity of this particular master. His rescue of the crew of a water logged American vessel succinctly demonstrates the basis for the fear of sailors on leaky vessels:

26 Oct. [At sea] 2nd mate and all seamen combined, refused to pump the ship out having 6 feet water in the hold unless I would put the ship before the wind and steer for the nearest port in the United States as the ship was not seaworthy wanting caboose and [having] leaky decks. I told them I could not do so with a cross sea running and that I considered the ship perfectly competent to continue her voyage and that everything as regards cooking and caulking the deck could be put to rights in a very short time, weather permitting. They continued of the same mind and went below and left the mate, carpenter and I to pump the ship out.

27 Oct. 4 pm. 2nd mate came to me and said that if I would say that I would put the ship back to the nearest port he could get them all to pump the ship out. I said that I wished the ship pumped out and I would go wind and weather permitting to the nearest port and half an hour afterwards they all turned to pump the ship out which they did by 11 pm one watch being sent below at 7 pm.

28 Oct. 9 am. Prepared and got the long boat out and saved nine men and the master of the American bark *Clara* from Shields to New York with coals and general cargo, 14 feet water in her hold.

29 Oct. 9 am. All hands came aft and wanted to know what I intended to do with the ship if I intend to put back or not, if not they would do no more duty. I replied I would think of it till noon.

5 pm. I called all hands aft and said I wished to come to some understanding with them that I still considered the ship fit to proceed on her voyage. They said they would not go further and when I respectively asked them to go they all refused with the same objections but they would work the ship to the nearest port.[40]

The log of the *Tara* indicates that her sailors were driven to a work stoppage in port as a last resort. They had been frustrated in attempts to take their case, relating to the unseaworthiness of their vessel, to a lawyer. On the voyage from Glasgow to Quebec most of the crew had supported one of their shipmates whose refusal to work had meant he was clamped in irons. In port most of the already disaffected crew were twice sent to prison for the offence of absence without leave, though they had requested leave to take their problems to legal authorities. Although the log is not very helpful on the point, it seems that much of the trouble was related to the pumping that was necessary, even in port. A new crew reaped the benefits: after a week of serious leakage on the way down the St Lawrence, the *Tara* returned to port to be discharged in order to discover the source of the problem. The original crew, had they but known, could have comforted themselves with the thought that the master, a doughty Prince Edward Islander, might have at last learned a lesson.[41]

More often the return to port, engineered by the crew, resulted in their arrest on charges of refusal to do duty or 'mutiny.' If solidarity was lacking among the crew, the defendants had little chance of successfully counteracting the charge.[42] Since the law tended to favour the party which took the initiative in court cases, charges of refusal to work, brought by the captain before the crew had seized the opportunity to demand a survey of the vessel, usually resulted in the sailors being convicted for their undue fastidiousness over the threat to their lives. In the case of the ship *Royal Saxon*, which returned to Saint John after sailing timber-laden for England in 1857, the dispute between the strikers and the master turned on the cause of the ten feet of water in the hold. The crew claimed the ship was leaky; the captain contended that the water had been 'shipped in a manner not unusual with heavily laden vessels in certain positions.' The magistrate believed the captain's explanation and sent thirteen sailors to the penitentiary. The editor of the *Morning News* could not refrain from a devastatingly anti-labour comment. 'Their punishment,' he wrote, 'was as mild as could be reasonably expected, and it will have the effect of teaching others besides the delinquents the danger of resorting to such conduct in future.'[43]

When the results of surveys demanded by sailor-defendants on refusal-to-work charges went against the sailors, relatively long prison sentences were meted out. Twelve crewmen of the ship *Governor Langdon* got four weeks in Quebec in 1880; four seamen of the ship *Seaforth* got ten weeks in Saint John in 1868. Fifteen crewmen, of the ship *Brunette*, whose work stoppage had caused their vessel to go aground near Digby, received twelve weeks in the penitentiary in 1864 after they had refused to accept the contention of the port wardens that the vessel was seaworthy. That same year in Halifax the seventeen-man crew of the *Excelsior* were also sent to jail for twelve weeks when the survey of the vessel bound to Liverpool from Saint John found the vessel safe. Four were reclaimed by the captain for the continuation of the voyage, while the rest, according to press rumours, were not long in jail during a busy season in the midst of the American Civil War. The crew of the ship *La Gloire*, bound for Bremen, claimed in Halifax that the ship's boats were bad and the vessel leaky, but the port warden thought otherwise, and once the magistrate was assured that the boats were in good order, the men were sent aboard and sailed for their destination. A similar decision was made by the Saint John port warden in the case of the *Flora P. Stafford* whose ten crewmen refused to work the vessel even to port. Four of the ten were allowed to languish in jail for two months while the other six were selected to be 'imprisoned' on board the vessel for the voyage to Liverpool. The Saint John port warden reached the same decision in the case of the *Vandalia*, whose crew protested that 'the vessel had a heavy list and the canvas could not be taken off her as she was heavy and therefore unseaworthy.' The captain reclaimed eleven of the dissidents for the voyage. Even in a case where the vessel, the *Edinburgh*, was proven to be unseaworthy, the ten vindicated crewmen were sent to jail for four weeks while the vessel underwent repairs.[44]

The problem with neatly categorizing sailors' protests is that it tends to oversimplify what were often extremely complex circumstances in which a number of labour grievances co-existed. An example of this complexity is provided by the *Agenora* during her visit to Quebec in 1858. Ten of the fourteen seamen stopped work on the vessel immediately on her arrival from Malta. They were sent to prison for three weeks, though their strike was apparently related to the poor conditions they had endured on the voyage out. When they were allowed back on board after two weeks in jail, they refused to join the vessel, an action which got them six weeks this time and discharge from the vessel. After clearing Quebec for Dublin, the remaining crew and the new hands stopped work on the ground that the vessel was making too much water. They forced the captain to return to port for a survey. The results of the survey, if indeed there was one, are not recorded in the log but that crew, too, was disposed of and another set of substitutes hired to work the passage to Britain. In all these changes of crew, the legitimate grievances became obscured and the possibility of securing remedies was lost.[45]

A third cause of work stoppages was infringement of the working practices to which sailors had become accustomed. It was usual, for example, for sailors newly signed-on not to go aboard to work until the vessel was on the point of clearing port. Eight crewmen of the barque *Tanmere* felt so strongly about this custom in Saint John in 1872 that they went to jail for twelve weeks rather than go aboard the vessel and get it ready for its voyage to Charleston. Ever vigilant about the observance of port hours, seamen objected to being called upon to perform duties at the whim of the master. Cornelius Outhouse refused to work on the schooner *Mower* because he was 'off watch.' For his intransigence he was beaten by the captain, a disciplinary action thoroughly endorsed by the magistrate. Seamen on fishing vessels, whose work differed in some respects from those on trading vessels, expected to be allowed to choose whether or not they fished on Sunday. In May 1883 the crew of the schooner *Elizabeth* refused to take their boats out onto the banks off Nova Scotia on the ground that it was Sunday. In court in Halifax a couple of weeks later, the magistrate upheld the rights of the seamen, the evidence clearly proving 'that the men were justified in the course they pursued, as it was entirely optional with themselves whether they should work on Sunday or not.'

The weather was always a cause for concern to seamen: at sea they had to work through fine weather and foul; in port, however, they expected to be treated like human beings rather than slaves. Six of the crew of the ship *Mary Jane* refused to clear the snow off the deck of their vessel in Saint John in February 1873 because it was raining and they had not been provided with oilskin clothing. Similarly, seven sailors of the ship *Star of India* refused to remove the snow from their deck in Halifax in January 1880 because they felt they were not getting their proper ration of bread. Too little food and too much work were the reasons for the interruption in the work of five seamen on the ship *Golconda* on the voyage from Liverpool to Halifax in 1870. Because the captain had failed to read them his charge of insubordination as recorded in the log they escaped a sentence like the six-week imprisonment passed on the crew of the *Star of India*. Overwork was also the complaint of several members of the packet ship *John Owens* who were brought to court for refusal in Saint John in 1856. The discipline on packet liners was notorious for making or breaking sailors and for producing that exceptionally hardened brand of seafarer known as a packet rat.[46]

Interruptions in work caused by legitimate grievances aroused some sympathy in port. A good illustration of the occasional disposition of the press to be hostile toward capital rather than labour is provided in a Halifax newspaper account of the work stoppage staged by six men on the barque *Moss Glen* on the passage from New York to Halifax in 1884. The seamen had been shipped in New York irregularly, and when they refused to work in that port in response to the captain's denial of permission for them to see the British consul, they were subjected to the shipboard assault of paid sluggers brought aboard to clobber them. Thereafter the badly injured men were overworked and underfed and once in Halifax they were again denied permission to go ashore to make a complaint against the master. After twenty-four hours they knocked off work.

The trial of the men on refusal-to-work charges revealed ample justification for their discharge. None the less the magistrate reached an unpopular judgment, which was designed to force the men to return to their jobs. They were sent to Rockhead prison when they stated 'they would rather go to prison for 6 months than return to the ship.' Only about a week later, however, they were taken from prison and forcibly put on board ship. As the vessel cleared for Dunkirk, the captain 'was heard to boast that he would make the b——s work their way across or starve them to death.' The editor of the *Morning Herald* condemned both the law and the law enforcement authorities.

It seems that there must be some law for doing all this – for taking men out of prison before the time is up – and sending them back to do that for which they were punished for not doing – but to laymen it looks very much like an exercise of arbitrary power and anything but justice. Seamen's counsel were not informed – indeed it was intimated that the captain would not attempt to take the men away – that other men were to be shipped in their place – otherwise proceedings would have been taken ere this to have the matter brought before the supreme court and the legality of their detention tested. The removal of the men from prison and handing them over to the captain, has all the appearance of a partizan dodge, rather than a judicial proceeding and looks like as if there were some truth in the complaint, not infrequently made, that things are sometimes worked in an underhand and tricky way at the police office.[47]

A somewhat similar attitude, even more sympathetic to labour because of the particular complaint of the sailors, was voiced by a leading organ of the denominational press in Halifax in 1877. Fiv. sailors of the barque *Pactolus* had refused to work in protest against the lack of a stove in the forecastle, an action for which they were sent to jail for four weeks. The Baptist *Christian Messenger* responded: 'We could ask if sailors were supposed to be humane beings, and unless there is something else the matter, whether this is not a case for the new society for Preventing cruelty to animals. What other men are put into a place to live without a fire when the cold is down to zero?[48]

While the men before the mast expected the observance of certain standards regarding work and rations, the proverbially abused cook expected to be allowed to pursue his calling without interference. Cooks therefore resorted to work stoppages when they were turned out of the galley. A cook named Wilson, on a barque in Halifax, was ordered out of the galley to work before the mast because the captain was dissatisfied with his cooking. He refused to accept the demotion on the grounds that he could produce certificates of competency and had been expected to cook without a sufficient number of utensils. He won his case and his discharge from the vessel but members of the crew meted out the punishment they thought he deserved by assaulting him before he left the vessel with his kit. The crew of the *George A. Holt* were more sympathetic about the fate of their cook, Alfred Morton, who refused to work at jobs about the vessel after he had been dismissed from the galley for incompetence and reduced in wages from £5 to £2 a month. He claimed he was unable to perform the duty of a seaman. He was reinstated in his job at the original wages after it had been proved in court that the sailors, on whose testimony the captain's case relied, had complained not about the quality of the cooking but about the quantity and that indeed Morton's 'cooking was as good as they had ever got on board any ship.'[49]

A fourth category of work stoppage, to protest against the violation of the contractual agreement, concerned such things as the nature of the voyage, the location of the work, and the payment of wages. The imprecision with which the articles defined the voyage was often to the advantage of the sailor, but misunderstandings were many. When five members of a brig's crew in New Brunswick waters in 1835 stopped work to protest against being taken to Dorchester rather than Saint John, they forced the captain to put into Saint John where they discovered that articles which specified discharge at a port or ports in New Brunswick did not necessarily mean Saint John. The work stoppage staged by the crew of the *Eunice Nicholas* in Saint John in 1872 was a classic plea for the recognition of sailors' rights. Like most seamen loyal to their vessel, they were involved in working the cargo but they drew the line when they were asked to pursue the loading from a timber-laden schooner alongside their vessel. As far they were concerned a schooner, woodboat or not, was an ocean vessel and it was not the vessel in which they had contracted to work. They steadfastly held out against what the magistrate decisively pronounced to be the customs of the port with a firmness which one reporter thought was 'worthy of a better cause.' Although they lost the case they demonstrated a significant measure of solidarity and 'evidently believed they were doing what is right.' In 1877 another instance of resistance to cargo-handling in Saint John found the magistrate supporting the sailors in their refusal to discharge the vessel since that responsibility was not specified in the articles.[50]

Work stoppages were sometimes precipitated by pecuniary considerations. For example, Thomas Ryan, a landsman from Limerick, worked his passage to Quebec in 1848 for two shillings a month but stopped working when he reached port. The magistrate pointed out that he had attached his signature to an agreement for a return voyage to Limerick at the two-shilling rate, but, recognizing that Ryan 'was an unsophisticated lad, fresh from the sod,' warned the captain that 'the sooner, Sir, you discharge that man, the better.' Six seamen of the steamer *Lady Head* stopped work because they alone among the crew had not been paid wages when the ship arrived in Halifax. When the captain paid them, they returned to their duty.[51]

Those seamen who were determined to avoid going or continuing on their contracted voyages often went to great lengths to expedite court proceedings which would, with luck, land them in jail rather than on board their vessels. Like other people they felt entitled to change their minds or to escape from engagements which might have been forced on them in the first place by crimps. John Bass of the *Kilblain* in Quebec in 1858 claimed that he would rather go to jail than return to work. John Garwood, carpenter of the *Indian Queen*, told the court in Halifax that he did not care what they did with him, he was 'determined not to go in the ship.' Henry Boswell and Henry Farrell, sailors of the brigantine *Nazarene*, told the magistrate in Halifax in 1876 that 'the vessel did not suit them.'

Thomas Scott of the *Lady Falkland* admitted to the Quebec magistrate that he refused to work in order to obtain a discharge from the ship, 'which was the worst he had ever been in.' William Baker and William Arnold escaped their duty on the brigantine *Edith*, shortly after it cleared Halifax for Puerto Rico in 1876, by refusing to work and being insolent and threatening to the mate. Henry McClure, seaman on board the brigantine *Sarah Carney*, similarly avoided a voyage to the West Indies by acting in a 'mutinous' manner after the vessel sailed from Halifax. His captain, fearful of the disturbance and incitement to disobedience which might occur, transferred McClure to a passing schooner with instructions to procure a warrant for his arrest.

Five seamen of the *Victory*, who refused duty in Quebec in 1848, explicitly demanded their discharge and the counsel they employed unsuccessfully tried to find irregularities in their articles which would not only acquit them of the charge but also lead to their legal discharge. The following day this ploy worked for one seaman among nine other crewmen of the *Victory* charged with refusing to do their duty. Since the articles had not been read to the seaman in question before be signed them, he was acquitted of the charge and discharged from the vessel.[52]

Whatever the cause of the work stoppage, a shipboard strike or mutiny involving the whole crew was a serious matter. In the case of large-scale stoppages occasioned by unsafe and unsatisfactory living conditions the solidarity of a crew sometimes prevented conviction and encouraged compromise. This is what happened in the case of the *Atlantic*, which was so poorly fitted out that a storm caused excessive damage to the forecastle and loss of the seamen's clothing. The difficulties between the captain and the crew were worked out before the magistrate found for the crew. In other cases the crew were favoured because of the manifold loopholes in the articles. The deal-laden barque *Gloire* had to put into Halifax after she left Saint John en route to Barbados in 1882 because the crew, worried about the unseaworthy nature of the vessel, 'had taken possession of the forecastle and threatened the lives of the officers.' With the help of three pilots from the Seal Island pilot boat *Lightning*, the officers locked up the mutineers and brought the vessel to port. Their sentence of three months' imprisonment was subsequently quashed on a legal technicality. Other mutinous crews benefited from a sympathetic ally on the bench. The work stoppage on the barque *Creole* in 1864, which occasioned her putting into Halifax after sailing from Quebec timber-laden for Belfast, was allegedly also caused by the crew's conviction that the vessel was unseaworthy. The magistrate concluded that the seamen's demand to put into port was justified, but on the ground that the captain and officers were completely intoxicated and totally unfit to discharge their duties.[53]

But in those instances where force rather than legal proceedings was likely to end mutinous behaviour, captains were not reluctant to clamp men in irons and lock them up until they had been intimidated into resuming work. Usually these shipboard conflicts saw the officers pitted against the seamen, though the work stoppage on the barque *Monteagle* out of Saint John en route to Liverpool in 1872 was led by the second and third mates. The captain avoided a trial by hiring two new mates and locking up eleven mutineers in the fo'c's'le, where it was thought they would yield 'to the persuasive influences of a dark forecastle and no grub.'[54]

The chances of conflict between officers and men seem to have been enhanced by racial considerations. At least three mutinies on vessels putting into Halifax in 1873–4 were blamed on the large proportion of blacks among the foremast hands. In the case of the *Moreland* mutiny in 1873, violence resulted in the shooting of one of the six blacks by the mate. The story of Peter Johnson, the wounded seaman, was that: 'While the vessel was off Sable Island, he complained to the captain the food supplied to the crew was small in quantity and not good, and also asked to have a friend who was then in irons released, as he was sick. The captain ordered him to work. Johnson said he could not do much for he had not had anything to eat for sometime.' It was then that the mate pumped twenty-two shots into the seaman's back. In the *Argo* mutiny in the summer of 1874, the mate's arm got broken in a scuffle with striking black sailors. The black crew which threatened the captain on the barque *Formosa* several months later were described in the press 'as an ill and hardlooking crew as have come into this port for sometime.'[55]

We have innumerable examples of consequences that occurred when crews, disenchanted with their conditions of work, took matters in their own hands either by depriving the captain of his command or by rendering his command inoperable. The *Signet*, sailing from Quebec in November 1861, carried a crew which included men who had already made an early voyage to Quebec that season and who had remained faithful after the vessel had reached Quebec from Gloucester in October. The master, however, might well have wished that the lot of them had deserted. The port stopover was characterized by considerable tension between captain and crew, particularly over the matter of the sailors' right to secure necessary personal supplies where they chose. Imprisonment for refusal and difficulties over the sailors' indebtedness to a local merchant drove a considerable wedge between the captain and the crew. The deteriorating relations were not enhanced by the crew's recollection of the outbound voyage which had taken an agonizing two and one-half months, the latter part on short rations. After leaving Quebec the crew worked, but in such a way that the navigation of the vessel was impeded. For instance, the master logged several seamen for poor steering; one of them, after being boxed on the ears, shouted: 'God blast your eyes you son of a Bitch who are you pushing.' The crew, having determined that the ship would not make it out of the river, allowed it to strike ground off Point De Monts in a tremendous gale which immediately occasioned the break-up of the vessel. Although all hands escaped, the suffering they had to endure in freezing conditions, and the loss of all their possessions, distinguish this wreck as the final protest of desperate men. Back in Quebec, the seamen defiantly refused to accept the balance of their wages decided by the arbitration of the shipping master who concluded that 'the loss of the *Signet* was caused by the mutinous conduct of part of the crew.'[56]

Those work disputes that were characterized by excessive violence were likely to end up in the superior courts.[57] Trials for murder often revealed details so lurid that the testimony became part of the Victorian seafaring lore of eastern Canada. Two cases tried in Halifax in 1866 and Saint John in 1875 continued to interest the public for years afterward. The celebrated murder of Captain Benson on the brigantine *Zero* occurred off the Nova Scotia coast in the late summer of 1865 after the vessel had loaded coal at Cow Bay, Cape Breton, and sailed for the United States. The small crew, consisting of a mate, two German seamen, a boy, and a black cook, had their grievances. Douglas, the mate, had been promised command of the vessel before it reached Cow Bay, but the captain had reneged on his promise and thereafter Douglas tried unsuccessfully to desert and, after being caught, did very little work. The two German seamen, hired in Sydney, discovered after joining the vessel that the captain intended to pay them $25 a month when they had shipped on the understanding that they would get $25 for an anticipated short run. The cook, Henry Dowcey, had undergone the indignity of being refused a berth on the vessel as a seaman, because the captain 'wanted to have a white crew,' and only after the original cook had proved unsatisfactory did he take on Dowcey, a friend of the mate's. All the members of the crew knew that the vessel was dangerously undermanned.

Douglas acted as ringleader of the dissatisfied crew. Finding himself at sea against his will, the mate encouraged the crew to take over the vessel, which they did by throwing the captain overboard. The task of stunning Benson with a belaying pin in order to facilitate his disposal fell to Dowcey, the cook, who did it out of loyalty to the mate. The crew then abandoned the plan of sailing to the West Indies but, before leaving the vessel in the boat for the shore where they separated, they knocked holes in the *Zero* in order to scuttle her. Unfortunately for them, the brigantine was salvaged and they were captured and brought to Halifax for a trial made possible when the boy, fifteen-year old Frank Stockwell, turned queen's evidence. The outcome of the supreme court trial was that Dowcey was hanged for the murder, whereas Douglas, the organizer of the deed, had his sentence commuted to life imprisonment. The ramifications were widely felt in Halifax, where the injustice of executing a black Catholic for a crime organized by a white Baptist aroused a range of racial and religious passions in a city the society of which reflected similar polarities.[58]

The other murder, on the *King Ceolric*, a new vessel en route from Saint John to Liverpool, was in itself the reason for the work stoppage by the eighteen crewmen. John Yealch was stabbed to death after the intoxicated crew became involved in a large-scale row shortly after sailing. George McNutt, a Saint John seaman, was condemned to death for the grisly murder. Since no one had actually seen him strike the fatal blow, the minister of justice commuted his sentence, and the doubts surrounding his guilt were such that he was pardoned in 1879 on the ground of sickness. His steadfast denial of his guilt and his exemplary behaviour in the penitentiary turned him into a local hero.[59]

LEGAL ACTION

Despite their frequent resort to extra-legal actions in the form of desertion or refusal to work, the latter of which sometimes assumed the proportion of violent mutinies, sailors were also the most litigious of nineteenth-century workers. The most common litigation initiated by seamen for offences against their persons concerned their ill-treatment at the hands of their captains and other officers. The editor of the *Morning News*, reviewing the complaints of seafarers in 1857, placed the responsibility for the volume of litigation squarely on the shoulders of the officers and blamed 'disorder' among seamen on the rough treatment they received at sea. He concluded that, to eliminate poor working relations between the bosses and the sailors, officers should be 'chosen by merchants for their affability and kindness of disposition.'[60] But instead of being noted for their affability and kindness, masters were notorious for such misdeeds as forcing sailors off their vessels despite the existence of the contract; clamping them in irons while in port instead of taking them to court; failing to pay them their wages; and leaving them in a port without their possessions.

Forcing sailors off vessels with the deliberate intention of leaving them behind became a noticeable transgression by shipmasters in the late 1870s.[61] The fact that sailors protested against such treatment by taking their captains to court is probably explained by a number of circumstances, including the worsening depression in shipping which made alternative engagements far less certain and the increasing sense of self-worth among sailors which was encouraged by Plimsollian reforms. When captains attempted to maintain the same high-handed, authoritarian level of control over sailors in port as they did at sea, they incurred the criticism of the courts. For example, when two seamen of the *Leonard Barry*, who had been shipped irregularly in New York, made dissatisfied noises about their lack of contract and wages when they reached Halifax, the captain accused them of intending to desert. He took them to the police station manacled and guarded by the vessel's watchman, 'who held a pistol in his hand, which he kept pointed directly at the men, all the time they were on the way.' In court the magistrate 'severely reprimanded the Captain for his unjustifiable conduct, and told him that it was an outrageous act to place manacles upon British subjects in a British port.' The Halifax stipendiary magistrate was similarly outraged in 1872 when two seamen of the Anchor line steamer *India* were handcuffed to an iron railing on their vessel in Halifax harbour after they had refused to sign articles, which they should have been asked to sign a month earlier in Ireland, and persisted instead in demanding their discharge. The seamen charged the master and third mate of the vessel with assault, a charge which was upheld in court because they had been manacled 'as a punishment ordered by the captain for disobedience of orders, not for the purpose of having them brought before the proper authorities for investigation into such a charge.' According to the magistrate, 'This was a high handed act to perpetrate after the ship had been anchored for hours in a British port.'[62]

Captains also made off with their sailors' wages. Captain Fash of the schooner *Etta* was fined forty dollars in Saint John in 1886 for paying off seaman Carlotta Taylor contrary to the Merchant Shipping Act and for attempting to defraud him of part of his wages. Fash was sent to the shipping office to settle with Taylor. Shortly after he slipped away to find the money for the settlement, his vessel was seen proceeding to sea. The master of another vessel in Saint John, the *Lizzie Burrill*, was charged by a seaman named John Campbell four years after he had been left behind in Saint John without the balance of his wages, an act which rendered the captain liable to a £100 fine. A concerned parent exposed a captain's misbehaviour regarding seamen's possessions in a letter to the *Shipping and Mercantile Gazette* in 1877. This Welshman's son had been imprisoned in Saint John for desertion and, for some reason, had not been put aboard his vessel when it sailed. The master had neglected to leave the deserter's sea chest at the jail which meant the sailor came out of prison with only the clothes on his back. Such negligence or design was patently illegal.[63]

Ill-usage was one thing; violent mistreatment supplies another dimension. The brutality of the seafaring life was well known in the nineteenth century. The editor of the Halifax *Morning Chronicle* squarely placed the blame on shipmasters and wrote at some length about the problem shortly after Captain John Michael of the brigantine *Nina*, enraged by drink and anti-Irish sentiment, shot his second mate, Daniel Duggan, through the head:

The late shooting case in our harbour, which has so narrowly escaped being instant murder, is only one of the many instances of brutal violence which are, unfortunately, too commonly to be placed to the account of merchant shipmasters. While there is no service which oftener presents examples of truly heroic courage, with regard to passengers – and even, sometimes, of attention and care with regard to the hands before the mast – it is, unfortunately, the fact that the merchant service has gained for itself an unenviable reputation for acts of brutal outrage upon the hapless and helpless crews which man it. The courts in every British and American port are continually crowded with actions for ill-usage, brought by seamen against the masters with whom they sailed. Experience has only too clearly proved that while a very small minority of these cases may be trumped up, the large majority are well founded. A merchant shipmaster is exposed by his position to all the temptations of the worst forms of tyranny. The sailor, too often leads a dog's life. Once at sea, the captain is an irresponsible tyrant. The restrictions and scrutiny, which, even in the Royal navy exist to regulate the conduct of the captain, are not supplied by anything half so effectual in the merchant service. It is true that the merchant shipmaster with an unruly crew, sometimes carries his life in his hands; but these cases are rare, infinitesimally rare, compared with the cases of brutal and wanton outrage of which the courts and the press are so often called on to take cognizance.[64]

Acts of brutality in port were generally surpassed in violence by those which occurred at sea. Offences committed at sea were normally tried at the first port at which the vessel stopped after the incident. The British shipping acts, the seamen's major protection against mistreatment, earned a reputation in Canada for being 'cruel and oppressive.' Yet nothing was done by either Britain or Canada until the early 1870s to implement effective punishment of captains and officers for ill-treatment of seamen. Until then convictions of captains and mates for mistreatment usually resulted in the imposition of a modest fine of a maximum of $20. In the 1870s offenders in the most serious cases were more severely punished as the seafaring reform movement encouraged more punitive sentences. Fines of up to $100 combined with jail sentences of up to six months became common and part of the fine could then be used to compensate the injured party. Local opinion, however, was not particularly impressed by the greater protection the amended legislation afforded sailors. The principles of the British Shipping Act of 1854, embodied in all subsequent legislation, were described by the editor of the *Quebec Mercury* as 'a pyramid of tyranny guilded [sic] by hypocrisy' and held responsible for the virtual enslavement of seamen. As a result sailors naturally preferred to protect their interests by extra-legal means rather than by submitting their grievances to the justice of the courts.

Sailors on foreign vessels could not be protected even by the inadequate Canadian or British shipping legislation unless the appropriate consul intervened. In Saint John in 1871, for example, an Irish sailor on the American barque *Calypso* sought a warrant against the captain and mates of his vessel who had beaten him without provocation on the passage from New York. Discovering that the vessel was American, the police magistrate sent the sailor to the American consul, whose co-operation was essential before a warrant could be issued.[65]

Court cases indicate that many of the sailors who were assaulted or cruelly treated clearly had experienced difficulties in carrying out their work because they were ill, a little slow or reluctant to perform their duties, or misunderstood orders because of language problems.[66] When Thomas Barrett was told to hook the mainstaysail sheet on a voyage from Liverpool to Saint John in the *Sirian Star*, he could not do it quickly because the hooks were rusty. For his slowness, he was hit by the captain and dangerously wounded with a tackle block by the over-zealous mate. Both captain and mate were convicted of assault but they did not regret their action, claiming that it was justified on grounds of the prevailing storm. The mate contended that he would have shot Barrett had he had a revolver.[67]

While the reasons for mistreatment varied widely and depended greatly on character and circumstance, some members of the crew were more likely to be seriously mistreated than others. Particularly vulnerable were boys (either green hands or cabin boys), stewards, cooks, and blacks.[68] Stewards were assaulted when the captain did not like his dinner, when the captain interfered with the steward's authority in the pantry, and when the steward would not oblige the captain by quitting the ship without his wages. Captain Penery of the *Edna M. Gregory* was convicted of aggravated assault on his steward, James Bradley, after the heavier penalties were introduced, and had to pay a fine of $100. He also gave the steward $20 by way of compensation for his injuries and paid him his wages in full for the period he was in hospital.[69]

The cook was able to maintain a greater distance from the captain than the steward or cabin boy but he also came in for his share of brutal mistreatment. Edward McIlwee was assaulted by his captain, J.F. Tucker, on the brigantine *Etta M. Tucker* while it was in the port of Saint John. The cook had succumbed to the need for an afternoon nap after over-indulging in drink.

The captain kicked and jumped on him until his whole face and part of his body and limbs were a mass of bruises. The magistrate told the captain that he could not be allowed to use his men as he would a dog; that sailors are not like other men and should be treated with a little leniency when in port, the mere fact of their getting drunk affording no excuse for such treatment of them as it was evident this man had suffered.

Alfred Butterworth, cook on the barque *Celeste*, stated in Halifax police court in 1867 that he had been punished at sea by being 'treed up' on a line between the mast and rigging with his feet off the deck.[70]

Black sailors were often mistreated in their capacity as boys, stewards, or cooks. Ebenezer Samuel, a black boy on the barque *Eunomia*, claimed that he was ill used by the officers on the voyage from Glasgow to Saint John, a charge which was not sustained because the captain countered it with an accusation of laziness. On arrival in Halifax in the summer of 1887 two black boys, Achilles Buckner and Humphrey Sawyer, charged the captain of their vessel, the Russian barque *Lyllie*, with assault. They stood a better chance than Samuel of arousing sympathy since they had been educated at a missionary school in Sierra Leone and could give more convincing evidence of ill-treatment, such as being beaten with belaying pins and rope and being forced to work non-stop night and day. Considerable dissatisfaction with the administration of justice was voiced in Quebec in 1865 when the captain and second mate of the *Jane* were acquitted in the murder trial of George Robinson, a 'Black Portuguese Pirate,' hired in Malaga. Without a body, the judge relied entirely on the interpretation of the medical evidence given by a local doctor. Ill-treatment was proved but so also was the poor health of the sailor, with the result that the officers were given the benefit of the doubt.[71]

Like Robinson, many of the sailors diabolically mistreated at sea did not live to bring charges against their malefactors. The prosecution of the officers then depended on the initiative of other crew members, as in the trial for murder of the mate of the barque *Kate Sancton* in 1883, or of the local authorities. When the attorney-general, police, and shipping master in Halifax each in turn refused to institute criminal proceedings against the captain and mate of the barque *Ivy* for the murder of seaman George Peirce in 1886, the vigilant Society for the Prevention of Cruelty brought charges against the two men.[72]

Trials for murder on the high seas frequently revealed gruesome details, but for excessive brutality it is hard to surpass the sadistic acts perpetrated by the masters charged with the deaths of two boys, one on the *Pandora* from Waterford to Saint John in 1844 and the other on the *Emma Searle* from Liverpool to Quebec in 1850. Andrew Lacey and William Ousely had similar problems. Lacey was described as being 'very filthy and disgusting in his habits'; Ousely was accused of 'a certain evil practice.' Both had to stop work because they had bowel complaints, which meant they were turned out of their quarters to suffer and defecate in the hold, being too weak to resort to the sides (the lee-bows) as was customary in vessels without sanitary facilities.

Their skin conditions, in Lacey's case ulcer-like sores, in Ousely's lesions which the captain claimed were venereal, were treated in a particularly vigorous manner. Off the Banks of Newfoundland, 'while the weather was severely cold, with ice floating about,' Captain Doyle of the *Pandora* ordered that Lacey 'be stripped stark-naked, and made one of the crew take a scrubbing brush and scour him, while the ulcers were breaking out, and running down his body in mattery streams.' While the sores were being bathed with spirits and covered with ointment, the captain allegedly 'stood over the boy with a rope, and every time he sung out or sighed from the pain the spirits caused, he would inflict a lash.' According to one witness, the master and mate of the *Emma Searle* ordered the crew to rub Ousely's face with his faeces and he was also scrubbed in cold salt water on deck at Captain Hesscroff's orders.

The results of these trials were largely inconclusive because no bodies were available for *post mortem* examination. The judge in Saint John decided that Lacey's death was caused as much by the crew as by the captain and dismissed the case against the captain. Despite the fairly clear-cut evidence in the Ousely murder trial in Quebec, the judge took into account the good character given to Captain Hesscroff and sentenced him to one month in prison. While these are two extreme cases of mistreatment, they amply demonstrate that shipboard minorities seldom gained the same legal protection as did the manly foremast hands.[73]

The civil action that sailors most frequently undertook centred on the recovery of wages. These were customarily paid in two instalments, one as an advance before the voyage began, the balance at the end of the contracted engagement. In between, customary supplies such as tobacco were doled out by the captain and sailors' families at home were sometimes provided for by allotment notes. In the course of the voyage, however, ample pretexts for wage disputes arose. Sailors laid formal complaints about their wages in three major circumstances: when, at the end of a voyage, they were denied the payment of the balance of wages; when their tally of what was owing them disagreed with that of the master or owner; or when they wanted to use a grievance over wages to obtain a legal discharge from their vessel. In addition to testimony given verbally by plaintiff and defendant, the articles were entered as evidence and often decided the case. When the sailor made his complaint, the burden of the defence fell on the captain or owner, who was not averse to entering a counter-complaint that could produce the effect of making the sailor the defendant in his own case.

The sailor's vulnerability to counter-charges was particularly obvious in the first type of case – suits brought to recover the balance of wages. Forced to make a formal complaint in order to remind the master of his non-compliance with the financial provisions of the contract, the sailor often found himself confronted with a conspiracy to deprive him of his wages. The reason was almost always the employer's unwillingness to pay a higher rate of wages. The court cases saw the captains making explicit assaults on customary practices of the ports in order to cheat crews of their balance of wages.

The captain's or owner's justification for refusing to pay the sailor his outstanding wages was usually the desertion of the sailor from his previous vessel or the vessel in question, a defence which met a mixed reception in the courts.[74] Sometimes the magistrates had to define what the court meant by desertion, in order to proceed with such cases. In a complicated case in 1849 involving four seamen who had deserted from the ship *Olive Branch* at Quebec three times in the course of the vessel's stopover and had sued for wages for the voyage from Middlesborough to Quebec after their return to London in another vessel, two of the four won their suits, for twelve pounds each, because the master had 'consented to their having their clothes, chests, and hammocks.' The magistrate interpreted this release of the sailors' property to constitute a formal discharge, despite the captain's plea that he was under duress, being threatened with the prospect of crippling delays as a result of processes instigated in the vice-admiralty court in Quebec.

A case in Quebec in 1850 for the recovery of wages by a seaman on board the vessel *Loodionah* from Liverpool via New Orleans forced police magistrate McCord to define desertion. The complainant left his vessel without permission, and when he returned ten days later to demand his clothes, the master told him to leave the vessel as he was considered a deserter. The seaman apparently went willingly without offering to resume his interrupted service. McCord summed up accordingly:

The evidence satisfies me that the complainant manifested no desire to return to his duty, but on the contrary evinced an intention of abandoning his vessel by demanding from the master his clothes. This act coupled with the previous prolonged absence of the complainant from his duty is conclusive evidence of desertion, in consequence of which the complainant has incurred the forfeiture of the wages claimed. It is with reluctance that I pronounce this judgment, because I am induced to believe that the forfeiture of so large a sum must press heavily upon the complainant, but ... feel I am promoting the interest of seamen and the trade of the port.[75]

In those cases where the desertion was proved by such documentation as the log or sailor's register ticket, the captain's refusal to pay wages was upheld and the sailor's wages were forfeited. When James

Welsh of the *Ann Kenny* sued for wages for the voyage from Quebec to London, being the balance of the £13 agreed to in the contract, the vessel's lawyer was able to produce a letter from the office of the registrar-general of seamen detailing Welsh's desertion from the *Juverna* and enclosing his register ticket. As a result Welsh forfeited his wages, the magistrate having to be satisfied with only the one penalty since Welsh was not in court on a charge of desertion.[76]

With the defendant in such cases acting as the accuser, sailors were often required to prove their innocence in order to render themselves eligible for the wages they claimed. In the late 1840s, when desertion was accepted in Quebec as a custom of the port, many seamen found themselves having to sue for their wages on return to Britain because masters and owners hoped to be able to avoid paying the contracted wages. This presented a difficulty for seamen because, until the abolition of register tickets in 1851, the British magistrates demanded the tickets as proof of regular discharge in Quebec. Although there was no legal requirement that seamen shipping in British North America possess register tickets, seamen hired without such tickets were very likely to end up forfeiting their wages.

Despite variations, the general trend was for the magistrates in the major British timber import ports to attempt from that great distance to influence the pattern of desertion in Quebec by requiring documentary proof from the sailor-complainant that he was not a deserter. Lt Brown, the British registrar-general of seamen, described the results in 1848: 'It has become the custom now for the master not to pay the crew their wages till they summons him; and upon summonsing them, if they cannot show that they were discharged from some ship at Quebec they are assumed to be deserters.' Brown went on to reveal the injustice which could be perpetrated on the sailor in these circumstances:

Upon the discharge of a Seaman the master gives him up his registered ticket. The magistrate requires that it shall be shown that the registered ticket was given up to the man in Quebec at his discharge before he will make an order for his wages. I think that that is straining the law to a great extent, because the man may have entered in Quebec without being a deserter. He may have come from some other port.[77]

Some magistrates were more willing than others to base their judgments on inference rather than legal proof. Justice Ballantine of the

Thames police court in London was one magistrate quite content to believe that the seaman was guilty unless he could prove his innocence. In a suit for wages by eight seamen of the barque *Canton* in 1847, which was resisted on the ground of desertion, Ballantine met his match in the sailors' counsel, a solicitor named Hodgson. Hodgson insisted that the contract was sacred and the balance of wages for a voyage from Quebec to London must be paid regardless of how the sailors happened to be recruited for the vessel. He deplored the way in which 'every mean artifice was adopted to deprive seamen, who shipped for high wages, of their hard earnings.' The seamen had shipped in Quebec for twelve pounds a month and their counsel argued that their manner of getting to Quebec to take advantage of this wage rate was irrelevant. 'If they came down from the skies,' he contended, 'it was no matter to him or any one else, if they had performed their part of the contract.' It seemed to Hodgson to be particularly nefarious that masters could be permitted to ship men in Quebec without ascertaining their status only to deny them their lawful wages in London on the ground that they were deserters. Hodgson was then forced to use his trump card, in order to encourage the magistrate to proceed with the cases rather than wait for various documentary evidence to arrive. He threatened to take the case to the court of admiralty, a course of action which was as much feared by shipowners and agents in England on account of the costs it would entail as were processes in the colonial courts of vice-admiralty in the British North American ports. As a result only three of the eight cases were postponed. Testimony revealed that the ship's agent had attempted to get out of paying the legitimate wages of at least two of the men by encouraging them to take one pound and thereby avoid being charged with desertion.[78]

A similar case in Plymouth that same year involved five seamen of the barque *William Bromham*. One obtained his wages immediately because he was a Dane with no previous experience in the British mercantile marine and another admitted to being a deserter, an admission the magistrate accepted without documentary proof, which meant the seaman forfeited his wages. The owners, however, offered to give the deserter part of his pay in recognition of their appreciation of his honesty. A third man admitted to being a deserter of some years' standing from the Royal Navy, while the two remaining seamen were unable to prove that they were not deserters from merchant vessels in Quebec. The three doubtful cases were adjourned for ten days, the magistrate being unwilling to countenance a longer postponement on the ground, put forward by the sailors' counsel, that the men would be without subsistence until their wage claims were settled.[79]

Justice Yardley of the Thames police court also worried about the inability of sailors without wages to await the arrival of documentary evidence. When John Gillingham, seaman of the ship *Argyle*, sued for wages earned in a voyage from Quebec to London in 1848, the likelihood of his being a deserter was so firmly established (he verbally admitted the fact to the clerk to the registrar-general of seamen) that Justice Ballantine would probably not have objected to dismissing the case, arguably a more humane course than waiting for evidence. Yardley however agreed with the sailor's lawyer that the man could not be deprived of his wages on the mere assertion that he was a deserter. Legal proof was required. In the mean time, Yardley required the owners to pay the wages into the court, from whence they would be given either to Gillingham, or, if he was proved to be a deserter within a week, to the owners of the vessel which had lost him by desertion and to the Seamen's Hospital Fund as required by law. The magistrate refused to delay the case longer than a week, because in a recent case of a similar nature which he had postponed for a month the two seamen had been put to 'great inconvenience and distress' and one of them had been compelled to put to sea, leaving his wages behind. Wage cases were a gamble and the sailor might be worse off for trying to secure the pay to which he was entitled if delays impoverished him.[80]

Occasionally wage cases gave the presiding magistrate the opportunity to chastize the captain for conduct contrary to that expected of him under the provisions of the merchant shipping legislation. The bench of magistrates at Boston, Lincolnshire, adopted a protective policy towards three seamen of the brig *Richard Watson* when their master justified his refusal to pay their wages on the pretext that they were deserters. While the men had clearly deserted from their vessels at Quebec, the magistrates upheld their claim and called the master's contempt of the contract fraudulent and disgraceful. They threatened to charge him with shipping deserters unless he immediately paid the complainants their eight pounds each. Justice Ballantine, who did not hesitate to penalize deserters, also thought that shipmasters did nothing to discourage the desertions which produced the wage cases. Commenting during the hearing of a wage case brought by a sailor of the *Juliet* for wages from Quebec to London, a case which the sailor won by convincing the court he had been recruited from the American merchant marine, Ballantine upbraided the captain:

I think the masters are as much to blame as the seamen. A vessel goes out to [sic] England with a crew at wages of £2.5s. or £2.10s. per month, and they all desert on reaching Quebec or some other port in our American colonies, for the purpose of obtaining high wages. The master of another ship, whose crew have also most probably deserted, receives them, and gives them £13 per month, and they are never asked for their register tickets or their certificates of service and discharge. You have no business to ship seamen without their tickets of discharge, unless they are Americans or foreigners.[81]

Conniving at desertion was another misdeed of captains. In Halifax in 1869 the crew of the *Evening Star* deserted and then, after the vessel was repaired, signed on again. When the captain refused to pay their wages on arrival in London because they were deserters, the magistrate ruled that the master had condoned the desertion by doing nothing to prevent it. He should have taken them to court in Halifax on a desertion charge. The sailors therefore were awarded their wages. In another case in Saint John in 1874, the master had withheld the wages of seamen hired on a monthly basis on the ground that the seamen would then desert. The magistrate would give no cognizance to this argument and insisted that the sailors' wages should be paid at the end of each month.[82]

While owners attempted to avoid paying wages when they mistrusted their own masters' accounts or when seamen used false names,[83] the other major defence against the payment of wages was the contention that freight (that is, profit) had to be earned before costs could be defrayed. The principle that 'freight was the mother of wages' had long prevailed, but by the 1830s it was seldom recognized as a legitimate pretext for withholding wages. Cases in 1850, after the shipwreck of the *Isabella* in the St Lawrence, and in 1876, after a schooner put back to Saint John in distress, upheld the sailor's right to his wages regardless of the financial affairs of the vessel. Similarly, the bankruptcy of the vessel provided no justification for withholding wages. Cases before the vice-admiralty court in Halifax brought by the crewmen of insolvent vessels were decided in the sailors' favour. The primacy of the sailors' lien in these cases usually meant that the vessels had to be sold to meet the sailors' demands. Sailors' rights to their wages were also upheld by the vice-admiralty court in cases of the abandonment of vessels by their owners and in those of salvage following shipwreck. When six seamen in Halifax claimed the salvaged material from the vessel *Warrior* for their wages in 1844, the defence held that the material had been sold to satisfy the vessel's creditors. The judge ruled that the wages must be paid because the seamen's lien took precedence over all other debts.[84]

Considerably more variation in both complaint and defence occurred in another type of action, brought by sailors to resolve differences of opinion between themselves and their captains or the owners over the *amount* of wages due them. The major disputes centred around deductions made by the captain; the captain's definition of the agreed wage rate; changes in wages due to disrating; or sailors' demands for additional wages. The deductions made by captains for fines, loans, and services varied greatly, the common aim being the determination to deduct all expenses they possibly could out of sailors' wages. The magistrates were generally sympathetic to the sailors in cases involving illness. In Liverpool in 1836 the master of the *Jane* was unsuccessful with his plea that he was not liable for the wages of William Cross because a replacement had been hired when Cross was injured by accident in Quebec. In Saint John in 1873 the magistrate refused to allow the master to deduct the ten dollars he had spent on medicine for the seaman-plaintiff. In the same port in 1883, the magistrate in the city court refused to allow the captain of the *Fannie L. Cann* to deduct from an injured seaman's wages expenses incurred by the detention of the vessel allegedly caused by the seaman's injury.[85]

Seamen rated as cooks frequently found themselves disagreeing with their masters over deductions. An English magistrate upheld a cook's right to the ship's fat and disallowed a deduction when the *Queen* arrived in London from Saint John in 1848. In Saint John in 1873 the magistrate disallowed the defence plea that the cook of the *Adelaide* had wasted provisions. The magistrate found also for Noah P. Williams, cook of the *Fred E. Scammell*, accused of careless cooking in Saint John in 1872. The captain deducted $6 a month from his wages to cover alleged wastage. Even if the magistrate was convinced that the cook was incompetent, he could not allow as evidence entries in the log since they had not been read over to the cook as required by law.[86]

Magistrates permitted captains to deduct amounts they had paid out in fines on behalf of seamen and amounts to cover equipment they had damaged on board ship or taken from the ship without permission. They also allowed deductions from wages to cover the time seamen served in jail during their engagements. One such deduction, from the wages of a seaman on the *Isabella*, upheld by a London magistrate in 1848, was accompanied by disallowances of three other types of deductions which the master wished to make from the wages of the same seaman. These were jail costs, broken handcuffs, and lost working time after the expiration of the jail sentence. The magistrate would not allow the jail costs incurred in Quebec, because his jurisdiction did not extend to the colonies; the cost of the handcuffs used when the seaman returned to his vessel from jail, because he claimed no unoffending British seaman should be treated in such a manner; or the lost working days, because the facts relating to the seaman's failure to work were not entered in the vessel's log.

Magistrates were also sometimes reluctant to let shipmasters capitalize on sailors' weaknesses. In Halifax in 1866, for example, the master of the brigantine *Florence* wanted to deduct from the wages of a seaman the amount paid to a replacement hired in Barbados when the seaman overstayed his shore leave and returned to the vessel incapacitated from drink. What else could the captain expect, argued the magistrate, when all the world knew that seamen given leave would get drunk and need time to recover from their excesses? Wilful leave of absence did however entail deductions, upheld by the courts, for substitutes' wages during the days lost.[87]

Seamen occasionally succeeded in resisting deductions related to seasonal and logistical aspects of their work. In the spring of 1846 a seaman of the schooner *Factor* was awarded wages by the vice-admiralty court for the winter period in which the vessel was detained by ice in the St Lawrence, though the captain claimed that he was not liable for wages during the detention. The same court awarded the crew of the *Jane* wages and cost of board for the period from the detention of their vessel by ice at Quebec to the opening of navigation in the St Lawrence. A young seaman named Frank King, who was threatened with deduction of three pounds for the transportation from his place of hiring to the place from which his vessel, the brig *John Good*, sailed, won his case in 1873 at least partly because he had acted unofficially as cook and steward on the return leg of his voyage from Sligo to Saint John. He also had the satisfaction of hearing the magistrate reprimand the captain for his shoddy treatment of the crewman.[88]

Disagreements between masters and sailors over the rate of wages could arise out of misunderstanding or attempts by the master to alter the contracted wages. A case heard in the Rochester, England, police court, involving three crewmen of the barque *Ava*, which had lately arrived at Chatham dockyard from Quebec, pitted the sailors' word against the captain's. The men claimed that they had been hired for fourteen pounds a month and that the captain had changed the articles to make it appear that they had been for the run to Britain instead of by the month. Since the voyage had taken two months, a large balance of wages was at stake. For some reason, the bench of magistrates decided to believe the sailors and awarded them the amounts they sought. Jeremiah Donovan, seaman on the schooner *Jesse Hoyt*, persuaded his captain at time of hiring to raise his wages from $20 to $25 a month and the change was recorded in the articles. When it came time for Donovan to collect his wages in Saint John, the port of discharge, the captain refused to pay the sailor more than $20 per month, a position which resulted in a wage suit.[89]

Seamen were likely to be less lucky in resisting deductions for incompetence, disability, or neglect of duty even though the magistrates were often suspicious that such charges were another artifice concocted by captains to avoid paying prevailing wage rates. The only protections a sailor had against disrating, or a lump sum deduction for a specified instance of incompetence, were the existence of some irregularity in the articles or the failure of the officers to comply with the statutory regulations for recording the relevant information in the log and informing the seaman in question of the content of the complaint.

In 1838 in Quebec four seamen of the *J.N. Bolton*, confronted with a defence based on incompetence, were awarded their full wages because the articles had been neither read nor explained to them, and their signatures had not been witnessed by the master or mate. While the magistrates understood that many poor-quality seamen had to be signed on in Quebec and Saint John where the demand was so high, they did not allow masters to take advantage of their recruits' incompetence. Three seamen of the vessel *Columbine* escaped deductions for incompetence on a voyage from Quebec to London in 1850, since the complaints had been recorded in the log book only when the ship neared the end of its voyage rather than at the time they had been provoked.

In 1856 a seaman of the ship *Monnequasi* won his wage case when it was discovered that the articles had been tampered with and that a charge of incompetence was supported merely by one late entry in the log of the voyage from Saint John to London. In Saint John in 1876 the defence of Captain William Lafferty of the brig *Alice M.* against Peter Halling's complaint failed because he had not inserted in the articles the proper printed regulations concerning the maintenance of discipline. Ships' officers also challenged deductions in their wages. In 1883 a Saint John magistrate found for mate John Kelley of the barquentine *Adria* when no mention by the captain of the alleged neglect could be found in the log. Even a Portuguese seaman in the British merchant service, who could neither speak English nor tell the stern from the bow, won his case in 1894; the entry in the log book recording the reduction in wages had not been read over to him.[90]

Magistrates insisted on their right to evaluate the quality as well as the quantity of the incompetence charges entered by the defendants. In Saint John in 1857 a defence by the owners of the schooner *Olive Branch*, based on the insubordination and failure to do duty of Edward Roach, failed to impress the magistrate because the captain was apparently a drunkard. As a result the magistrate agreed with the complainant's counsel who held that no forfeiture of wages could occur except in cases of gross insubordination and then only at the magistrate's discretion. Another seaman, Roff Ray, who had already suffered what the Saint John magistrate considered an unjust imprisonment in a Havana jail, was awarded full wages in 1873 on the ground that the magistrate did not consider his conduct on the brig *Annie Barker* sufficiently reprehensible to warrant any deduction.[91]

The cases in this category most frequently lost by seamen were those in which they had been disrated in the course of the voyage from able seaman to ordinary seaman with their full knowledge. But the failure of captains to comply with the regulations pertaining to disrating again favoured the sailors. This is illustrated by a case won by several mariners of the *Edmond* in Saint John in 1887. Although they were clearly not able seamen as they claimed, the captain delayed telling them about their disrating and the resultant reduction in their wages until three days before the vessel reached its port of discharge.[92]

Sailors also instituted wage suits from time to time to attempt to secure additional wages for duties performed either in a different capacity to that for which they had contracted or for a longer period of time. When John Tufts, seaman of the schooner *Bloomer*, sued for wages as acting cook in 1871, he was supported by his captain who disagreed with the owners' refusal to acknowledge his extra duty, which had relieved them of the cost of hiring another hand. Similarly, the boy-steward of the schooner *Victory* won his case for $5 extra a month as payment for his services as cook after the regular cook had been discharged. The sailors of the ship *James Gibb* found to their chagrin that the court refused to award them wages up to the date of the arrival of the *James Gibb* in London because they had been discharged in Plymouth en route despite the understanding that the port of discharge would be London. When James Hunter tried to obtain the full balance of wages for the run to Britain in the *Ellen Atlee*, after the vessel had been wrecked during the first night out, the court felt he was unsuccessful in establishing his claim that the failure of the sailors to fulfil their contract was owing to the negligence of the captain. Instead of being awarded $20, therefore, he received $6 for the extra duty involved in salvaging cargo.[93]

One category of seamen had virtually no chance of receiving fair or regular remuneration at the end of a voyage: the men who had performed duties without signing articles. While contracts did not always protect seamen, in the absence of such agreements, sailors' rights were usually disregarded by the courts. Two seamen shipped on board the *Rory O'More* in Quebec in 1847, but because the master's position was not then filled and 'they were shoved on board in a hurry' they did not sign the papers. Despite the fact that they had been promised £13 a month by the crimp and were able to prove their bona fides by producing register tickets and discharge certificates, the London magistrate settled their wages on the basis of an arbitrary £6 rate, much to the seamen's disappointment. Although stowaways were often placed on the articles after their discovery, they had no right to demand regular employment and probably had little idea of what would happen to them if they were not given the protection of the contract. A case in Saint John in 1866 turned on the credibility of the plaintiff and defendant. The seaman-plaintiff claimed he had been enticed aboard at Liverpool by the captain and promised a fair wage and that he had performed a seaman's duty during the voyage, statements that were corroborated by two of his shipmates. The captain-defendant, however, described him as a stowaway without rights. Without evidence of an official hiring in Liverpool, the court decided for the captain. The exploitation of stowaways sometimes masqueraded as benevolence on the part of the master. A case in point is that of Charles Stephen Coilard, a black who escaped from slavery in

Cuba, getting himself to Jamaica where he secreted himself on board the *Sinope* bound for Saint John. Coilard took Captain Brown to court in Saint John to try to recover twenty dollars for two months' service. When he discovered that he was liable to prosecution for stowing away, he forsook the suit, 'muttering to himself about the rigor of the law.'[94]

Yet another kind of wage litigation was sometimes initiated by sailors in order to obtain a discharge from the vessel. Often their rights to discharge depended on the description of the voyage. As time passed, judicial decisions, which found that the description of the voyage was too vague, had the effect of encouraging captains and shipping masters to tighten up their wording. Cases in Quebec, such as those pertaining to the *Jupiter* in 1835, the *Varuna* in 1855, the *Cambula* in 1858, and the *Golden Eagle* in 1860, indicated that a contract was not an agreement to go anywhere in the world; and that the contract should give the sailor a 'reasonable intimation of the intended voyage.' In 1874 a case before the vice-admiralty court in Quebec established that a sailor who signed articles for a voyage which subsequently and unexpectedly brought the vessel back to Quebec from Brazil and Barbados before proceeding to the United Kingdom was no longer obliged to stay by the vessel for the Atlantic crossing.[95]

Misunderstandings about the nature of the voyage or anxiety to get away from the vessel encouraged sailors to bring actions, often unsuccessfully, pertaining to the duration of their contracts, the failure of their vessels to proceed directly to the port of discharge (which was a critical factor for sailors who were paid by the 'run'), the visit of their vessels to ports which they were not expecting to enter, and their entitlement to the payment of wages before the expiry of the contract.

In their use of the articles, sailors won as wide a variety of cases as they lost. A typical suit in Saint John in 1845 resulted in the discharge and paying off the crew of the barque *Sea Nymph* because they claimed the articles had not been read over and explained to them as required by law. In an appraisal of this case a local barrister complained that the legislation encouraged perjury, and that it was indefensible that the contract should be voided 'by the non-observance of certain minor formalities,' when the shipping acts were primarily designed to secure 'a large, constant and ready supply of seamen.' But if the crew could effectively lie about the explanation of the articles, the captain, who was always more likely to be believed in any case, could successfully claim the existence of a verbal agreement with the crew in the absence of appropriate written articles. Shipmasters were known to admit that they were at fault in not observing to the letter regulations relating to articles and logs. They also failed to secure the stipulated witnesses to the signing of the contract. Five seamen of the *Hero* won their wage case in Quebec in 1864 because they had not been shipped in the presence of the British consuls in the ports of Antwerp and New York. The captain, too, had to ensure that his signature headed the crew list or the crew would gain their discharge. Sailors' contracts were also not binding on them in circumstances where the ownership or the command of the vessel changed while the vessel was in port.[96]

Wage-discharge cases could be more complex or controlled more by human considerations than the technicalities of the form and observation of the articles would imply. Two sailors of the barque *Kingston* took their master, Alex Murray, to court in Saint John in 1857 because he failed to keep his promise to pay them off, a promise made as their condition for bringing the vessel to port. They wanted to escape a master who was continually drunk and who underfed and abused his crew. Their lawyer, a man usually reluctant to plead sailors' cases, argued and won a case which he championed because of the treatment of the crew by the master.

In contrast, John Kerr, prominent in Saint John legal circles a decade and a half later, was never reluctant to plead sailors' cases and indeed earned a reputation as the 'seamen's friend.' A man of considerable integrity, he none the less knew that his fees in sailors' cases depended on his success: if he won, the master or owner paid his bill, if he lost, fees were often unrecoverable. We find him therefore taking the trouble to advice sailors against going to court in those circumstances which were unlikely to favour them. He advised William Williams, a mulatto steward on the *Julia A. Merrit*, that he would lose a wage and discharge case in which his only defence was the health of his wife, who 'had cut her hand so dangerously that he thought he could not leave home.' On failing to secure his discharge from the captain, Williams had left the ship, taking his clothes with him. This action, explained Kerr, could be interpreted as desertion. In order to avoid litigation, Kerr applied to the owners of the *Julia A. Merrit* and succeeded in persuading them to stay their proceedings against Williams for desertion. All this, according to one newspaper account, was performed without charge by Kerr.[97]

IMPORTANT

TO

SEAMEN!

DESERTIONS AT QUEBEC.

IN consequence of the inconvenience to which Ship Owners are subjected by the *Desertion* of Seamen at *Quebec*, and the extortionate Wages demanded for the return Voyage to the *United Kingdom*; the Legislative Assembly of Canada have passed an Act adopting the Provisions of the 8th & 9th of Victoria, cap. 116, the Act for

The Protection of Seamen from Crimps.

The Law comes into operation on the 1st of January, 1848. From and after that date no Seaman shall be Shipped at *Quebec*, or the Ports on the *St. Laurence*, except by the Owner, Master, Ship's Husband, or the Licensed Shipping Master, appointed for that purpose; every Seaman will be required to produce his **REGISTER TICKET** and **DISCHARGE** from his last Ship, or satisfactorily account for not producing them; and *Deserters* will incur the punishment of imprisonment and hard labour. Under these Regulations, which will be adopted in all the *Colonies*, the breach of Articles, so disgraceful to Seamen will be obviated, and a check put to the extortions now practised upon them by the *Crimps* at *Quebec*, and other Ports:—

THE LORDS OF THE ADMIRALTY

have deemed it necessary to make these Regulations public, in order that Seamen may not plead ignorance of the law, should they violate their Agreements, and thereby incur the punishment which will henceforth certainly be inflicted upon *Deserters*.

J. H. BROWN,

Registrar General of Seamen.

CUSTOM HOUSE, LONDON,
   21*st October*, 1847.

Handbill of 1847 warning British seamen about the Quebec shipping act

The ice-coated ss *Nova Scotian* entering Halifax harbour in 1882

Rescue of shipwrecked survivors of the *Reward* off Saint John in 1872

The eastern end of Champlain Street in the heart of Lower Town, Quebec

Reed's Point, Saint John, the scene of many sailortown brawls

Duke Street, Saint John, ca 1870
(seen from Germain Street, looking west across the harbour towards Carleton)

Crew of the *Agnes Sutherland*, a long-range cargo vessel of 1,134 tons, ca 1875

OPPOSITE PAGE

TOP Capt Farquhar (seated) and crew of the ss *Harlaw*,
a Halifax coastal vessel, 16 August 1895

Capt Bethel, officers, and crew of the ss *Fastnet*, with
customs official (in spotted tie), in Halifax, ca 1897

William Lord
at the peak of
his career

Drying sails and sailors' clothing in Saint John harbour

LEFT A sailing vessel, the *Paramatta*, loading timber alongside the steamship *Nether Holme* at Quebec

Cronan's wharf, Halifax

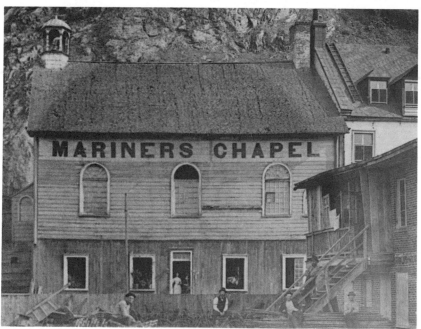

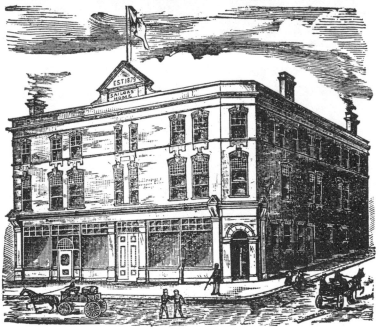

New Sailors' Home, Upper Water Street at Bell's Lane, Halifax, 1888

TOP Kent Marine Hospital, Saint John,
built in 1884 to replace the original wooden structure

THE QUALITY OF JUSTICE

Over the century sailors' wage cases revealed the changing biases of the courts and the central involvement of third parties in the process of litigation. The most significant change in the court review of wage cases was the transfer of the overwhelming majority from vice-admiralty to magisterial jurisdiction. Most sailors' wage cases before the mid-1830s in Quebec and the early 1840s in Halifax went to the vice-admiralty courts, where residual mercantilist notions made the judge the special protector of the transient, vulnerable seafarer. Because of its operation on the basis of a fee structure, from which sailors were protected by a form of legal aid, the vice-admiralty court was an expensive proposition for owners and often intimidated them sufficiently to produce a settlement with their employees out of court.

It is symptomatic of the middle-class nature of the colonial reform movements in both Lower Canada and Nova Scotia that one of the grievances was the cost of justice which accrued to merchants in the vice-admiralty courts, costs which ensured the humble sailors a fair chance of victory in their battles over wages and working conditions.[98] The vice-admiralty court also offered sailors the advantage of being able to bring collective suits, and thereby demonstrate solidarity and camaraderie, something they were unable to do in the common-law courts where their actions had to be individual ones. Moreover, suits in the vice-admiralty court could be instituted against the vessel in cases where its sale was necessary to satisfy a claim for wages. By the mid-1850s, however, the limitation of £20 for vice-admiralty wage suits introduced in the previous two decades was increased to £50, which, to all intents and purposes, meant an end to vice-admiralty jurisdiction in wage cases.

Wage cases which were resolved by summary jurisdiction were not necessarily less successful for sailors. As long as the common-law courts continued to operate on a system of fees paid to magistrates, it was in the magistrate's interest to find in favour of the sailor, because sailors defeated in court seldom had any money to pay the costs. While the shipping interests ranted and raved about the corrupt colonial magistrates, the sailors more often collected their wages from these unsalaried justices. A few statistics have survived for the 1840s and tell us something about the sailors' success rate in wage cases tried in the unreformed lower courts. In 381 wage cases tried in Quebec police court in 1846, wages were awarded in 54 cases, 167 cases were dismissed, and 160 were withdrawn. Some of the latter were undoubtedly settled out of court to the sailors' satisfaction, if what was happening in Saint John is anything to go by. In Saint John, before the appointment of a stipendiary magistrate, the magistrates' interest in the outcome of sailors' wage cases was the subject of an investigation which clearly revealed the tendency of justices, such as Benjamin L. Peters, dependent on fees, to find for the sailor-plaintiffs. An examination of the results of the wage cases tried by Peters for the three years 1844 to 1846 indicates that of the 217 cases, 76 were decided in favour of the sailors, 40 cases were dismissed, and 101 were withdrawn. Detailed information on the cases shows that 61 of the 101 withdrawn cases were decided out of court to the satisfaction of the sailor-plaintiffs. The sailors therefore won 63 per cent of their wage cases either through litigation or more often through threat of litigation.[99]

After the appointment of stipendiary magistrates, sailors were confronted with a bench which clearly favoured capital in its legal battles with labour. C. Secretan jr, a lawyer in Quebec, succeeded in reversing a judgment by Justice John Maguire against ten sailors of the ss *Ontario* in 1854 by removing the case to the superior court by means of a writ of *habeas corpus*. He was scathing in his view of the anti-labour bias of both the law and the magistrate's court. He considered that the laws, 'bad and oppressive as they are, if justly administered by public servants unbiassed by the disgraceful and hateful propensity of favouring the rich,' could be made to work relatively humanely. But in Quebec the laws were administered by the allies of 'a parcel of worthies who fatten and thrive upon the brute labour of unfortunate sailors in return for whose slavery they are ever ready to bundle them into prison without trial.' The shipowning and merchant class had become 'robbers and pilferers of seamen's wages under cover of acts of parliament passed for the express purpose of enabling them to navigate their ships "gratis".'[100]

Robbery and pillage were prominent in a number of arbitration hearings before the magistrates. Arbitration was encouraged by the threat of suits against which masters knew they could not successfully defend themselves. In 1869 the captain of the barque *Mary E. Campbell* was found to have fraudulently substituted a new set of articles to prevent the sailors from securing their wages at Saint John as had been originally agreed. In the controversial *Gladstone* case in 1870 arbitration was agreed to in order to avoid taking the matter to the vice-admiralty court, the amounts at issue being outside the jurisdiction of the magistrate's court. The evidence revealed that the captain had been trying to force four of his seamen off the vessel without their wages after a voyage in which they had received inhumane treatment at the hands of a tyrannical master. The decision of the police magistrate in this case was confirmed by a judge of the New Brunswick supreme court, and the determination of the actual awards was then handed over to the shipping master whose decision for the payment of $869.55 was legally binding on both sides under the provisions of the merchant shipping legislation. Although this case did not formally come before the courts, the Saint John lawyer John Kerr was the strategist for the sailors and received considerable kudos for his expert handling of the investigation.[101]

In the magistrate's court, where the vice-admiralty tradition of protecting the sailors was lacking, the sailor's chances of winning his case were negligible without the intervention of a third party. Lawyers such as Kerr, who protected the sailor against employer, could be acting on their own in a purely professional capacity or they could be acting as the courtroom agents of sailortown crimps. In either guise, lawyers often took up sailors' cases with enthusiasm. Charles Doherty, for example, refused to accept defeat in a rather clear-cut case in Saint John in 1872 when a sailor of the ship *Coronet* tried to recover wages after refusing to sign the articles. When the magistrate found for the captain, Doherty 'expressed his determination to carry the matter to a higher court and if need be, to the highest court in the Dominion.' The city court was apparently high enough – the judgment on this appeal was for the plaintiff.[102]

Lawyers who seem to have specialized in sailor cases did not do so out of the goodness of their hearts or because they were advocates of sailors' rights. Shipping law provided both a challenge and a livelihood. John Kerr, for instance, did not confine himself to arguing for sailor-plaintiffs and -defendants. Although he acted as counsel for captains less regularly, he could with equal effect champion their side in shipping cases. Despite the lack of any ideological commitment to the sailors' cause, his great talents and persistence as an advocate won for him the respect of the seafaring class.

Kerr knew how to play on the weaknesses of shipowners and masters. One of these weaknesses was their dependence on short port calls and the rapid transport of freight from port to port. A case in 1876 involving the American ship *Joseph Clarke* aptly illustrates Kerr's talents as a tactician. Six sailors, who had received advances of $15 each, were charged with refusal to do duty and proceed to sea. Claiming that their vessel was unseaworthy, they applied to the American consul in Saint John who ordered a survey of the vessel which found her all right. Since the men could not pay back their advances, having used the money to reimburse their boarding masters, they were unlikely to escape jail sentences for their breach of contract. Having ascertained the seriousness of the case against them Kerr questioned the nature of the survey since the ship had not been put up on blocks. A cursory survey was not, according to his intepretation of the law, a proper survey. Furthermore, if the captain was determined to go ahead with the legal proceedings, Kerr would insist that each man be tried separately. The owner, who was in port, was primarily concerned with the dispatch of the vessel but the judge decided that the vessel must stay in port to await the outcome of the case. Faced with the prospect of detaining the vessel because of the necessary court appearances of the captain for each of the six cases, the owner decided to absorb the loss sustained by the payment of $90 in advances, discharged the six obdurate crewmen, and sent his vessel to sea.[103] Men with legal training were often the only people able to sort out the complexities of sailors' contracts, hedged as they were with so many statutory provisions as well as precedents both in the port in question and in ports throughout the empire. Cases which strictly followed the letter of the law could often favour the sailor, but the inflexibilities and inconsistencies of the contractual arrangements were often unfavourable to sailors.

The forensic skill of lawyers was often joined to the interest of the crimp whose influence as the major third party intervening between sailor and shipmaster determined to a considerable extent the legal complaints brought by sailors. The regularity with which the crimp encouraged the sailor in legal actions in Quebec was summarized by an official of the British Board of Trade in 1848: 'Their practice, is, in the first place, to endeavour to convict the masters of ships arriving there of some breach of the provisions of the Merchant Seamen's Act and thus to get the men discharged. If they do not succeed in this they offer them facilities for deserting.'[104]

The crimp obviously wanted to gain control of the sailor's earned wages in addition to engrossing most of his unearned advance money, paid over as the prelude to the next shipping engagement. Litigation was therefore a necessary first step. A captain explained in 1858 how crimps enticed sailors through litigation.

In the month of June last I arrived at Quebec from Havannah, with a crew with which we had left Liverpool a few months before, at £2.10s. per month wages; but no sooner had we dropped our anchor in the St. Lawrence than we were boarded by crimps, who of course informed our men that the wages from Quebec were £10 per month, which was the case, and in the course of the next few days I received summonses from nine of the crew, claiming the balance of wages, amounting to about £11 each. This I determined to resist, as they had signed articles in Liverpool to proceed to a port or ports in the West Indies, or wherever freight might offer, and to a final port of discharge in the United Kingdom, the voyage not to exceed 12 months. This you would have thought, was binding enough: but no. The magistrate decided that the men were entitled to their discharge, and I had to pay them the full balance of their wages, together with £15 costs to their attorney. But how much of this money did the men receive? About £5 each out of their £10 or £11, as they had each agreed to pay their attorney £5, he paying them their balance in Quebec currency instead of in sterling money, and one man to whom there was £5.10s. only due, receiving 10s and the lawyer £5.[105]

The crimps encouraged sailors to go to extreme lengths, some of which bordered on the absurd, to secure their discharges. Most of the concocted cases were based on alleged violations of the crew agreement or shipping regulations. The crimps, for example, were blamed for the proliferation of suits in Quebec in the late 1840s for the non-delivery of lime or lemon juice, the anti-scurvy treatment provided for in the British statute 7 & 8 Vic, cap 112, sec 18. Sailors won fifteen of the twenty-nine lime juice cases they brought to court in 1846. Police Magistrate William McCord was 'decidedly of opinion that Limejuice regulations ought to be repealed as to vessels coming direct to these colonies,' a repeal which came into force in 1850. Until then, however, whole crews commonly complained of the captain's failure to observe the regulation, complaints which, given the absence of scurvy, were clearly designed to obtain the discharges encouraged by the crimps. Several such cases in the early summer of 1848 display the flimsy nature of the sailors' claims. In one case the sailors had not acquired their lime juice on one day about three weeks after sailing but the hearing revealed that they had not gone to collect it. In another case the men had not got their juice because they had refused to take it when it was offered. A third case which occupied two and a half courtroom hours was dismissed because the sailors had taken weekly rather than daily rations of lime juice at their own request. Their insistence that they had not received their daily dose included evidence that some of them had not obtained their allowance on the '33rd of April'![106]

Since the hand of the crimp was apparent in sailor-initiated discharge cases, it is not surprising that anti-crimping legislation seriously undermined the sailor's ability to challenge his employer. After the enactment in 1853 of the Canadian statute to prevent desertion, for example, sailors' wage cases in Quebec dropped from 128 in 1852 to 60 in 1853 to only 47 in 1854. Since crimps were recognized by the shipping interests to be the evil geniuses of sailortown, many of the emendations of maritime labour law in the middle decades of the century were aimed more at these land-based managers of sailors' labour protests than at the sailors themselves. But since crimping offences were part and parcel of shipping offences, what applied to the crimp also affected the sailor. This had serious implications when it came to changes in appeal procedures. Under imperial shipping law until 1874, a zealous lawyer could appeal a sailor's or a crimp's case to a higher court by means of a writ, usually that of *certiorari*. But the campaign to curb crimping and crimp-inspired legal actions by sailors reached a climax at the very time (1873) that the federal government finally produced its own major shipping law, the Seamen's Act. That law removed the right of appeal from all parties involved in shipping cases.[107]

Subsequently justice for sailors became far less certain. That uncertainty was demonstrated by the grossly unjust imprisonment, for absence without leave, of a sailor of the schooner *Glenera* in Saint John in 1887 by the police magistrate of Portland. The decision was allowed to stand by Justice Tuck of the supreme court who construed that appeal, even in the form of *habeas corpus*, was denied by the Canadian Seamen's Act. He argued that although the lack of appeal seemed hard in this particular case, yet it was 'very probably intended for the protection of the sailor, as the ship's master is generally in a better position than the sailor to continue litigation.' The good judge, however, totally misinterpreted the real intention of the clause, which was to reinforce the summary nature of shipping cases in order to prevent the interruption in sailing schedules caused by appealed shipping cases.

Sailors also misinterpreted the intention of the act by confusing it with the actual effect, which was to give the occupation of seafarer a second-class status in the area of the legal rights of working people. In 1891 a Halifax shipmaster, for example, deplored the failure of an 1890 amendment to the Seamen's Act which would have enabled 'the toilers of the sea to become repossessed with the same privileges as the farmer, tradesman, labourer or steamship agent.' The amendment restored *certiorari* in an attenuated form, but the debate in the Commons revealed the concern of legislators for profit rather than justice. Referring to shipping litigation, A.G. Jones, a shipowner and MP for Halifax, claimed:

Connected, as I long have been, with the shipping interests of the country, I have found it of the greatest advantage to be able to deal with these questions promptly. When sailors engage to ship on board a vessel, and which they have always done some days before the vessel is about to proceed to sea, and when, as it very frequently happens, they refuse to go on board, we can deal promptly with them by bringing them before a magistrate, and if they still refuse to go on board a vessel, he has the power to send them to gaol for a certain time. If the Act requires longer delay, and that the captain and witnesses also remain, together with the ship, until and appeal is heard, it will cause very great hardship and loss to the shipowner. If the Act contemplates that, it is one that will be strongly opposed by the shipping interests.[108]

What began, then, as an attack on crimps, ended up looking like an attack on the occupation of seafarer. Without a Canadian navy to contribute to the formulation of state marine policy and encourage greater regard for seafarers, the new federal government largely ignored the interests of the merchant marine. This belittling of the sailor's status would seem to suggest that, in less than half a century, the underlying rationale of the courts had changed. The earlier mercantilist-inspired emphasis on protecting sailors' rights had given way to a ruthless preoccupation with expediting the business of shipping as befitted the new pace of life and work in the highly competitive age of steam. During this transition the 'crimps of hell and goblins damned' vied with middle-class urban 'reformers' for the sailor's flesh, soul, and purse.[109]

5

Crimps and reformers

An examination of the rise and decline of crimping is central to an understanding of the character of sailortown. Not only was the relationship between sailors and crimps the determining factor in establishing the features of the labour market, but also most of the measures taken by government to control the supply of sailors and regulate their conduct ashore were meant to interfere with the activities of the crimps. As the reputed evil geniuses of dockside society, crimps were challenged by shipping masters and court proceedings. Their influence over sailors was contested at another level in local communities by reform elements striving to establish sailors' homes to rescue seamen from the degradation and debauchery of the crimps' dens.

The crimps who flourished in the second half of the nineteenth century were recruited principally from two groups: unofficial suppliers of seamen and boarding-house-keepers. In the days before the existence of government shipping offices, it was the legitimate business of a handful of men in each port to act as employment agents supplying shipmasters with sailors. When their activities became illegal about mid-century they became crimps ipso facto. Before the establishment of the respective government shipping offices, Patrick Comerford of Saint John and John Wilson of Quebec were two such free-enterprise sailor agents who depended, at least partly, on shipping seamen for their livelihood. Comerford was subsequently chosen as Saint John's first government shipping master. Wilson's comparable experience as a sailor-broker did not result in his appointment to the same position in

Quebec. The explanation of this divergent treatment may lie in part in their respective attitudes towards drink: Comerford was a temperance advocate, whereas Wilson was a publican.[1]

Wilson's career as a middleman in the sailor labour market was ruined by his demotion to the status of a crimp after the Quebec shipping act of 1847. He had come to Canada in 1833 to join other members of his family after twelve years' employment in an attorney's office at Gray's Inn in London. Thwarted in his intention to practise civil law in French Canada, he turned to the business of supplying sailors, a livelihood he undoubtedly combined with giving legal advice to litigious sailors. At the time of the selection of the first government shipping master (1847), Wilson found he was precluded from applying for the position because he was the keeper of a tavern. He had to disqualify himself for the same reason in 1848, when three deputies were temporarily appointed by the Quebec Board of Trade to assist Shipping Master Hawkins. One of the these deputies was a son-in-law of Wilson's, which led Hawkins to suspect a conspiracy led by Wilson, whom he described as 'a chief of the gang of crimps.'

After his tavern burned down in the summer of 1849, Wilson moved to the States and tried his hand at shipping seamen in New Orleans. Unable to resist the pull of Quebec, he returned from his seasonal domicile in Dayton, Ohio, during the summers of the early 1850s to aid owners and masters (including Gilmour and Co, according to his own account) to find seamen, an activity which put him clearly on the wrong side of the law. Hawkins prosecuted him five times for his illegal supplying of sailors; he was convicted twice. Hawkins was afraid of this accomplished and experienced labour agent and also jealous of his previous income, which he believed to have been £600 a season. Displaced from his living by the repeated prosecutions, Wilson turned his resentment into a campaign to discredit the shipping master's office. In particular he criticized its monopolistic nature and continued to do so, adding suggested remedies, to the highest government officials for at least two decades after the opening of the office. He demonstrated, at least to his own satisfaction, that he could ship men at lower wages than those prevailing at the government office. As a result, he advocated the reform, not the abolition, of the government hiring system through the establishment of three or four shipping offices, 'which would create competition and civility.' There is no reason to believe with Hawkins that Wilson was a rogue. He did not resort to the violent tactics of sailor-stealing which were more typical of the new brand of crimps. He was merely a supplier of labour and went about that business until he was squeezed out by the combined impact of the shipping office and the more ruthless crimps.[2]

Another, much larger, category of crimps was drawn from the boarding-house-keepers who supplied the sailors' economic and social requirements ashore. As late as the mid-1860s in Saint John many sailors' boarding-house-keepers were also engaged in various kinds of labouring activities or shopkeeping, particularly liquor selling, but over the next two decades more highly specialized boarding masters emerged. The boarding-houses, kept initially by dozens of small shopkeepers and workers, were the major recruiting ground for the private employment agents such as Comerford and Wilson before the establishment of government shipping offices, and the official shipping masters in Saint John and Halifax cheerfully continued to rely on them; in Quebec such reliance was bitterly resented.

The close proximity of the sailor to the boarding-house-keeper provided opportunities for both comradely and exploitative relationships. In the boarding-houses sailors, especially deserters, could be secreted, entertained, disciplined, and cajoled. Limiting the length of Jack's stay was of more concern to the boarding master than to the boarder. As long as food, drink, accommodation, and companionship were available, the sailor was content to take advantage of the hospitality. An experienced sailor with his wits undimmed by drink undoubtedly exercised some discretion in the choice of vessel and voyage he was willing to embark on at his host's behest.

For the average sailor, however, the sojourn ashore was up and new employment chosen for him when his money ran out or his credit had been used up to the extent of his advance of wages. On being placed aboard his next vessel, the sailor could depend on receiving the rate of wages maintained by the boarding-house-keepers and the largest possible advance, much of which stayed with the boarding master to pay legitimate expenses. The temptation was often irresistible, however, for the boarding-house-keepers, who lived a marginal and often seasonal existence, to exact a high rate of interest for discounting an advance note, to inflate a sailor's bill with drinks he did not consume, or to overcharge him for his seafaring kit or cheat him by leaving out essential items, the omission of which was discovered only after the vessel was on the high seas. If the sailor was at risk in the boarding-house, the boarding master also took his chances with the sailors. The debts of boarders, for example, could not be recovered by retaining their effects, which was prohibited by law. Moreover, unforeseen interference in the progress of voyages, such as shipwreck, could leave the boarding-house-keeper out of pocket because of unredeemable advance notes.[3]

Since contemporaries seem to have applied the term *crimp* to anyone who became involved in manipulating the sailor labour market, most nineteenth-century boarding-house-keepers qualified as crimps. Of all the boarding-house-keepers in Saint John late in the century, only one was considered by sailors' home reformers to be a respectable, law-abiding citizen rather than a disreputable crimp. Yet the crimps' continued activities owed much to their status as residents. Not only were they more permanent elements in sailortown than the seamen, but also they owned or rented property and exercised the right to vote. The crimps' ability to evade the law and pursue their business owed much to their successful integration within the social fabric. In both Saint John and Quebec crimps were reputed to have considerable political clout. Hawkins claimed that in Quebec the 'crimps have not only the votes, but it is a lamentable fact that they keep the polls during the election days!!' They were thought to be able to influence elections, the police, and the bench.[4] Before the 1870s they were let off very lightly in the courts when they were arraigned for infractions of the shipping law. In Saint John, for example, sailor-snatching cases were often resolved by the crimp's initiative in offering to provide suitable substitutes for the sailors who had gone missing through his efforts.

Since no man was in a position to understand the advantages and disadvantages of crimping better than the sailor, the boss crimps were often drawn from the ranks of seafarers tired of traversing the seas. Ex-sailors or resident sailors turned to crimping as a natural extension of their nautical experience. Their status in the sailortown sub-culture was probably quite high though gradations existed among the crimps themselves.

Sometimes the term *crimp* was used to describe the hired man who did the dirty work for the boarding-house-keeper. Usually referred to in sailortown literature as 'runners,' the crimps' hired hands were the men who performed – either in concert with the crimp, or, in the last three decades of the century, instead of the crimp – the act of stealing or enticing sailors. The stiffer penalties against crimping in the 1870s encouraged the sailortown bosses to supervise the manipulation of the labour market from a safe distance and leave the runners to take the 'rap.' The runners were usually seamen who had themselves only recently deserted.[5]

At the bottom of the crimping hierarchy was the lowliest runner; at the top, the well-established property owner on the waterfront. Whether the crimp was an ex-sailor or merely a product of marginal port society in which sailors were the crucial prey, he usually came from proletarian origins like the sailor. Whatever differences might have existed between crimp and sailor, they were not therefore differences based on class, and they were not based on ethnicity or race. Sailortown society was eminently adaptable to the demands of sailor-clients. We find, therefore, black crimps catering to black sailors and Norwegian crimps catering to Norwegian sailors.[6]

Because of the illegal nature of their activities, crimps did not operate wholly independently of each other. They banded together to ensure the maximum protection and success for their business; the most prominent organizational example was the Boarding House Keepers Association of Saint John. In the halcyon days of Quebec shipping, crimps there operated in gangs in order to secure a large proportion of the sailor business and conduct their raids on vessels with dispatch before the river police descended. In 1869 the ship *Home* was 'boarded by the crews of no less than seven crimping boats,' only minutes after the vessel had dropped anchor at the ballast ground. The *Monarchy* was similarly invaded by more than twenty crimps before the ropes had scarcely been made fast to the posts.[7]

The crimps considered themselves to be the masters of sailortown in much the same way as shipmasters considered themselves to be the bosses on board their vessels. For this reason, crimps exercised strict control over sailors as their property once they came ashore. Their insistence that their rights be recognized was clearly illustrated by their conflicts with captains who came ashore to look for their sailors. In these circumstances, and despite the existence of formal crew agreements, the crimp was not averse to resorting to violence against the captain to demonstrate the point. As crimps grew bolder, they began to extend their notions of property even to the vessel itself, which they began to treat as a mere extension of sailortown.

For their audacity, however, individual members of the various crimping fraternities could not entirely escape the arm of the law. Crimps were brought to court charged with a variety of offences covered by the shipping acts, the most common being harbouring deserters; taking away sailors' effects; forcibly removing seamen from their vessels; going on board ship without permission; loitering near a vessel; being found in a boat alongside a vessel. After the passage of the colonial acts establishing shipping offices, crimps were charged also with shipping seamen contrary to law and with exacting blood money or fees from captains for supplying them with sailors.

Since crimping involved the desertion of sailors, it was not uncommon to find sailors and crimps arraigned in court in connection with the same incident. The crimp's status as a resident helped to ensure that he was often acquitted, while the transient sailor bore the punishment alone for what he might have been encouraged or coerced into doing. A certain amount of public indignation resulted from the perceived injustice of punishing sailors for desertion, while the crimps who caused the desertion escaped.[8] Probably the best explanation for this outcome, however, lies in the importance given to maintaining the labour supply: the sailor was the essential commodity. It was his return to his work which was crucial to the employer, not the punishment of the crimp.

Since the real crackdown on crimping did not occur until the 1870s – a period in which the sail-based economy itself entered its long decline – the crimps or, less pejoratively, the boarding masters, remained the bosses, albeit the disputed bosses of sailortown, for the whole period under review. They acted as a major impediment to the achievement of the kind of unrestricted labour market desired by the shipping industry and the government. The degree to which crimps interfered also with the real interests of the sailors is a more contentious matter. In the discussion that follows, an attempt will be made to describe, for each port in turn, the features of crimping and the progress of the sailors' home movements as an antidote to crimping. We will conclude with an assessment of the nature of the controversial relationship between crimp and sailor.

QUEBEC

Nineteenth-century Quebec was notorious for its crimping and for its disregard of the welfare of the sailor. Its crimps became the bane of the honest sea captain, the arch-enemies of the non-resident shipowner, and the embarrassment of a commercial community which bred and protected them. Their activities increased steadily in intensity, peaking in the 1850s and 1870s in particular. Their success in evading punishment encouraged them to undertake more daring exploits for securing sailors, until their outrages brought down on their heads some of the most stringent summary legislation (the Seamen's Act of 1873) that the new federal government had yet enacted. In their resort to chicanery, force, assault, and murder, the crimps of Quebec could hold their own with their counterparts in New Orleans, San Francisco, or Shanghai.

Crimping in Quebec was caused by factors which applied equally to the other Canadian ports: the shortage of seamen; the opportunities for irregular practices encouraged by the peculiarities of the labour market, especially the advance note system; and the sailors' disposition for changing ships frequently. The shortage of labour in Quebec was so severe that it turned the seaman into a high-priced commodity whose 'arranged' desertion became the staple trade of the Lower Town of Quebec. Even without a severe and almost continuous shortage, the kind of private employment agent who emerged to facilitate the arrangements between restless sailors and the masters of under-manned vessels was not likely to be inhibited by business ethics from overstepping the bounds of legitimate brokerage. The vested interest of crimps in the shortage of supply meant that they did not hesitate to create an artificial shortage when necessary by secreting sailors in their dockside accommodations. The manipulation of the labour market attracted to it also the more disreputable elements in sailortown; their proximity to criminality could produce a particularly ruthless approach to crimping.

The sailors themselves also contributed to the prevalence of crimp-ing. Many of them wanted to leave their ships because of the treatment meted out by masters or the inadequate wages, and they were happy to seize on the alternative opportunities provided by the crimps. The familiar picture painted by establishment sources of the helplessness of sailors, whose kidnapping happened only when they had been drugged by alcohol or narcotics, is misleading. Many sailors were crimped because they wanted to be crimped. They even paid to be crimped. When a sailor told his new captain in 1849 that he needed an advance of £6.10s out of his £12 monthly wages for the two days he had been ashore, the captain asked him how he could have spent so much money in so short a time. In reply the sailor said: 'In the first place, I pay one pound for being crimped out of my ship. I then pay a pound of entrance-money to the house; and then, another pound is considered all right to treat the company. Then there is 10s. for putting me on board the other ship. The rest is spent on tobacco and grog.'[9]

The features associated with the crimping of merchant seamen were similar wherever they occurred in the world of nineteenth-century shipping. What concerns us about Quebec is why the business of crimping thrived and did so continuously during Quebec's shipping heyday. It made the Lower Town of Quebec seem to observers like a raw, frontier town in the wild American west. The two major reasons for its continuance were the connivance of almost every element in dockland and the distinctive geographical features of the port, which rendered efficient supervision of shipping and of sailortown virtually impossible.

Connivance with crimping does not seem to have been rooted in bribes or the payment of hush money. It was too deeply ingrained in society for such practices to have become necessary. Instead the regulation of the sailor market by the crimps was the accepted practice. Without resident shipowners to interfere with established procedures, dockside stood united against the half-hearted efforts by reformers to root out the perpetrators. Even the justices were considered to be allies of the sailortown bosses. The police magistrate of Quebec during one of the contentious periods of the crimp debate in the 1850s was J.I. Maguire. His critics thought they discerned a distinct connection, far from coincidental, between Maguire's previous success as a sailors' lawyer and his magisterial tendency to let off the members of the crimping establishment very lightly indeed.[10]

While the crimps were escaping punishment, the deserters were not, and the victimization of the sailor pricked the consciences of the Quebec middle class. The *Morning Chronicle* claimed in 1857 that the attempts to eradicate the problem of crimping and desertion 'punished the stranger and generally left the resident of the city unpunished.' Embarrassed by this contradiction and concerned for the reputation of the port, the local authorities tried to lay the blame elsewhere. So it transpired that the shipmasters became the scapegoats. Shipping Master Johnson explained to the imperial Board of Trade in 1869 how visiting masters allegedly used the crimping system to their own advantage:

[The crimps] can afford to give the masters a pecuniary consideration for an opportunity of inducing the crew, or part of it to desert – the master avoids paying any fee for discharge of crew; the seaman forfeits his arrears of wages [and] all the effects he may have on board and the crimp gains the advantage of boarding the sailor at a dear rate, until he can engage him on board of some other ship at a much higher rate of wages – so high that a large advance is made nominally to the sailor but in reality to the crimp, who can thus afford a pecuniary consideration to the master, for taking the men of his hands.[11]

It would be difficult to prove that shipmasters connived at crimping; but it would be unrealistic not to admit that the masters of vessels who regularly traded out of Quebec would not have adjusted themselves to the prevalence of a practice that they had demonstrably failed to stop. Their local associations, their initiative in encouraging the river police force, and their support for the government shipping office were all evidence of a preference for changing the traditions of labour supply in the port. But by the mid-1850s, with a shipping office in place and a police force in regular operation, the situation had not improved. The experience of Edward Jones, master of the barque *Honor*, demonstrates this failure:

On my arrival at Quebec, 24th July, seven of my crew deserted. I searched the house where the men boarded twice; the first time I failed in taking any of them. The next day the boarding master brought the men before me on the race course, and dared me to touch one of them. For a week I met and saw them walking the street or sitting before the door, which so annoyed me that I made a second attempt to capture them and succeeded in taking two and put them in jail till the ship was ready for sea, the 22nd Aug., when the police took them on board. I left the ship in a river boat to post some letters before getting underway, and during my absence, at 4 pm, 10 men came on board armed and forcibly took the men out of the ship, the boarding master at their head.[12]

Often faced with threats of violence by crimps and unable to exact any degree of loyalty from their crews, captains were naturally tempted to make the best of a nasty state of affairs and come to terms with reality. As a result, many captains did not pursue deserters and did not attempt to prosecute crimps. It was said at the time that it was to the captain's advantage to aid and abet the crimps, since by getting rid of the crew, the owners were saved the expense of their wages.

This complicity by masters was publicized during the crimping controversies of the mid-1850s and the early 1870s. A correspondent to the *Quebec Mercury* claimed in 1856 that 'that much abused man, the boarding master, is not the root of the evil – the shipmaster is the root of the evil.' He described a scenario in which the master indirectly but clearly gave permission for the crimping of his crew. A boarding master with whom the captain had imbibed a bottle of brandy asked: 'Captain, do you think your crew will stop by you this voyage?,' to which the captain answered: 'I wish to goodness the d——d scoundrels were gone from me now, so long as I knew nothing of it, or did not see them go; for I owe some of them about £7 a man, and that will pay any extras I may have to give a man for the run home.' The captain's integrity was further questioned in this instance by the speculation that he probably put the wages of £7 into his pocket after his crew had been crimped, the conclusion being that captains who were willing to sell their crew would not hesitate also to steal their employees' wages. By 1872, it was 'notoriously known that sea captains, when they have a "disliked" member of the crew, when there are large arrears due to their sailor, or when they have illtreated the sailors and fear punishment, permit crimps to board their vessels to steal their men, and that these very captains share in the booty.' For example, while two seamen were awaiting the court hearing of their suit against their master for their wages and discharge on the ground of the irregularity of their articles, they were 'run off by a notorious Champlain-Street crimp.' Since this kidnapping rid the master of troublesome litigation as well as the payment of the men's wages, the press concluded that the crimping must have happened at the master's request.[13]

Despite the notoriety of the behaviour of some captains towards their crews, the argument that masters encouraged the designs of crimps does not stand up to scrutiny. In those instances where compliance occurred, it was unwilling compliance and it followed the manifest failure of the local authorities to eradicate a system which had been for a long time openly criticized by associations of visiting sea captains convened for that very purpose. The attitude of a British captain, unsupported by authority in a 'British' port, may well have been: 'If you can't beat them, join them.' After all, it was getting the port work done and clearing Quebec as quickly as possible, not retaining all his crew, that remained the captain's major consideration. To the masters 'time is everything. There are ships which during the season, ply regularly between Quebec and some port in the old country; and upon the number of their trips, and the nature of their cargo, it depends whether they turn out to their owners profitable speculations or not.'[14] In these circumstances captains had to avoid delays in manning their vessels.

More important, however, it is highly questionable that the captain really saved money by getting rid of his crew. He always had to ship men at much higher wages in order to replace his deserters and financially the shipowner or charterer would be out of pocket. Moreover, sailors seldom arrived in Quebec with sufficient wages owed to them to interest a greedy master. Cases might have arisen where the traditions of Quebec provided a suitable opportunity for a captain to rid himself of a crew that he considered particularly troublesome and from which he feared mutiny or worse on the return voyage. But in general the evidence does not support a charge of willing complicity on the part of a significant number of captains. The keenness with which the government of the new dominion endeavoured to blame visiting captains for the continuance of crimping was therefore a sign of petulant self-defence in the face of mounting British criticism of crimping.[15]

Unlike the local authorities, who preferred not to interfere with the crimping that helped to sustain the economy of the Lower Town, shipmasters displayed no such reluctance. Irate, highly provoked captains often took it upon themselves to deal with the crimps, having little faith in the ability of the water police to catch the crimps or in the impartiality of the courts that tried them. In these circumstances captains were sometimes driven to violence to protect their sailor labour. The two best-known incidents of this nature in the port of Quebec involved the captain of the *Rhea Sylvia*, David Price, who in October 1854 shot to death two runners (in a party of six from Burke's boarding-house on Champlain Street) who boarded his vessel, and the captain of the *Rivoli*, Napoleon Pelletier, who in the fateful summer of 1872 killed a crimp, James Dillon, with an axe. The editor of the *Quebec Mercury* took the opportunity of the acquittal of Captain Pelletier of the charge of manslaughter to distribute the blame for crimping somewhat wider than usual. 'The past summer,' he suggested, 'should certainly be a lesson to our commercial men, for they must in a great measure be held responsible for the many acts of violence then committed; for did they not offer great pecuniary profits to keep up the traffic in seamen it is beyond a doubt that men would not run the risk of the gallows simply to serve the purposes of others.'[16]

While there was a chance that the crimp would meet his just desserts at the hands of the shipmaster, the likelihood prevailed that the shipmaster would be throttled for interfering with the business of the crimp. Captain Hawes of the ship *Sir Harry Smith* was assaulted in 1855 by a gang of eight crimps who boarded his vessel to take away the clothes of one of his crew. In 1866 Captain Moore of the ship *Transit* was beaten unconscious at mid-day in the Place d'Armes by three crimps, villains supposedly employed by a boarding-house-keeper whom the captain was prosecuting for harbouring his seamen. [17]

The problems raised by the connivance of the community and the pragmatism of the shipmasters were magnified by the geography of the port. Geographical considerations were both physical and climatic in nature. Contemporaries usually contrasted the physical features of Quebec with those of its rising competitor on the St Lawrence – Montreal. At Montreal ships docked at the wharves and could be supervised by a largely land-based river police force. Ships at Quebec, in contrast, moored in the river and in coves within a ten-mile radius of the Lower Town. It was virtually impossible to patrol that very considerable stretch of water with twenty-five water policemen and one patrol boat. The crimps learned to take full advantage of both the immunity from interception provided by the water, rowing their little boats under the very bows of the ships for the purpose of luring away sailors, and the safety afforded by the cover of darkness, prosecuting most of their business at night. Both these techniques proved to be more than enough to defeat the attempts of the police to supervise the shipping of the port. The apprehension of crimps and runners remained a hit-and-miss affair. Moreover, like most other dockside elements in Quebec, the water police (drawn themselves from seafarers) were suspected of conniving with the crimps. They were accused of living in sailors' boarding-houses, themselves keeping such boarding-houses, warning crimps of impending arrest, and resigning from the police force to follow the crimping business. Accordingly the rumour spread that 'the majority of the most successful crimps in this port were formerly employed in the River Police.' [18]

The climatic problem concerned the seasonality of shipping caused by the winter freeze-up of the St Lawrence. Boarding-house-keepers who could not make a living in winter compensated for the interruption by crimping in the summer and by leaving port on a regular basis at the close of the shipping season. A North Shields shipowner revealed an understanding of the pressures that seasonality produced: 'The Quebec season only continues during "shipping months" and the boarding-house keepers and others who depend upon the shipping for their existence or keep during the winter have to make as much of it as possible, and thus engage, either directly or indirectly, in this disgraceful system of crimping.'

The first known crimping incident of the season was usually noted by the Quebec newspapers as being as significant as the arrival of the first vessel. The report of the opening of the 1854 season was typical:

The first arrival from sea this year is the ship *Glencairn* from Glasgow with a general cargo. No time was lost in mooring the vessel to a convenient wharf for discharging her goods; and no time was lost by the crimping fraternity to hold a survey on the said ship. When at the wharf the establishment's conclusion having been come to, that, although she had gallantly made her way through almost impenetrable barriers of ice, the fatigues her crew must have undergone during such a hazardous voyage, required relaxation, and the professional fraternity of Champlainers were reported to have cast lots for the privilege of breaking cover and securing the first WOOD-COCK of the season.

The well-known migration of the crimps at the end of the shipping season induced the magistrates to reduce their prison sentences in order to expedite their removal and relieve the port, for a few months, of their troublesome presence. The seasonality of these activities meant that the attack on crimping, before 1873 at least, was never pursued with the same determination which might have been applied in a year-round port. The seasonal adaptability of crimps suggests, too, that they were characterized by a degree of shrewdness that stood them in good stead during the Quebec crimping season.[19]

Because of their historical notoriety as villains and as powerful manipulators of the sailor labour market, the crimps of Quebec deserve a place in nineteenth-century biography. While they could not publicly boast of their illegal occupation, they were far from anonymous. There may have been hundreds of them, even more if the count includes runners. English shipping interests believed there were 200 to 300 crimps in Quebec at mid-century, composed of 'the lowest characters in the city, whose whole occupation is to encourage every species of disorder and profligacy amongst the seamen frequenting the port, and to entice them to defraud their employers by desertion.'[20]

Although many of them were, like the sailors themselves, birds of passage, the crimping business remained lucrative enough to attract the same characters to Quebec, season after season, during the buoyant years of the commercial economy. One such crimp was Jim Ward, whose career serves as an instructive example of a number of the distinctive characteristics of crimping in Quebec. Ward may not have been entirely typical since his exploits were apparently world-renowned in seafaring circles of his day. Canada's best-known maritime antiquarian, F.W. Wallace, claimed: 'Ward was perhaps the most notorious crimp in Quebec and is credited with some particularly daring and reprehensible deeds. Yet, from what I can learn of this man, he did not appear personally as a criminal character to his fellow-townsmen, although few shipmasters could say a good word for him.' Wallace's assessment nicely captures the ambiguous reputation enjoyed by the crimps. By the time of Ward's death in 1891, however, a Quebec paper was willing to admit that he had 'in the palmy days of crimping here, kept a sailor's boarding house at Diamond Harbor and gained a good deal of unenviable notoriety for his wayward doings.'[21]

Like many other crimps before and after, Ward entered the business as an experienced seafarer. When he was tried in October 1856 with three others for loitering about the *Lord Metcalfe* 'lying at anchor in the river and not giving a satisfactory account of their business near the vessel,' he was identified as a seaman who was not a resident of Quebec. On this occasion he was sent to jail for one month and fined two pounds. Given the more usual resort to a straight fine at this period, Ward's stiffer sentence may indicate that he had not yet established himself as a regular member of the protected sailortown community.

Ward's conviction did, however, come at a time when all eyes in north Atlantic shipping were turned towards crimping in Quebec as a result of the revelations printed in *The Times* of London and in the *Shipping and Mercantile Gazette* by Henry Fry, shipowner and Lloyd's agent in Quebec. His condemnation of crimping, which implied that it was carried on with the connivance and to the profit of virtually every merchant and public official in the port, prompted the governor-general to demand an investigation of the matter. Ironically enough, it was conducted by John Maguire, the not-unbiased inspector and superintendent of police.

With Quebec's reputation badly sullied, local partisans leapt to the defence of their beleaguered city and counselled more severe penalties against crimps. Ward's case was reviewed in the midst of controversy by the Quebec *Morning Chronicle* and worried the editor for a number of reasons. Ward's testimony seemed to indicate that he was also acquainted with crimping in New Orleans and raised the possibility that crimping in Quebec was controlled internationally. The editor was sure that Ward would have been operating under a local bossman who might clear as much as £800 during the season, while agents such as Ward made £100 to £200 out of the illegal trade in seamen. It also looked very bad when a dangerous character such as Ward, who brandished a revolver, was given the minimum sentence. The one month in jail was justified by the magistrate, however, on the familiar ground that the accused would be released in time to clear out of Quebec for the winter season. But the maximum fine of £5 had not been inflicted, on the ground that Ward was a seaman. It was this reduction that particularly irked the editor, since the designation of seaman 'would apply to the majority of the most blood-thirsty pirates, but would be deemed a very insufficient reason for lessening the amount of their punishment.'[22]

Over the next few years Ward adjusted himself to the customs of the port and became prominent in crimping circles. In 1864, for example, we find him actively engaged like other Champlain Street crimps in kidnapping seamen, not to man vessels, but to sell to the Union army for use as cannon fodder in the American Civil War. The extent of the power of the crimping establishment was well illustrated in 1866, when several instances of Ward's business practices were cited by the Quebec collector of customs to explain to the Colonial Office in London why officials encountered so much difficulty in placing regularly discharged seamen, especially shipwrecked seamen, on vessels clearing for Britain. Ward's mode of operation revealed the extent to which shipmasters were at the mercy of the crimps. They had to submit to the desertion of a proportion of their seamen, desertions that were arranged by the crimp, and then had to accept as substitutes seamen supplied often by the same crimp at a wage rate also determined by the crimp. As a result, seamen outside the control of the crimps – those whose unemployment had not been arranged by them – had great difficulty finding jobs and the shipping master had virtually no influence over the establishment of the wage rates.[23]

The accusations of Ward's involvement in this pattern of manipulation were based on two examples. In the case of the ship *David*, Ward crimped eight of the seamen. Captain Pennington apparently knew that his seamen were with Ward, but he declined to look for them. When the deputy shipping master asked the captain to hire some discharged seamen before he shipped any deserters, Pennington refused. He claimed that the ship's owners had made a bargain with the boarding-house-keepers and he was afraid his head would be broken if he acted otherwise. He had no choice but to take his men from Ward and the other crimps.

The other case cited illustrates the crimp's influence over the shipping office. Ward was apparently in the habit of going with the shipmasters to the shipping office to make sure that the crimp's wage rate was entered on the official articles. In the arrangement of the financial terms the captain, in this instance of the ship *Simonds* of Saint John, negotiated with his prospective crewmen through Ward. When the sailors, prompted by Ward, refused to consider the shipping office wage rate of £9 for the run, and insisted on the crimp's rate of £10, the shipping master put Ward out of the shipping office. Alone with Captain Heatherington, the deputy shipping master convinced him to leave the hiring of the seamen, at £9, to the government office. Outside the shipping office, however, the captain entered into a *tête-à-tête* with Ward that resulted in the immediate return of the captain to the shipping office to demand again the £10 rate. Although the shipping master tried to dissuade the captain on the ground that he was raising the wages of the port, Heatherington claimed that he was helpless in the matter since he had been forced to engage the men from Ward at £10.[24]

Like most crimps, Ward was not averse to resorting to violence. In 1867 a seaman named O'Neil charged him with attempting to stab him with a clasp knife. The incident developed during a row in a house of which Ward was the reputed proprietor. In the newspaper account of the case, the outcome of which was not reported, Ward was described as 'a noted crimp and boarding-house keeper for sailors.' The reference to his 'reputed' proprietorship of the house in which the row occurred may indicate that Ward controlled more than one hostelry for sailors.[25]

Ward's unsavoury reputation and coercive tactics as a crimp are best illustrated by an incident involving a young seaman on the new Quebec ship *Atlantic* in 1869. The vessel left Quebec on 16 November and, as we have seen, put into Halifax on 27 November, the crew having refused to work when their living conditions deteriorated during a gale. They were supported by Halifax's stipendiary magistrate for their refusal to proceed on the voyage and had apparently been shipped in Quebec by Ward. He had supervised the signing of the articles at £7 for the run, with a £5 advance, before the impotent Quebec shipping master. One of the seamen, however, a man signed up as Thomas Cassels, absconded before Ward could deliver him on board. The substitute, chosen also by Ward, was a Liverpool boy of fifteen named Thomas Turner who, on arriving in Quebec on the steamer *Gaspé* from Pictou, entered Ward's boarding-house, was immediately 'shanghaied' and put aboard the *Atlantic* shortly before she sailed. He was told by Ward that he must answer to the name of Thomas Cassels, able seaman, but Ward would not give him Cassels's £5 advance, supplying Turner instead with one red shirt. When the boy objected, he was 'ill-used' by Ward and thereafter he was afraid to admit his identity until the crew was mustered on the way down river. The captain, on hearing his story, refused to allow the boy to return to Quebec in the steam tug. When he described his experiences to the rest of the crew, the boy discovered that Ward was considered 'the biggest rogue in Quebec.'[26]

Ward probably abandoned Quebec in the 1870s when crimping became a felony. His runners were prosecuted under the 1871 act against crimping which was a prelude to the more severe measures in the 1873 Seamen's Act. What we know about Ward's circumstances at the time of his death in 1891 make it possible to speculate about the likely direction of his subsequent career. He died in Savannah, Georgia, a major cotton port, where he had earned his living as 'a full fledged boss stevedore' and a reputation as a valuable citizen.

As we have seen, the seasonal nature of shipping activities in Quebec encouraged dockside labour and business interests to migrate seasonally to other shipping ports where they could pursue similar activities in the winter. The southern American ports of Galveston, New Orleans, Mobile, Savannah, and Charleston offered employment in cotton, and that of Pensacola, in timber. As F.W. Wallace noted, Quebeckers became important elements in the society of Pensacola, Mobile, and Savannah, at first on a seasonal basis, but by the 1880s, with the decline of Quebec, on a permanent basis. It seems very likely that Ward had been a part of that seasonal migration to the southern ports as early as the mid-1850s. Like other displaced Quebeckers of the age of sail, he eventually took up a year-round domicile. Exactly why, as a resident of Savannah, he turned to bossing cotton screwers rather than seamen, is another story, but his transition over forty years from a seaman to a crimp-cum-boarding-house-keeper in Quebec to a steve-dore in Savannah is one of the best illustrations we have of the intimate relations between these various petit-bourgeois and proletarian elements in sailortown society.[27]

While Ward may have earned a reputation as the most notorious of the Quebec crimps, other names occur just as frequently in the uniformly anti-crimp sources on which we must rely. Some of the better-known crimps operating in Diamond Harbour were Thomas O'Leary, whose activities spanned the 1850s and 1860s; Dominick

Dempsey, who flourished in the 1860s; and Thomas Harrington, who appears in Quebec sources from the 1860s to the 1880s. Violence and criminality characterized the careers of these demi-monde figures. O'Leary, better known as 'Bludgeon,' boarded vessels, harboured deserters, and helped Royal Navy seamen to desert by shipping them on foreign merchant vessels. He made a spectacular escape from a knife attack by one of the seamen he shipped on board the *Mamelon* in 1859 by seizing the end of a rope and springing overboard. Dempsey harboured deserters, crimped sailors for the Union army (he was prepared to shoot his recruits, if necessary), graced the street with his drunken presence, created a row at the shipping master's office, and in 1868 was indicted on a charge of larceny from the ship *Beverley*. Both Dempsey and O'Leary were implicated in a boarding-house affray in Champlain Street in 1864 that resulted in the death of a seaman.

Thomas Harrington was convicted of the crimping offences of loitering in a boat, going on board a vessel without the permission of the master, and harbouring seamen. In 1879 he was apprehended in his house in Champlain Street after he had taken Frederick Smith from the ship *Transit*, lying at Sillery, but he escaped punishment on technical grounds. The next year, however, he incurred one of the heavy sentences for crimping that obtained under the tougher legislation of 1873. His violent tactics were described in a 'Horrible Fight' with another Diamond Harbour crimp in 1875. They agreed to this set-to to settle a quarrel at 2 a.m. on a spring morning. After 'tearing, biting, kicking and gougeing,' both had 'their noses chewed off.' 'The whole affair,' read the press report, 'was horribly disgusting, and is reprobated by the district in which the combatants live, as debasing and brutal.'[28]

While it is impossible to unravel the hierarchy that might have prevailed among crimps, we are clearly not dealing with 'a set of rascally Jew crimps' as described by W.H.G. Kingston in 1856. There must however have been some internal organization and the widespread acknowledgment of a set of crimping rules. Certainly this was the case in Saint John, where much of the business was open and above board. In Quebec crimping remained an underworld activity, but the absence of much documented conflict of a sustained nature among the crimps themselves would seem to suggest the existence of a disciplined code of operations. The shipping master claimed in 1868 that 'crimps hold meetings to fix the rate of wages, and cause it to be understood among disengaged seamen, that any man who dares to ship on lower terms will be *fearfully beaten*, and in some cases, if the men have shipped at lower wages at the shipping office, than those decreed by the crimps, they are beset with sticks and knives in the street.'[29]

The suggestion occasionally arises that the crimping establishment of Quebec may have been controlled from outside the port, maybe from outside the country. Ward's apparent acquaintance with crimping in New Orleans was not unique in the 1850s. A letter in the *Quebec Mercury* in 1856 referred to 'those sharpers who come from New Orleans &c. during the summer months, and leave again with their pockets full of sailors' hard earnings in the fall.' Two other sailor-snatchers of the decade, Michael Redman (or Redmond) and Christopher Sheridan, were part of the New Orleans connection. Redman, thwarted in an attempt to avenge himself against a shipmaster, threatened that 'if it was in four years from this, that he would have Captain McNeil's life, that he would catch him in New Orleans or some other place.' Sheridan, who assaulted the mate of the ship *Spartan* in early June 1859, was described as a runner for a sailors' boarding-house in Champlain Street who had recently arrived from New Orleans.[30] The mobility associated with seasonality could indeed have encouraged the infiltration of alien criminal elements. But we cannot go so far as to say that a chain of command existed from the humblest runner to the most powerful crimp to the leading Quebec underworld figure to the boss of organized crime in New York or New Orleans. Rather we should acknowledge that the international nature of sailortown activities, like shipping itself, could have produced a degree of external control of Quebec's dockside.

It was more likely, however, that the chain of command led to the offices of Quebec's respectable shipping interests, particularly the shipbuilders and merchants. The editor of the *Quebec Mercury* complained in 1873: 'It is patent to those who frequent Peter Street that these crimps are in the pay of shipowners who most recklessly and unscrupulously obtain the completing of crews for their own vessels by the denuding of others.' He pointed out one way in which owners and brokers were implicated:

A crimp employed to furnish seamen, took a man to a merchant's office, a consignee, to have shipped as a seaman. The consignee, instead of giving the advance note of £6 sterling to the seaman, gave it to the crimp, who refused to give it to the seaman unless the latter paid him $10. This is of common occurrence amongst the merchants of lower town, who, in this open and direct manner assist the crimping system.[31]

With the crimps of sailortown anxious for his custom, how did Jack fare in all this frenetic kidnapping of his person and selling of his labour? The sources are too biased to permit a balanced view of the advantages and disadvantages of crimping. Reports of the disadvantages predominate and must therefore occupy most of our attention. But the possible advantages must not be lost sight of. As Ward's influence over the wage rates indicates, the crimps were often responsible for setting higher wages than those that the shipping master was willing to condone. After sailors were induced to desert by the crimps with the promise of better earnings, they joined together in a united front which drove up the wages of the port, thereby defeating the attempt of the shipping office to regulate the wage rate.[32] Admittedly, a portion, often one-half, of the run money went to the crimp in the form of an advance, most of which was not passed on to the sailor as cash. But this is not to say that Jack did not sometimes get his money's worth out of the services provided in the boarding-house. Moreover, British court cases prove that the Quebec deserter was likely to end up recovering a greater balance of wages on discharge in Britain than he would have done had he stuck to his original agreement. This undermines the contemporary argument about the disadvantageous relationship between sailor and crimp.

The effect of the higher wage rates probably affected also the wages of native sailors, though such men were few and far between in Quebec. Residents were not directly aided or intimidated by the crimps, but if there were financial benefits to be gained from the crimps' control of the sailor labour market, native sailors would have shared them. Experienced seamen, particularly those who regularly sailed on vessels in the Quebec trade, undoubtedly learned how to work the system to the maximum advantage. Inexperienced non-English- or non-French-speaking, or dissolute sailors, in contrast, would often find themselves at the mercy of what was clearly a parasitical system much open to abuse.

The disadvantages to the sailor, objectively perceived, could be very severe indeed. But some of them might not have seemed so serious to the sailor. This consideration may apply in particular to the sailor's apparent lack of control over the voyage on which he was shipped.

When he was dumped on board in an intoxicated state, he did not have the slightest notion of where he might end up in a month or six weeks. In Quebec, however, this was not a very serious consideration since the vast majority of vessels were carrying timber to British or other northern European ports. Sailors crimped in Quebec were not therefore likely to wake up and find they were on the way to Australia or South America, though seamen kidnapped for impressment into the Union army in the 1860s were in for an unpleasant surprise.

Crimping destroyed the sailor's freedom to sell his labour as he chose, interfered with the length of time he might want to spend in port, and subjected him to harsh discipline when he tried to resist the orders of his boarding master. Seamen who did not like the arrangements made by their boarding-house-keeper for their next ship might try to escape from the engagement but in so doing they exposed themselves to recapture and forcible return to the vessel chosen by the crimp.[33]

The crimps were not averse to punishing the sailor even when his failure to fall in with the plans for his disposal was not his own fault. The practice of arresting seamen in Quebec for bogus debts became a popular way of enforcing such discipline in sailortown. Although the sailor could not be held for debts owed to his boarding master, the law had nothing to say about other creditors. An affidavit sworn by seaman John Synott in 1853 revealed he was induced to leave his vessel, a coaster which traded between Quebec and St John's, in August 'by a party of shore people, with whom I was induced to get drunk and keep away from the ship and finally leave her, taking my chest, hammock &c. away with me to the boarding house of James Burke in Champlain Street,' where he was discovered by his captain and sent to jail for thirty days for desertion. When the vessel was ready to sail several days later, he was placed on board by the police; he was apparently glad to be back and sorry that he had been badly advised on his earlier course of action. A few hours later the bailiff arrived with Burke, the boarding-house-keeper, to arrest Synott for indebtedness to one Timothy White. Synott was taken from his vessel, but his irregular papers meant he was not admitted to the jail and was therefore enabled to go to the shipping master's office, where he swore that the debt of £12.10s to White was entirely fraudulent and complained bitterly about the loss of his clothing, bed, and other property which had been taken out of the vessel and impounded by the bailiff. While the captain had thereby lost his crewman, the seaman had lost his vessel and, without possessions, was left completely at the mercy of the boarding master and the bogus creditor.[34]

The disadvantages to the sailor were also likely to affect his personal safety. The violence associated with crimping is well documented and was a constant feature of life in sailortown, on the wharves, and on vessels in the harbour. At the hands of crimps and their underlings, reluctant or obstreperous seamen were beaten, stabbed, or shot; they were robbed as well as being victimized by being forced often to take the total 'rap' for their involuntary desertion. The violence had to reach fatal proportions before it stirred much excitement, but it was none the less common throughout the period. In 1857 an apprentice of the brig *Robert and George* 'was beaten in a most brutal manner by a crimp for refusing to desert from his ship.' In 1858, a crimp, John Doran, struck a seaman in the face and on the back of the head with his fists. A seaman named Andrew Wilson, of the *Royal Victoria*, was severely cut in the head by a Champlain Street runner in 1868.[35]

The year 1872, however, was a vintage one for 'crimping ruffianism.' The key to the extent of the violence, as one British Board of Trade official speculated, was the anti-crimping act of 1871. With the threat of prison sentences rather than fines now hanging over them, the crimps themselves refrained from boarding vessels, leaving that branch of the business entirely to the runners, 'men of the most ruffianly and desperate character.'[36] The brutality of the thugs illustrates the problem implicit in tighter legislation: it created worse conditions than the ones it was designed to correct. The accounts of extreme incidents that year are legion. Captain Mowlan of the ship *Redan* reported that a man armed with a revolver came on board and, having unshipped an iron belaying pin, went to the forecastle where he gagged and beat a seaman and took him from the ship by force, the crew being afraid to interfere with an armed man. The next day six sailors were forcibly removed from the barque *Asta*, at anchor in the stream, one of them, the boy, crying all the while. Three days later the boatswain of the *Becher des Ambardais* was stabbed in the thigh by three crimps as he and the third mate tried to go on board. And several days after that, a runner, Patrick Dooley, picked a quarrel with a seaman named Charles Bradford; the latter was wounded by a pistol shot.[37]

The best-known violent crimping incident in Quebec in 1872 became a *cause célèbre*. It was the early season murder of a Scandinavian sailor on the Yarmouth-registered vessel *N. and E. Gardner*, after he had refused to leave the vessel with crimps. The audacious crimps shot

Pnufs through the head and made off with his clothes and several of his shipmates. Despite broad daylight, his murderers escaped and the consequent lack of a culprit to punish for what was regarded as a most heinous crime meant that the reputation of Quebec was condemned by all and sundry, including the British government, the federal government, spokesmen for the other ports, and the local business community. Many violent incidents had occurred in the previous twenty years, but the murder of Pnufs seemed to demand a concerted attempt to end crimping once and for all. It took an incident as nasty as this one to produce effective measures against crimps.[38]

This brings us to an analysis of the ways in which crimps were dealt with by the law. On the whole, until Pnufs's murder, they were treated very lightly indeed. The sentences they received distinguished between active and passive crimping in the sense that when there was a chance that the fault and initiative might lie with the sailor instead of the crimp, the latter was merely fined. The notion of passive crimping was particularly evident in cases of harbouring deserters, the crimping offence most often brought against boarding-house-keepers. From the 1830s until the act of 1871 came into force, individuals charged with harbouring deserters were almost always fined £10 or $40. The active and violent crimping offences elicited jail sentences as well as fines. The Quebec shipping act of 1847 established a maximum sentence of three months at hard labour for incidents which involved forced desertion. Over the next twenty-five years the offences to which one- to three-month jail sentences plus a fine averaging $20 were applied included possession of seamen's clothing and loitering near a vessel or boarding a vessel. Most other crimping offences were covered by fines set out in the Canadian act of 1853. The major defect in that law, until corrected by the federal legislation of 1871, was that no imprisonment was stipulated in lieu of non-payment of fine. This meant that crimps who could not or would not pay the fine got off scot-free.[39] Furthermore, the way the defendants received the sailors' clothing and the manner in which they loitered provided them with ample means of escape under a law that was very precise when subjected to the searching eye of a sharp lawyer. Christopher Sheridan, for example, was released by means of a writ of *habeas corpus* in superior court after his conviction by Justice Maguire was found to be defective on the ground that he had not received the sailors' clothing from a 'boat' as the law specified.[40] In a notable proportion of crimping trials reported in the press, the defendants were acquitted through lack of evidence. In other incidents the crimps escaped because captains or owners failed to prosecute them. Both local comment before the 1870s and the animus subsequently reflected in the Seamen's Act of 1873 indicate that society in Quebec was really outraged by crimping incidents only when they involved gang action and violent tactics. Otherwise the illegal traders of sailors' flesh were allowed to flourish unhindered.

The Pnufs murder and several other outrageous crimping incidents in the summer of 1872 were largely responsible for the changes in the anti-crimping legislation. The Seamen's Act clearly identified the problem as a shipboard one and set out penalties of two to three years in penitentiary for persons unlawfully boarding vessels, with a more severe penalty of five years for those who went aboard vessels armed. Thereafter such persons found aboard vessels in Quebec were given these relatively long sentences, a measure which seems to have removed some of the violence from crimping. Moreover, no crimp was any longer simply fined for the less serious offences. Both harbouring and enticement cases incurred imprisonment for a period of three to nine months. The act also deprived the offender of his normal legal rights by denying access to jury, and to appeal either by *certiorari* or *habeas corpus*. For the first time the public viewed the shipping law with some concern. What had happened to the guarantees enshrined in Magna Carta?

But doubts about the excessive nature of the legislation proved unnecessary insofar as the crimps were concerned. The declining number who remained in business made sure that they removed themselves from the actual execution of the crimping and the more severe sentences were borne by the underlings whom they hired as runners. Sailors, either as runners or active seafarers, therefore again bore the brunt of the legislation. The crimps remained protected members of society, apparently so skilful in their manipulation of their runners that the latter failed to implicate the bosses. The new law, then, was apparently not designed to strike at the heart of the problem, but rather to control the excesses. The conscience of the liberal press occasionally winced at the injustice of it all. When several sailor-runners were sent to the penitentiary in August 1876, the newspapers commented:

We think it looks a little strange that all of them should have been staying in the same sailors' boarding-house, the proprietor of which would naturally be anxious to get sailors; and knowing the danger of going on board ships himself, would get strangers, who were in ignorance of the danger in which they were placing themselves, to do it. We admit the necessity of having such a law as the present one, but we think a clause should be inserted making it a punishable offence for parties inducing any sailor going on board a ship other than his own. It looks as if we wanted a Plimsoll around.

For his part, however, the minister of marine cheerfully reported in the late 1870s that the Seamen's Act was being so strictly enforced 'that masters of ships state that there is no port either in England or elsewhere where they or their crews are so well protected as in Quebec.' Since the imposition of the more severe penalties coincided with the decline of the port, the crimping establishment was probably deterred as much by economic as by legal restrictions.[41]

The crimps in Quebec certainly never had to worry about interference from middle-class reformers who, in other ports both in Canada and elsewhere, achieved a foothold in sailortown through the establishment of sailors' homes. Quebec proved to be infertile ground even for sailors' institutes and coffee-houses, though missions to seamen enjoyed some success. Two seamen's missions – one maintained by the Quebec City Mission and the other by the Church of England – had an almost continuous existence from the 1850s. Providing services in a number of languages on bethel ships and in the Mariners' Chapel, the jail, and the marine hospital, the missions maintained also some facilities in which sailors could practise temperance and read magazines or write letters, activities which were encouraged by the missionaries as alternatives to the attractions of the taverns. These missions supplied a token of concern for the sailors' welfare without producing a sailors' home movement.

Since the sailors' home movement generally derived much of its inspiration from a desire to destroy crimping, Quebec was very unusual among major nineteenth-century trading ports in its failure to establish a sailors' home. Routing out the crimps by reforming sailortown was often discussed but never aggressively pursued. The little interest there was in sailors' homes tended to be expressed by a range of urban do-gooders, ranging from clergymen through shipowners and merchants to newspaper editors, and by critics of the status quo prevailing in Quebec, especially foreign visitors and reformers in other ports.[42]

Apart from the usual interest in trying to emulate institutions which had been tried elsewhere, the motives of the sailors' few 'friends' in Quebec tended to fall into two categories. One interest was in rescuing Jack from the evils which beset him in port and endangered his morals, his health, and his pocket book. The vast majority of sailors in Quebec were, after all, strangers and incapable of avoiding the prevailing pitfalls. Instead of friends to make their stopover comfortable, they had to endure the attentions of the harpies of sailortown out to deceive, defraud, and degrade them, a fact well understood in the ports in which Quebec trading voyages originated. To Liverpudlians at mid-century, for example, the port of Quebec was 'the most conspicuously noted for the demoralization and ruin of sailors of any port in the British dominions.' While there was a realization that it would be difficult, perhaps impossible, to wean Jack away from the rum bottle, the exponents of rescue tended to be moralists who saw as part of the design a chance also to rescue Jack from himself: to do away with the drunkenness, the spendthrift habits, and the debaucheries for which he was famous. The other motive of the sailors' home advocates was to clean up sailortown, particularly the crimping dens. It was thought that by preventing the sailor's contact with the crimps, his behaviour was less likely to lead to his punishment in court for offences relating to his contract or his rowdiness. Prevention then would be more effective than punishment in reforming Jack.[43]

If the motives for establishing a sailors' home in Quebec were timely, the circumstances were not. First, Quebec was not a port of discharge for sailors. As a result, articled men stayed on their vessels or, if they deserted, they were accommodated by the crimps in sailors' boarding-houses. The few discharged sailors were not likely to have been sufficient to fill a sailors' home. This was in sharp contrast to Halifax where engagements often ended, as they did increasingly in Saint John. Second, Quebec's completely seasonal shipping militated against the formation of a voluntarily supported institution. In winter a sailors' home would have to be turned to some other purpose and no such purpose was envisaged. A third reason for the weakness of the sailors' home movement was provided by the opposition of the sailortown bosses and businessmen, the crimps and publicans who frowned on alternative forms of accommodation for sailors. In the late 1840s Thaddeus Osgood, an evangelical moral reformer, tried again and again through the medium of public meetings to convince the society of Quebec of its duty to seamen. In the end, his plans, which included a whole range of programs and services for seamen, were thwarted by the liquor interests of the Lower Town which would not countenance the prospect of temperance establishments.[44]

Yet another reason for the failure of the Quebec public to respond to the suggestions for sailors' homes made by Osgood and other outsiders was the relative weakness of the Protestant middle class. It was the members of this group who were responsible for voluntary associations which promoted amelioration and social control in urban society. The marked absence of a practical paternalism or evangelical benevolence in the Quebec community was not a reflection just of the weakness of Protestantism. It also reflected class residential patterns. In Quebec the sailortown proletariat and the Upper Town bourgeoisie lived far apart and the sub-culture of sailortown thrived in greater isolation than in either Saint John or Halifax. The distance – both physical and social – between merchant seamen and 'respectable' society in Quebec also owed much to the lack of native sailors. The kind of active benevolence that the sailors' movement needed required a degree of self-interest. In Quebec, such self-interest simply did not exist.

SAINT JOHN

Contemporaries said a good deal less about crimping in Saint John than in Quebec, and yet the features of the activity in the two ports seem to have been very similar. Sailors were relentlessly pursued by their boarding-house-keepers whose tidy profits depended on the sailors spending their wages and advances and joining the vessels chosen for them by their sailortown masters. When the sailor tried to protest or escape his 'servile bondage,' he was flouting a deeply entrenched structure of authority which enjoyed what amounted to the force of law in the local community. Undoubtedly the more permanent nature of the boarding-house establishment in Saint John (as compared with Quebec) enabled the crimps to become even better integrated into local society. To the boarding masters their own respectability was never in doubt. When his reputation was impugned by a sea captain, James Miller, Saint John's leading boarding-house-keeper, felt compelled to counter the attack in the local press by rational argument rather than on the streets with fisticuffs. Not only were they respectable, but also they were powerful, so powerful that it was not beneath the dignity of a lieutenant-governor to visit them personally in an attempt to keep them in line in the 1820s, or so the story went in 1837. They were much less frequently referred to as 'crimps' and felt exceedingly insulted when designated as such. Their social mobility may not have been any greater, but, unhampered by Quebec's seasonality, they were clearly in a better position to own property and to diversify their activities beyond the basic dockside pursuits than were their counterparts on the St Lawrence.

Certainly they did not think of themselves as law-breakers: their self-perception and degree of power in the port produced a much more open system of free-enterprise manipulation of the labour market than in Quebec. The major cause for this seems to have been that the crimps of Saint John operated in conjunction with the government shipping office in a largely co-operative manner, whereas in Quebec the shipping master openly resented the yoke of subordination to the sailortown bosses. The personnel of the Saint John shipping office were more closely acquainted with maritime pursuits (they included ex-shipmasters) and did not bring to their work predispositions against the customary supply system. Moreover, from 1864, with antecedents perhaps of a much earlier date, the boarding-house-keepers of Saint John were openly organized in an association which effectively ruled the port.[45]

The Boarding House Keepers Association was formed to provide some form of financial security for boarding masters in the face of legal interference with the customary advance note system in the early 1860s. The Saint John association adopted a procedure which antedated by some twenty years a similar one introduced in the major hiring port of Cardiff in the 1880s. Instead of yielding to the local pressure to redeem advance notes three days after vessels sailed, the association insisted on the payment of an advance in cash (what M.J. Daunton, the historian of Cardiff, calls a 'demand note'). In return the boarding masters guaranteed the delivery of their men on board ship – something that had always been necessary under the advance note system in order to enable them to cash the note but was clearly at the crimp's discretion in circumstances where the cash was already in hand.

A set of association rules was therefore needed to make sure that the boarding masters did their duty; otherwise the sailor supply system in Saint John would have deteriorated into chaos. Accordingly the association maintained very strict regulations in an attempt to earn the trust of shipmasters and shipowners and ensure its own respectability as a group of businessmen. While further research is necessary to determine how long the cash advance system survived in Saint John, it is known to have persisted beyond the implementation of the Seamen's Act of 1873, which provided for a five-day advance note. The shipping master reported in the year the act became operative: 'Up to the present time the shipowners have not combined to establish the five day notes, as directed under the Act, they paying the advance in cash to the boarding masters who, having control of the seamen, refuse to let them ship until the merchants promise to advance the cash in the same manner as before the present Act became law.' The vigour with which the boarding-house-keepers stood up to the shipowners in Saint John was a major feature of the sailortown power structure. None the less, this defiance did not stop the local authorities from calling the Boarding House Keepers Association a deplorable combination, and when the boarding masters began exacting a bonus of five dollars per seaman from the shipmasters during seasons of severe shortage of labour, the alarmists cried 'blood money' and compared Saint John to San Francisco.[46]

The association's effective control over the labour market meant that seamen were forced to ship in the capacity demanded by the crimp. Ships' logs indicate that such men often had to be disrated in the course of the voyage. When Benjamin Gritten of the *Celeste* was disrated from able to ordinary seaman after sailing from Saint John, he acquiesced readily, saying that it was the boarding master who had shipped him as an able seaman. Similarly Walter Pryce acknowledged his deficiencies as a seaman on the *Kate Troop* in 1870. When the officers noticed that he was not able to steer properly or perform the other duties of able seaman, Pryce 'was questioned as to why he shipped as such. He stated that this was but his second passage having never made a voyage. Knew himself not to be what he had shipped for, an AB, but was induced by his boarding master to sign as such to get more advance and that he did not so much [out of] regard [for] the wages as to obtain a passage to England.'[47]

The Boarding House Keepers Association, in keeping with its counterparts elsewhere, was not averse to using violence, but the effective manner in which it successfully manipulated sailors, shipmasters, and shipping masters through tact and influence meant that violence was a lot less common than in Quebec. The actual methods of shipping sailors were very similar in the two ports. The Saint John crimps set the wages, encouraged desertion with the promise of higher wages, and supplied the vast majority of seamen for ocean-going voyages. As time went on the control of the supply was concentrated in fewer and fewer hands.

When enticement or force was deemed necessary, the crimps of Saint John operated through gangs and protected themselves by employing runners to do the dirty work. In 1859 the *Reliance* was boarded by some fifteen to twenty crimps who attempted to remove the seamen by force. The deception practised on runners by the crimps, which was clear in Quebec in the 1870s, was also revealed in Saint John. In 1874 one of the four men who boarded the brig *Guide* was captured and turned out to be a mere boy who said 'that when he went to the vessel with the others he had no idea that they intended to steal sailors.' But the bosses themselves were not immune from appearances in the courts on crimping charges. They were prosecuted for offences similar to those of their counterparts in Quebec. Yet when the crack-down on crimping became possible in Saint John after 1873 through the introduction of stiffer penalties, the middle-class response was dismay that such sentences could be handed down through summary process. Whether the reaction indicates a real concern for civil rights or an acknowledgement that the punishment of crimps had always been merely *pro forma* remains open to question.[48]

The reported crimping cases in Saint John emphasize the usual theme of exploitation: the sailor's fate as a crimped sailor was seldom arranged with his approval. William McFadden, a well-known crimp in the middle decades of the century, got into minor trouble – an 'abusive language' charge – when he went on board a vessel to retrieve one of his boarders who was trying to ship against the boarding-house-keeper's wishes. But we have evidence that the crimps could also act in response to the sailor's wishes. When the brigantine *Harmony* returned to Saint John a few weeks after shipping a Saint John crew, most of the crew deserted. Augustus Delph, the young West Indian steward, also wanted to leave the vessel and he turned for help to George Blair, the sailors' boarding-house-keeper who had originally secured him the place on the *Harmony*. Blair obliged but both sailor and crimp were apprehended by the police. As an articled sailor, Delph was sent to jail for eight weeks for being absent without leave while Blair was excused only after he had agreed to pay back the twenty-six-dollar advance he had obtained from the captain of the *Harmony* when the hiring had occurred. Two other deserters were apparently more successful in 1879 when they clambered over the stern of their ship, the *Queen of the North*, and dropped into a small boat which was following in the wake of the vessel as it sailed out of the harbour. They were men who had refused to work while in port the previous week and had been sent to jail until the vessel was ready to clear. Since they were then forcibly put upon a vessel with which they were clearly dissatisfied, the chance to escape in a crimp's boat was one they eagerly embraced.[49]

The boldness of Saint John crimps may owe something to the facility with which they escaped punishment even when caught. Robert Lee of Britain Street is a good case in point. He was implicated in the June 1871 case of two deserters, a Welshman and a Dane, from the British brig *Caroline*. The sailors were apprehended in his boarding-house and in the alley-way outside and sent to jail for four weeks or until the brig was ready to sail. The captain testified that Lee had been on board his vessel for the purpose of persuading the seamen to desert and yet he got off with no more than a caution from the magistrate about harbouring deserters. The captain had apparently intended initially to charge Lee with enticement or wilfully harbouring the sailors but dropped the charge when Lee undertook to furnish the vessel with a man to replace yet a third deserter who had not been captured.

Such circumstances undoubtedly encouraged Lee to press his luck far beyond a mere defence of his behaviour. In the summer of 1873 he twice took Police Sergeant Patrick Owens to court and charged him with assault after the law officer had entered Lee's boarding-house looking for deserters. On the first occasion the policeman had apparently erred by not showing Lee his search warrant. On the other occasion, when the policeman was looking for six deserters from a Norwegian barque, he was careful to show his warrant and did not manhandle anyone in the house. At his second trial for assault, the policeman explained that 'the noise and tumult caused by the plaintiff and his wife about showing the warrant was for the express purpose of giving time for said sailors to escape by the back way.' Lee was apparently not worried that his crimping activities would get him into trouble: he was secure in the knowledge the role of the crimp in Saint John was taken for granted.[50]

An earlier example of the audacity of boarding-house-keepers is provided by John Fitzgerald, who was fined twenty pounds in 1860, 'the full penalty for harbouring and secreting a seaman.' He had openly gone about his business, frequently visiting the barque *Mary Anne* despite the prohibition of the master, and had told the master 'plainly he meant to steal his sailors.' A well-known late-century boarding-house-keeper, John Richards, blatantly refused to deliver up the clothes of one of his boarders, Olaf Olsen, who was confined to jail for desertion from the barque *India*. The sailor apparently owed Richards money, and it was only when the insistent creditor was threatened with a charge of enticement, which carried a three-month prison sentence, that Richards agreed to give up Olsen's clothes. Luckily for Richards, the purpose of the action had been to regain the belongings for the sailor, not to punish the crimp.[51]

Some of the rights claimed by the crimps of Saint John resembled pre-industrial notions of customary justice. For example, crimps could be relied on to act with considerable chagrin when their plans were thwarted. Daniel Costigan, another active boarding-house-keeper, was abruptly halted in his work aboard the *Queen of the North* in 1879 when the watchman made him a prisoner. For whatever reason, the watchman did not hold his man until the captain returned on board and when Costigan got on shore, without his quota of deserters, he 'pelted the ship with stones, deal ends, or whatever he could find moveable.'[52]

The best-known nineteenth-century crimp in Saint John was James Miller of Germain Street, the boss of sailortown, who was the number-one supplier of seamen for vessels leaving the port. Described as a member of the sailortown aristocracy, Miller, known locally as 'Spud Murphy,' owned by the early 1870s a first-class residence in the lower cove area. Despite his prominence and undoubted influence in the sailor supply business and as a property-owner in sailortown, Miller was implicated over the years in the kind of crimping activities and violent relations with sailors that might be expected of *lumpen* elements in dockside society. Even when he was clearly the leader in the field, he continued to be intimately involved in the mechanics of crimping, including the violence.

Miller's career raises an important question about the status of the sailortown bosses. How could his claim to respectability be upheld when his tactics were so disreputable? The answer seems to be that it was his power, not his respectability, that determined his secure position in society. Miller's respectability was entirely a matter of self-perception. His influence, in contrast, was obvious every time he was brought face to face with the forces of law and order, because he was always able to arrive at some accommodation which answered the needs of the labour market. In Saint John the crimps were forgiven their occasional outrages, outrages which continued to characterize society at the bottom, because their general utility as 'employment agents' was widely recognized and the customs of that business were deeply embedded in the fabric of everyday life in sailortown.

The information on Miller's career in the 1870s, 1880s, and 1890s in Saint John reveals three kinds of violent or semi-criminal activities. The first type was straightforward crimping. In August 1873 Miller was implicated in a crimping attempt aboard the American vessel *Annie Camp*. We know about this incident only because the accompanying violence resulted in an assault charge against the first mate for shooting one of the crewmen. The affray occurred after Miller pulled alongside in a boat, undoubtedly looking for sailors to entice. He made contact with the crew and tried to engage their interest by offering them tobacco, something they had been without during the month-long voyage from Liverpool. The court case, which resulted in the acquittal of the mate, did not deal specifically with the attempted crimping, though the magistrate remarked that he knew that 'no boarding-house-keeper would take the trouble of nearing a vessel for the purpose of giving sailors tobacco.' He also 'expressed his regret that there was no reciprocity between the British and American governments in this matter so that crimps, who board vessels as soon as they arrive in port might be arrested and severely punished.'

In 1878, in another crimping incident, Miller was caught on the barque *Orontes* by the captain in the act of assisting an articled seaman to carry off his clothes. Despite the contempt he expressed at the time of his capture for both the shipmaster and the magistrate, he avoided imprisonment by supplying the vessel with another seaman. By 1893 Miller had become involved in crimping sailors from Norwegian vessels, a more dangerous enterprise than looting American vessels, because Norway and Britain had a reciprocal agreement covering shipping matters. He arranged for the desertion of two of the crew of the barque *Ararat* and supplied them to the *Orontes*, a vessel well known to him. After the Norwegians were apprehended, Miller was arrested on a charge of inducing them to desert, but it never reached the court because he paid a lawyer to settle the matter. Miller get off scot-free except for the court costs.[53]

Second, Miller's relations with his sailor clients were by no means pacific. He may have used his influence to escape the repercussions of crimping; he used his knife, his fists, and his feet to establish his dominance over Jack. In 1879 he was in court for stabbing a sailor, but the sailor failed to appear to prosecute. Ten years later he was committed on a charge of brutal assault on a Norwegian sailor in his boarding-house. Apparently he had refused to give the sailor twenty-five cents of the $17.50 advance in wages that he held to cover the costs incurred and as security for the Norwegian's fulfilling his new shipping engagement. Miller's acquittal demonstrates the difficulty the stranger had in establishing the credibility of his story against that of the resident, no matter how notorious. The same consideration applied in the trial of Patrick Fitzgerald, a seafarer who was accused of assaulting Miller at Reed's Point in 1874. Fitzgerald was found guilty, to which he responded that 'justice was all on the side of the boarding masters in this city.' Indeed if Miller was typical of the generality of Saint John boarding masters, we have conclusive evidence that the legal interference with crimping in Saint John was minimal.[54]

The lack of effective interference was certainly not related to the orderly way in which the business of enticement, boarding, and shipping sailors was conducted. For a third feature of Miller's activities relates to disorder in his boarding-house, presumably a typical sailortown hostelry. Included among the customary activities of sailors in these houses was fighting with their fellow boarders, and while the boarding master may have intervened to preserve the tranquility of his house, it does not seem likely that his authority in his house was as dominant as the authority of the master aboard ship. Whether or not the boarding-house-keeper turned a blind eye to what went on, he went to some lengths to try to avoid unfavourable publicity. Miller, for example, tried to cover up two violent incidents in his house in 1890 and 1891: he did not succeed in these cases; over the years he may have been more successful with others. In 1890 a sailor died in his boarding-house after he had been thrown down the stairs. The next year a drunken row in the house resulted in the serious stabbing of another sailor.[55]

Disorderly dockside activity in Saint John does not seem to have produced the same degree of reaction as at Quebec. Saint John society and the absentee shipowners and charterers who used the port appear to have learned to live with crimping and its attendant influences. They did not go out of their way to provoke the crimping establishment by trying to mount effective opposition. Their major initiative in this direction produced the Boarding House Keepers Association which thereafter ruled sailortown. In the 1870s the attempt by the shipping establishment to break the back of the association was singularly unsuccessful. The surprising lack of a shipowners' association, in a port which contained sufficient owners to maintain such an organization, seems to suggest that the status quo operated sufficiently in the interests of the commercial community to discourage it from a serious attack on the prevailing labour supply system.

Moreover, the citizens of Saint John were not subjected to the same degree of hostile comment from critics of crimping as were those of Quebec. In the 1840s and 1850s, for example, the persistent condemnation of the irregularities in the sailor labour markets of the timber ports made by the London *Shipping and Mercantile Gazette* was only infrequently directed towards Saint John. A shipmaster's letter of 1851 that described the 'sharks and their minions on the beach of St. John (N.B.), with a curse on their victim, hurrying him into the boat to be conveyed to the ship' was the exception, not the rule. The greater involvement of British shipowners in Quebec at that period helped to protect Saint John against the acquisition of an equally bad reputation.[56]

Increasingly thereafter, fewer non-resident shipowners were using the port of Saint John, and the local owners undoubtedly had links with past practices, including crimping, that made accommodation possible in the New Brunswick port. Here no group of shipowners ever organized a water police force to supervise the misdoings of the sailortown population. Various parties in Saint John were well aware of the existence of river police in Quebec and Montreal and occasionally alluded to the lack of such a force in Saint John, but that is as far as the matter went. Unabashed laissez-faire continued to predominate in Saint John. Indeed, if there was a lesson to be learned from the Quebec experience, it was that the greater the interference, the more serious the nature of the crimping incidents.

The Saint John shipping master understood the advantages of the easy-going arrangements. 'Crimping exists to a considerable extent,' he reported in 1870, 'but neither shipowners or agents make any effort to recover the men, their indifference having a tendency to keep wages down, while more stringent measures would induce the boarding masters to secrete the men in the country until the sailing of the ship they were taken from. This would create a scarcity, and wages would go very high.' Accordingly a suggestion by Saint John's Board of Trade in 1883 – that shipowners had been negligent in prosecuting crimps and needed to hire a trouble-shooter to undertake prosecutions on their behalf – fell on deaf ears. A similar reluctance to prosecute crimps is discernible in the tendency of Saint John magistrates to avoid passing the harsh sentences for crimping set out in the federal Seamen's Act of

1873 by claiming that they lacked jurisdiction over offences that appeared to have been transformed from the status of misdemeanours to that of felonies.[57]

In Saint John, however, considerably more interest than in Quebec was aroused in the idea of reforming sailortown rather than punishing its denizens. The interest took the form of an intrusion into sailortown of the so-called sailors' friends – missionaries, businessmen, and middle-class women – whose major enthusiasm was the establishment of a sailors' home. Saint John shared with Halifax two major periods of heightened activity in this regard, the first in the middle part of the century, the second towards the end of the century, reflecting to some extent the respective moral and social reform movements in urban society.

In its call for a sailors' home in 1844, the grand jury seemed primarily concerned with securing the sailor 'from all temptations to vicious indulgence to disturb the peace or violate the laws.' By 1846 plans for a home had been launched with a wide range of support from merchants, and the project received even a grant from the legislature. The merchants who backed the proposed establishment professed to be worried about 'the loose morals and degraded habits of Seamen,' particularly as 'a considerable part of the expenses of Police and administration of Justice have arisen from the disorders in Society caused by this class of men.' But the overriding idea seems to have been that the home would separate the sheep from the goats, that only the moral, steady seamen would board in the sailors' home, that indeed dissolute characters would be denied accommodation. The segregation would provide in one location a pool of first-class sailor material for hiring and would therefore become the favoured recruiting ground for masters and owners. Segregation, then, not reform, was the primary objective. Given the sailor's propensity for drinking ashore, abstinence was another goal of the planners of the 1840s.

The depression of the late 1840s delayed the implementation of the scheme until 1853. Then the home opened its doors only with the help of further funds from the New Brunswick government. It probably did not interfere with the boarding-house-keepers' control of the labour market and it clearly did interfere with the drinking habits of its boarders. It went bankrupt in 1857. Subsequently the backlash against the Bording House Keepers Association produced some noises about the desirability of a sailors' home to which all non-resident seamen should be compelled to go, but no sailors' home was attempted again until 1890, the interim activities of the Mariners' Friend Association, established in 1864, being entirely missionary in character.[58]

By the end of the century, middle-class women had become deeply involved in rescue work and reform movements in Saint John. Yet prospects for extending their efforts to include merchant seamen were not very promising. The Women's Christian Temperance Union had already tried and failed to sustain a combined coffee room and reading room for sailors. Its failure did not deter a woman named Mary Hutchinson who, with her father's money and the examples of Halifax, St John's, and Montreal before her, built a 'palatial' sailors' home on St James Street, which was centrally heated, lighted by gas, and endowed with running hot and cold water and indoor wcs. Hutchinson hoped that the home would become self-supporting. She refused to conduct any public campaigns to support the institution at its inception or to save it from an early demise. She welcomed the voluntary help of the women who formed the Ladies' Seamen's Friend Society in 1891, but the assistance of a handful of women was an insufficient mainstay. Moreover, despite warnings against running a 'straight-laced home, with a gospel meeting every evening,' Hutchinson would not compromise her principles in order to attract greater business. When it became clear by 1894 that the home could not pay its running expenses, its doors were closed after an existence of only four years. Not enough public support could then be encouraged by the seamen's friends to take over this private venture.[59]

The Saint John boarding-house-keepers were probably not unduly perturbed by the initial establishment of the Hutchinson home, which accommodated about forty men. But by 1892, the home had begun to act as a minor source of supply for the shipping office, the attraction for shipmasters being cheaper sailors, since Mary Hutchinson required no blood money. This incursion into the sacred realm of the boarding-house-keepers demanded a vigorous response. They adopted a 'boycott' whereby they refused to provide seamen for any vessel that engaged a proportion of its men from the sailors' home. As a result, shipmasters discharged their sailors' home recruits. Lack of prospects for shipping through the home in turn discouraged the patronage of sailors. The boarding masters, however, graciously provided alternative boarders for the home: they encouraged Hutchinson to take in 'sick and broken-down sailors' from their houses – 'their own wrecks,' as it were – who required charity and would be unable soon to re-enter the sailor labour market. The reformers persisted in believing that the boarding-house-keepers viewed 'a home where sailors are induced to remain sober, where they are persuaded and assisted to bank their money or to send it to their families and where seamen are protected from thieves and gamblers, and loose women and rum, as a menace and an offence.'[60]

While the boarding-house- and tavern-keepers had a vested interest in an unreformed sailortown, the attitude of the shipping interests towards sailors' homes changed from one of support to one of indifference. The active involvement of shipowners, builders, and merchants was prominent in the ventures in Saint John in the 1840s and 1850s. Indeed the Chamber of Commerce was instrumental in airing the subject of sailors' homes in the initial discussions of 1846. Thereafter, however, the matter was allowed to drop and the control of sailortown was fully relinquished to the Boarding House Keepers Association. Business interest was revived only in 1893 when Mary Hutchinson indicated her inability to carry on with the management of her sailors' home. A committee, which included merchants and manufacturers, mostly far removed from shipping, expressed a willingness to assume responsibility for the home if its regimen could be altered to make it more attractive to sailors and less of a moral prison. They were apparently unable to reach agreement with the owner, who persisted with her venture a few months longer, at the same time expressing her dependence on the shipowners of the port. If they 'would only speak a good word for it,' she told a newspaper reporter, 'there would be no difficulty in keeping it open, for many of the sailors simply go where they are directed.' To the sailors' home, however, they were not directed.

The hostility of the crimps and the lack of interest on the part of the shipowners explain partially the failure of the sailors' home in Saint John. But the sailors too must have contributed to its failure. Those who neither deserted nor were crimped may nevertheless have still preferred the boarding-houses. Ultimately however the failure of the sailors' home movement was determined by the alteration in the character of the port as sail gave way to steam and Saint John gave way to its better placed competitors. On its closing in 1894, the home was succeeded by a seamen's mission building in Water Street, with the limited aims of providing gospel meetings and a reading room, which is what the earlier missions in Saint John and Quebec had done decades before.[61]

Halifax provides the least evidence of crimping, but the most evidence of interest in reform. Crimping in the Nova Scotia capital seems to have differed significantly in character and extent from that in the other two ports. It did not reach serious proportions, to judge by contemporary opinion, until the 1880s. Its rarity was noted in 1869. What sporadic crimping existed was characterized by two features. Many of the seamen crimped were not employed on merchant vessels but were members of the Royal Navy, the North American squadron of which frequented Halifax in the summer. In 1861, Thomas Ward, who kept a boarding-house for merchant seamen, was charged with assisting seamen to desert from the navy. Two other boarding-house-keepers, William Agnew and Thomas Webb, were actively involved in crimping naval sailors in 1870. Webb was himself a former member of the navy and Agnew was affluent enough to be able to pay a $100 fine for concealing naval deserters. The terms of employment of naval seamen were more discouraging than those of articled merchant seamen; the attraction of desertion into the merchant service was clearly better remuneration. Thomas Carroll encouraged Henry Longstreet to desert from HMS *Ariadne* by offering to 'get him three times as much pay as he received in the navy.'[62]

The other feature of sporadic crimping in Halifax pertains to the crimps themselves. They tended to be disreputable semi-criminal elements. Their range of sailortown transgressions was broader than that pursued by the crimps of Saint John and Quebec. Nicholas Berrigan, for example, was a Newfoundlander who kept a boarding-house on Upper Water Street and had a reputation as a 'bad character.' During seven months in 1875–6 when he was busy boarding sailors in his house, he was accused variously of being one of a gang of harbour pirates, selling liquor without a licence, selling liquor on Sundays and to minors after he had acquired a licence, illegally retaining the money of a sailor, and receiving stolen goods. Cornelius Buttomore was another colourful character whose activities included, at least for the short time he was actively engaged in crimping, the proprietorship of a sailors' boarding-house. His name appears on a crew agreement of

1873, which means he was supplying shipmasters with labour from among his boarders. He was convicted of rape early in 1874, and when he jumped bail in connection with an assault case in the spring of the same year he was described as a man 'of unenviable notoriety, who for some years kept a den known in other countries as a crimp shop in Lower Water Street.'[63]

Eventually the crimping of merchant sailors became a problem in Halifax because of two changes in the nature of the sailor labour market. First, the government shipping office, established in 1873, represented the first serious interference with the free operation of the labour market and probably created the conditions under which crimping was able to thrive. In addition, the federal Seamen's Act, which came into force the next year, directed greater attention towards prosecuting crimps. Second, since crimping and desertion went hand in hand, crimping could not flourish until desertion became common. As a port of discharge for many sailors, Halifax was not traditionally a port prominent for desertion. Towards the end of the century, however, this situation changed with the increasing volume of foreign shipping using the port. Unlike sailors whose engagements ended in Halifax, the sailors on foreign vessels were under contracts as were the majority of seamen visiting Quebec and Saint John. Their only options in Halifax were to stay by their vessels or to desert. The crimps became actively engaged in inducing foreign sailors to desert, because their manpower was now needed. This apparent shortage of supply, particularly in the 1880s, may have been tied to the marked increase of out-migration from the shipping centres and the accompanying decrease in the availability of local seafarers for manning the West Indian and transatlantic fleets. The attention of the Halifax crimps seems to have been directed to Norwegian vessels in particular. The year 1883 was especially active for crimps and the local press feared that unless some effective measures were taken 'Halifax as a port of call will speedily earn for itself the unenviable reputation which a few years ago made Quebec so notorious among shipmasters.'[64]

The ingenuity of the crimps active in Halifax at this time is well illustrated by the case of Hendrick Gullickson, a sailors' boarding-house proprietor, and his runner Peter Hendricks, who specialized in stealing sailors from Norwegian vessels in the harbour and secreting them, not in the crimp's house, but in a fishing smack. From the small vessel the sailors were sent on to new engagements on vessels round the coast. At what point they began this mode of operation it is impossible to determine but Gullickson, who was crimping sailors in 1883, went on merrily with impunity until July 1884 when he was apprehended, convicted, and sent, along with his runner, to prison for three months at hard labour.[65]

While crimping was seldom prosecuted thereafter, with the shipping master claiming in 1886 that Halifax had no crimps, the enticement of foreigners continued. The *Morning Herald* reported in 1890 that 'Norwegian, Danish, Russian and other continental sailors get poor pay compared to mariners of the English and American merchant marine; so it takes very little persuading to get them to desert; and it is an easy matter to secrete them for the few days foreign ships remain in port.' While crimping, by its nature, was always aimed at the non-resident, it took on what amounted to a 'racist' twist in Halifax when it was aimed almost exclusively at the foreigners on vessels owned and manned outside the English-speaking shipping world.[66]

In the mean time the sailors' home movement came to fruition in Halifax. Although it began as early as the 1820s with the British and Foreign Seamen's Friend Society, reformist concern for sailors became significant only in the 1840s. In order to win the support of the shipping interests, the sailors' friends pointed to the beneficial effects that sailors' homes would have on the seaman's conduct at sea. Temperate seamen, imbued with Christian deference, were likely to perform their seafaring duties with greater loyalty, assiduity, and sobriety and thereby enhance the employer's prospects of profit. Certainly the longest-lasting sailors' home was governed by a set of rules and regulations that reflected middle-class notions of the qualities desired in wage earners of the industrial age: punctuality, hard work, temperance, thrift, and obedience. Interestingly, what the seamen's friends failed to do to improve the sailors' value as employees and their prospects as mariners was to teach them anything about seamanship.

In Halifax at least two small-scale sailors' homes were attempted unsuccessfully in the 1840s. The second venture grew out of the activities of the local seamen's mission of 1844, known as the Bethel Union, and the inspiration derived from a visit of Boston's missionary to seamen, E.T. Taylor, in 1846. While bethel services were held under the auspices of the City Mission (1852–68) and briefly in the late 1850s by a missionary sent out by the British Missions to Seamen, no other home materialized until 1862, when the London sailors' home provided the inspiration for Haligonians. The short life of this voluntarily supported institution, even with wide-ranging endorsement from the city's businessmen, and the failure of a number of other schemes in the 1860s and 1870s were caused by the predominant local interest in naval rather than in merchant sailors. Since most of the impetus behind the establishment of a home for 'bluejackets' came from the temperance movement, considerable conflict arose between the seamen's friends and the admiral commanding the North American squadron, who refused to deny his men their grog.

It was not until the late 1870s that the futility of combining efforts with the naval authorities fully dawned upon Halifax reformers. Then a sailors' home, which enjoyed a life of almost twenty years, developed out of a night hostel set on foot by James S. Potter, a dour Scot and Presbyterian city missionary, and the recent interest shown by the city's élite in the welfare of seamen, generated by the establishment in 1878 of a branch of the Church of England's St Andrew's Waterside Church Mission. The highlight of those twenty years was the opening of a new building in 1888. Conceived as a golden jubilee memorial, the home was located on the corner of Upper Water Street and Bell's Lane, slightly north of the earlier rented premises between George and Duke streets. It immediately experienced financial difficulties. Despite a $10,000 bequest from Sir William Young, the friends were unable to discharge a debt for a similar amount which the $26,000 project had incurred. Like Hutchinson's home in Saint John, the Halifax venture was not self-supporting and its debts steadily mounted. Among the appeals launched to save the home were futile applications to the British government to provide an annual grant for the facilities provided for naval sailors, who outnumbered the civilian boarders for the first time in 1889. Deteriorating finances finally forced the home to close in 1896.[67]

While it may have been unrealistic for the projectors of sailors' homes to have believed that such enterprises would pay for themselves, the sailors' home movement in the nineteenth century failed for reasons other than inadequate financial backing. The seamen's friends had powerful opponents to contend with, ranging from boarding-house- and tavern-keepers, to shipping interests, to the sailors themselves. As a rival to private enterprise in sailortown, the sailors' homes aroused the opposition of boarding master and liquor seller (frequently one and the same person) because they attempted to interfere with traditional hiring practices and because they were run on strict temperance principles. As a hiring device, the cosy arrangement whereby the government shipping master's office in Halifax was housed under the same roof as the sailors' home represented a critical piece of anti-boarding-house propaganda. The message clearly was that seamen boarding in the sailors' home would have priority when it came to filling the requests for crewmen placed with the shipping master. The manager, James Potter, proudly reported soon after the home opened that, in the first quarter of 1880, 121 of his 180 boarders had been shipped. Since Halifax boarding masters were not as vocal as their Saint John counterparts, their response is difficult to gauge, though they did criticize the home as a bogus charity. The marriage between the sailors' home and the shipping office was however short-lived, the two agencies going their separate ways on the opening of the new sailors' home in 1888.[68]

The liquor sellers, for their part, had good reason to be perturbed by the Halifax sailors' home because it not only afforded competitive accommodation but its manager also challenged the right of liquor sellers to exist in sailortown. This extreme stand represented the personal vendetta of James Potter, who spent his spare time pursuing violators of the liquor licensing laws. Initially, in the early stages of his management of the home, he received considerable civic support for his attempt to impose a ban on the sale of liquor in the vicinity of the sailors' home. By the late 1880s, however, the public and the Seamen's Friend Society itself had become disenchanted with Potter and unwilling to back his campaign for prohibition, which was being conducted through the highly controversial Law and Order Society. In addition to the liquor issue, accusations that his management of the home was self-serving, autocratic, heartless, and excessively puritanical resulted in a confrontation between Potter and the board, leading to the manager's resignation in 1891. His Halifax supporters claimed on his departure that the Seamen's Friend Society had listened to the clamour of the liquor interests against Potter's temperance activities and appeased them by dismissing him. After a brief sojourn in Saint John, during which he supported Miss Hutchinson's efforts, Potter moved west to take 'charge of the work among seamen on inland waters,' which resulted in the establishment of the Royal Arthur Institute at Port Arthur, an interest he pursued until his death in Toronto in 1921.[69]

In Halifax the local supporters of the sailors' home movement and such allied activities as missions to seamen constantly complained about the lack of support from the very shipping interests that the projects were likely to benefit. Only a handful of the many shipowners and shipping agents participated actively, including A.G. Jones, who was involved in trade through Halifax, and T.E. Kenney, the largest Halifax shipowner of the 1880s, who had little involvement in the port's own trade. Both were federal politicians with self-interested reasons for supporting good causes. By the time of the construction of the new home and the formation of the Seamen's Friend Society, even this token support had been lost, very few of the shipowners subscribing to the building fund or acting as directors. Since this development coincided with the separation of the shipping office and the sailors' home, we are left to conclude that the earlier modicum of interest shown in the home by shipowners and agents was more concerned with economy than reform.

On the basis of the scanty evidence we have, it appears that by 1890 local shipping firms requiring seamen went to the sailors' home only when the boarding houses were empty. The reason suggested was the disrepute into which the home had fallen under the management of the fanatical James Potter. A.W. West, prominent in the port's West Indies trade, claimed that he could not 'get one of his captains to go to the home to get a crew, they look on the home as the last resort in such a case.' West, however, was a property-owner in sailortown. His tenants sold liquor and they may also have kept boarding-houses. Since the sailors' home functioned as a rival to the commercial facilities for seamen, it may have incurred the hostility of local landowners whose property was already suffering an increasing burden of taxation and whose tenants' livelihood was being endangered by the temperance campaign.[70]

If the sailors' home threatened the investment of the shipping interests in local property, it also called on them for financial contributions at a time when their profit margins in the shipping business were rapidly diminishing. The unhealthy state of their trade discouraged concern for the welfare of their employees. In fact the shipping interests were fed up with regulations designed to protect the sailors and considered the reforms of Samuel Plimsoll, the real sailors' friend, to be a threat to Canadian shipping. Shipowners who preferred laissez-faire at sea may also have adopted a laissez-faire attitude towards the welfare of the sailor ashore. In fact their lack of interest in local reformist schemes, whatever the limitations of those schemes, was indicative of an unfeeling attitude towards their employees in general.[71]

If the petty shopkeepers and shipping magnates of sailortown generally scorned the sailors' home, what was the atttitude of the sailors themselves? We have no way of knowing what kind of sailor willingly patronized this establishment. They were referred to in reports as 'the best class of sailors.'[72] If they tended to be temperate, family men who appreciated facilities for writing letters home and opportunities for saving money, they represented a minority in a work-force that was, regardless of nationality, overwhelmingly young, single, and at best semi-literate.[73] Undoubtedly there were sailors who preferred the sailors' home, but a much greater number wanted to spend their time in the more tolerant social atmosphere of boarding-houses, taverns, eating-houses, and shops. The sailors probably viewed Potter and others of his ilk as a fanatical form of crimp. He was certainly as anxious as any boarding-house-keeper to get his men aboard ship. At the sailors' home and from its keeper, the boarders got the discipline of the boarding-house but without its ameliorating influences.[74]

Nevertheless, the sailors' homes did perform some useful functions, which differed entirely from those of the crimps' boarding-houses. The Halifax home proved its earnestness to operate as a non-profit-making venture by cashing sailors' advance notes without charge. It also provided seamen with ample opportunities to take the temperance pledge, secure medical attention, and transmit allotment notes to their families. In addition it was a refuge for two special categories of sailors. One was that of shipwrecked sailors, whom the federal and foreign governments boarded in it until transportation could be arranged to convey the unfortunate crews back to their home ports. The other category comprised unemployed and destitute sailors of whom there must have been many in slack seasons and lean years. Since Potter's first venture in 1876 had been a refuge for the destitute homeless, regardless of occupation or sex, his subsequent concentration on sailors would tend to suggest that, in his experience, seamen formed the most numerous group of vagrants in the city.

The sailors' home of 1879 retained, as a separate department, a night refuge for destitute seafaring men whose only alternatives were the jail or the poorhouse. Without immediate prospects of shipping engagements, unemployed sailors were unlikely to find places in sailors' boarding-houses. Potter in fact claimed that the night refuge sheltered 'friendless and moneyless sailors, who have been kicked from boarding houses because they have nothing to pay.' For the Seamen's Friend Society the refuge became the most costly and therefore least satisfactory aspect of the operation. But, by the time the sailors' home had virtually ceased operations as a hostel for merchant sailors in the mid-1890s, the refuge may have been rendered unnecessary by the Salvation Army's establishment of a refuge and shelter house on Hollis Street which undoubtedly catered to the destitute sailors of the port. Contemporaries in Halifax, as in Saint John, tended to attribute the failure of the home to the transition from sail to steam.[75]

AN IDENTITY OF INTEREST

Since crimps and reformers were not in fact so very different in their approach to the sailor labour market and their manipulation of the seamen whom they attracted to their facilities, why did Jack so overwhelmingly prefer the boarding-house to the sailors' home? It seems likely that he saw his relationship to these elements in terms that we would objectively describe as class ones. The crimps or boarding masters belonged to the same class as the seaman before the mast. Often mariners themselves or, if not, long-time residents of sailortown, they shared a community of interest with the visiting sailors. They only infrequently took each other to court, they rescued each other in difficult circumstances, and they banded together against authority both on ship and shore.[76]

The sailors depended for assistance in their wage disputes on the greater familiarity with port life enjoyed by the boarding-house-keepers. In Quebec, especially, the authorities tended to blame the crimps for strikes and see the sailors as mere tools in their hands. Although it may be true that the initiative for holding out for higher wages came from residents better acquainted with seasonal and market trends than from the transient sailors, the dispersed nature of both the labour force and the places of work made it impossible for the sailortown bosses to apply successful pressure on the shipping office and shipmasters without the large-scale co-operation of the seamen themselves. During many seasons seafarers were in a state of passive refusal to ship, engineered and maintained by the boarding masters through their tight control over when and at what wages shipping articles were signed. Even in instances where the initiative for a strike appeared to come from the seamen, the call for a cessation in engagements went out to the boarding-houses, where most of the prospective strikers could be located.[77]

Undeniably, the relationship between seamen and crimps was often marked by violence, but it was a violence that was self-generated, not one imposed from the outside. That the relationship involved exploitation cannot be denied either, but it was exploitation characteristic of the urban lower classes, not of the capitalist over the propertyless or the rich over the poor. A letter from a 'Seaman' in the Saint John press in 1873 tried to lay out this perspective. Defending blood money as a bonus that the boarding master heartily deserved, the seaman identified the sailors' aggressors and robbers to be the masters and owners of vessels whom the sailors had frequently to take to court 'in order to recover their hard earned wages.' Verbal attacks on boarding masters by shipmasters he likened to defamation of character.[78]

The failure of crimps and sailors to appear to be equal partners in an enterprise beneficial to both was caused more by the transitory nature of the sailor labour force than by a fundamental cleavage of interest between crimps and deserters. Indeed it was the transiency of the sailors that produced and nurtured the crimping establishment. Sailors themselves could easily slip into crimping either as runners or, for those who stayed in one place long enough, as boarding-house-keepers. The seasonal nature of shipping, particularly in Quebec, meant that crimps might turn to sailoring to get them out of the St Lawrence in the winter season, returning with the first vessels in the spring. Clearly the interchangeability of the roles of crimp and sailor was in no way replicated by the relationship between the sailor and the reformer. Reformers, particularly seamen's missionaries, sometimes brought seafaring credentials to their work, but they were not about to transform themselves into hands before the mast, even for a season. In those instances where reformers may have come from the same class as sailors, they had experienced sufficient upward mobility to remove themselves, both socially and psychologically, from the prevailing culture of sailortown.[79]

Another distinguishing feature of crimping that strengthens its connection with seafaring was its marginal nature. While this marginality can be demonstrated in a number of ways, the most striking example is the connection between the poor and outcast and crimping. James Prendergast is a case in point. Both his wayward existence and his seafaring experience marked crimping out as a likely extension of his activities. In Saint John, at least in the period before the boarding-house ring became exclusive and predominant, we find another example. Peter Talty was fined forty dollars for enticing a sailor to desert from the ship *Admiral* in 1863. The evidence in this case is interesting, because the principal witness was another Saint John resident named Daniel Shugrue, who was employed as a night watchman on the ship when Talty came on board to help the deserter collect his belongings. According to Shugrue, who was a close neighbour of Talty's, he did not interfere with the proceedings, beyond telling Talty he was foolish to take such a risk, because, 'as Talty was a poor man with a large family,' Shugrue 'thought he might as well have the man as any one else.'[80]

In contrast, the sailor was likely to feel totally alienated from the reformer and his sailors' home. Admittedly, the sailors' 'friends,' as they liked to call themselves, were not likely to assault or cheat poor Jack, but their primary interest was to turn him into something he was not: a sober, serious, well-behaved man who would pose no threat, in terms of his behaviour, to the established society of the port. He was unacceptable as he was; he needed protection against the crimps because his employers needed protection against the crimps' manipulations of wage rates. It was no coincidence that campaigns for sailors' homes accompanied periods of heightened crimping activity.[81] The sailors' best interests were seen by his social betters to be those of his employers. The hand that the middle-class reformers extended to the sailor was an iron hand in a velvet glove, a hand that belonged to associates of the shipowners and the shipmasters, not of the men before the mast. To the sailor therefore the reformer appeared as an outsider entering sailortown to form alliances with the shipmasters and shipping merchants and to interfere with the customary practices of deserting, boarding, and hiring. The crimps and sailors demonstrated a consciousness of their community of interest again and again in the face of interference from 'upper town' society. Their attacks against the Quebec shipping office, their strikes for higher wages in all three ports, and their failure to support the sailors' homes were, each in its respective ways, conclusive evidence, not of the manipulation of sailors by crimps, but of the identity of interest between crimps and sailors.

Epilogue

The familiar sailortown of crimps and seafarers died with the passing of the sailing ship. A new pattern and rhythm of sailors' lives ashore accompanied the ascendancy of the steamship. Seamen working on steamers that did business in Halifax, Saint John, and Quebec were only briefly in port and needed far fewer facilities than they had done as sailors. For the remaining large sailing vessels, the pressure to compete with steam meant that the obsolete freighters stayed in port as short a time as possible and that shore leave for the crew was rare. The need for the ports to discipline sailors correspondingly diminished. As the Saint John *Sun* explained in 1893:

The St. John of today is vastly different from the St. John of twenty years ago. Then the deals exported went in sailing vessels, many of which paid their crews off here. Now the steamers do a very large part of the business and their crews always stay by them. The foreign vessels visiting the port retain their crews as a rule. This leaves only the men who come here in vessels flying the British flag to be provided with boarding houses.[1]

Port calls were transformed by forces beyond local control, forces which, ironically, operated in the interests of the reformers because they shortened a sailor's stopover and sufficiently improved his conditions of employment (often by making him an employee of a steamship company) to lower the rate of desertion. In a sense, then, the failure of the costly sailors' homes in Saint John and Halifax signalled the passing of the problem that had stimulated the philanthropy of the seamen's friends. As a commentator remarked retrospectively in regard to the defunct Halifax sailors' home in 1897, 'The changing conditions of the port had largely swept away the source it was designed to succor and be sustained by. "The sailors are not here".'[2] The reduced traffic could neither sustain the sailors' homes nor support the extensive boarding-house network. By the turn of the twentieth century boarding masters too were abandoning sailortown or converting their houses into working-class tenements.

At the same time, the world-wide demise of the sailortown of the pre-steam age was accompanied by a redefinition of the sailors' place of work. During most of the nineteenth century the place of work was not coterminous with the vessel. Instead it followed the sailor like a shadow wherever he went. Surrounded by masters day in and day out, on ship and on shore, the seafarer could not escape the context of his employment. In port he remained specifically a sailor, never becoming a plain labourer or working man. In effect he lacked a private domain. His activities were supervised by shipmaster, shipping master, and boarding master. Indeed the status of the nineteenth-century sailor was more analogous to that of an apprentice than that of a free wage labourer. No wage labourer was subjected to the same mixture of rigorous discipline and patronizing solicitude as the sailor. Society confirmed the analogy between sailor and apprentice through its perception of sailors as 'boys' and its interpretation of seafaring as a juvenile stage in a man's life-cycle of work.

These ineluctable characteristics of seafaring life changed in response to the late nineteenth-century mechanization of the occupation. Gradually the diffuse nature of the sailors' work-world disappeared. Work became focused on the ship, in a reduced number of ports, and in a greater specialization of shipboard jobs. For their part, the masters of the sailors' work-world were affected by the centralization and bureaucratization of the shipping industry. The shipmaster became the servant of the shipowner or steamship company, the erstwhile private shipping master became a public employee or an outlaw, and the boarding master eventually lost his supremacy and learned to take his instructions from emergent sailors' unions.

Since the changes attendant on the transition from sail to steam were accompanied in Halifax, Saint John, and Quebec by economic dislocation, the characteristics of the nineteenth-century sailortowns of Canada were soon lost amid the nostalgic and frequently misleading reminiscences of apologists of the age of sail. Inevitably a detailed examination of sailortown and its clients dispels much of the romanticism associated with 'golden age' mythology. Instead we encounter the stark reality of a vital but transitory labour market. Its legacy was a mixed one, containing both negative and positive elements. Because seafarers belonged to a declining sector of the economy, were subject to rigid maritime labour law, and were divided among themselves by ethnicity, race, and language, they left few serviceable traditions to their steam-age successors in the twentieth century.

In the responses seafarers stimulated ashore, however, important precedents were created. The government was forced to take cognizance of the chronic shortage of manpower and stepped in to try to regulate sailors' employment for the sake of law, order, and shipping profits. State involvement led also to the establishment of a water police force to promote the interests of business, a theme not unfamiliar in the history of Canadian labour relations. While the enactment of Canadian merchant shipping acts drew on British precedents, such legislation was repressive enough by the late nineteenth century to serve as a warning to a wider sector of the labour force. Similarly, the bias of the courts in favour of the shipowner rather than the sailor underscores the way in which the legal system changed to strengthen the power of the economic élite. If the one progressive response by the public appears to have been the encouragement of health and welfare measures for sailors, it was a grudging one. These various responses by govenment and business were inspired by the sailors' collective weaknesses. But if the weaknesses of the seafaring work-force – transiency, seasonality, contractual obligations, and isolation – were unique features, the attitude of the state to the merchant marine was not. Similar measures would be effectively directed against other groups of workers in the emergent industrial age.

Maritime labour statutes

The following is a list of most of the major statutes comprising Canadian maritime labour law. Excluded are the acts relating solely to sick, shipwrecked, and destitute mariners, and seamen on inland waters.

GREAT BRITAIN

5 & 6 Wm 4, cap 19 An Act to amend and consolidate the laws relating to the merchant seamen of the United Kingdom, and for forming and maintaining a register of all seamen engaged in that service (1835)

7 & 8 Vic, cap 112 An Act to amend and consolidate the laws relating to Merchant Seamen; and for keeping a Register of Seamen (1844)

13 & 14 Vic, cap 93 An Act for improving the Condition of Masters, Mates and Seamen and maintaining Discipline, in the Merchant Service (known as the Mercantile Marine Act, 1850)

14 & 15 Vic, cap 96 An Act to amend the Mercantile Marine Act, 1850 (1851)

15 Vic, cap 26 An Act to enable Her Majesty to carry into effect the Arrangements made with Foreign Powers for the Apprehension of Seamen who desert from their Ships (known as the Foreign Deserters Act, 1852)

17 & 18 Vic, cap 104 An Act to amend and consolidate the Acts relating to Merchant Shipping (known as the Merchant Shipping Act, 1854)

30 & 31 Vic, cap 124 An Act to amend the Merchant Shipping Act, 1854 (1867)

32 Vic, cap 11 An Act for amending the law relating to the Coasting Trade and Merchant Shipping in British Possessions (1869)

34 & 35 Vic, cap 110 An Act to amend the Merchant Shipping Acts (1871)

36 & 37 Vic, cap 85 An Act to amend the Merchant Shiping Acts (1873)

38 & 39 Vic, cap 88 An Act to make provision for giving further powers to the Board of Trade for stopping Unseaworthy Ships (1875)

39 & 40 Vic, cap 80 An Act to amend the Merchant Shipping Acts (1876)

43 & 44 Vic, cap 16 An Act to amend the Law relating to the Payments of Wages and rating of Merchant Seamen (1880)

43 & 44 Vic, cap 43 An Act to provide for the safe carriage of grain cargoes by Merchant Shipping (1880)

45 & 46 Vic, cap 76 An Act to amend the Merchant Shipping Acts, 1854 to 1880, with respect to Colonial Courts of Inquiry (1882)

46 & 47 Vic, cap 41 an Act to amend the Merchant Shipping Acts, 1854 to 1880, with respect to Fishing Vessels and Apprenticeship to the Sea Fishing Service and otherwise (1883)

51 & 52 Vic, cap 24 An Act to amend the law with respect to the Appliances to be carried by British Merchant Ships for Saving Life (1888)

52 & 53 Vic, cap 46 An Act to amend the Merchant Shipping Act, 1854, and the Acts amending the same (1889)

57 & 58 Vic, cap 60 An Act to consolidate Enactments relating to Merchant Shipping (1894)

CANADA (to 1867)

47 Geo 3, cap 9 An Act to prevent the desertion of Seamen and others in the Sea Service; to punish all persons encouraging such Seamen and others to desert or harboring or concealing them hereafter, and to repeal certain Acts therein mentioned (1807)

6 Wm 4, cap 28 An Act to promote less expensive means for the recovering of wages due to Seamen of vessels belonging to or registered in this Province (1836)

6 Vic, cap 4 An Act to amend the Act therein mentioned (47 Geo 3, cap 9) relative to the desertion of Seamen, and others in the Sea Service (1843)

10 & 11 Vic, cap 25 An Act for regulating the Shipping of Seamen (1847)

11 Vic, cap 5 An Act to amend the Act for regulating the Shipping of Seamen, and to fund the fees payable under the said Act (1848)

13 & 14 Vic, cap 25 An Act to extend certain Provincial Acts, to Foreign Merchant vessels (1850)

16 Vic, cap 165 An Act more effectually to prevent the Desertion of Seamen (1853)

22 Vic, cap 105 An Act respecting the prompt and summary administration of Criminal Justice in certain cases, Sect. 15 (1859)

22 Vic, cap 43 An Act for more effectually preventing the desertion of Seamen (1859)

NEW BRUNSWICK (to 1867)

7 Geo 4, cap 12 An Act to repeal all the Laws now in force for the regulation of Seamen, and to make more effectual provision for that purpose (1827)

3 Vic, cap 62 An Act to make more effectual provisions for the Regulation of Seamen in this Province (1840)

8 Vic, cap 87 An Act to make provision for the regulation of Seamen shipped on board or belonging to all Ships or Vessels registered in or belonging to the Province of New Brunswick, while such Ships or Vessels shall be within the precincts thereof (1845)

12 Vic, cap 50 An Act for regulating the Shipping of Seamen at the Port of Saint John (1849)

13 Vic, cap 27 An Act to continue an Act to make provision for Seamen shipped on board of Vessels belonging to this Province (1850)

15 Vic, cap 61 An Act to continue an Act for regulating the Shipping of Seamen at the Port of Saint John (1852)

16 Vic, cap 36 An Act to amend an Act regulating the shipping of Seamen at the Port of Saint John and extend the provisions thereof to other Ports and places being Sea Ports in this Province (1853)

Revised Statutes of New Brunswick, 1854, Title 14: Of Seamen, chap 86: Of Regulations for Seamen; chap 87: Of Regulations for shipping Seamen at the Port of Saint John.

30 Vic, cap 21 An Act to amend Chap. 87, of the Revised Statutes (1866)

NOVA SCOTIA (to 1867)

6 Wm 4, cap 48 An Act relating to the Merchant Seamen of this Province (1836)

4 Vic, cap 50 An Act for facilitating the recovery of Seamen's Wages (1841)

Revised Statutes of Nova Scotia, 1851, Title 21: Of the Regulation of Trade in Certain Cases, chap 76: Of shipping and seamen

Revised Statutes of Nova Scotia, 1864, Title 21: Of the Regulation of Trade in Certain cases, chap 75, part 1: Of Shipping and Seamen

CANADA (post-1867)

32 & 33 Vic, cap 32 An Act respecting the prompt and summary administration of Criminal Justice in certain cases, Sect. 16 (1869)

34 Vic, cap 32 An Act for more effectually preventing the desertion of seamen in the Port of Quebec (1871)

35 Vic, cap 39 An Act respecting the Shipping of Seamen in Nova Scotia (1872)

36 Vic, cap 56 An Act respecting Deck Loads (1873)

36 Vic, cap 129 An Act respecting the shipping of Seamen (known as the Seamen's Act) (1873)

42 Vic, cap 27 An Act to amend 'The Seamen's Act, 1873' (1879)

53 Vic, cap 16 An Act to amend 'The Seamen's Act,' chap 74 of the Revised Statutes (1886) (1890)

57 & 58 Vic, cap 44 An Act further to amend the Revised Statutes (1886) chap 77, respecting Safety of Ships (1894)

Notes

ABBREVIATIONS

ANQ	Archives nationales du Québec, Quebec
AR	*Acadian Recorder*, Halifax
BT	Board of Trade Papers, Public Record Office, London
CO	Colonial Office Papers, Public Record Office, London
DS	*Daily Sun*, Saint John
DT	*Daily Telegraph*, Saint John
DTribune	*Daily Tribune*, Saint John
EE	*Evening Express*, Halifax
HBrit Col	*Halifax British Colonist*
HH	*Halifax Herald*
HMC	*Morning Chronicle*, Halifax
HMJ	*Morning Journal*, Halifax
HMP	*Morning Post*, Halifax
HMS	*Morning Sun*, Halifax
JHA	*Journal of the House of Assembly*
MF	*Morning Freeman*, Saint John
MH	*Morning Herald*, Halifax
MHG	Maritime History Group Archives, Memorial University, St John's

MN	*Morning News*, Saint John
MT	*Morning Telegraph*, Saint John
MT	Papers of the Marine Department, Board of Trade, Public Record Office, London
N	*Novascotian*, Halifax
NBC	*New Brunswick Courier*, Saint John
NBM	New Brunswick Museum, Saint John
NMM	National Maritime Museum, London
PAC	Public Archives of Canada, Ottawa
PANB	Provincial Archives of New Brunswick, Fredericton
PANS	Public Archives of Nova Scotia, Halifax
QBT	Quebec Board of Trade Papers
QG	*Quebec Gazette*
QM	*Quebec Mercury*
QMC	*Morning Chronicle*, Quebec
RCRCL	Royal Commission on the Relations of Capital and Labor
SJMJ	*Morning Journal*, Saint John
SJMP	*Morning Post*, Saint John
SMG	*Shipping and Mercantile Gazette*, London
UHJ	*Unionist and Halifax Journal*
WC	*Weekly Chronicle*, Saint John
WT	*Weekly Telegraph*, Saint John

CHAPTER ONE : The sailor labour market

1 *SMG*, 26 Nov. 1847; *MN*, 30 Sept. 1863; *DT*, 10 Mar. 1871; *HMC*, 10 June 1876, 2 Mar. 1877
2 *QMC*, 2 June 1852; *DT*, 26 Dec. 1868, 9 Apr. 1872; *MN*, 18 Nov. 1872; Royal Commission on Unseaworthy Ships, Great Britain *Parliamentary Papers*, XXXIV, 1874, Minutes of Evidence, No. 13,387; Arthur Lower, *Great Britain's Woodyard: British America and the Timber Trade, 1763–1867* (Montreal 1973), 146
3 *QG*, 16 Sept. 1840; *MN*, 17 May 1843; *DT*, 1 June 1869; *MN*, 28 Oct. 1872; *HMC*, 25 Mar. 1873, 26 May 1874

4 Most vessels visiting Montreal had to clear from Quebec. *QM*, 10 July 1863

5 *QMC*, 11 May 1854, 28 May 1859, 11 May 1860; *MN*, 8 Apr. 1869; *HMC*, 30 Apr. 1872; *QM*, 6 Aug. 1872. A good description of the hazards of Atlantic crossings in winter is 'The Winter at Sea,' *HMJ*, 24 Feb. 1862. The hazards were increased when adverse gales lengthened the passages, *HMC*, 16 Jan., 2 Mar. 1877.

6 *DS*, 10, 11, 14 Mar. 1879

7 Petitions of John Alexander of Alexander, Barry & Co, 19 Jan. 1842, and Adam and Davidson, 22 Jan. 1842, PANB RLE/842, pe 1, No. 3, and pe 4, No. 82; Report of the Controller of Customs on the annual returns of Trade and Navigation for New Bruswick in 1860, *MF*, 18 July 1861; *HMC*, 5 Apr. 1872; *DT*, 26 Apr. 1873, 30 Sept. 1879; *SMG*, 27 Dec. 1880; *QM*, 1 Oct. 1881; *DS*, 30 Sept. 1884, 2 Oct. 1885; William Lord, *Reminiscences of a Sailor* (2nd ed, Edinburgh and Glasgow 1894), 40, 43; Lower, Wood-yard, 240–1

8 *QG*, 25 Oct. 1847; *QM*, 3 June 1851, 15 Nov. 1865, 14 Apr. 1874, 15 Nov. 1879; *QMC*, 20 Oct. 1852, 6 June 1872, 3 Nov. 1874; Albert Faucher, 'The Decline of Shipbuilding at Quebec in the Nineteenth Century,' *Canadian Journal of Economics and Political Science*, XXIII (1957), 195–215

9 *QMC*, 30 May 1860, *QM*, 3 Nov. 1886. Samuel Plimsoll, British Liberal MP, campaigned in the 1870s for improvements in the working conditions of merchant seamen.

10 *HMC*, 29, 30 Nov. 1869; Lord, *Reminiscences*, 26

11 *QM*, 25 Nov. 1852; Lord, *Reminiscences*, 12, 24–30. *Dorchester* was a fictitious name.

12 *QMC*, 5 Nov. 1852

13 *QG*, 9 Nov. 1836; ANQ, AP.G 219/2, QBT Minutes, 20 May 1851. For criticism of captains too readily shipping deserters in Quebec, see *SMG*, 26 Nov. 1847, 11 Nov. 1848. In general the literature does not support the view that desertion was a form of disguised immigraiton, though occasional references occur to deserters going inland: for example, *QMC*, 4 May 1848. There is also some indication that seafaring on the Great Lakes attracted deep sea sailors inland from Quebec. See Report of the Shipping Master, Quebec, for the year ending 30 June 1870, Canada *Sessional Papers*, IV, 1871, vol. 3, No. 5, App. 12, 117.

14 *QMC*, 23 Aug. 1851, 10, 24 Nov. 1855, 7 July 1858, 2 Aug. 1859. The effects on freight are described by Wm. Graves & Son, Shipowners, New Ross, Scotland in *QM*, 18 Sept. 1852. The demand for seamen and level of wages followed closely the shipbuilding graph used by Faucher, 'Decline,' 196 and Lower, *Woodyard*, 262.

15 Desertion of Seamen and the Crimping System at Quebec, 10 July 1849, BT 1/479/2425/1850

16 *QM*, 5 Oct. 1852, 6 Jan. 1853; *QMC*, 24 Feb. 1854

17 ANQ, AP.G 219/1, QBT Minutes, 4 Apr. 1840 and 22 May 1841; *NBC*, 6 Mar. 1847; *SMG*, 26 Nov. 1847; *QMC*, 8 Mar. 1854; *N*, 11 Aug. 1856; *QM*, 6 June 1857; *HMC*, 6 Mar., 8, 16 Apr., 30 May 1878. On both apprenticeship and training ships as sources of supply in Britain, see Stephen Jones, 'Blood Red Roses: The Supply of Merchant Seamen in the Nineteenth Century,' *Mariner's Mirror*, LVIII (1972), 437–41.

18 The notable exceptions were the registrar-general of seamen and the *Shipping and Mercantile Gazette*, through the latter saw it merely as a temporary expedient until stringent measures could be taken against Quebec crimps. Brown to Ward, 30 Dec. 1847, BT 1/468/50/1848; ANQ, AP.G 219/4, QBT Minutes, 5 Apr. 1852, 7 Apr. 1862; *QG*, 5 June 1839; *QMC*, 27 May, 6 and 7 June, 4 July 1848, 6 June 1851, 31 Mar. 1852; *SMG*, 20 Apr. 1852; *QMC*, 11 May 1852, 8 Apr. 1856; Halifax *Sun*, 24 June 1857; *QM*, 2 Oct. 1852, 12 Apr. 1862, 27 June 1865, 12 Oct. 1875; William McCord to Attorney General Drummond, Canada *Sessional Papers*, XI, 1852–3, App. No. 8, A.A.A.A., 13; Wm. Graves & Son to Earl of Elgin, ibid, 24

19 *MN*, 16 Feb. 1848; *QMC*, 11 May 1852; *QM*, 5 Aug. 1875

20 *QM*, 6 Oct. 1859, 3 Nov. 1870, 12 Oct. 1875; 'Discharge of Seamen at Foreign Ports,' from *SMG*, reported in *HMC*, 17 Jan. 1871

21 ANQ, AP.G 219/1, QBT Minutes, 22 May 1841; *QG*, 5 June 1839, 17 Dec. 1845; *QMC*, 1 July, 23 Aug. 1851, 24 Nov. 1855; *QM*, 26 Mar. 1853

22 *MN*, 20 Dec. 1841; *SMG*, 6 Nov. 1847; *NBC*, 8 Dec. 1849; *WT*, 24 Oct. 1862; *MN*, 16 Oct. 1865; *QM*, 11 Nov. 1876; *DS*, 27 Oct. 1879

23 *NBC*, 28 July 1838, 11 Sept. 1841; *QMC*, 26 July 1847; *N*, 4 Sept. 1848, 20 Aug. 1849; *MN*, 15 Aug. 1851, 15 Apr. 1853, 17 Oct. 1855, 5 Sept. 1856; *MF*, 29 Nov. 1866; *DT*, 17 June 1869; *QM*, 20 July 1874; Minister of Marine's Report, li, Canada *Sessional Papers*, VII, 1874, vol. 3, No. 4; Faucher, 'Decline,' 205; Peter D. McClelland, 'The New Brunswick Economy in the Nineteenth Century,' PHD. thesis, Harvard University, 1966, 200–29

24 J. & M. Ward & Sons to Gibbs Bright & Co, 29 July, 28 Nov. 1840, NBM, Ward Papers, Letter Book, 16 Dec. 1839–13 Nov. 1844; Henry Labouchere's memorandum on New Brunswick acts, 29 Mar. 1841, CO 188/75, f.33; Petitions of John Alexander, 19 Jan. 1842, PANB RLE/842 pe 1, No. 3; John Wishart, 18 Jan. 1842, ibid, No. 4; Milby and Thomas, 21 Jan. 1842, ibid, No. 15; Adam and Davidson, 22 Jan. 1842, PANB RLE/842 pe 4, No. 82, and 1 Feb. 1842, ibid, pe 10, No. 187; Willard Buchanan & Co, 3 Feb.

1842, PANB RLE/842 pe 7, No. 160; Stephen Wiggins, 25 Jan. 1843, PANB REX/PA Miscellaneous, Imported Seamen 1842–3; QG, 18 May 1840, 9 Mar. 1846; MN, 25 Feb. 1848, 21 Mar. 1849

25 N, 2 June 1856; RCRCL, Evidence – Nova Scotia, 57

26 HMC, 21 Nov. 1877

27 Ibid, 16 Jan., 4 Feb. 1873

28 HMJ, 11 Aug. 1856

29 N, 27 Mar. 1854; HMC, 14 Nov. 1872, 22 Mar. 1873, 1 June, 25 Dec. 1874, 15 Jan., 11 Feb. 1875, 5 May, 21 Nov. 1877

30 N, 13 Oct. 1851; MN, 21 June 1861. A Quebec newspaper reported 150 desertions in Halifax in the space of a few days, QM, 25 June 1861. The admiral instituted marine patrols to keep his sailors in check, HMJ, 28 May 1862; N, 1 Aug. 1864; MN, 1 Aug. 1864; HMC, 2 Aug, 1864, 19 Oct. 1872.

31 RCRCL, Evidence – Nova Scotia, 57

32 QG, 31 Mar. 1847; QMC, 2 June 1852

33 Not all shipmasters shared the enthusiasm for a police force, a scepticism they demonstrated by refusing to pay the voluntary tax of ½d per ton. The tax was increased to three farthings per ton in 1845. ANQ, AP.G 219/1, QBT Minutes, 6 June 1839, 4 Apr. 1840; AP.G 219/2, QBT Minutes, 14 June 1845, 6 Apr. 1846, 30 Apr., 20 May 1851; QG, 5, 19 June, 23 Sept. 1839; QM, 20 May, 3 June 1851

34 ANQ, AP.G 219/4, QBT Minutes, 5 Apr. 1852; QMC, 2 July 1851, 30 Sept. 1856; QM, 30 Aug., 8 Nov. 1856, 30 Nov. 1864, 16 Oct., 14 Nov. 1865, 27 Nov. 1868, 25 Oct., 22 Nov. 1871

35 QMC, 1, 4, 11 June 1872; HMC, 8 June 1872; QM, 7, 25 Nov. 1872; QM, 12 May 1874; QMC, 1, 2 May 1876, 14 May 1877; HMC, 5 Jan. 1878; QM, 30 Apr. 1879, 25 May 1881, 30 June 1882. The duties of the force are described in the Report of Quebec Water Police, for the year ending 30 June 1869, Canada Sessional Papers, III, 1879, vol. 4, No. 11, App. K, 251.

36 Canada, House of Commons, Debates, 2nd Sess. 7th Parl., vol. 1, 11 Apr. 1892, 1225–6; 3rd Sess. 7th Parl., 24 Mar. 1893, 3021–2; QM, 12 Apr., 22 July 1893

37 The Admirality notice of the legislation, which was exhibited for the benefit of sailors in all the seaports of the United Kingdom, was headed: 'Important to Seamen – Desertions at Quebec,' MN, 6 Dec. 1847. For Hawkins' appointment, see QMC, 17 Aug. 1847.

38 QMC, 24 May 1848. For local reaction to the first year of the operation of the shipping master's office see Report of the Special Committee on an

Act for regulating the Shipping of Seamen, with minutes of evidence,
Canada *Sessional Papers*, VIII, 1849, App. No. 3, R.R.R.R. See also *QMC*,
27 May 1848; *QG*, 8 May 1849; *QMC*, 23 June 1849. Most of the official
correspondence and background documents relating to the establishment
and first year of the office are printed in Return of Correspondence
between the Imperial and Canadian Governments, and between the latter
and any private individuals, with reference to the Act to regulate the
Shipping of Seamen at the Port of Quebec, Canada *Sessional Papers*, VIII,
1849, App. No. 2, W.W.

39 'Desertion of Seamen and the crimping system at the Quebec,' 10 July
1849, BT 1/479/2425/1850; Extracts fromthe *Freeman's Journal and Commercial Advertiser*, BT 1/468/50/1848; *QMC*, 19 June 1848, 9 May, 1, 2 Aug.,
1 Sept., 17 Oct. 1849; Report of the Special Committee on an Act for
regulating the Shipping of Seamen

40 Repeal of the 1847 act was defeated three times in the Canadian assembly, according to John Wilson; Wilson to President of the British Board of
Trade, 10 Nov. 1867, CO 42/665/12120, ff. 497–514; *QMC*, 10 and 11
June, 1 July 1851; *QM*, 3 June 1851, 17 Aug., 5 Oct., 20 Nov. 1852; *QMC*,
8 Apr. 1856

41 *QG*, 20 Oct. 1841; *QM*, 1 Sept. 1849, 3 June 1851

42 Hawkins to Brown, 15 Dec. 1848, BT 1/468/50/1848; Hawkins to Brown,
29 June 1850, BT 1/479/2425/1850; *QMC*, 9 Aug. 1851, 20 Oct. 1852

43 *SMG*, 15 Aug. 1849. Documents relating to the operation of the shipping office between 1849 and 1853 are printed in Return of Correspondence between the Government of this Province and the Imperial Government, or between either of them and any person or persons, on the
subject of the Seamen's Shipping Act, Canada *Sessional Papers*, XI,
1852–3, App. No. 8, A.A.A.A.

44 *QMC*, 23 Jan. 1858

45 ANQ, AP.G 219/4, QBT Minutes, 7 Nov. 1854; QBT Petition to Legislative
Assembly, 19 Feb. 1856; QBT Minutes, 22 Apr. 1856, 4 Apr. 1864. Hawkins
defended his performance in *Remarks upon the Desertion of Seamen at the
Port of Quebec* (Quebec 1852), PAC Pamphlet Collection 1-2323. Wilson
claimed to be one of the two chief suppliers of seamen for vessels after
Hawkins' death. *QMC*, 4 July 1854; *QM*, 7 Sept. 1854; *QMC*, 7 Aug.
1855; *QM*, 29 Mar. 1856

46 *QMC*, 16 Aug. 1858; Return of Correspondence, 17, Canada *Sessional
Papers*, II, 1869, vol. 6, No. 65; Wilson to President of the British Board of
Trade, 10 Nov. 1867, CO 42/665/12120, ff. 497–514; Minister of Marine's
Report, 7, Canada *Sessional Papers* II, 1869, vol. 4, No. 12

47 *Harvest Home* (No. 38758), 1873, BT 99/409
48 Petition, 31 Jan. 1849, PANB RLE/849 pe 12, No. 409; Return of Correspondence, 18, Canada *Sessional Papers*, II, 1869, VOL. 6, No. 65
49 *MF*, 26 Apr. 1864; see J. Fingard, 'Masters and Friends, Crimps and Abstainers: Agents of Control in 19th Century Sailortown,' *Acadiensis*, VIII 1 (autumn 1978), 22–46.
50 The fines were either $4 or $8 per man. *MF*, 20 Oct., 18 Dec. 1866, 28 Mar., 6 Aug. 1867, 30 Jan. 1868; *MN*, 3 Feb., 25 May 1868; *DT*, 26 Oct. 1870
51 Minister of Marine's Report, 52, Canada *Sessional Papers*, IV, 1871, vol. 3, No. 5
52 Report of the Saint John Shipping Master for year ending 30 June 1870, Canada *Sessional Papers*, IV, 1871, vol. 3, No. 5, App. No. 13, 118
53 Wilson to Governor General, 29 Mar. 1852, PAC, RG 4, C 1, vol. 346, No. 476; Toronto *British Colonist*, 20 May 1853; *MN*, 22 May 1865
54 *UHJ*, 4 May, 25 July 1866; *HMC*, 2 Nov. 1872, 1 July 1874
55 *HMC*, 18 Jan., 22 Mar. 1873
56 For Bligh's controversial appointment see *HMC*, 13, 19 Dec. 1878, 1, 3, 6, 8, 11 Feb. 1879; RCRCL, *Evidence – Nova Scotia*, 55. The act of 1873 tried to require the shipping of sailors on foreign vessels before the shipping master. See Minister of Marine's Report, lii, Canada *Sessional Papers*, VII, 1874, vol. 3, No. 4. On Saint John, see Fingard, 'Masters and Friends,' 34.
57 Extract from *Freeman's Journal and Commercial Advertiser*, BT 1/468/50/ 1848; *QM*, 9 Oct. 1852; J. Havelock Wilson, *My Stormy Voyage through Life*, I (London 1925), 77

CHAPTER TWO: Patterns of seafaring life

1 *Janet Kidston* (No. 32993), 1859, Log, BT 98/6178
2 Lord, *Reminiscences of a Sailor* (2nd edn, Edinburgh and Glasgow 1894)
3 *MH*, 30 Jan. 1882
4 Prendergast frequently appeared in the local news columns of the newspapers and in police and jail records: *HMC*, 9 Oct. 1869; 22 May, 7, 8 Aug., 2 Sept., 5 Nov. 1874; 17 July, 13, 14 Sept. 1875; 12 Feb., 8 Aug., 23, 25, 27 Oct. 1876; 5, 6, Mar., 15 Nov. 1877; 18 Apr., 1 Oct., 7, 11 Dec. 1878; 29 Apr., 5, 28, 30 Aug., 8 Dec. 1879; *MH*, 1 Mar. 1880; 19 Dec. 1881; 30 Jan., 5 Oct. 1882; *AR*, 29 May 1888; Halifax Police Court Minutes, 1 Feb. 1871; 23 Apr., 21 May, 18 June, 6, 7 Aug., 1 Sept. 1874; 25 Nov. 1884, PANS, RG 42, Series D; Halifax Prison Registers, 1869–1879, PANS, RG 35–102, Series 18B; Halifax Stipendiary Magistrate Records, xxx, Return

of Persons before the Police Court, 1877–1891, PANS, RG 42, Series D. Prendergast cannot be clearly identified in the city directories, though there are entries of the name with spelling variations that also occur in the other material: Pendergast, Pendergrast, and Prendergrast. My man is probably the James Pendergrast on page 26 of the 1871 census of ward 3 in Halifax city. It is in the Returns of Persons before the Police Court that his occupation is identified most often as a seaman, though he is occasionally listed as a mason or labourer, and a man of the same name is identified in the directories for most of the 1880s as a wharf builder.

5 *MF*, 22 Nov. 1859, 14 July 1863

6 Reminiscences of Harris H. Barnes, PANS, MG 1, vert ms file. His service on the *Hutoka* is recorded in the vessel's articles: *Hutoka* (No. 46004), 1863, MHG.

7 *MN*, 15 Nov. 1879

8 *DS*, 7 Mar. 1894

9 *HMC*, 12 June 1878

10 *MN*, 2, 3, 4, 5, 7, 8, 10, 19, 23 Nov. 1870; *DS*, 4, 7, 10, 17, 19, 21 Nov. 1870; *MF*, 5, 22 Nov. 1870

11 *MF*, 6 July 1875

12 *HMC*, 7 July 1875

13 *MF*, 8 July 1875

14 *MF* and *MN*, 13 July 1875. For F.W. Wallace's description of the duties of stewardesses, see *Wooden Ships and Iron Men* (London and Toronto 1924) 186.

15 *Privateer* (No. 64634), 1883, MHG

16 *Marabout* (No. 85504), 1882, and *Celeste Burrill* (No. 90875), 1886, MHG

17 *Mary L. Burrill* (No. 85542), 1883, MHG

18 *Abbie S. Hart* (No. 80611), 1883, and *Ecuador* (No. 71008), 1883, MHG

19 *Lottie Stewart* (No. 66873), 1883, MHG

20 *Robert S. Besnard* (No. 80394), 1883, MHG

21 *Vendome* (No. 80638), 1882, 1883; *City Camp* (No. 59298), 1888, 1889, 1890; *Constance* (No. 88673), 1884, 1885, 1886; *Kelvedale* (No. 80087), 1881; *Marabout* (No. 85504), 1882, 1883, MHG

22 *Wealth of Nations* (No. 54391), 1868, Log, MHG. For a stewardess of sterling quality, see Wallace, *Wooden Ships and Iron Men*, 241–8.

23 Coasting vessels were legally defined in New Brunswick in 1868 as 'vessels owned in this province, or from any port in British North America, or from a fishing voyage'; *MF*, 8 Oct. 1868.

24 NBM, Canada, Department of Transport, Port of Saint John, Coast Book No. 2, 1883–1886.

25 RCRCL, *Evidence – Nova Scotia*, 57–8
26 The thirty-vessel sample from the engagement books for coasting vessels is made up of every seventh vessel. The vessels in chronological order of their first 1883 engagement are:

Vessel	Official no.	Tons	Port of registry
Acacia	66928	98	Saint John
Alba	85974	91	" "
May Flower	59168	70	" "
Ariel	80045	90	" "
Julia S.	79975	82	" "
W.M. Mackay	85984	97	" "
Nellie Bruce	85987	117	" "
Champion	66956	114	" "
C.Y. Gregory	85509	88	" "
James Watson	80033	97	" "
Victoria	66959	92	" "
Howard Holder	64600	93	" "
Annie Gale	85981	96	" "
Annie Simpson	80012	169	" "
Temperance Bell	64454	78	" "
Mary Pickard	66963	89	" "
Jessie	59186	72	" "
Westfield	85574	80	" "
Sea Bird	59200	80	" "
Evergreen	59234	106	Saint Andrews
A.G. Blair	85584	80	Saint John
Comrade	59162	66	" "
Reporter	85588	121	" "
Sarah	72334	117	" "
Riverdale	85590	83	" "
Mary L. Dunn	80095	179	" "
Maud W.	80060	82	Chatham
Jeddo	64588	103	Saint John
Linnet	59118	28	" "
James Rourke	85572	85	" "

27 NBM, Coast Books No. 2, 1883–1886 and No. 3, 1886–1889
28 New Brunswick, *JHA*, 1861, App. No. 5: Annual Returns of Trade and Navigation for the Province of New Brunswick for the year 1860, 3–4

29 *DS* and *MN*, 5 May 1883. The wages recorded in the shipping master's engagement books for seamen on the coasting vessels in 1883 range from $12 to $25 per month, but cluster mainly around $18–$20.

30 NBM, Canada, Department of Transport, Port of Saint John, Port Entry Journal, 1878–1887. As in the case of the coasters, cargo information is from the newspapers.

31 With the exception of the *Broomhaugh*, the articles of which are in BT 99/1401, the papers for the steamships are in the MHG collection of crew agreements. The vessels in alphabetical order are:

Steamship	Official no.	Tons	Port of registry
Beaconsfield	76646	1436	North Shields
Bessarabia	78733	1644	Liverpool
Borghese	63698	2044	Glasgow
Broomhaugh	83907	2095	Newcastle
Caduceus	70687	1860	London
Chilian	65881	2113	Liverpool
Cydonia	70415	1692	North Shields
Glentruim	73399	1319	Dundee
Hesleden	72651	1535	West Hartlepool
Minnie Irvine	67531	1076	″ ″
Rossend Castle	76203	1728	Newcastle
Sicily	76395	1877	Liverpool
Stanmore	63009	1951	″
Streonshalh	78863	1588	Whitby
Widdrington	79227	1581	North Shields
Winchester	87047	2199	London

32 RCRCL, *Evidence – Nova Scotia*, 56

33 Pickford and Black Shipping Registers, 1 Sept. 1880–28 Nov. 1887, PANS, MG 7, No. 43. The fifteen steamships, the articles of which are to be found in the MHG collection of crew agreements, include in alphabetical order:

Steamship	Official no.	Tons	Port of registry
Acadia	56164	697	Glasgow
Assyria	63808	1249	″
Australia	63750	1456	″
Caledonia	47833	1396	″
Caspian	63758	1717	Montreal

Steamship	Official no.	Tons	Port of registry
Chiswick	65587	796	London
Dorian	60400	667	Glasgow
India	60406	1592	"
Nova Scotian	21380	2081	Montreal
Peruvian	47845	1845	"
Polynesian	67994	2023	"
Prussian	60403	1776	"
Sarmatian	63844	2160	"
Scotland	62293	1694	London
Sidonian	63770	850	Glasgow

34 *Hibernian* (No. 33526), 1863, MHG
35 Of 1,309 seamen engaged on coasting vessels in Saint John in 1886, 88.5 per cent were from the Atlantic region, including 31.8 per cent from Saint John itself; NBM, Coast Books No. 2, 1883–1886, and No. 3, 1886–1889. The shipping master claimed proudly in 1878, several years before we have extant engagement books, that 1,870 of the 3,664 seamen shipped in Saint John were Canadians. Although this figure includes the coastal engagements, it would none the less seem to indicate, on the basis of the shipping master's enthusiasm, that the number of native seamen was on the increase. In 1878, 696 were from the United Kingdom, 404 from Scandinavia, and 309 from the United States: Report of the Shipping Master, Saint John, for the year ended 31 Dec. 1878, Canada *Sessional Papers*, XII, 1879, vol. 3, No. 3, App. No. 84, 387.
36 RCRCL, *Evidence – Nova Scotia*, 55
37 I am grateful to David Alexander for this calculation, which is based on a random sample from his data on 3,000 Canadian and 3,000 foreign seamen serving on Yarmouth-registered vessels between 1863 and 1899.
38 NBM, Port Entry Journals, 1878–1887 and 1887–1896
39 NBM, Port Entry Journal, 1878–1887
40 NBM, Canada, Department of Transport, Port of Saint John, Shipping Register (Record of engagments on deep-sea vessels), No. 2, 1881–1887. The entries correspond very closely to the entrances and clearances in newspaper shipping columns. Of the 297 voyages, 51 relate to non-British vessels. All the articles for the 97 sailing voyages (some vessels entered and left the port twice) are housed in the MHG collection of crew agreements. ACO = account of crew only; D = discharged; Out = outbound articles only.

Vessel	Official no.	Tons	Port of registry	Desertions
Abbie S. Hart	80611	1487	Yarmouth	14
Ada Barton	64581	620	Saint John	8
Addie H. Cann	71021	672	Yarmouth	5
Ailsa	43623	474	Ayr	2
Alruna	64513	188	Saint John	Out
Annie Troop	54401	511	" "	Out
Antwerp	66982	573	" "	Out
Arabia	71048	986	Dorchester	2
Arklow	72291	769	Saint John	5
Artisan	80086	1155	" "	13
Asia	85599	1398	" "	Out
Asiania	48228	1192	" "	17
Bachelors	61806	655	Yarmouth	8
Ben Lomond	45201	986	Liverpool	6
Bertha Anderson	71057	544	Dorchester	ACO
Bittern	85604	397	Saint John	Out
Calcutta	29273	983	Dundee	0
Camperdown	23436	945	London	10
City of Charlottetown	74173	302	PEI	0 (D)
Cora	75865	232	Yarmouth	Out
Curlew	80085	330	Saint John	Out
David	6121	947	" "	(1) 6
"				(2) 8
David Taylor	59268	599	" "	Out
Director	66889	702	" "	(1) 0
"				(2) 4
Dunsinane	68269	303	Dundee	2
Dusty Miller	45458	595	Liverpool	0
Ecuador	71008	1080	Yarmouth	(1) 10
"				(2) 10
Eunomia	18449	446	Glasgow	6
Euphemia	80633	1406	Yarmouth	(1) 9
"				(2) 12
Eurydice	51058	1246	Saint John	(1) 10
"				(2) 12
Favonius	85608	1525	" "	Out
Fred B. Taylor	85540	1798	Yarmouth	11
Gateshead	56064	550	Newcastle	0
G.P. Payzant	61456	623	Swansea	4

Vessel	Official no.	Tons	Port of registry	Desertions
G.S. Penry	72260	749	Saint John	7
Henry	34891	1095	" "	8
Herald	85597	1398	" "	Out
Hypatia	54487	730	" "	9
Jane Law	59901	1319	Glasgow	12
John Boyd	64041	644	Digby	4
Katahdin	80031	1205	Saint John	12
Kate Burrill	61817	690	Yarmouth	0
Kate Sancton	57145	677	"	(1) 6
" "				(2) 8
Kentigern	75458	835	Saint John	7
Lady Hincks	60000	714	London	11
Lepreaux	72254	779	Saint John	10
L.H. Deveber	64532	599	" "	Out
Lottie Stewart	66873	763	" "	(1) 10
" "				(2) 7
Lydia	71001	1239	Yarmouth	22
Maiden City	79973	841	Saint John	6
Mark Twain	72327	792	" "	10
Marquis of Lorne	80003	1209	" "	9
Mary L. Burrill	85542	1455	Yarmouth	Out
M & E Cann	66669	920	"	12
Melbourne	57113	621	"	6
Milo	66687	684	"	(1) 9
"				(2) 0
Morning Star	60668	280	Salcombe	5
Moss Glen	80000	893	Saint John	Out
Napier	59846	1177	Quebec	1
Noel	72606	812	Maitland	9
Onoway	71317	420	Sackville	ACO
Orontes	79980	763	Saint John	6
Palermo	57488	799	Annapolis	(1) 0
"				(2) 7
Paramatta	80046	967	Saint John	8
Peruana	1497	442	Glasgow	0
Plevna	77656	656	Liverpool	(1) 0
"				(2) 7
Privateer	64634	906	Saint John	8
Roycroft	57471	619	Annapolis	Out

Vessel	Official no.	Tons	Port of registry	Desertions
Sarah B. Cann	61802	757	Yarmouth	(1) 8
" "				(2) 2
Scammell Brothers	85616	1218	Saint John	Out
Scotia Queen	57186	423	Glasgow	5
Scotscraig	52574	246	Dundee	0
Scotswood	77643	252	Liverpool	1
Seaward	64518	686	Saint John	7
Souvenir	71040	860	Yarmouth	8
Stowell Brown	66937	1418	Saint John	13
Syringa	64599	628	" "	5
Tamar E. Marshall	85681	1270	Digby	4
Thomas N. Hart	80625	1491	Yarmouth	1
Twilight	53855	778	Londonderry	(1) 6
"				(2) 11
Vancouver	74311	1403	Yarmouth	11
Vandalia	85605	1422	Saint John	Out
Vanduara	80637	1410	Yarmouth	8
Vandyke	80607	1409	"	13
Wildwood	85586	1548	Saint John	25

41 Deserters in the 1880s did not seem to be deterred by the suspension in Britain of the practice of paying advance wages. They had not received the benefit of a month's wages in advance (only the token one shillin)g and therefore were leaving behind outstanding wages, unlike their predecessors who had the benefit of the first month's wages before the British legislation of 1880. See agreements (listed in note 40) for *Asia*, Liverpool, 14 Oct. 1883; *Curlew*, Glasgow, 31 Oct. 1883; *Ecuador*, Liverpool, 15 Sept. 1883; *Herald*, Liverpool, 6 Oct. 1883; *Kate Sancton*, Liverpool, 13 Oct. 1883; *Scammell Brothers*, Liverpool, 10 Nov. 1883.

42 Great Britain *Parliamentary Papers*, LIX, 1873, Paper 83: Return of the Crews of Merchant Ships which have been committed to Prison in the years 1870, 1, 2 for refusing to proceed, 259

43 *HMC* (from *SMG*), 17 Jan. 1871

44 These versions of the songs are from Stan Hugill, *Shanties and Sailors' Songs* (London 1969), 169–70, 212–13, 143–4, 180–1

45 *Ben Lomond* (No. 24978), 1858, BT 98/5416

46 Saint John shipowners and merchants were asking insurance companies to enforce temperance principles on British and colonial vessels as early as 1843: *MN*, 25 Mar. 1843.

47 *Lady Hincks* (No. 60000), 1883, MHG
48 *Simonds* (No. 13740), 1867, Log, BT 99/336
49 *Milton Lockhart* (No. 33303), 1871, Log, MHG
50 *Larne* (No. 7815), 1857, Log, BT 98/4854
51 *Bellcarrigg* (No. 10544), 1863, Log, BT 99/149
52 *Lady Falkland* (No. 12926), 1858, Log, BT 98/5233
53 HMP, 8 Jan. 1845

CHAPTER THREE: The rhythm of port life

1 *QMC*, 4 May 1872, 26 Apr. 1877
2 *HMJ*, 29 Apr. 1857
3 *QG*, 18 Dec. 1835, 13 Jan. 1836, 21 Jan. 1848
4 *MF*, 13 Dec. 1866; *MN*, 28 Jan. 1867, 31 Dec. 1873; *MF*, 6, 27 Jan. 1874
5 *QMC*, 16 Dec. 1853
6 *MN*, 11, 25, 29 Jan. 1841
7 *QMC*, 12, 13 Nov. 1856
8 *QG*, 9 Dec. 1846; *QMC*, 4 July 1856
9 *QM*, 7 Nov. 1878
10 *QMC*, 8 Oct. 1856
11 Ibid, 3 June 1859. Sheridan was in fact released on a legal technicality by a higher court and his ineffective prosecution serves as a good example of the defects in the laws against crimping; *QMC*, 5 Oct. 1859.
12 *QM*, 7 Apr. 1876; *QMC*, 10 Oct. 1878, 23 Sept., 10 Oct. 1879; *QM*, 6 Oct. 1891
13 *QM*, 10 July 1876
14 *QG*, 20 June, 18 July 1854
15 *QM*, 9 Dec. 1856
16 NBM, Log Book of the Barque *Achilles*, 1846
17 *DS*, 25, 29 Apr. 1882; shipping columns, *DS*, 24, 25, 26, 27 Apr., 1, 4, 5, 6, 8, 9, 12 May 1882
18 *EE*, 3 June 1874; *MH*, 22 Feb. 1886. John Grierson, sailors' missionary in Halifax, estimated that the arrival of 3,751 vessels with 41,696 sailors in 1881 probably meant 2,000 different vessels and 25,000 different men; First *Annual Report* of the Halifax Seamen's Mission, 1881, 9. Chaplain Robert Wyllie of the St Andrew's Waterside Church Mission claimed in 1879 that there were seldom less than 500 seamen at a time in the port of Halifax in summertime; Our Sailors. St. Andrew's Waterside Church Mission for Sailors, Fishermen and Emigrants. *Report for 1879*, 48. It is

possible to compute roughly the number of sailors ashore for years late in the century from newspapers which list the vessels remaining in port each day. As an example, the Halifax *Morning Herald* was consulted for 1886. The number of vessels in Halifax at the middle of each month was: January: 26, February: 29, March: 20, April: 85, May: 59, June: 70, July: 65, August: 80, September: 77, October: 104, November: 64, December: 102. On the basis of the federal Trade and Navigation statistics for Halifax there were about 10 seamen to a vessel during the 1880s. It is possible to suggest therefore that, except for the winter months of January, February and March, when there were between 200 and 300 merchant sailors in port, the number of seamen ashore averaged from 600 to 1,000. The listings in the *Morning Herald* do not include fishing vessels whereas the Trade and Navigation statistics do include fishing vessels.

19 *QM*, 30 Aug. 1856. Acting shipping master John Dunscomb claimed that same year that 'there are sometimes 8,000 persons afloat in this port at one time'; Dunscomb to Provincial Secretary, 21 Oct. 1856, Canada *Sessional Papers*, xv, 1857, App. Vol. 6, No. 37.

20 *QM*, 23 May 1850; *QMC*, 12 May 1854, 7 Aug. 1856; *QM*, 1 Feb. 1859

21 *QMC*, 14 May 1852 (from *New Brunswicker*), 3 June 1852

22 For example *QMC*, 8 June 1872

23 *QG*, 6 Mar. 1848

24 *Signet* (No. 5757), 1861; Log, NMM; *Jessie Boyle* (No. 1051), 1868, Log, MHG; *Chevalier* (No. 1755), 1869, Log, MHG; *Laura B.* (No. 64490),1873, Log, MHG; *Mary Jane* (No. 65971), 1873, Log, MHG

25 *James McHenry* (No. 10592), 1858, Log, BT 98/5210; *Agenora* (No. 32878), 1858, Log, BT 98/5488

26 *Cap Rouge* (No. 26821), 1860, Log, BT 98/6825; *Signet* (No. 5757), 1861, Log NMM; *Margaret Ann* (No. 6133), 1868, Log, MHG

27 *Mary Jane* (No. 65971), 1873, Log, MHG; *Lady Westmoreland* (No. 24177), 1866, Log, MHG; *Flying Foam* (No. 47603), 1869, Log, MHG; *Astoria* (No. 24915), 1862, Log, NMM

28 *Birmingham* (No. 6055), 1860, Log, BT 98/6380; *Squando* (No. 36194), 1860, Log, BT 98/6908; *Whirlwind* (No. 15953), 1866, Log, MHG

29 *Effingham* (No. 26825), 1860, Log, BT 98/6825; *Whirlwind* (No. 15953), 1866, Log, MHG

30 *Astoria* (No. 24915), 1862, Log, NMM

31 *Signet* (No. 5757), 1861, Log, NMM; *Almira* (No. 24915), 1860, Log, BT 98/6905; *Chevalier* (No. 1755), 1869, Log, MHG

32 *Madawaska* (No. 5606), 1859, Log, BT 98/5686; *Bellcarrigg* (No. 10544), 1863, Log, BT 99/149; *Chevalier* (No. 1755), 1869, Log, MHG

33 *Simonds* (No. 13740), 1867, Log, BT 99/335; *Strathblane* (No. 60389), 1870, Log, MHG; *Jessie Boyle* (No. 1051), 1868, Log, MHG

34 *Eliza* (No.15069), 1869, Log, MHG; *Lady Westmoreland* (No. 24177), 1866, Log, MHG; see also *John Davies* (No. 14358), 1860, Log, BT 98/5536

35 *Almira* (No. 35553), 1860, Log, BT 98/6905; *G.M. Carins* (No. 28179), 1871, Log, BT 99/756

36 *John Davies* (No. 14358), 1860, Log, BT 98/6536. The entries have been arranged in chronological sequence whereas in the log they are unsystematically recorded.

37 Hugill, *Shanties and Sailors' Songs* (London 1969), 202; *Commerce* (No. 22299), 1858, Log, BT 98/5339; *Signet* (No. 5757), 1861, Log, NMM

38 *DS*, 28 Apr. 1883, 24 Apr. 1884, 6 Aug. 1884; *MH*, 15 July 1886; *DS*, 15, 19 July 1886; *MH*, 12 May 1884, 22 May 1886

39 *DT*, 15, 16, 26, 27 Feb. 1877; *MF*, 15, 17, 27 Feb. 1877; *MN*, 15, 16, 26 Feb. 1877; *MH*, 15 July 1886; *DS*, 31 July 1886

40 *QM*, 12 Dec. 1892; *Labor Gazette*, Apr. 1905, 1050

41 *MN*, 19, 20 Apr. 1877; *MH*, 23 Jan. 1886; *QM*, 30 May 1887. In 1877 about 27 per cent of the loading in Saint John was still being handled by sailors, ie 300 labourers to 80 sailors at work.

42 *DT*, 10 Oct. 1870; *HMC*, 1 Jan. 1878. For more detail on this topic, see J. Fingard, 'The Decline of the Sailor as a Ship Labourer in 19th Century Timber Ports,' *Labour / Le Travailleur*, II (1977), 35–53

43 *N*, 9 Sept. 1856; *MN*, 16 June 1871; *HMC*, 21, 23 Sept. 1876; *MN*, 23 July 1879; *DS*, 5 Nov. 1881

44 *MF*, 8 Feb. 1872; *Little Fury* (No. 54392), 1872, Log, MHG

45 *MF*, 11 July 1876

46 *Almira* (No. 35553), 1860, Log, BT 98/6905; *MF*, 7 Mar. 1872; *HMC*, 30 Jan. 1873; *Mary Jane* (No. 65971), 1873, Log, MHG; *Chancellor* (No. 45923), 1874, Log, MHG; *HMC*, 16 Feb. 1874; *MN*, 15 Feb. 1875

47 *HMC*, 24, 26 Feb. 1876, 16, 20 Jan. 1877

48 *DS*, 5 Jan. 1888

49 *HMC*, 30 Nov., 4 Dec. 1872, 11 Dec. 1875, 14 Jan. 1879; *N*, 8 June 1836

50 *Astoria* (No. 24915), 1862, Log, NMM

51 *MN*, 26 May 1874; *HMC*, 21, 23 Oct. 1879. See also *QG*, 5 June 1835; *QM*, 24 Oct. 1864; *MN*, 10 May 1870; *MF*, 29 Apr. 1873; *Queen of Hearts* (No. 38756), 1873, Log, BT 99/928; *MN*, 13, 15, 16 May 1876; *QM*, 7 Aug. 1879; *QMC*, 9 Oct. 1858

52 *QG*, 29 June 1859; *MF*, 19 June 1869; *HMC*, 2 Sept. 1873; *MF*, 11 July 1876; *QM*, 16 Aug. 1864; *MN*, 4 Nov. 1870; *Larne* (No. 7815), 1857, Log, BT 98/4854; *QMC*, 11 Oct. 1854; *Margaret Ann* (No. 6133), 1868, Log, MHG

53 *Milton Lockhart* (No. 33303), 1871, Log, MHG; *QG*, 2 June, 25 Sept. 1871

54 *DS*, 19 Feb. 1880, *MN*, 19 Feb. 1880; *DS*, 20 Mar. 1885; *QMC*, 11 Oct. 1854; *DS*, 26 Aug. 1887

55 *DS*, 28 Apr. 1883; *AR*, 27 Apr. 1893

56 *QMC*, 11 Sept. 1847, 25 May 1859; *QG*, 10 Nov. 1865

57 *DT*, 4 Apr. 1868; *QM*, 20 July 1875; *QG*, 26 May 1865

58 *Australia* (No. 15848), 1863, Log, MHG; *UHJ*, 2 Oct. 1867; *Mabel* (No. 64570), 1873, Log, MHG; *QM*, 1 June 1881

59 *MF*, 6 Aug. 1870; *QM*, 20 Oct. 1874; *DT*, 25 Jan. 1866; *QM*, 20 Oct. 1874, 19 July 1875

60 *DT*, 27 Oct. 1873; *MN*, 2 Mar. 1874; *HMC*, 11 Nov. 1874; *QMC*, 16 Sept. 1857; *MF*, 6 Aug. 1870; *MN*, 6 Aug. 1870; *QMC*, 16 Oct. 1851, 20 Oct. 1859; *HMC*, 9 Nov. 1874; *QM*, 24 Oct. 1878; *MN*, 25, 26 Nov. 1878

61 *QMC*, 20, 26 Sept. 1876

62 *N*, 5 June 1865

63 *DS*, 2 Apr. 1880

64 *QG*, 4 Nov. 1835; *SMG*, 9 Sept. 1880

65 *Spruce Bud* (No. 43976), 1869, Log, MHG

66 Draft by Farrer, 11 Aug. 1864, MT 9/19/2254/1864

67 For example, *Crimea* (No. 33161), 1870, Log(2), MHG

68 *DS*, 30 June 1880

69 *MN*, 20 Dec. 1870

70 *QMC*, 12 Sept. 1857; *HMC*, 12 Dec. 1872. See also *HMC*, 19 Mar. 1874.

71 *DS*, 30 June 1880

72 Ibid, 2 Apr. 1880

73 *MF*, 25 Aug. 1868

74 *QG*, 22 Jan. 1836; *QMC*, 27 July 1847; Douglas to Casault, 26 Nov. 1850, CO 42/575/2884, ff.102–4; ANQ, AP.G 219/4, QBT, Memorial to Elgin, 27 Dec. 1852; *QMC*, 29 May 1886; Canada *Sessional Papers*, XIV, 1880–1, vol. 6, No. 11, App. 16

75 Canada, House of Commons, *Debates*, 2nd Sess. 1st Parl., vol. 2, 3 June 1869, 598–602, 5th Sess. 3rd Parl., vol. 2, 22 Apr. 1878, 2101–3, 3rd Sess. 6th Parl., vol. 2, 1 Apr. 1889, 934–5, 2 Apr. 1889, 977. For details on the failure to preserve the marine and immigrant hospital and the sale of the building to the Asylum of the Good Shepherd, see Reports of Minister of

Marine, Canada *Sessional Papers*, xxiv, 1891, vol. 7, No. 7, 35–6; xxv, 1892, vol. 8, No. 10, 63–5.

76 Minister of Marine's report, xlii, Canada *Sessional Papers*, vii, 1874, vol. 3, No. 4; ANQ, AP.G 219/2, QBT Minutes, 9 Dec. 1843; *QM*, 1 July 1863; *Annual Report*, Quebec Board of Trade, 1889–90

77 *QMC*, 6 Aug. 1877

78 *QG*, 15 June 1835

79 *SMG*, 30 May 1849; *QG*, 18 Oct. 1848, 29 July 1854; ANQ, AP.G 219/2, QBT Minutes, 28 Jan. 1851, and Dean to Leslie, 3 Mar. 1851; *QMC*, 25 June 1851; Correspondence, CO 42/646/7967, ff.160–77

80 Sykes to Board of Trade, 28 Feb. 1870, CO 42/690/3102, ff.385–91

81 *QM*, 10 Nov. 1883

82 *QMC*, 29 May 1866

83 NBM, A95, Minutes of Commissioners of Marine Hospital, 1822–7, 1 Nov. 1822; Minister of Marine's report, xcix, Canada *Sessional Papers*, xxvii, 1894, vol. 9, No. 11

84 New Brunswick, *JHA*, App. 1842, 1848, 1854, 1860

85 *MN*, 16 Apr., 18 Mar. 1872

86 *DS*, 30 June 1880, 15 Feb. 1884

87 *MN*, 9 Sept. 1850; *DS*, 30 June 1880

88 *MN*, 24 June 1877; *DS*, 26 Dec. 1884

89 Canada, House of Commons, *Debates*, 3rd Sess. 6th Parl., vol. 2, 2 Apr. 1889, 977–9; Saint John *Globe*, 8, 15 Apr. 1889; *DS*, 12 Apr. 1889; W. Bayard's Report on the Saint John Marine Hospital, 29 Oct. 1889, Canada *Sessional Papers*, xxiii, 1890, vol. 12, No. 16, App. 15; *DS*, 20, 24 Jan., 2 Feb., 28 Oct. 1893; Canada, House of Commons, *Debates*, 4th Sess. 7th Parl., vol. 1, 6 Apr. 1894, 843–4

90 Halifax *Nova Scotia Royal Gazette*, 1 June 1814; *HMP*, 4 Nov. 1844; *MN*, 18 Dec. 1844

91 *AR*, 17 Mar. 1860

92 *N*, 9 Sept. 1856; Halifax *Reporter*, 10 Apr. 1862

93 *MH*, 15 Jan. 1880, 13 Oct. 1881

94 *MH*, 23 Apr. 1886

95 See the *Annual Report*s of the minister of marine in Canada *Sessional Papers*.

96 Halifax Stipendiary Magistrate Records, xxx, Return of Persons before the Police Court, 1877–1891, PANS, RG 42, Series D

97 See Simon Houfe, 'Poor Jack: The Mendicant Sailors of Regency London,' *Country Life*, 3 May 1979, 1381, 1384.

98 *QG*, 20 Oct. 1841; *MN*, 17 May 1843; *EE*, 31 Jan. 1859; *HMJ*, 2 Feb. 1859; *HMS*, 2 Feb. 1859; *MN*, 9 Feb. 1859; *QMC*, 7 July 1876

99 *N*, 3 Aug. 1846

100 *HMJ*, 4 Dec. 1854

101 *MF*, 22 June 1871; *MN*, 4 July 1871, 4 May 1878; *QM*, 22 May 1879; *MF*, 6 Dec. 1870; *MN*, 4 Nov. 1871

102 *MF*, 1 May 1866

103 *QG*, 6 June 1836, 18, 20 June 1838, 27 Jan. 1847; *MN*, 2 June 1847

104 *MN*, 25 July 1870; *HMC*, 18 June 1872, 25 May 1874

105 *HMC*, 19 Feb. 1878

106 *HMC*, 6, 10 Sept. 1869. While aggravated assaults of the type described below were also frequently attributed to drink, drunkenness was also combined with a range of lesser but newsworthy offences such as 1) carrying an offensive weapon (usually the prohibited sheath knife); 2) smashing windows, a common form of protest; 3) resisting the police; 4) dangerous driving in 'borrowed' horse and carriage; and 5) indecent exposure: 1) *QM*, 15 May 1865; *MN*, 11 Oct. 1871, 14 June 1872; *DT*, 17 Oct. 1873; *MN*, 6 Apr. 1874, 7 Dec. 1875; *MF*, 27 July 1876; *SMG*, 26 Nov. 1877; *DS*, 8 Aug. 1878; 2) *QMC*, 4 Aug. 1857; *MF*, 15 Aug. 1867; *QM*, 31 Aug. 1870; *HMC*, 13 Oct. 1876, 26 Apr. 1877; *MF*, 7 Nov. 1877; 3) *MF*, 13 Jan. 1863; *WT*, 16 Jan. 1863; 4) *MN*, 30 Aug. 1869; *MF*, 19 June 1873; 5) *MF*, 17 Sept. 1870.

107 *QM*, 23 Oct. 1860; *WT*, 24, 31 Oct. 1862; *QM*, 11, 16 June, 18, 27 July, 10, 26 Aug. 1863; *MN*, 2 Oct. 1863, 1 June 1864

108 *QM*, 12, 25 July, 17 Sept. 1864; *MN*, 28 Sept., 7 Nov. 1864; *N*, 13 Mar. 1865; *MN*, 29 May, 13 Oct. 1865

109 *DS*, 21 May 1886; *QG*, 26 Oct. 1835; *MF*, 3 Feb., 14 May 1872; *MN*, 13, 14 May 1872

110 *QG*, 12 Oct. 1863; *MF*, 5, 6, Aug. 1878; *QG*, 16 Nov. 1866; *HMC*, 31 Oct. 1878; *MN*, 9, 10 Dec. 1872, 6 Jan. 1873

111 *HBrit Col*, 13 Sept. 1853; *HMC*, 11 Aug. 1876; *QG*, 23 Sept. 1867. The discovery of sailors and women engaged in illicit sexual activities occurred sometimes by accident. One such case in Halifax in 1883 led to the prosecution of the proprietress of a house on South Brunswick Street and the women who resided there as, respectively, the keeper and inmates of a house of ill fame; *MH*, 2 Nov. 1883.

112 *MN*, 13 June 1871; *DS*, 5 Nov. 1883, 9, 28 July 1885; *HMC*, 27 July 1868

113 Helen Creighton (collector), *Songs and Ballads from Nova Scotia* (Toronto 1932), 105–6. Reprinted with the permission of Dr Creighton

114 *MH*, 23 Dec. 1885; *HMC*, 22 July 1871; *MH*, 22 Feb. 1884; *HMC*, 16 Sept. 1876.
115 *HMJ*, 20 Nov. 1854; *MF*, 30 May 1867
116 *MH*, 19 Feb. 1883; *DS*, 21 Jan. 1884; *MH*, 4 Dec. 1889, *HMC*, 17, 19 June 1873. For stealing from crew, see *QM*, 2 Dec. 1858, *MN*, 21 Dec. 1864, 15 Nov. 1865, 6 May 1867, *UHJ*, 22 Mar. 1869, *DT*, 29 Nov. 1872, *MF*, 24 Jan. 1874, *HMC*, 5 Dec. 1874. For broaching cargo, see *HMC*, 16 Nov. 1867, *MN*, 8, 11, 27 May 1869, *HMC*, 16 June 1869, *MF*, 30 June, 5 July 1870, *MN*, 5 July 1870, *HMC*, 9 Sept. 1871, *MN*, 16 May 1872, *HMC*, 2 July 1872, *QM*, 29 May 1883.
117 *MF*, 16 Nov. 1869, 13 Jan. 1863
118 *MF*, 9 Apr. 1872, 27 June 1871; *MN*, 29 Sept. 1871, 5 May 1879; *DS*, 25 June 1883; *QMC*, 5 Sept. 1850; *MN*, 9 June 1873, 26 Nov. 1878
119 *QM*, 2 Dec. 1858 (Summary Jurisdiction Act); *MF*, 30 May 1871; *DT*, 29 Nov. 1872; *MN*, 10 Dec. 1872 (Dominion Criminal Act); MN, 31 July 1873
120 *UHJ*, 29 Mar. 1869; *MF*, 1 Nov. 1870, 13 June 1871
121 *QG*, 20 Mar. 1840; CO 42/701/8895, ff.363–9
122 *MN*,12 Apr. 1873, 19 Feb. 1874

CHAPTER FOUR: The sailor's labour rights

1 Statistics of Crime, Quebec, showing the number of persons brought before the Inspector and Superintendent of Police and other Magistrates, 1 Jan. to 31 Dec. 1854; PAC, RG 4, B 14, vol. 22.
2 'Desertion of Seamen and the Crimping System at Quebec,' 10 July 1849, BT 1/479/2425/1850; Canada *Sessional Papers*, XI, 1852–3, App. A.A.A.A., 3; Sixth Annual Report of the Shipping Master's Office, Quebec for the Year 1853, PAC, RG 4, C 1, vol. 331, No. 355; *SMG*, 19 Oct. 1857
3 *Commerce* (No. 22299), 1858, Log, BT 98/5339; *Kilblain* (No. 15437), 1858, Log, BT 98/5265; *Birmingham* (No. 6055), 1860, Log, BT 98/6380
4 Great Britain, *Parliamentary Papers*, XXVIII, 1847–8, Report of the Commissioners appointed to inquire into the Condition, Prospect, and Management of the Merchant Seamen's Fund, 456, Nos. 27, 28
5 *SMG*, 16 Nov. 1847, 1 Aug. 1849; *DS*, 22 Dec. 1883
6 *QG*, 20 July 1857; *HMC*, 1 July 1862; *QG*, 17 July 1867; *DS*, 21 Aug. 1883; *QG*, 15 Oct. 1851; *DS*, 2 Dec. 1889
7 These were the most commonly prosecuted sailor offences defined in

shipping law. To document their occurrence would be to list most of the police reports for nineteenth-century shipping seasons. For random examples of cases for Halifax in 1853 see Halifax Police Court Minutes, 1, 9, 21, 24 June, 7 July, 5, 14, 28 Oct., 3 Nov. 1853, PANS, RG 42, Series D; for Quebec in 1863 see *QM*, 28 May, 2, 3, 16, 17, 27 June, 10, 14, 22 July, 20 Oct. 1863; for Saint John in 1873 see *MN*, 30 Jan., *DT*, 3 Feb, 17 Oct., *MF*, 18 Oct., *DT*, 7 Nov., *MN*, 29 Nov. 1873.

8 *QG*, 14 July 1852; *DT*, 13 Nov. 1873

9 *UHJ*, 8, 20 June 1866; *HMC*, 19 June, 10 Nov. 1866

10 *DS*, 14, 16 Mar., 1 Apr. 1887

11 *QMC*, 16, 29 May 1848, 5 Apr. 1850; *SMG*, 6 Nov. 1847; *MN*, 19 Nov. 1856

12 *QMC*, 3, 10 July 1858; *WT*, 9 July 1863; Halifax Police Court Minutes, 7 July 1864, 24 Mar. 1871, 4 June 1851, 9, 21 June 1853, PANS, RG 42, Series D; *MN*, 13 Mar. 1857; *MF*, 18 May 1867; Halifax Police Court Minutes, 18 Oct. 1871, PANS, RG 42, Series D; *HMC*, 14 June 1873; *MN*, 17 Apr. 1872; *MF*, 10 Oct. 1872; *MH*, 16 Nov. 1881; Halifax Police Court Minutes, 11 Nov. 1881, 21 June 1853, 9 Sept. 1864, 14 July 1871, PANS, RG 42, Series D; *DT*, 3 May 1872; *MF*, 18 Oct. 1873, *MH*, 16 Nov. 1880; *DT*, 3 May 1872; *DT*, 3, 7 Nov. 1873; *MN*, 27 Oct. 1856; *MN*, 14 Aug. 1871; Halifax Police Court Minutes, 22 Apr. 1862, PANS, RG 42, Series D; *HMC*, 17 Aug., 29 Nov. 1872; Halifax Police Court Minutes, 24 Apr. 1874, 6 Sept. 1854, 24 Aug. 1868, PANS, RG 42, Series D; *HMC*, 9, 10 June 1874

13 *MF*, 20, 23 Oct. 1866

14 Halifax Police Court Minutes, 1 June 1864, PANS, RG 42, Series D

15 Ibid, 7 Sept. 1855

16 Ibid, 29 Nov. 1859; *MN*, 3 June 1869

17 Examples of sentences in Saint John in 1870: ordered on board, *MN*, 7 July 1870; four months at hard labour, *MN*, 30 Aug. 1870; four weeks in jail, *MF*, 20 Oct. 1870; six weeks in jail or till vessel sailed, *MN*, 20 Oct. 1870; four weeks in jail or till vessel sailed, *DT*, 26 Oct. 1870; jail till vessel sailed, *MN*, 3 Nov. 1870; four weeks in jail, *MF*, 17 Nov. 1870; allowed to return on board, *MF*, 24 Nov. 1870; 1) ten days in jail 2) two weeks in jail or till vessel sailed, *MN*, 28 Dec. 1870

18 *MF*, 24 Sept. 1867; *MF*, 13 June 1868; *MN*, 27 Nov. 1868; *MN*, 30 Aug. 1870; *HMC*, 14 June 1873, 24 Dec. 1872, 20 Mar. 1873; *MH*, 6 Dec. 1881

19 *AR*, 21 Feb. 1893

20 *WT*, 28 Nov. 1862; *DT*, 2 Sept. 1876

21 *SMG*, 16 May, 8 Aug., 5 Oct., 16 Dec. 1850

22 Ibid, 10 Oct. 1850, 14 Nov. 1851

23 Ibid, 27 Nov. 1839, 9 Dec. 1847, 19 Aug. 1850, 15 Dec. 1847
24 Ibid, 13 Sept. 1851, 5 Sept. 1851, 10 Oct. 1851, 31 Dec. 1852, 28 Jan. 1857, 18 Mar. 1857
25 Ibid, 30 Oct. 1872, 29 Aug. 1854
26 QM, 4 July 1872; HMC, 27 Sept. 1872; MH, 16 May 1883; MF, 18 Dec. 1860; DT, 7 Nov. 1873; Halifax Police Court Minutes, 20 July 1868, PANS, RG 42, Series D
27 MF, 24 Sept. 1867; MN, 10 April 1871; Halifax Police Court Minutes, 4 Aug. 1854, 1 May 1856, PANS, RG 42, Series D; QM, 25 June 1869; Halifax Police Court Minutes, 7 Aug. 1854, PANS, RG 42, Series D
28 QG, 27 Jan. 1847
29 'Desertion of Seamen at Quebec,' November 1848, BT 1/468/50/1848
30 HMJ, 13 Dec. 1854; QMC, 9 June 1858; QM, 2 Nov. 1861; QM, 24 June 1863; WT, 16 July 1863; MN, 29 May 1867; MN, 12 July 1867, 10 July 1868; UHJ, 27 July 1868; MN, 21 July 1870; QM, 5 Nov. 1870; MF, 19 Dec. 1872; HMC, 10 Dec. 1873; HMC, 2 Mar. 1874
31 MF, 19 Dec. 1872; DT, 29 Aug. 1870; MF, 12 Dec. 1867; N, 12 May 1856; Halifax Police Court Minutes, 1 May 1856, PANS, RG 42, Series D
32 DT, 5 July 1873, 14 May 1877
33 In a large number of instances of work stoppages reported in the press, we are left to speculate on the motives of the sailors. In forty-two such representative cases before the courts in the three ports between the late 1840s and the early 1880s, slighty over half were actions against two or more seamen and the sentences for all the cases varied widely, from being sent back on board on promise of good behaviour to twelve weeks in prison for continual disobedience or second offences to six months in one case where an assault was also proven. Only two of these undetailed cases resulted in acquittal and only three more in the option of a fine instead of imprisonment. QMC, 3, 7 June 1848; QM, 23 Oct. 1858, 6, 14 July 1863; HMC, 25 June, 11 Aug. 1864; MN, 15 Sept. 1865; UHJ, 6 Oct. 1865; HMC, 19 Sept. 1865; MN, 15, 18 June 1866; MF, 30 Oct., 13, 17 Nov. 1866; MN, 24 Dec. 1866, 16 Jan., 10 May 1867, 3 Apr. 1868; QM, 24 July 1868; MN, 5 Sept. 1870; QM, 8, 12, 17 Oct. 1870, 2, 3 May 1871, 23 May, 6 July 1872; MN, 20 Nov. 1872, 14 July, 20 Sept. 1873; HMC, 19 May 1874; MN, 15 June 1877; HMC, 20 Mar. 1878; MN, 24 Aug. 1878, 13 Feb. 1879, 30 Apr. 1879; MH, 15 May 1880; DS, 30 May 1882, 10 Sept. 1884
34 MN, 21 Oct. 1863, 16 Jan. 1867; HMC, 6 Oct. 1873, 30 May 1874; QM, 1 Oct. 1879; DS, 18 July 1884; DT, 4 Oct. 1869; HMC, 1, 5, 8 Mar. 1875, MN, 1 to 6 Mar. 1875

35 *MH*, 24 Jan. 1883; *HMC*, 28 Sept. 1870; *DS*, 4, 9 Apr. 1888
36 *HMC*, 10 May 1875; *HMC*, 13, 15 June, 17 Dec. 1874; 24 Apr. 1876. See
   Conrad Dixon, 'Lascars: The Forgotten Seamen,' in R. Ommer and G.
   Panting ed, *Working Men Who Got Wet* (St John's 1980), 265–77.
37 *MN*, 24 July 1857; *QMC*, 16 May 1848; *MF*, 1 May 1866
38 Halifax Police Court Minutes, 4 June 1861, 10 Sept. 1881, PANS, RG 42,
   Series D; *HMC*, 27 Nov., 28 Dec. 1871; DeMill to Cannon Miller & Co, 12
   Sept. 1846, NBM, DeMill Letter Book, A233
39 *QMC*, 25 June 1858; *MF*, 14 May 1867; *SJMJ*, 15 May 1867; *MH*, 5 Oct.
   1882; *MN*, 6 Oct. 1841
40 *Mary Stewart* (No. 25693), 1858, Log, BT 98/5435
41 *Tara* (No. 24207), 1861, Log, NMM
42 *MN*, 17 Sept. 1866; *HMC*, 21 May 1877, 25 June 1879; *MN*, 27 Sept. 1880
43 *MN*, 3 June 1857
44 *QM*, 13 July 1880; *SJMJ*, 22 July 1868; *MF*, 23 July 1868; *MN*, 23 May 1864;
   N, 1 Aug. 1864; *MN*, 1 Aug. 1864; *HMC*, 2 Aug. 1864; *N*, 26 Sept. 1864;
   HMC, 3 Nov. 1875; *DS*, 23 Nov., 27 Sept. 1883; *MF*, 22 Dec. 1859
45 *QMC*, 3 July 1858; *Agenora* (No. 32878), 1858, Log, BT 98/5488
46 *DT*, 21 Nov. 1872; *DS*, 22 May 1884; *MH*, 8, 16 May 1883; *DT*, 10 Feb.
   1873; *MH*, 3 Jan. 1880; *HMC*, 19, 20, 21 May 1870; *MN*, 19, 21 Nov.
   1856
47 *MH*, 9 Oct. 1884
48 *HMC*, 29 Jan. 1877; Halifax *Christian Messenger*, 31 Jan. 1877
49 *HMC*, 15, 16 May 1878; *MN*, 9 July 1879.
50 DeMill to Robinson, 22 Sept. 1835, NBM, DeMill Letter Book A233; *MF*,
   7, 9 Nov. 1872; *DT*, 6, 7, 8 Nov. 1872; *MN*, 7, 8, 9 Nov. 1872; *DT*, 24
   April 1877
51 *QMC*, 19 June 1848; *HMC*, 5 Oct. 1872
52 *QMC*, 6 July 1858; Halifax Police Court Minutes, 24 June 1864, PANS, RG
   42, Series D; *HMC*, 7 June 1876; *QM*, 30 Oct. 1858; *HMC*, 18, 19 May
   1876; *MH*, 24 Mar. 1882; *QMC*, 16, 17 May 1848
53 *HMC*, 29, 30 Nov., 1, 10 Dec. 1869; *DS*, 24 Aug. 1882; *MH*, 25 Aug.
   1882; *N*, 21, 28 Nov. 1864
54 *HMC*, 9, 11 May 1872; *MN*, 27 Feb. 1875; *QMC*, 2 Sept. 1876; *MN*, 16
   Apr. 1872
55 *HMC*, 9, 13, 14 Aug. 1873; *HMC*, 16, 17 June 1874; *HMC*, 2, 3 Oct. 1874
56 *Signet* (No. 5757), 1861, Log, NMM
57 For example, *Albert Gallatin*: *DT*, 29 July, 31 Aug. 1865; 3 July, 23 Dec.
   1869; *MN*, 7, 11 Aug. 1865; *Alice Roy*: *UHJ*, 5, 7, 8, 11, 14, 17 May 1869
58 The papers in Halifax and Saint John are full of this case in the autumn

of 1865 and winter of 1866 but the above account is based on a compendium compiled from Halifax newspapers in pamphlet form, a copy of which can be found in the Akins collection of PANS: 'Summary of Judicial Proceedings relating to the murder of Captain Benson, on board the Brig Zero.' Ten years later the murder was discussed again when Douglas stabbed a warden in the penitentiary: HMC, 9, 10 Oct. 1876. In 1879 Dowcey was remembered as the one occupant of the death cell in the Halifax county jail: HMC, 30 Sept. 1879.

59 MF, 6, 8 July 1875; HMC, 7 July, 10 Nov. 1875; MN, 5, 6, 7, 8, 13 July, 18, 19, 21, 25, 27, 28 Aug., 16 Nov. 1875, 14 Oct. 1878, 14 Jan. 1879

60 MN, 22 Apr. 1857

61 Ibid, 29 Sept. 1876, 8, 9, 25 Jan. 1877

62 HMJ, 3 Feb. 1864; HMC, 5, 6, 9 Mar. 1872

63 DS, 29 Sept. 1886; MH, 30 Sept. 1886; MF, 7 May 1881; SMG, 27 Apr. 1877. Captains were also notorious for starving their men: MH, 4 Dec. 1889.

64 HMC, 26, 27, 29 Dec. 1871, 5, 6 Jan., 9 Apr. 1872. For a trumped up charge see MN, 17 Dec. 1872.

65 Minute by Farrer, 8 Feb. 1858, MT 9/4/1461/1858; DT, 24 May 1877; QM, 19 July 1866; HMC, 9 Mar. 1872; QM, 11 Oct. 1880; MN, 9 Aug. 1871

66 For examples of convictions in a variety of cases see MF, 17 Oct. 1863; HMC, 5 June 1865; QM, 10 Aug. 1866; UHJ, 12 Feb. 1868; SJMJ, 26 Oct. 1868; MN, 12 Apr. 1869; MF, 26 Mar. 1870; DT, 30 Jan. 1872; MF, 17 Feb. 1872; MN, 10 June 1873; MF, 12, 14, 17 June 1873; MN, 23 Oct. 1873; MN, 10 Feb. 1876; MF, 10 Feb. 1876; MF, 26 Aug. 1876; MN, 21, 22 Mar. 1877; MN, 11 June 1877; DT, 24 Sept. 1877; MH, 25 Feb. 1880; MH, 12 Aug. 1881; MH, 10 Jan. 1883.

67 MN, 24 Feb. 1874

68 Ibid, 14 Apr. 1858; MN, 12 Aug. 1873; MN, 18 May 1857; N, 26 Apr. 1858; MF, 20 June 1868; MF, 7, 9 Mar. 1876; HMC, 31 Jan. 1877

69 QM, 23 Oct. 1860; QM 20 July 1863; MN, 7 Jan. 1873; MF, 1 July 1876

70 MF, 28 Dec. 1871; HMC, 13 Feb. 1867

71 DS, 14 Aug. 1883; AR, 20 June 1887; QM, 12, 13, 15 July 1865

72 MN, 10, 11 Apr. 1883; MN, 13 Nov. 1886

73 MN, 1 July 1844; QMC, 6, 11, 13, 15, 18, 20, 22, 25 Nov. 1850

74 QG, 12 Mar. 1834; DT, 11, 15 Sept. 1866

75 SMG, 1 Aug. 1849; QMC, 12 Aug. 1850

76 SMG, 6 Nov. 1847, 21 Aug. 1850

77 QG, 17 Dec 1845, 31 Mar. 1847; Great Britain, Parliamentary Papers, xxviii, 1847–8, Report of the Commisssioners appointed to inquire into the

Condition, Prospect and Management of the Merchant Seamen's Fund, 457

78 *SMG*, 6 Nov., 15 Dec. 1847, 4 Jan. 1848

79 Ibid, 25 Nov. 1847

80 Ibid, 4, 10 Jan. 1848

81 Ibid, 16 Nov. 1847, 20 Jan. 1848

82 *UHJ*, 20 Jan. 1869; *MF*, 4 Aug. 1874

83 *SMG*, 5 Feb. 1848; *QMC*, 24 Feb. 1854; *MF*, 15 July, 5 Aug. 1869

84 *QC*, 25 Aug. 1850; *DT*, 8 Dec. 1876; Halifax Vice-Admiralty Court Papers, PANS, RG 40, vol. 12, file 30 (1838); vol. 18, file 135 (1844); vol. 20, files 169, 173 (1852), files 177, 178 (1853); vol. 22, file 204 (1860); vol. 23, files 222, 223 (1865); vol. 30, file 334 (1876); vol. 31, file 336 (1876); vol. 44, file 479 (1887)

85 *WC*, 21 Oct. 1836; *MN*, 7 Apr. 1873; *DS*, 27 June 1883

86 *SMG*, 8 Dec. 1848; *MN* and *MF*, 22 Apr. 1873; *MN*, 28, 30 Dec. 1872

87 *MN*, 6 June 1872, 24 May 1873; *HMC*, 31 Oct. 1874; *SMG*, 30 Aug. 1848; *UHJ*, 9 May 1866; *MN*, 16 Nov. 1855

88 *QG*, 1 May 1846; *MN*, 23 Jan. 1873

89 *SMG*, 20 Jan. 1854; *MN*, 17 Sept. 1875

90 *SMG*, 3 Nov. 1847, 26 Jan., 14 Aug. 1848; *QG*, 31 Oct. 1838; *SMG*, 14 Oct. 1850, 3 Sept. 1856; *DT*, 23 Aug. 1876; *DS*, 5 May 1883, 7 Mar. 1894

91 *MN*, 20 Feb. 1857, 18, 24, 28 Mar. 1873

92 SMG, 3, 6 Nov., 9 Dec. 1847, 25 Aug. 1848; *DS*, 7 Dec. 1887

93 *MN*, 3 Apr. 1871; *AR*, 18 May 1889; *SMG*, 5 Feb. 1848; *DT*, 16 Feb. 1867

94 *SMG*, 25 Nov. 1847; *DT*, 1 Sept. 1866. Coilard's suit was for $17.50, the captain having given him $2.50; *MN*, 10 Apr. 1873.

95 *QG*, 13 July 1835; *QMC*, 17 Oct. 1855, 6 July 1858, 10, 11 July 1860, 1 July 1874

96 *MF*, 24 Nov. 1879; *MN*, 25 June 1873; *DS*, 6 Feb. 1883; *QG*, 13 July 1838; *NBC*, 5 July 1845; *QMC*, 30 Oct. 1851; *QM*, 22 Oct. 1864; *QG*, 19 Nov. 1847; *MN*, 27, 31 Jan. 1873; *MF*, 1 Feb. 1873

97 *MN*, 6 Mar. 1857, 10 Apr. 1873

98 *QG*, 23 June 1832, 28 Oct. 1833, 30 Oct. 1833, 1 Nov. 1833, 6 Nov. 1833, 5 May 1834, 6 Aug. 1834, 31 Oct. 1834, 1 Dec. 1834, 28 Oct. 1835, 25 Nov. 1835, 29 Jan. 1836; *N*, 4 May 1837; Nova Scotia, *JHA*, 1839, App. No. 10, 1839–40, App. No. 88; PANS, RG 1, vol. 314, No. 83; *HMP*, 18, 20 Mar. 1841; Nova Scotia, *JHA*, 1842, App. No. 7; *QMC*, 8 Apr. 1853; D.A. Sutherland, 'The Merchants of Halifax, 1815–1850: A Commercial Class in Pursuit of Metropolitan Status,' PHD. thesis, University of

Toronto, 1975, 308. The Halifax Vice-Admiralty Court Papers which were consulted for this study reveal the features set out below. For insights into the earlier importance of this court for sailors in the eighteenth century see R.B. Morris, *Government and Labor in Early America* (New York 1946), ch 5.

99 *SMG*, 25 Aug. 1849; *QG*, 27 Jan. 1847; A Return of prosecutions by seamen, PANB, RLE/847 re 5; *MN*, 16 Feb., 10 Mar. 1848

100 *QMC*, 24, 27 June 1854

101 *MN*, 1 May 1869; *MN*, 2, 3, 4, 5, 7, 8, 10, 19, 23 Nov. 1870; *DT*, 4, 7, 10, 17, 19, 21 Nov. 1870; *MF*, 5, 22 Nov. 1870. See 55–6.

102 *MN*, 17, 26 July 1872

103 Ibid, 31 Aug., 1 Sept. 1876; *DT*, 1 Sept. 1876

104 Memorandum by Northcote on Desertion at Quebec, BT 1/468/50/1848. According to the shipping interests in Saint John, John Kerr was in league with the Boarding House Keepers Association.

105 *QMC*, 23 Jan. 1858

106 *QG*, 27 Jan. 1847; *QMC*, 31 May, 3, 5 June 1848

107 Sixth Annual Report of the Shipping Master's Office, Quebec for the year 1853, PAC, RG 4, C 1, vol. 331, No. 355; Statistics of Crime ... , 1 January to 31 December 1854, PAC, RG 4, B 14, vol. 22; Canada, House of Commons, *Debates*, 5 May 1873 (Seamen's Desertion Bill), 9 May 1873 (Desertion of Seamen), Library of Parliament, Debates reported by newspapers – Ottawa, *Times*, Toronto, *Globe and Mail*

108 *DS*, 22 Nov. 1887; *MH*, 8 Jan. 1891; Canada, House of Commons, *Debates*, 4th Sess. 6th Parl., vol. 1, 10 Apr., 5 May 1890, 3153, 4400–3

109 *QMC*, 8 June 1848

CHAPTER FIVE: Crimps and reformers

1 Petition of Patrick Comerford, 2 Feb. 1847, PANB RLE/849, pe 9, No. 297. Ward Brothers of Saint John used Comerford's services in their home port; see NBM, Ward Papers, Packet 4, Advance notes, crew of the *Avon*, February 1847. Wilson was employed by Ward Brothers as their Quebec shipping master; Ward Papers, Packet 5, Disbursements of the ship *Avon*, 14th voyage, Quebec 1847.

2 *SMG*, 27 Sept. 1849; *QMC*, 17 Oct. 1849, 31 July 1852; *SMG*, 24 Sept. 1852; *QMC*, 25 July 1853; *QM*, 7 Sept. 1854; Hawkins to Brown, 15 Dec. 1848, BT 1/468/50/1848; Wilson to Brown, 7 July 1848, BT 1/469/1613/1848; Hawkins to Brown, 18 Jan. 1850, BT 1/479/2425/1850; Wilson to Governor General, 2 Dec. 1850, and Wilson to Provincial Secretary, 21 Feb. 1851,

PAC, RG 4, C 1, vol. 288, No. 2548; Wilson to Governor General, 29 Mar. 1852, and Wilson to Lt General Rowan, 27 Mar. 1854, PAC, RG 4, C 1, vol. 346, No. 476; Wilson to President of British Board of Trade, 10 Nov. 1867, CO 42/665/12120, ff.497–514

3 MF, 29 Nov. 1866, 6 Apr. 1872; HMC, 11 Feb. 1875, 25 Nov. 1876; MH, 10 Mar. 1883

4 DS, 29 Apr. 1890; HMP, 4 Feb. 1841; QM, 11 June 1872; QMC, 13 Oct. 1853, 22 Oct. 1856

5 QM, 10 Nov. 1860; Minister of Marine's report, 42, Canada *Sessional Papers*, v, 1872, vol. 4, No. 5

6 MH, 29 June 1889; MF, 8 Dec. 1863, 3 Nov. 1868; MN, 4 Nov. 1868; see below, 233. Since women often engaged in boarding-house-keeping, they too participated in crimping. Minister of Marine's report, 42–4, Canada *Sessional Papers*, v, 1872, vol. 4, No. 5

7 QG, 30 July, 4 Aug. 1869. Reference to gangs of crimps boarding vessels appear in the Quebec press in the autumn of 1856: QMC, 10, 25 Oct. 1856.

8 HMC, 14 June 1866; DTribune, 16 Oct. 1873; DT, 1 May 1877

9 QM, 1 Sept. 1849

10 QMC, 10 Nov. 1856; Toronto *Leader*, 1 Dec. 1856

11 QMC, 16 Jan. 1857; Johnson to Board of Trade, 14 Oct. 1869, CO 42/682/13496, ff. 180–8

12 QG, 1 Sept. 1856

13 QMC, 2, 4 June 1857; QM, 9 Dec. 1856, 6, 14 June 1872

14 QMC, 22 Oct. 1856

15 Report of a committee of the Privy Council of Canada, 26 Oct. 1872, CO 42/708/11194, No. 76, ff. 486–9

16 QMC and QG, 10 Oct. 1854; QM, 16, 17 July 1872; QMC, 17 July 1872; QM, 2, 4 Nov. 1872

17 QG, 24 May 1855; QMC and QG, 26 Oct. 1866; QM, 3 Nov. 1866

18 QM, 6 June 1862; QM, 28 May 1857; QMC, 30 Sept. 1856

19 QMC, 12 July 1872; QMC, 18 May 1854, 28 May 1859, 11 May 1860; QMC, 15 Sept. 1849, 5 Oct. 1859

20 QMC, 1 July 1851

21 QM, 31 Oct. 1891; F.W. Wallace, *In the Wake of the Wind-ships* (Toronto 1927), 118

22 QM, 4 Oct. 1856; SMG, 10 Sept., 22 Oct. 1856; QMC, 1, 8 Oct., 10 Nov. 1856; Return of Papers relative to Desertion of Seamen at Quebec, Canada *Sessional Papers*, xv, 1857, App. vol. 6, No. 37

23 QM, 27 Sept. 1864; QMC and QG, 28 Sept. 1864; QM, 5 Nov. 1864; Canada *Sessional Papers*, II, 1869, vol. 6, No. 65, 14, 15

24 Correspondence respecting complaints of Dunscomb, collector of customs, about his difficulty in inducing masters to engage shipwrecked seamen, including Parker to Dunscomb, 23 Nov. 1866, CO 42/661/154, ff. 120–3. The ship's articles for that voyage indicated that four able seamen – two American, one Irish and one German – were engaged at £10 for the run to Greenock and received advances of £5. They replaced four able seamen who had deserted – two Irishmen and two Swedes who had been hired in Greenock at £3.15s a month with advances of £2. Two ordinary seamen – an American and a Swede – were also hired at Quebec at £8 for the run, with £5 advances; one of them was probably a substitute for a sailor drowned at sea on the outbound voyage. See *Simonds* (No. 13740), 1866, MHG.

25 *QG*, 28 Oct. 1867

26 *HMC*, 29, 30 Nov., 1, 10 Dec. 1869

27 Minister of Marine's report, 42, Canada *Sessional Papers*, V, 1872, vol. 4, No. 5; *QM*, 31 Oct. 1891; Wallace, *Wind-ships*, 64–6. Within Quebec itself, the close connection between seafaring, ship labouring, and boarding-house-keeping was noted in an acrid newspaper letter in 1839 in which a shipmaster claimed that another correspondent who signed himself as 'Old Mariner' was 'a labourer, and keeps what he calls a boarding-house, and what any man in his senses would call a mad house, drinking, swearing, &c encouraged within its walls, delude the poor sailor from his duty'; *QG*, 19 June 1839. For Ward's transformation in the south, see Wallace, *Wooden Ships and Iron Men* (London and Toronto 1924), 102.

28 O'Leary: *QMC*, 28 July 1857, 24 June 1858; *QG*, 27 June 1859; *QM*, 11, 12 Sept. 1860, 24 Oct. 1863. Dempsey: *QM*, 20 June 1863; *QMC*, 2, 24 Sept. 1864; *QM*, 22 Oct. 1864, 5 Oct. 1866; *QMC*, 5 Oct. 1866; *QM*, 22 July 1868. Harrington: *QM*, 17 June 1863, 6 Sept. 1871, 10 Oct. 1873; Report of Quebec River Police, 1879, Canada *Sessional Papers*, XIII, 1886, vol. 6, App. No. 43; *QM*, 18 Aug. 1880; *QMC*, 16 Apr. 1875

29 Kingston, a prolific writer of children's sea stories, was a founder of the British Missions to Seamen. W.H.G. Kingston, *Western Wanderings or, A Pleasure Tour in the Canadas* (London 1856), II, 115; see also I, 87; Shipping Master's Report, Quebec, 1868, Canada *Sessional Papers*, II, 1869, vol. 6, No. 65, 17

30 *QM*, 9 Dec. 1856, 26 May 1857; *QMC*, 28 May 1857, 3 June 1859

31 *QM*, 6, 24 June 1872, 20 Jan. 1873

32 *QMC*, 23 May 1848, 26 Oct. 1850

33 *QM*, 14 July 1884

34 *QMC*, 27 Aug. 1853

35 *QM*, 26 May 1857, 30 Oct. 1858; *QG*, 1 June 1868

36 T. Gray to Colonial Office, 6 July 1872, CO 42/710/6924, ff.476–82. Minister of Marine's Report, 42, Canada *Sessional Papers*, v, 1872, vol. 4, No. 5

37 *QG*, 31 May 1872; *QMC*, 1 June 1872; *QM*, 4, 10 June 1872

38 *QM*, 29, 30 May 1872; *QMC*, 30 May 1872; *QM*, 5 June 1872; *MF*, 18 June 1872; Canada, House of Commons, *Debates*, 4th Sess. 1st Parl., vol. 3, 3 June 1872, 945–7; CO 42/708/11194, ff. 484–9; CO 42/710/7895, f. 149; CO 42/710/6924, ff. 476–82

39 *QG*, 6 Oct. 1856; Maguire to Terrill, 16 Feb. 1857, *Canada Sessional Papers*, xv, 1857, App. vol. 6, No. 37; Extract from Dunscomb's letter, CO 42/673/13879, ff. 147–51; *QMC*, 6 June 1872

40 *QMC*, 5 Oct. 1859

41 *QM*, 29 May 1873; *QMC*, 18, 23 Aug. 1876; *QM*, 18 Aug. 1876, 9 Sept. 1878; Minister of Marine's Report, xxx, Canada *Sessional Papers*, xi, 1878, vol. 1, No. 1

42 Kingston, *Western Wanderings*, ii, 115; Minister of Marine's Report, 51–2, Canada *Sessional Papers*, iv, 1871, vol. 3, No. 5

43 *QMC*, 7 Apr. 1852; *QG*, 28 Mar. 1851; *QMC*, 12 Apr. 1852; *QG*, 18 Jan. 1843; *QMC*, 8 June 1872, 27 Apr. 1876

44 *QG*, 20 Oct. 1847; *QMC*, 27 Oct. 1847, 30, 31 Oct. 1848, 10 Oct. 1849

45 *SJMP*, 25 Apr. 1864; *DT*, 10 Jan. 1873; *QG*, 23 Oct. 1837; *MF*, 11 Sept. 1860

46 *MF*, 26, 28 Apr., 10, 12 May, 11 June 1864; *DT*, 27, 28 Dec. 1872, 14 Jan. 1873; *Leonide* (No. 46156), 1871, Log, 13, MHG. One association rule required extra payment from the shipmaster for putting seamen on board on Sunday. *MF*, 11 Feb. 1873; Fingard, 'Masters and Friends, Crimps and Abstainers: Agents of Control in 19th Century Sailortown,' *Acadiensis*, viii 1 (Autumn 1978), 28–31; M.J. Daunton, 'Jack Ashore: Seamen in Cardiff before 1914, *Welsh History Review*, ix (1978), 182–4. Report of Saint John Shipping Master for year ended 30 June 1874, Canada *Sessional Papers*, viii, 1875, vol. 4, No. 5, App. 19, 80

47 *Celeste* (No. 53570), 1867, Log, MHG; *Kate Troop* (No. 52163), 1870, Log, MHG

48 *MN*, 2 Aug. 1844; *MF*, 15 Feb. 1866; *MF*, 9 June 1859; *MN*, 12 Oct. 1874; *MF*, 12, 14 Nov. 1874; *MN*, 16 Nov. 1874

49 *MN*, 25 July 1864. McFadden had earlier been caught loitering on the water alongside various vessels. *MN*, 10 July 1859; *MF*, 27 Aug. 1859; *DT*, 29 Aug. 1872, 28 Apr. 1879

50 *MN*, *MF*, and *DT*, 1 June 1871; *MN*, 3 June, 29 July 1873; *DTribune*, 4 June 1873; *DT*, 30 Sept. 1873

51 *MF*, 11 Dec. 1860; *DS*, 22 June 1891
52 *DS*, 16 Apr. 1879
53 *MN*, 8, 9, 16 Aug. 1873; *DT*, 8, 16 Aug. 1873; *MN*, 16 Nov. 1878; *DS*, 10 May 1893
54 *DS*, 27 Sept. 1879, 25 Nov. 1889; *MF*, 22 Jan. 1874
55 *DS*, 30 June 1890, 8 Sept. 1891
56 *SMG*, 4 Apr. 1851
57 *DTribune*, 16 Oct. 1873; Report of Saint John Shipping Master for year ending 30 June 1870, Canada *Sessional Papers*, IV, 1871, vol. 3, No. 5, App. 13, 118; *DS*, 5 July 1883
58 Presentment, Dec. 1844, PANB, R 67.5, RMU Csj 1/11; Petition, 19 Feb. 1846, PANB RLE/846 pe 13, No. 277; *QG*, 9 Mar. 1846; *MN*, 6 July 1846; *NBC*, 16 Jan. 1847; Petition, 2 Feb. 1849, PANB RLE/849 pe 9, No. 297; *MN*, 20 May 1853, 15 Mar. 1854, 12 Nov. 1856; *DTribune*, 30 Dec. 1872
59 Saint John *Progress*, 15 Dec. 1888; Saint John *Globe*, 11 Feb. 1889; *DS*, 7 Feb. 1890, 20 Jan. 1894
60 *DS*, 24 Jan. 1893
61 *MN*, 2 Mar. 1846; *DS*, 20 Apr. 1893, 9, 14 Mar. 1894
62 *HMC*, 4 Nov. 1869; *UHJ*, 3 Dec. 1866; Halifax Police Court Minutes, 14 June 1861, PANS, RG 42, Series D; *HMC*, 27, 29 Aug. 1870, 9 Nov. 1872
63 *HMC*, 31 Dec. 1875, 17 Feb., 11 May, 21 July 1876; *HMC*, 23 Nov. 1872, 14 June 1873; *Tancook* (No. 66676), 1873, MHG; *HMC*, 22 Jan., 30 May 1874
64 *N*, 19 May 1883; *MH*, 12 Oct., 7, 19 Nov. 1883
65 *MH* and *AR*, 31 July 1884; *N*, 9 Aug. 1884
66 RCRCL, *Evidence – Nova Scotia*, 55; *MH*, 13 May 1890, 31 Jan. 1891
67 *AR*, 28 Aug. 1841; first and second *Annual Reports* of the Halifax Bethel Union, 1846, 1847; *N*, 3 Aug. 1846; see also retrospective letter of G. Ray Beard, *MH*, 19 Mar. 1886; Minutes of the Halifax City Mission, 2 July 1862, PANS, MG 4, No. 42; *Annual Report* of the Halifax City Mission for 1862, 10; *MH*, 23 Jan. 1886, 29 June, 29 July 1889. At the end of the century some non-commercial sleeping accommodation for sailors was still available under the auspices of the Seamen's Friend Society, but that was patronized largely by naval sailors; *AR*, 27 Jan. 1899.
68 *MH*, 15 Apr. 1880, 8 Mar. 1883; *AR*, 29 June 1889.
69 *MH*, 9, 19 Nov. 1880; *AR*, 9 Jan. 1889; *MH*, 14 Jan., 6 May 1889; *HMC*, 9 Dec. 1890; *DS*, 27 Apr. 1891; *HH*, 16 Dec. 1921
70 The Halifax capitalists who were prominent in the venture were outside shipping: men such as S.M. Brookfield, master builder and company director, and J.C. Mackintosh, stockbroker, civic politician, and company director. The fortunes of the Halifax sailors' home can be traced through the *Annual Reports* of the Halifax Sailors' Home, 1880–7, and of

the Seamen's Friend Society, 1888–93, some of which are extant only in the newspapers; *HMC*, 1 Dec. 1890; *AR*, 9 Jan. 1889.
71 *DS*, 22 Jan. 1891, 2 Nov. 1893
72 *MH*, 23 Jan. 1886. We do know the rating of the boarders. Boarders in Halifax Sailors' Home, exclusive of naval sailors (source: *Annual Reports*):

	1880	1881	1882	1883	1884	1885	1886	1887	1888	1890	1892
Masters	19	16	15	14	13	14	11	17	16	14	20
Mates	88	89	88	76	61	75	51	62	39	41	56
Cooks/ stewards	80	62	96	63	70	90	66	71	48	54	49
Able seamen	536	644	550	552	441	434	363	515	349	304	548
Ordinary seamen	58	70	71	52	74	48	32	25	22	47	43
Engineers	10	5	12	6	9	5	8	4	4	–	–
Firemen	17	19	58	28	43	41	23	33	13	47	62
Carpenters	–	8	–	11	4	14	6	–	–	6	12
Fishermen	–	–	–	–	–	61	100	41	117	221	95
Boys	7	–	–	–	–	–	–	–	–	–	–
Doctors	–	–	–	–	–	1	1	–	–	–	–
Cattlemen	–	–	–	–	–	16	16	–	–	–	–
Total	815	913	890	802	715	799	661	788	608	680	885

73 See David Alexander, 'Literacy among Canadian and Foreign Seamen, 1863–1899,' in Ommer and Panting ed, *Working Men Who Got Wet* (St John's 1980), 3–33.
74 *AR*, 9 Jan. 1889
75 *HMC*, 25 Apr. 1890; *HH*, 31 Jan. 1893; *MH*, 18 Mar. 1880, 9 Nov. 1882, 23 Feb. 1883; *DS*, 30 Aug. 1888; *MH*, 24, 25 Dec. 1889; *AR*, 7 Nov. 1896, 17 Feb. 1897
76 *MF*, 18 July 1868; *MN*, 12 Oct. 1878; *DS*, 27 Sept. 1879; *HMJ*, 29 Dec. 1854; *QM*, 9 Sept. 1870
77 *QM*, 7 July 1865; *QMC*, 21 Apr. 1877
78 *DT*, 14 Jan. 1873
79 *MH*, 24 Dec. 1879, 19 Mar. 1886
80 *WT*, 16 Jan. 1863
81 *QMC*, 17 July 1851; ANQ, AP.G. 219/6, QBT Minutes, 19 Mar. 1872

EPILOGUE

1 *DS*, 26 Jan. 1893
2 *AR*, 17, 18 Feb. 1897

Bibliographical essay

Two of my articles, one dealing with the cargo-handling aspects of the sailor's job in nineteenth-century Quebec and Saint John and the other with hiring and boarding practices in Halifax and Saint John, complement and supplement this book. They are 'The Decline of the Sailor as a Ship Labourer in 19th Century Timber Ports,' *Labour / Le Travailleur*, II (1977), 35–53, and 'Masters and Friends, Crimps and Abstainers: Agents of Control in 19th Century Sailortown,' *Acadiensis*, VIII 1 (autumn 1978), 22–46. My interest in sailors ashore arose originally out of a preoccupation with the historical predicament of people on the social and economic margins of pre-industrial society in urban Canada. These more general studies of poverty focused largely on seasonality and middle-class attitudes: 'The Winter's Tale: The Seasonal Contours of Pre-Industrial Poverty in British North America, 1815–1860,' Canadian *Historical Papers*, 1974, 65–94, and 'The Relief of the Unemployed Poor in Saint John, Halifax, and St. John's, 1815–1860,' *Acadiensis*, V 1 (autumn 1975), 32–53.

The more specific approach, which the shift in focus to seafarers entailed, turned up remarkably little in the way of helpful secondary sources. Apart from a plethora of descriptive accounts of ships and compilations of marine statistics, the Canadian literature, until recently, centred on the works of F.W. Wallace, particularly *Wooden Ships and Iron Men* (London and Toronto 1924) and *In the Wake of the Wind-Ships* (London and Toronto 1927). The critical work emerging from the Atlantic Canada Shipping Project at Memorial University, some of which has been published, has begun to fill in many of the gaps, particularly as regards the nature of investment by Maritimers in shipping and the patterns of trade pursued by Maritime-owned vessels. The first three volumes of proceedings of the conferences held as part of the project were published before the completion of this manuscript: *Ships and Shipbuilding in the North Atlantic Region* (St John's 1978), edited by K. Matthews and G. Panting; *The Enterprising Canadians: Entrepreneurs and Economic Development in Eastern Canada, 1820–1914* (St John's 1979), edited by L.R. Fischer and E.W. Sager; and *Volumes not Values: Canadian Sailing Ships and World Trades* (St John's 1979), edited by D. Alexander and R. Ommer. The fourth, *Working Men Who Got Wet* (St John's 1980), edited by R. Ommer and G. Panting, reveals the richness of both the source materials and approaches for studying merchant seafaring.

Outside Canadian historiography, some of the issues addressed in this study have found their way into American and British literature. On the American side the reader can consult J.C. Healey, *Foc's'le and Glory-Hole: A Study of the Merchant Seaman and His Occupation* (New York 1936), R.B. Morris, *Government and Labor in Early America* (New York 1946), E.P. Hohman, *Seamen Ashore: A Study of the United Seamen's Service and of Merchant Seamen in Port* (New Haven 1952), H. Weintraub, *Andrew Furuseth: Emancipator of the Seamen* (Berkeley and Los Angeles 1959), E.T. Jackman, 'Efforts Made Before 1825 to Ameliorate the Lot of the American Seaman: With Emphasis on His Moral Regeneration,' *American Neptune*, xxiv (1964), 109–18, J. Lemisch, 'Jack Tar in the Streets: Merchant Seamen in the Politics of Revolutionary America,' *William and Mary Quarterly*, 3rd Series, xxv (1968), 371–407, and I. Dye, 'Early American Merchant Seafarers,' *Proceedings of the American Philosophical Society*, cxx 5 (October 1976), 331–60.

Important British sources include G.S. Graham, 'The Ascendancy of the Sailing Ship 1850–85,' *Economic History Review*, 2nd Series, ix (1956–7), 74–88, R. Brown, *Waterfront Organisation in Hull 1870–1900* (Hull 1972), S. Jones, 'Blood Red Roses: The Supply of Merchant Seamen in the Nineteenth Century,' *Mariner's Mirror*, lviii 4 (Nov. 1972), 429–42, and 'Community and Organisation – Early Seamen's Trade Unionism on the North-East Coast, 1768–1844,' *Maritime History*, iii (1973), 35–66, E.L. Taplin, *Liverpool Dockers and Seamen 1870–1890* (Hull 1974), and M.J. Daunton, 'Jack Ashore: Seamen in Cardiff before 1914,' *Welsh History Review*, ix 2 (1978), 176–203. Although not scholarly accounts, the books of Stan Hugill are extremely valuable. These comprise his three collections of songs – *Shanties from the Seven Seas* (London 1961), *Shanties and Sailors' Songs* (London 1969), and *Songs of the Sea* (New York 1977) – and his guide to *Sailortown* (London 1967).

Although there are signs that the seafaring work-force is attracting renewed attention, the fruits of these researches have not materialized early enough to benefit this study. Like other pioneering work, *Jack in Port* is therefore based almost entirely on primary research. The richest source, as the notes amply attest, is provided by newspapers. Archives in their own right, the press of commercial cities recorded for posterity daily shipping statistics, frequent court cases, including those based on maritime labour law, legislative debates, and reports of boards of trade, seamen's missions, seamen's friend societies, and sailors' homes. Press accounts of marine disasters and sailors' misfortunes ashore provide some unique insights into the everyday hardships of the seafaring life. Apart from the regular secular press of the three major seaports, the most important newspaper for my purposes was the London *Shipping and Mercantile Gazette*.

Government documents of a great variety, both manuscript and printed, provided detail on policies, controversies, laws and regulations, and statistics. The major collections on the English side are the papers of the Board of Trade, the Marine Department of the Board of Trade, and the Colonial Office in the Public Record Office in London and a variety of inquiries, royal commissions, and select committees recorded in the British Parliamentary Papers. The relevant Canadian government sources include the sessional papers of the pre-Confederation colonies and of the dominion, particularly the Trade and Navigation statistics and the reports of the Department of Marine. Commons debates, statutes, evidence given to the RCRCL, the Saint John shipping master's records comprising the Department of Transport collection at the New Brunswick Museum, the provincial secretary's correspondence for the Canadas at the Public Archives of Canada (RG 4), the extensive collection of New Brunswick assembly papers in the Provincial Archives of New Brunswick (RLE), and the Halifax city police court and prison records and vice-admiralty court papers at the Public Archives of Nova Scotia (RG 42, 35, 40) allowed me to isolate common, representative, and special features in the three ports. For recreating the structure of seafaring in the nineteenth century, I was able to draw on the most valuable official marine collection in existence – the crew agreements and official ships' logs of British-registered vessels, about 80 per cent of which are located at the archives of the Maritime History Group at Memorial University, and others, in smaller portions, in BT 98 and 99 at the Public Record Office and in the Woolwich repository of the National Maritime Museum.

The other original documents used to supplement and broaden the major collections of newspapers and government documents, all of which are detailed in the notes, are the papers of the Quebec Board of Trade, selected seafarers' memoirs, unofficial ships' logs, seafaring novels, shipowners' and agents' papers and records, pamphlets of critics of seafarers' working conditions, and various useful nineteenth-century compilations of seafaring practices such as the English *Maritime Notes and Queries: A Record of Shipping Law and Usage*. By piecing together this variety of sources, it has been my intention to try to capture the perspective of the seafarer and thereby provide an authentic appreciation of the ethos of sailortown.

Index

Picture credits

Handbill of 1847	Public Record Office, London, England: Board of Trade Papers 1/469/1613/1848
Nova Scotian	*Canadian Illustrated News*, 18 March 1882
Reward	Ibid, 21 December 1872
Champlain Street	Archives nationales du Québec (ANQ), Quebec City: fonds L.P. Vallée
Reed's Point	Courtesy New Brunswick Museum (NBM), Saint John
Duke Street	NBM
Agnes Sutherland	Maritime Museum of the Atlantic (MMA), Halifax
Harlaw	MMA
Fastnet	MMA
William Lord	William Lord, *Reminiscences of a Sailor*, 2nd edn (Edinburgh and Glasgow 1894)
Loading timber	ANQ: fonds J.E. Livernois
Drying sails	NBM
Cronan's wharf	MMA
Champlain Street	ANQ: fonds P. Gingras
Mariners' Chapel	ANQ: fonds Wurtele
Kent Marine Hospital	NBM
New Sailors' Home	Halifax *Morning Herald*, 4 May 1888

The Social History of Canada

General Editors:
Michael Bliss 1971–7
H.V. Nelles 1978–

This book

was designed by

ANTJE LINGNER

and was printed by

University of

Toronto

Press